CYBERSECURITY AND LEGAL-REGULATORY ASPECTS

CYBERSECURITY AND LEGAL-REGULATORY ASPECTS

Editors

Gabi Siboni
Tel Aviv University, Israel

Limor Ezioni
Academic Center for Science and Law, Israel

World Scientific

NEW JERSEY · LONDON · SINGAPORE · BEIJING · SHANGHAI · HONG KONG · TAIPEI · CHENNAI · TOKYO

Published by

World Scientific Publishing Co. Pte. Ltd.

5 Toh Tuck Link, Singapore 596224

USA office: 27 Warren Street, Suite 401-402, Hackensack, NJ 07601

UK office: 57 Shelton Street, Covent Garden, London WC2H 9HE

Library of Congress Control Number: 2020951595

British Library Cataloguing-in-Publication Data
A catalogue record for this book is available from the British Library.

CYBERSECURITY AND LEGAL-REGULATORY ASPECTS

ISBN 978-981-121-915-3 (hardcover)
ISBN 978-981-121-916-0 (ebook for institutions)
ISBN 978-981-121-917-7 (ebook for individuals)

For any available supplementary material, please visit
https://www.worldscientific.com/worldscibooks/10.1142/11793#t=suppl

Desk Editors: Balamurugan Rajendran/Sylvia Koh

Typeset by Stallion Press
Email: enquiries@stallionpress.com

Printed in Singapore

Preface

The rise of threats and challenges in the realm of cybersecurity reveals and provisions the ongoing evolution of various aspects. This book encompasses an array of articles written by experts across different sectors and from around the world, discussing varying dynamics of legal and regulatory aspects of cybersecurity. Examining various undercurrents, developments, and opportunities of cybersecurity regulation on an international, regional, and national level. The book particularly examines the risks and obstacles businesses and society face with the evolution of the internet and the formation of cybersecurity management to prevent cyber harm.

It provides an analysis on the EU's cybersecurity policy framework, regulations and legislations in cyberspace in Latin America and the Caribbean, as well as a case study from Asia. It also explores the use of the class action mechanism and escalation control, strategic fatalism, and the role of cybersecurity.

The book further examines rising cyber threats and challenges in maritime order, an emerging risk arena, while considering the role of non-state actors in the growing influential space for international corporations, as well as the implication of hacking back under international law.

This book suggests several policy and regulatory strategies to enhance cybersecurity and the global information society with emphasis on ethics, human security, and human rights; influence operations; and the combination of technological attacks and manipulation of Content. It will be useful to policy makers, lawyers, law students, regulators, researchers, IT professionals, law students, and any individuals interested in seeking a general understanding of cybersecurity governance and legislation.

Prof. Dr. COLONEL (res.) Gabi Siboni
Prof. Dr. Adv. Limor Ezioni
December 2020, Israel

About the Editors

Gabi Siboni is a National Security Specialist and the former Director of the Military and Strategic Affairs Program as well as of the Cyber Security Program at the Tel Aviv University's Institute for National Security Studies (INSS). Prof. Siboni is also the editor of the journal *Cyber, Intelligence, and Security*. He serves as a Senior Consultant to the IDF and other Israeli security organizations, and is also a Professor for cybersecurity at the Francisco de Vitoria University, Madrid, Spain. He has published more than 100 peer-reviewed articles and several books about National Security and Cybersecurity.

In addition, Prof. Siboni is the chief methodologist of the IDF's Research Center for Force Deployment and Buildup. In this scope, he develops Strategic & Operational concepts for various domains including: Integrated Combat in complex and densely populated areas, Cyber defense and Cyber warfare, Cognitive and Influence operations, and more. He also develops methodologies for Computerized Simulation for various needs including for Military Operations.

Prof. Siboni is a Specialist in geopolitical risk analysis with expertise extending to corporate strategy and operations, physical security, cybersecurity of large organizations, with application of bespoke methodologies and analytical processes. He is a consultant in a wide range of fields, including: Cyber Security, Information Technology, ICT & Cloud Risk Management, and Strategic Planning. He has extensive proven experience in Decision Support Systems (DSS) related to Cyber Security Investment, and Security & Safety Control Systems.

Prof. Siboni holds a B.Sc. and an M.Sc. in engineering from Tel Aviv University and a doctorate in Geographic Information Systems (GIS) from Ben-Gurion University.

Limor Ezioni. Adv. is the former Dean of Law at The Academic Center of Law and Science and a highly requested lecturer in many academic institutions. Alongside her vast academic work, Ezioni has published three books and numerous articles on the Criminal Law field as well as on Cyber Law, Cyber Crime, and the Liability of Content Providers and Site Operators.

Within the scope of her work at the cyber defense program at the INSS, Ezioni engages in a variety of legal, regulatory, and ethical aspects regarding minors in cyber space.

Ezioni specializes in Criminal Sex offenses and Crimes against Minors as well as Minors in Criminal Law. Alongside her vast academic work, Ezioni has published several books, the first, *Incest* (2009), and the Second, *Filicide* (2016), are the only Hebrew law books on these subjects in Israel and are used by judges and law scholars alike. Her third book is *Minors in Criminal Law* (2019). Her fourth book, *Unsafe Home*, in English, will be published this year, 2020, in the United States.

Ezioni has also published numerous articles, in Hebrew and in English, on the criminal law field on: repressed memories, female genital mutilation, pornography, sex trafficking, family sex offences, online bullying and minors in the cyber world, and more.

Ezioni is the head of her own law firm. She is also freelance consultant on a variety of legal and regulatory subjects in different parliament committees as well as for public and privately held companies in the business sector.

About the Contributors

Benjamin Ang is a Senior Fellow and Head of the Cyber and Homeland Defence program in the Centre of Excellence for National Security (CENS), a policy research think tank based at the S. Rajaratnam School of International Studies (RSIS) at the Nanyang Technological University, Singapore. He leads a team of researchers studying and publishing on policy, legal and regulatory aspects of cybersecurity, international cyber norms of behavior, cyber conflict, security issues in digital technologies including 5G, blockchain, smart cities, social media, and AI, as well as disinformation, foreign interference, and gray zone hybrid threats. He is a former Lawyer, former CIO, and Certified Network Administrator. He also volunteers on the executive committee of the Internet Society Singapore Chapter.

Guillermo Arce is currently Associate Dean for International Relations and Marketing & Branding Professor at UFV School of Business and Law (Universidad Francisco de Vitoria, Madrid). Dr. Arce owns a Marketing PhD from UAX (Madrid) and a Marketing Diploma and Mass Media Degree from UCM (Universidad Complutense de Madrid).

He has complemented his background in Marketing and Communication with a Research Master's, and several courses about management, strategy, sales, and communication. His field of research is mainly focused on the internet, social networks and their influence on Teenagers, and understanding the profile that future society and companies will be demanding from them.

He has an extended professional career as an entrepreneur, in his own marketing company, and has also worked as Team Leader, Sales and Marketing Director for several International companies and industries. Nowadays, he works as a consultant and company trainer for different brands such as AMEX, PASCUAL, and FUTJITSU.

Annegret Bendiek is a political scientist of the research division "EU/Europe" at the German Institute for International and Security Affairs (SWP). Since 2005, she has been researching fundamental issues of European foreign and security policy and is a Lecturer in the postgraduate program "Master's of European Studies" at Freie Universität Berlin and Technische Universität Berlin. In 2014, she was appointed to the planning staff of the Federal Foreign Office for the project "Review 2014: Rethinking Foreign Policy." In 2013, she was a Robert Bosch Fellow at the Transatlantic Academy "The Future of the Liberal Order" and a Visiting Fellow at the German Marshall Fund in Washington, D.C. In addition to her research and publication activities, she advises governments, international institutions, and companies on European foreign and security policy as well as on regulatory issues in cyber security and digitization at EU level.

Stephen J. Cimbala is Distinguished Professor of Political Science at Penn State University (Brandywine). An award-winning Penn State teacher, Dr. Cimbala is the author of numerous works in the fields of nuclear strategy, arms control, and other national security topics. His recent publications include the book *The United States, Russia and Nuclear Peace* (Palgrave–Macmillan: 2020).

Emma Corcodilos graduated from Stockton University in 2019 after dedicating her final semester to research in Washington, DC, at the William J. Perry Center for Hemispheric Defense Studies and the National Defense University. Emma is currently a paralegal specializing in natural disasters and insurance fraud. In college, Emma participated in social science research as a Research and Data Analyst, wrote for the University's newspaper, edited for the South Jersey Culture and History Center's yearly publication, and participated in the National Model United Nations. She has a B.A. in political science and pre-law studies.

Naomi Elimelech Shamra is the Director of the Treaties Department in the Ministry of Foreign Affairs of Israel since 2018. Among other things, she gives legal advice on bilateral agreements. She also leads the Israeli negotiations team over the multilateral treaties of the Council of Europe, as well as cybercrime treaties. In the past, Ms. Elimelech-Shamra was the Deputy Director of the same department, and before that — Deputy Director of the Department for Civil and Diplomatic Law. She is also a qualified diplomat. Ms. Elimelech Shamra holds LLB (cum laude) and LLM (magna cum laude) degrees from the Hebrew University of Jerusalem, in which she also taught civil law, labor law, and criminal law. She also taught at the Academic Centre for Law and Business in Ramat Gan.

Deborah Housen-Couriel is a member of the Advisory Board of the Hebrew University Cyber Security Research Center–Cyber Law Program and teaches cyber law and policy at the Law Faculty of Hebrew University and at IDC Herzliya. She was a member of the International Group of Experts that drafted the Tallinn Manual 2.0; and is currently a Core Expert on the Manual on International Law Applicable to Military Uses of Outer Space (MILAMOS) project. At the international level, she serves as Chair of Working Group D of the Global Forum on Cyber Expertise. Deborah is an alumna of Wellesley College (B.A.), Hebrew University (LL.B and LL.M), and Harvard Kennedy School (MPA-MC). She currently serves as the Chief Legal Officer and VP Regulation of Konfidas Digital Ltd., based in Tel Aviv, specializing in cybersecurity, data protection strategies, and cyber incident response.

Eva Pander Maat is a PhD Candidate at City University in London. Her research project is an EU external relation research on the implementation of environmental protection provisions in the EU's Free Trade Agreements. Previously, she worked as an intern in the Research Division EU/Europe at the German Institute for International and Security Affairs (SWP) in Berlin.

José María Ortiz Ibarz is currently the Rector of the Villanueva University in Madrid. A Doctor in Philosophy, with Extraordinary Prize for his Bachelor's and Doctorate degrees, he was Dean of the School of Philosophy and Letters of the University of Navarra and Vice Rector of

Students. He has been the Vice President for Academic Planning and Faculty, Secretary General, and Director of Human Resources at the Universidad Nebrija, and Dean of the Law and Business School at the Universidad Francisco de Vitoria in Madrid. He joined HayGroup in 1998 as Director of Corporate Governance; he was also responsible for the utilities and family business sectors. For six years he has led numerous projects in major companies in Spain, Chile, Mexico, Argentina, Brazil, Portugal, Andorra, and France. He has published twelve books on Philosophy and Management, forty scientific articles in specialized journals, and more than two hundred collaborations in the economic press.

Eyal Pinko (Cdr. (ret.)) is a Senior Research Associate in the International Institute for Migration and Security Research (IIMSR), Senior Analyst and Reporter of defense and security at Israel Defense, and the CEO of cybersecurity firm InMotion.

Beatriz Vila Ramos is currently Vice Dean of Institutional Relations of the Faculty of Legal and Business Sciences and Director of the University Master's Degree in Law (access and practice of law) at the Francisco de Victoria University of Madrid in Spain. A Doctor and Professor accredited by ANECA, she has been teaching at the UFV since 1996, subjects related to the field of Constitutional Law. She has published several articles and books related to political philosophy, parliamentary law, minors and is currently working on issues related to fundamental rights and technology.

Boris Saavedra is a retired Venezuelan Air Force General Officer, He has devoted more than 30 years to academic activities, both in Venezuela and the United States. He successfully completed all courses and specializations in air operations as a combat pilot. He graduated from the higher Military Studies course at the École Supérieure de Guerre Interarmées of France (1983–1986) and the Higher National Defense Course at the Institute of Higher Studies in National Defense of Venezuela (1988–1989). In addition to his doctorate from the Gutiérrez Mellado Institute at the National Distance Education University in Spain (2014), he has an MA in International Policy and Practice from George Washington University in the U.S. (2003). Dr. Saavedra is currently an Associate Professor at the William J. Perry Center for Hemispheric Defense Studies, located at National Defense University in Washington,

DC, a position he has held since 1998. Before assuming this position, Dr. Saavedra was the Chief of Academics at the Inter-American Defense College (1996–1998).

David Siman-Tov (Lt. Col. (res.)) is a Senior Researcher at the Institute for National Security Studies' (INSS) Lipkin-Shahak Program for National Security and Democracy in an Era of Post-Truth and Fake News. He formerly served in the Israeli intelligence community, and also serves as Deputy Director of the Institute for the Research of the Methodology of Intelligence at the Israeli Intelligence Heritage and Commemoration Center.

Chagai Vinizky is a Senior Lecturer on property law, contract law, class actions, and Judea and Samaria law and director of legal clinics at the Academic Center for Law and Science, Adjunct Lecturer at the Hebrew University, Head of the Begin Institute of Law and Zionism, and a Military Judge (res). Dr. Vinizky was a member of a professional team appointed by the Prime Minister to formulate construction regulations in Judea and Samaria. Dr. Vinizky published a book on class actions (with Adv. Aviel Flint), edited two collections of articles (with Dr. Harel Arnon), published articles in the fields of property, contracts, intellectual property, and law applicable in Judea and Samaria in legal journals in Israel and the United States, and authored position papers on the Basic Law: Israel as the Nation-State of the Jewish People and the application of Israeli law in Judea and Samaria. Member of the Israel Bar Association since 1998.

Ohad Zaidenberg is a Senior Cyber Intelligence Researcher at ClearSky who focuses mainly on attacks in the Middle East and is an expert on Iranian affairs. Former Researcher and Commander at Unit 8200, and Founder of CTI League.

Acknowledgments

We would like to deeply thank Ms. Gal Sapir, a researcher at the Institute for National Security Studies (INSS), who assisted us throughout the entire process and provided valuable insights and contributions. Without her dedication and help we would not have been able to complete this book.

Contents

Chapter 1

Cyber Crisis Management and Regulation

Limor Ezioni[*,‡] *and Gabi Siboni*[†,§]

*Dr. Limor Ezioni Law Office, Tel-Aviv, Israel

*†Military & Strategic Affairs Program,
Cyber Security Program — INSS, Tel-Aviv, Israel*

‡le@limorezioni.com

§gabriel@g-bina.com

Abstract

Companies and organizations operate through central computers, managing large databases, some of which contain confidential and classified information. This agency of cyberspace has become essential for information retention and management across countries and continents in a broad and applicable way. This chapter will describe the cyberspace and its risks, regulations, and legislation that exist in the State of Israel and globally.

1.1. Introduction

At present, organizations find themselves administrating and managing information and their environment through cyberspace online, and this has increasingly become the norm and a required measure for ongoing business management. Companies and organizations operate through central computers, managing large databases, some of which contain confidential and classified information. This agency of cyberspace has become essential for information retention and management across countries and continents in a broad and applicable way. Materials that were previously filed and stored in the organization's archives can now be obtained and accessed at any time online. Today, the cyber realm also dominates many other capacities related to the human environment. Over the years, online technology has entered our lives in a way that shadows every individual and organization. Everyone surrounds themselves with online tools. The term "online" here encompasses use of computers, websites, smartphones, social networks, telecommunications providers, navigation satellites (known as GPS), technology regulation sensors, and smart systems, among others that provide wide access to information.[1]

All these technological innovations are fertile ground for a more comfortable, accessible, and smarter life, which is accomplished by remote human control through content servers. However, the less ideal situation is one in which useful technological tools are compromised by a cyberattack or encounter a crisis that has significant altering effects, as a result of a third party with malicious intent or technological delinquency.[2] Under such circumstances, associate user(s) need to manage the cyber crisis most efficiently, which will reduce the degree of damage and vulnerability to the infrastructure and the organization as a whole, which can sometimes consist of several complex operations in parallel.[3] It is important to note that cybersecurity is now a priority for all businesses and individuals.

Cybersecurity is an important aspect of life, and its increasing importance can be attributed to our growing dependence on technological developments. Every household or office now has computers loaded with

---

[1] Major systems are now seamlessly integrated in everyday life, such as wearable smart systems; regulation and detection sensors; biometric reservoirs; floating systems, such as skimmers, autonomous vehicles, and more.

[2] For example, Russia's intervention in the 2016 US election campaign. See: https://www.cfr.org/backgrounder/russia-trump-and-2016-us-election (accessed on September 18, 2020).

[3] Boin, A., P. Hart, E. Stern and B. Sundelius (2017). *The Politics of Crisis Management-Public Leadership under Pressure*, New York: Cambridge University Press, 2017, 2nd Edition, pp. 3–4.

personal data. It is important to consider this while constantly developing the field of cybersecurity to protect the individual and the society at large as well.[4] The remedy in this case is a complete attack on malicious actors and their intents while arming ourselves with firewalls, VPNs (virtual private networks), and IDS (intrusion detection system), which can enhance the cybersecurity field and protect our lives from being compromised online and, eventually, offline.[5] Cybersecurity is a necessary component of our lives because all the data regarding security, health, personal, and financial information are stored on the Internet. For example, CNBC has compiled the biggest five data breaches in tech history, and all of them were caused by hacking, poor security, or both. The companies that were affected are big global players on the Internet and financial sectors, such as Yahoo, First American Financial Corp., Facebook, Marriott International, and Friend Finder Networks. The lack of strong cybersecurity in these instances caused problems for over a billion people worldwide in total.[6] Malicious actors such as hackers can cause damage or steal from a potentially abundant pool of unsuspecting victims.

This chapter will describe the cyberspace and its risks, regulations, and legislation that exist in the State of Israel and globally. Furthermore, it identifies ways to manage a cyber crisis and explains the reasons and need for a comprehensive and regulatory legislation for managing such crises.

The constantly evolving cyber world is a productive and amazing invention, replete with progress, development, thought exploration, and creation. It is a new frontier with modern and complex challenges that need to be addressed with utmost priority. Nonetheless, conduct in the cyber world, as well as in the physical (real) world, must follow rules, procedures, and regulation in order to avoid a situation in which the absence of government intervention causes a state of chaos among the population and poses a danger to the society and the economy. The cyber world has a longstanding reputation of being the Wild West where businesses and individuals alike can trade products and ideas, and individuals with virulent and malicious aspirations can produce unlimited damage.

---

[4]Khan, M. (2017). "Computer Security in the Human Life," *International Journal of Computer Science and Engineering*, **6**: 35–42.

[5]*Ibid.*

[6]https://www.cnbc.com/2019/07/30/five-of-the-biggest-data-breaches-ever.html (accessed on September 18, 2020).

1.2. The Uses and Users

Computing and Internet tools are a major factor in the organizational behavior of many companies affecting the economy, and those in the financial, insurance, computing, cellular, banking, and public sectors have increased their use of online cyber computing. These companies, which provide essential online services based on cyber infrastructure, comprise a large audience of online service providers and users.

The development of cellular networks is a great example of the ongoing use of the Internet and the provision of services from the communications field, while simultaneously using them as a service provider based on telecommunications providers.[7] The growing use of data transfer and the need to cope with a large database creates the need for telecom providers to deal with this type of load. Cellular companies must improve and update their services regularly so that this load will not be felt by the customer and especially ensure it will not lead to an incident in the manner of providing the service and information security. The crisis faced by the Israeli cellular company Pelephone in 2018 is an example of how the use of a telecommunications provider and the need to increase the carrier's capability caused communication failures that began as a minor incident with escalating consequences. Although the incident was not attributed to the malicious intent of a third party, it could have snowballed into a major security crisis if it had been the case.[8]

The organizational structures, such as those listed at the beginning of this chapter, contribute greatly to the sustenance of an economy.[9] These companies are of great importance and significance to the ongoing functionality of the state and its economy[10] and have become leaders in public opinion

---

[7]Kuczyski, K. (2019). *Principles of Cyber Law and Policy*, Module 1.

[8]*The Marker* (2018). "9,000 clients abandoned Pelephone, damage could reach M9 NIS/ Year (Hebrew)." Available at: https://www.themarker.com/advertising/.premium-1.6491395 (accessed on September 18, 2020).

[9]This is reflected in the ongoing business management, hiring, research, and development of the various fields.

[10]Public relations with private companies have undergone a great change over the years. For years, companies have tried using public relation bodies and employees who believe in the company, to lead a change in the public opinion about their image. This change was due to the understanding that public opinion is important and that they must change the situation in which the organization is the quiet factor in society, which responds only in times of crisis. See: Regester, M. and J. Larkin (2005). *Risk Issues and Crisis Management*, 3rd Edition, pp. 39–40.

among the general population. In some situations, given their power and importance, companies have even found themselves taking an active part in influencing social decisions, which is not a primary goal of their business.[11]

Despite many companies in the economy being listed as belonging to the private sector, the clear interest of the state is to maintain the existence of these companies and their tremendous contribution to the advancement of the political and state order in general. This necessitates the enlistment of the state to help those companies make the most secure choices when online, thus helping to preserve their integrity. Therefore, one can see the significant connection between the existence of the organization, the interests of the country in which it exists, the connection between the director of work relations, and the ongoing business process.

1.3. Crisis Management

The field of crisis management is in control of a wide range of actions within private and public companies alike. The field, which began its significant growth in the late 1990s,[12] led to the important consciousness that an organization might be involved in an incident which may develop into a crisis.[13] A crisis as defined is something that varies from domain to

---

[11]An example of a situation in which private sector companies are taking an active role in leading social processes is to mobilize many companies in the economy to promote the surrogacy law in 2018. See: "High-Tech companies recruiting for help: Funding for surrogacy for employees," *The Marker*. Available at: https://www.themarker.com/technation/1.6291590 (accessed on September 18, 2020).

[12]The term "crisis management" was first coined by Howard Chase in 1979. The term stemmed from the understanding that an organization must take an active part in the day-to-day conduct of nationals and share information regularly. This is to change the public's perception of private companies at that time, given that this was a real problem and led to stricter corporate legislation. In this way, when the organization finds itself in a crisis, it does not respond to the crisis after it has happened, but prefers to share with the public about its conduct in advance. In such a situation, when companies and organizations are faced with situations where laws and regulations are set regarding their conduct, companies will be in a position where they do not have to defend themselves against lawmakers who want stringent legislation that results from the lack of sharing and knowledge of processes. This will lead to a situation in which public opinion about these companies is positive in light of transparent conduct, which will help the company in preventing stricter laws against it. See: Regester, M. and J. Larkin (2005). *Risk Issues and Crisis Management*, 3rd Edition, p. 40.

[13]Crisis management theory is an area that has also gained momentum in the last decade, with the understanding that when a company faces a crisis, it should ideally be managed

domain and as the incident, develops, it leads to the development of a real crisis in the field in which it occurs. In this area, many studies are underway to find the best way to deal with the trigger event when it arrives and, if the catalyst has developed into a crisis, determine how to proceed in the most efficient way to tackle it. In a way that will minimize the damage and prepare for the arrival of the crisis, crisis management also examines the steps taken through planning, control, analysis, and communication.[14] First, one must understand the crisis and its nature.[15] A crisis, as defined in this chapter, refers to a situation in which an undesirable situation exists within an organization, person, or group, which can create chaos and disorder, thereby posing a threat.[16] The chaos that can create the crisis can lead to undesirable consequences in the areas where it exists, such as economics, health, security, nature and the environment, government, and politics. A crisis is a critical and important period in the life of the organization and requires immediate and urgent consideration that will place it as a priority when it occurs. In order to deal with the exigencies, it is first necessary to identify the type of crisis and determine whether it is a visible one in which the dangers it poses are clear and can be resolved expediently, or whether it is a crisis that has not yet been identified and could lead to unknown results.[17]

1.4. Crisis Preparation and Risk Management Planning

The development of the field of crisis management has led to the understanding that a crisis must be managed properly, and that the most

---

to prevent the crisis from collapsing and operating. Since the development of the crisis management field, there have been many studies in the field to assist the body or organization meeting this crisis and to outline, before and after, the rules of conduct and prevention during the crisis.

[14]Regester, M. and J. Larkin (2005). *Risk Issues and Crisis Management*, Chartered Institute of Public Relations, 3rd Edition, p. 44.

[15]Boin, A., P. Hart, E. Stern and B. Sundelius (2017). *The Politics of Crisis Management — Public Leadership under Pressure*, 2nd Edition, p. 5.

[16]A dictionary reference and research-based definition of crisis.

[17]Boin, A., P. Hart, E. Stern and B. Sundelius (2017). *The Politics of Crisis Management-Public Leadership under Pressure*, 2nd Edition, p. 6.

effective way is to prepare for its arrival through the existence of a crisis management plan and preparedness.[18]

According to Meng's approach,[19] presented in a number of different literature sources, the first part of the life cycle deals with the first stage, i.e. the early identification of the potential crisis and its source as a crisis management aid.[20] The second principle deals with a systematic response of the organization to the crisis and its effects at internal and external levels.[21]

Every stage of the life cycle of the crisis is an opportunity to save the organization from risk costs and damages that may result from the realization of the crisis.[22]

The first stage is a significant part of preparing for a crisis, where the thinking and understanding take place; and where the structure or operations of the organization may create incidents that can lead to a potential crisis. Understanding an action as a cause that can lead to an incident can aid in proper preparation; the origin can therefore pave the way to the remedy of the crisis. In order to swiftly and effectively identify the potential incident, it must be done by the experts in the field in which it exists. This provides the tools necessary for identification. Once the existing potential is identified that indicates that an incident could threaten the organization, if the response is accurate and correct, the majority of the incident can be averted, thus preventing the emergence of a crisis and changing the outcome of the incident.[23]

The second phase deals with the discovery of the incident. The stage at which the incident was already taking place may have intensified to become a crisis. The discovery phase is a significant step. Getting the information out to the public can lead to an intensification of the incident and result in an ever-growing crisis. According to Meng's approach,[24]

---

[18] Regester, M. and J. Larkin (2005). *Risk Issues and Crisis Management*, 3rd Edition, p. 45.

[19] Meng, M. B. (1987). "Issues management today," Unpublished Thesis, Bingham Young University.

[20] Meng, M. B. (1992). "Early identification aids issues management," *Public Relations Journal*, March.

[21] Regester, M. and J. Larkin (2005). *Risk Issues and Crisis Management*, 3rd Edition, p. 68.

[22] Deloitte (2016). "Cyber crisis management: Readiness, response, and recovery," p. 2.

[23] Hanna, N. (1985). "Strategic planning and management: A review of recent experiences," World Bank Staff and Working Papers No. 751, Washington DC, USA.

[24] Meng, B. M. (1992). "Early identification aids issues management," *Public Relations Journal*, March.

the discovery of his incident and his attempts to overcome it are the real pinnacle of the crisis. At this point, when the incident is at an initial stage and has not yet grown into a real crisis, dealing with it must be made the topmost priority. It may not be devastating for the company at this stage but overlooking it may turn this avoidable crisis into a credible threat to the organization. Deflecting the incident that has not yet developed into a full-blown crisis can be a critical stage in its development. Therefore, in order to prevent the threat from materializing into a crisis, coping with it as early on as possible could mean the success or failure of the company. Most often, communication intervention enters within the timeline toward the end of the second phase and before the transition to the third phase. The first two stages comprise early crisis management and the identification and detection of the incident. In the third and fourth stages, the degree of stress involved in the incident and the actual crisis form a significant part of the decision-making and management of the crisis.

The third stage in the timeline is the phase in which the organization's population must be incorporated into full cooperation to lead the eradication of the crisis.[25] Such a situation is divergence from the status quo: inter-departmental teamwork becomes key, and those with different areas of expertise may be called upon to cooperate in order to achieve a common goal. In this respect, media intervention and public interest already exists, and the showcase of cohesion within the organization can have a positive impact on preserving its image. A positive image of unity can be advantageous in dealing with the crisis and removing the threat. In addition, communication is primordial when a crisis has erupted to inform and guide the narrative to avoid damage. Miscommunication poses a real threat that can be tangibly estimated as the potential for harm can be great. When the crisis is fully presented to the public, this can put pressure on the governmental authorities and can lead to the understanding that they must act in favor of the organization. Certain threats directed toward major companies can have severe consequences which can become a threat not only for the organization in question but the State itself. It can be understood in two ways — the incident has become a crisis in terms of crisis intensity, the magnitude of the threat, and the immediate need to eradicate it. When a disruptive event occurs, which jeopardizes the organization, it is measured by the nature of its response to the crisis and

---

[25]Regester, M. and J. Larkin (2005). *Risk Issues and Crisis Management*, 3rd Edition, pp. 50, 52.

its ability to isolate and overcome it, while at the same time promoting a unified message regarding the crisis.

The fourth and final stage of the life of a crisis deals with its solution and damage recovery. When the crisis culminates, it is a situation in which the organization must make decisions on conditions that do not necessarily match its needs, goals, or desires. Such a situation usually happens when a governmental authority intervenes in a crisis and sets rules or regulations in order to calm down and restore the situation to normal.

These four stages represent the two important principles of crisis management: (1) Identification and (2) Response. They are a theoretical model for the stages of a crisis from its development to its end. A successful crisis management strategy would require the efforts of everyone in the company (including all the employees) to save it from the threat.

1.5. The Effects of Cyber Crisis

Alongside all the advantages of cyber technology, the risks must not be understated. The increasing reliance of our society on modern and complex digital systems, especially in the operations of critical national infrastructure, increases the risks of disruptive or destructive attacks in many significant ways.[26] Online systems contain limitless amounts of software and boundless vulnerabilities, with the number of possible attacks also being aggressively limitless.[27] The development of the cyber field over the past decade has led to the study of the subject by many companies and has initiated the understanding of the significance of a security breach or cyber threat within the organization. In light of the conclusions gathered on the subject, which originated in cases that have occurred in the State of Israel and around the world,[28] it is now understood that companies worldwide are constantly at risk of security breaches that can be attributed

---

[26]Choraś, M., R. Kozik, A. Flizikowski, W. Hołubowicz and R. Renk (2016). "Cyber threats impacting critical infrastructures," doi: 10.1007/978-3-319-51043-9_7, pp. 141–142.

[27]*Ibid.*

[28]An example of cyber hacking experienced by American television company HBO in 2017, in which content and episodes were stolen from the TV series *Game of Thrones*. There, the company had to deal with the burglars by negotiating to prevent leakage of confidential information about the unpublished episodes and scripts. See: https://www.theguardian.com/technology/2017/aug/21/game-of-thrones-hbo-hackers-threaten-leak-of-season-finale (accessed on September 18, 2020).

to phishing practices,[29] including those targeted at networks, sites, credit card data, secret databases, and other security incidents.[30] For example, in September 2019, Microsoft revealed a severe security crisis, when browser software launched by hackers threatened the security of its users who, in using the Explorer browser, exposed themselves and their data to the hackers. In response to the crisis, Microsoft worked to launch a new version that contains important security updates and warned the general public to avoid using the browser in its unsafe version and to update to the latest version as soon as possible.[31]

Understanding the risks associated with cyber breaches and access to sensitive information has motivated the development of the field of information security and cyber protection. Keen awareness of how critical security is to companies in the cyber field is especially important to avoid incidents that could develop into a crisis. Given the exposure of many companies to risks that could jeopardize their reputation, lead to information leakage, and disrupt operations, many companies and organizations have started working with cyber protection entities to develop internal security practices to tackle such situations.[32] Simultaneously, studying this field and integrating crisis management with cybersecurity prepares organizations in the event of unforeseen threats and malicious actors to combat this modern-age menace in the best manner,[33] in light of the company's ability to defend itself in the cyber field, which is an area that can never guarantee a safe breakthrough.[34] Therefore, when a company faces its current management, it must outline a policy for managing this crisis before it develops into a

---

[29]The phishing method is an expression of sensitive information is stolen through phishing on the Internet. Usually, after phishing, cyberattack is likely to occur.

[30]Deloitte (2016). "Cyber crisis management: Readiness, response, and recovery," pp. 1–14.

[31]Aten, J. (2019). "800 million Microsoft Windows 10 customers just got an urgent warning to update their software now." *INC*, September 19. Available at: https://www.inc.com/jason-aten/800-million-microsoft-windows-10-customers-just-got-an-urgent-warning-to-update-their-software-now.html (accessed on September 18, 2020).

[32]Deloitte (2016). "Cyber crisis management: Readiness, response, and recovery," pp. 1–14.

[33]ראה את אתר. See: https://www.cisecurity.org/ (accessed on September 18, 2020).

[34]Deloitte (2016). "Cyber crisis management: Readiness, response, and recovery," pp. 1–14.

crisis and identify preventive measures that can aid in its defense. How the crisis is managed may determine the future of the company and whether it can continue after such a setback.

When a cyber incident occurs in an organization, there is sometimes a tendency to see the incident as associated with the technology department. A technological solution can often remedy the situation, but it may also be the catalyst and therefore the inaction of other departments could significantly lower the success of the recovery. Even if the crisis originated on the technological level, it in no way means that other departments must not cooperate in order to put in place contingencies to isolate and contain the threat. The managers and employees alike have a duty to cooperate between departments to find solutions.[35]

When preparing for a cyber crisis in a company, Meng's crisis management principles can be used, as mentioned above, with the leading principles being the company's preparation and preparedness for the cyber crisis and its response.[36] To these principles, we will add the relevant variables to the nature of the crisis and the type of crisis, i.e. whether it requires a long or short response time, an operation strategy, and the restoration of the company after the crisis has ended. When classifying the type of crisis as a cyber crisis, there are other principles that we must apply in order to deal with it in the best and most appropriate manner. First, we will understand what a cyber crisis is and identify which areas of the organization's business may be at risk. For this purpose we will take the example of a situation in which a company is in crisis, as the company's confidential information is stolen by an external party which demands a ransom from the management in order not to use the same information (concerning the company's customers, employees, etc.). Information theft can have devastating consequences for the organization's reputation and ongoing functioning.

Now, there are a number of possible situations when dealing with the same incident from the moment one identifies it as a crisis. In the approach supported by the authors, the company must reach the stage when it encounters a cyber crisis in which it is ready for any eventuality and can avoid surprising elements which could have a paralyzing effect.

---

[35] *Ibid.*

[36] Regester, M. and J. Larkin (2005). *Risk Issues and Crisis Management*, 3rd Edition, p. 48.

This means that the organization and its employees must develop important tools that will prepare them for any type of incident.

1.6. Preparing for the Crisis

Although cyber crisis occurs primarily through technological means, it can affect the entire society. Therefore, a company must prepare to deal with such a crisis in the best possible way. The existence of a team of experts who are responsible for policy planning, thinking, control, and preparedness for the fourth-coming crisis will lead to a high state of readiness.[37] This is when engagement with crisis management is a pre-planned component, outlining policy and conduct.[38] Through such a team, management of a crisis preparedness plan and exercises simulating a true situation should be employed.[39] In order to prepare for the crisis, the crisis management team, in collaboration with the employees and through active simulations of real-life situations, must understand what risks the organization may encounter during its near and current life cycle. Understanding this will help in early identification of the crisis as it begins to exist.[40] When a dedicated team sits with executives and stakeholders from all departments in the company, any department can flag the risks exist in its field, thereby avoiding potential incidents.[41] Therefore, an existing crisis management plan ensures an optimal simulation according to pre-selected indices. Similar to fire drills, cyberthreat exercises can help safeguard the company from a variety of threats. There is no better teacher than the enemy itself. The company actors that will play critical roles must develop analytical skills to:

---

[37]Mitroff, I. I., P. Shrivastava and F. Udwadia (1987). "Effective crisis management," *The Academy of Management Executive (1987–1989)*, **1**(4): 283–292.

[38]According to Cyber Deloitte's experts, in order to manage the best response, the company must coordinate and practice using six key phases: policy, strategy, technology, business operations, risk and adjustment, and finally rehabilitation and repair. See: Deloitte (2016). "Cyber crisis management: Readiness, response, and recovery," pp. 1–14.

[39]*Ibid.*

[40]Regester, M. and J. Larkin (2005). *Risk Issues and Crisis Management*, 3rd Edition, p. 43.

[41]*Opt. cit.*, p. 48.

(1) better comprehend, synthesize, and leverage complex scenarios that may arise;
(2) identify and create intelligence requirements through practices such as threat modeling;
(3) understand and develop skills in tactical-, operational-, and strategic-level threat intelligence;
(4) generate threat intelligence to detect, respond to, and defeat focused and targeted threats;
(5) learn about different sources of threats to collect adversary data and how to exploit and pivot off of it in terms of protection from competitors or malicious actors; and
(6) establish structured analytical techniques that are successful in any security role through interdepartmental cooperation.

1.7. Planning the Response

A managed crisis is a crisis that did not surprise its managers. The company must understand that it must always be prepared, that it is exposed to risks in its field, and should formulate an orderly plan in response to a crisis that includes different types of threats. The company must classify the information it contains, i.e. the most important information that requires the utmost security and the information that will cause less harm. When such a classification is done in crisis management planning, the existing response will be based on the injury and its severity. Classifying the information according to its importance and confidentiality will help to understand the intensity of the crisis and the actions required to end it and minimize the damage caused, while simultaneously making technological attempts to recover what was taken.

Response planning, which is an important strategy for management, is planning the outlined policies and line of conduct. From any simulation conducted within the company that emulates a true crisis, the lessons relevant to the situation in which the company experienced a real crisis must be derived. At the same time, it should be noted that a company must understand that it is not possible to prepare accurately for a real crisis due to the element of surprise that arises with each individual threat as it occurs. The real crisis will be different from the manufactured simulation, and organizational managers must be flexible in their thinking on how to implement the plan. In a real crisis, the plan's guideline will be used with reference to what is happening, given the difference between a theoretical plan and a state of reality in the field. Therefore, an understanding of the existing reality and the ability to adapt the theoretical plan to the existing situation is required.

For example, the stealing of a customer list could be an incident that would lead to a serious crisis in which the information regarding important customers of the company present in the same list could reach third parties with the possibility of access by competing companies.

1.8. Executing the Response to the Crisis

Crisis response is a stage that consists of the early comprehension and addressal of a crisis.[42] An early perception that the incident could indeed become a crisis is that it can, at the same time, prevent its development and lead to coping when the dimensions of the incident are still in its initial stages.[43] At the bottom line is the response to the crisis. First, the crisis may have led to a meeting of the company's capabilities and its ability to respond fully. In order to manage a crash, the company must restore these capabilities at the earliest opportunity for that type of crisis can have a crippling physical effect. This is to curb the existing pygmy and to prevent the incidents.[44] This means that, as the company's war with the technological crisis wages, it must simultaneously continue to deal with its customers, business partners, employees, regulators, and investors who have been affected or may be affected by the crisis. When this kind of deadlock occurs, a lack of communication and explanation related to the company can lead to a situation where regulatory or business decisions are made about it without giving an opinion. Therefore, the company must make use of the media available to it, such as the press, TV, and social media, while creating a secure communication interface with its employees and customers for the purpose of transmitting and updating messages. This communication is a critical step that a company can take by giving proper reference and explanation of what is happening. The company must understand that using the media properly can save it from a situation

---

[42]Comfort, L. K. (2007). "Crisis management in hindsight: Cognition, communication, coordination, and control," *Public Administration Review*, December: 189–197.
[43]*Ibid.*
[44]Deloitte (2016). "Cyber crisis management: Readiness, response, and recovery," pp. 1–14.

where there is concern that the company is a "sinking ship" and explain what crisis it is experiencing and give real solutions and deadlines on how to get back to a functional status quo. The company must create a message page with detailed reference for their clients. This page must be created by consulting with the public relations and corporate spokesperson, contacting the public with details of what is happening while protecting strategic data. Proper communication during a crisis is a critical and important means available to the company when it is being attacked. By using proper communication, it can minimize present and future damages that may result from the crisis. With the rise of digital and social media, customers expect a swift response to any issues that arise, because companies have the technology to address them. Social media can be useful at the communication stage to leverage supporters that may not be directly affiliated with the company and may give the message a more authentic perception. It is also important to acknowledge the victims of the crisis (if there are any) irrespective of whether the company is to blame or not; empathy can play a great role in the crisis and can rally more support from the public for the organization. When a crisis occurs, the company must not play the blame game, even if it is not culpable; this is a sign of weakness and can shake the confidence of shareholders, employees, and the public at large. Amid a crisis, the organization under attack is also put under a microscope, and every move it makes is going to be judged by the public. It is better to be upfront and transparent than plead ignorance or stonewall. The message must be uniform throughout both inside and outside the company.

Second, during the crisis, the company will be required to respond to situations and the exceptional issues that arise from the crisis. The company must understand that it may have to respond to such requests and acknowledge their significance, which represents the dynamism required during the crisis and leads to cooperation between shareholders and customers. In addition, the company may be required to respond to various regulatory requests in order to lead to cooperation and exit from the crisis. These are all things that, in advance planning, can be predicted for the most part, and accordingly the reaction is planned. This can hasten response time and therefore eliminate the crisis at a much faster pace.

Another significant thing that the company must do during the crisis is partnering with its employees, managers, and partners in secure ways.[45]

---

[45] Deloitte (2016). "Cyber crisis management: Readiness, response, and recovery," pp. 1–14.

If the company's information systems are hacked, its communications systems and other entities are also likely to be attacked. Preparedness to create an alternative communication system, secured by strict rules, will assist in the ongoing conduct of the crisis and will lead to healthy work processes in the company.

1.9. Ending of the Crisis

The end of the crisis is the final stage of the process, which began with identification and continued response. Now, the organization needs to rebuild from the damage and recover from the incident. Rapid rehabilitation and quick return to routine will create a sense of security among customers, employees, and management, as it can be concluded that the crisis has passed, and recovery and learning are taking place quickly and efficiently.

At the same time as the company is recovering from the crisis, it must undertake an in-depth crisis learning process. The company must understand where it went wrong, what caused the incident, and how to prevent such a crisis in the future. Company executives, in collaboration with the crisis management team, should study the same case, understand how the design structure should change, and identify the new rules that should be outlined in accordance with the conclusions of the debriefing. These conclusions are an important process along the way, as it allows for re-learning of the dangers that exist and examines the company's ability to respond. When the crisis is cyber in nature, information security of the company is of utmost importance and so is the ability to take backup actions to prevent a systems crash.[46] Therefore, in a situation where the company's vital capacity has been compromised, it must ensure the existence of alternative safety nets that will be put into operation to neutralize the main means of experiencing the crisis.

It is important to understand that a crisis can prove costly for the company. This can be reflected in unplanned costs, damaged reputation, customer abandonment, and a decline in stock value, but in such a situation, it is necessary to understand what the crisis does. The crisis provides us with a fertile ground for immediate decision-making and conclusions. Creating change in security processes, policies, and organizational planning is an

---

[46]Pelephone's crisis is an example of supplier transfer.

example of these possible changes. When the dust has settled, this is the time to take stock and optimize its results and realize that now it is possible to influence the conduct and operations of the organization quickly and effectively.[47] After the incident occurs, the company has the power to formulate guiding principles that must be adapted and established by a new policy. This can be reflected in the conduct of the security routine in the company, in the conduct of information assets, the company's vigilance measures, and understanding how any action can lead to a cyberthreat. When these are done in parallel with the company's ability to recover, the ability to return to normal operation alongside the rehabilitation affected by the crisis is quickened.[48]

1.10. The Need for Law and Order

Just as many cyber vulnerabilities exist in the private sector, many risks exist for state-of-the-art organizations as well.[49] Cyber legislation is paramount in order to set standards to monitor the actions for the public; it can also address the issues that can affect order and governance.[50] The digital world is a wild paradise full of knowledge but void of geographical borders which challenge the rule of law. This means every country on a global scale must be on the same page and cooperate in order to protect the citizens of the world.[51] Therefore, informed and developed cyber behavior is both a political and social interest, given the importance of the vital means for the state and its citizens and the importance of the functioning of private sector companies that exist in the country.[52]

---

[47]"In the early phase of President Obama's tenure, which coincided with the depths of the financial crisis, his Chief of Staff, Rahm Emanuel, famously remarked: "You never want a serious crisis to go to waste.""

[48]Deloitte (2016). "Cyber crisis management: Readiness, response, and recovery," pp. 1–14.

[49]*Reuters* (2017). "Ukraine power outage was a cyber attack: Ukrenergo." January 18. Available at: https://www.reuters.com/article/us-ukraine-cyber-attack-energy/ukraines-power-outage-was-a-cyber-attack-ukrenergo-idUSKBN1521BA (accessed on September 18, 2020).

[50]Kamble, R. (2013). "Cyber law and information technology," *International Journal of Scientific and Engineering Research*, 4: 789–794.

[51]*Ibid.*

[52]"Cybercrime causes direct and indirect financial damage. Examples of direct damages are stolen money, lost time, damages that businesses can pay for damages caused to their

Today, the cyber realm contains sparse legislation on the subject, which allows each company to decide on different organizational policies, even making it difficult for cyber companies to play a significant part in this risk.[53] By using the various cyber practices, such as phishing methods that are usually accompanied by cyberattacks, the possibility of an attack collapsing a company and crippling its operations is a clear and present danger for the economy.

At the legal level, it can be seen that in the State of Israel, hacking through technological means is addressed by the enactment of the Computer Law. The Computer Law refers to offenses committed against a computer, such as disruption and interruption, illegal computer penetration, and software-prohibited operations and attributes those acts to a criminal offense that causes the perpetrators to be prosecuted. In addition, the Computer Law refers to actions that establish grounds for tort in accordance with the Tort Ordinance.[54] Thus, there is a possibility of receiving compensation as a remedy when this was done due to the defendant's negligence.[55]

But is the Computer Law, setting aside norm-setting sanctions, sufficiently effective in a situation where in many cases it becomes difficult to reach the offending identity or its geographical location?[56] Moreover, in light of the existing technological development and the many breakthroughs that are being made,[57] is this the right way to deal with this phenomenon? This question establishes the need for understanding the

---

customers, and loss of economic value information (e.g. customer list and credit information). Indirect damages can be reflected in a company's credit rating being compromised for its information security, loss of business opportunities, decreased customer actions due to the loss of security in the cyberspace, as well as expenses associated with defending against future attacks. In addition, cybercrime causes unfinished damage, such as privacy." Extract from: State Comptroller's Report for 2015, Annual Report 67B, p. 1860 TS.

[53] Siboni, G. and I. Sivan-Seville (2018). "Regulation in the cyber space," *Memorandum No. 190*, INSS, p. 79.

[54] The Tort Order (New Version), 1968.

[55] Section 9, The Computer Law, 1995.

[56] In the hacker crisis experienced by American television company HBO, the hacker was Iranian, residing within Iranian borders. This led to difficulty in further prosecution by the US. See: *Reuters* (2017). "U.S. prosecutors charge Iranian in 'Game of Thrones' hack," November 21. Available at: https://www.reuters.com/article/us-cyber-hbo-indictment/u-s-prosecutors-charge-iranian-in-game-of-thrones-hack-idUSKBN1DL1YT (accessed on September 18, 2020).

[57] State Comptroller's Report 2015 — Cybercrime widely uses "dark networks" and sophisticated technological operations using both advanced technology that differs the

state's existing regulation and guidance. Following the enactment of the Computer Act, governmental bodies were established in 2017. As part of the national cyber defense, companies defined as national critical infrastructure, are guided by the national cyber directorate to improve their cyber defences. Private sector companies receive references from a sector regulator of the company domain, which are, for the most part, not mandatory requirements.[58]

Given the lack of mandatory regulation on the subject, companies and organizations have increasingly become in need of, practices, and prevention in line with the development of research in the field, primarily by external companies and the consumption of cyber insurance to cover existing risks.[59]

After investigating the field of crisis management, which comprises a wide variety of crises, such as political, environmental, social, and economic crises, cyber crises management can be seen as an effective tool to signal the company's readiness, given the understanding that there is a higher chance of dealing with a cyber crisis in an effective way, with the crisis identified and the ensuing response already practiced in an organized manner. Through a cyber regulator, a mandatory policy will be laid down in the manner in which the company's behavior in the economy will be given more coverage, resulting from government involvement. The government's involvement in cyber regulation may be argued against, for reasons of private sector control and additional oversight of the organization's operations. But in the long run, given the increasing vulnerability and status of cyber technology in the State of Israel and in the world, this is a fitting solution to the need to maintain a functioning Israeli economy.

1.11. Summary

In this chapter, we briefly reviewed a crisis management model and adapted it to the cyber world, and highlighted the need for information security among private and public organizations.

---

crime and malware to take millions of innocent hosts across the world under cybercrime commands on other computers and servers.

[58] Siboni, G. and I. Sivan-Seville (2018). "Regulation of the cyber complex," *Memorandum No. 190*, INSS, p. 81.

[59] Shoshan, A. (2016). "Most cyber hacks: For healthcare and financial services," *The Marker*. Available at: https://www.themarker.com/markets/1.2895808 (accessed on September 18, 2020).

The cyber field is experiencing the highest number of crises in the economy, and it is the need of the hour to address and try to help companies and organizations not get into such crises due to preconceived behavior. As we have seen in this technological world, the possibility of an organization ensuring a secure environment for its secret repositories is always at risk. This risk is the reason why accurate crisis management plans should be applied to try and predict the crisis that may occur. Early identification of the incident, the understanding that the incident may be a crisis, along with a response that includes communication and proper organizational conduct, can help reduce the damage that may be caused. The need for a dedicated team whose purpose is to prepare for crises is an immediate need in the technological world. It is worth examining for larger companies to create a new department that would solely be dedicated to crisis management.

The difficulty arises with the fact that, within the economy, each organization practices a different degree of crisis management and preparation, depending on its budgetary abilities. However, prevention and protection must put on the top of the agenda, and security measures must be put in place by specialists that work for these companies.

Unique regulation that will be tailored to the cyber world and will be a guiding and binding factor for those organizations can be one of the solutions on the way to preventing these crises, as it will monitor the company's actions and how they are prepared to tackle a crisis. Such regulation will help reduce gaps between the readiness of different organizations and may even save companies from devastating crises. The clear interest is that companies and economic organizations must continue to exist and that we must do everything we can to keep them safe in a world full of dangers. The future of the State of Israel as a Western state that is on the path of research and development lies in the continuing ability of these companies to exist and develop.

The advancement offered by technology has the potential to contribute to research and development and to create an advanced, tailor-made living environment, but this can only be achieved when done safely, efficiently, and willingly. It is noteworthy to summarize that readiness, response, and recovery are key elements in managing any crisis. Security, vigilance, and resilience play a great role in managing a threat which could turn into a crisis. Technical, forensic, and investigative capabilities are vital to preserving evidence and analyzing control failures, security lapses, and other conditions related to the incident. In addition, organizations should implement both proactive and responsive technology solutions to mitigate future cyber incidents. When it comes to incident and crisis management, readiness is an evolutionary state. What you were ready for yesterday may be the last thing cybercriminals have in mind today.

Chapter 2

The EU's Cybersecurity Policy: Building a Resilient Regulatory Framework

Annegret Bendiek[*,‡] *and Eva Pander Maat*[†,§]

*German Institute for International and Security Affairs — SWP
Berlin, Germany*

†*University of London, London, United Kingdom*

‡*Annegret.Bendiek@swp-berlin.org*

§*Eva.pander-maat@city.ac.uk*

Abstract

The European Union (EU) plays a coordinating role on cybersecurity and primarily aims to build a cyber-resilient regulatory framework. Its cybersecurity policy is delineated by the foundational Treaties and has been shaped by two concepts: the internal market rationale and resilience. The internal market rationale entails that the EU is legitimized to formulate a common policy and promote harmonized standards on cyberissues because the regulation and protection of the internal market require it to do so. Resilience is the core concept in the EU's cybersecurity strategy and represents the capacity to resist and regenerate. The EU aims to achieve deterrence by resilience. Following the strong path dependency of the internal market rationale, cybersecurity policy in all domains of EU competence is eventually accessory or complementary to the resilience of the internal market. However, cyber-security as a cross-cutting policy concern has also had a significant spill-over effect into domains other than the internal market, namely the Area of Freedom, Security and Justice, the Common Foreign and Security Policy, and the Common Security and Defence Policy.

2.1. Introduction

The free trade of data has spurred globalization and led to an increasingly interconnected world. Cyberspace and the Internet were long seen as a source of economic growth, a place primarily belonging to businesses and customers. The EU, too, has long seen the digital world through an economic lens with a free trade perspective. Even today, "data transfers are seen as crucial to revive the slowing European economy."[1] Over time, however, concerns about the privacy rights and security of individuals in cyberspace have grown, and cyberthreats on the European soil have surged. According to the European Cybercrime Centre, "cybercrime continues to take new forms and new directions"[2]; "In a 12-month period, [...] over 2 billion [[data-]breaches] were reported, all impacting EU citizens to some degree"[3]; "Malware attacks [have been taken] to a level where they can be an impossible challenge for national law enforcement agencies to handle alone"[4]; and "Attacks are used not only for financial gains but for ideological, political or purely malicious reasons."[5]

In response to these concerns, cybersecurity quickly ascended to the top of EU's political and legislative agenda in the past two decades. This study sets out how the EU's approach to cybersecurity, as delineated by the foundational Treaties, has been shaped by two concepts: the internal market rationale and resilience. The former represents the regulatory policy argument that largely determined how the EU's approach to

---

[1]Bendiek, A. and M. Römer (2019). "Externalizing Europe: The global effects of European data protection," *Digital Policy, Regulation and Governance,* **21**(1): 32–43, 37.

[2]European Cybercrime Centre (2017). *Internet Organized Crime Assessment 2017* (The Hague: European Union Agency for Law Enforcement).

[3]*Ibid.*

[4]European Cybercrime Centre (2018). *Internet Organized Crime Assessment 2018* (The Hague: European Union Agency for Law Enforcement).

[5]*Ibid.*

cybersecurity has been developed in the past three decades. The latter is the core concept in the EU's cybersecurity strategy as it has matured in the past years.

In this study, the term "cybersecurity" is understood to entail "the safeguards and actions that can be used to protect the [civilian and military] cyber domain [...] from those threats that are associated with or that may harm its interdependent networks and information infrastructure."[6] Such threats, referred to as cyberthreats, can be military, hybrid, or (conventionally) criminal in nature. At first sight, cyberthreats affect the internal and external security domains.[7] Many international actors, therefore, establish their cybersecurity policy primarily in these domains. However, cyberthreats also significantly affect the economic and (foreign) political domain. Cybersecurity is therefore a cross-sectional policy challenge, prone to create spillover effects from the security domain into other domains.

The EU is a supranational, multi-level governance institution with characteristics of both a federal state and a traditional intergovernmental organization.[8] The foundational Treaties, as per its signatories, transfer sovereign powers to the EU.[9] These powers are exercised with direct effect in Member States' jurisdictions.[10] Competences not conferred upon

---

[6]This definition is taken from the EU's Cyber Security Strategy, *JOIN* (2013) Vol. 1 final (Brussels, February 7, 2013).

[7]Internal security is commonly used to refer to crime, civil protection, and law and order inside the state, whereas external security refers to defence and deterrence between states. See, amongst others, Eriksson, J. and M. Rhinard (2009). "The internal — external security nexus: Notes on an emerging research agenda," *Cooperation and Conflict*, **44**(3): 243–267.

[8]Grimm, D. (1995). "Does Europe need a constitution?" *European Law Journal*, **1**(3): 282–302; Habermas, J. (1995). "Remarks on Dieter Grimm's '*Does Europe Need a Constitution?*'" *European Law Journal*, **1**(3): 303–307; Kuper, R. (1998). "The making of a constitution for Europe," *Contemporary Politics*, **4**(3): 285–297; Caporaso, J. (1996). "The European Union and Forms of State: Westphalian, Regulatory or Post-Modern?" *Journal of Common Market Studies*, **34**(1): 29–52.

[9]The Treaty on European Union (TEU) and the Treaty on the Functioning of European Union (TFEU).

[10]The doctrines of direct effect and the supremacy of European law were established by the European Court of Justice in its landmark cases Van Gend & Loos and Costa ENEL. European Court of Justice, Case 26-62, "Van Gend en Loos," February 5, 1963; European Court of Justice, Case 6/64 "Costa v ENEL," July 15, 1964. See for in-depth coverage of

the EU remain to lie with Member States.[11] Because the Treaties do not mention cybersecurity as such, the EU does not have an explicit competence for a common policy on cybersecurity. Moreover, the EU's competences in the internal and external security domain — as noted, often the primary domains of cybersecurity policy — are limited to coordinative efforts, such as a finite extent of minimum harmonization, expertise pooling, and the steering of industrial investment. Regardless, the EU has found itself confronted with increasingly salient cybersecurity concerns. Cyberthreats on European soil significantly impact the EU's economy and society. The elimination of internal borders makes the EU particularly vulnerable to cyberthreats. Facing these concerns, the EU has grappled to formulate a common cybersecurity policy. The juxtaposition between the strong intention within EU institutions to regulate cybersecurity and the limited legal competences to do so lies at the core of this study. Perhaps strikingly, the EU has incrementally constructed a common cybersecurity policy which currently stretches across four policy domains. This study investigates the EU's cybersecurity policy and its creation within the context of constitutional constraints.

Because competences for cybersecurity strictly speaking still lie with Member States, the study of the EU's cybersecurity policy must recognize the EU as a multi-level governance actor in a policy structure subject to both intrainstitutional and intergovernmental forces.[12] Following an institutionalist method of analysis, institutions do matter, and the Commission strategies and cases by the European Court of Justice are critical junctures in the development of the EU's cybersecurity policy.[13]

---

both doctrines Chapter 3 (Competence) and Chapter 9 (Supremacy) in Craig, P. and G. de Burca (2015). *EU Law. Text, Cases and Materials*, (Oxford: Oxford University Press).

[11] Article 4(2) TEU.

[12] Thelen, K. (2004). "Historical institutionalism in comparative politics," *Annual Review of Political Science*, **2** (1999): 369–404; Pierson, P. (2004). *Politics in Time: History, Institutions, and Social Analysis* (Woodstock, UK: Princeton University Press, 2004).

[13] This approach to the role of institutional actors in historical institutionalism is promulgated by Bell and beautifully demonstrated by Schmidt's account of the role of the ECJ in a historical institutionalist account of European integration. See Bell, S. (2011). "Do we really need a new 'constructivist institutionalism' to explain institutional change?" *British Journal of Political Science*, **41**(4): 883–906; Schmidt, S. K. (2012). "Who cares about nationality? The path-dependent case law of the ECJ from goods to citizens," *Journal of European Public Policy*, **19**(1): 8–24; Schmidt, S. K. (2018). *The European Court of Justice and the Policy Process: The Shadow of Case Law* (Oxford: Oxford University Press).

This study takes a particular interest in regulatory policies. In political science terms, regulatory policies can be distinguished from distributive and redistributive policies.[14] Both distributive and redistributive policies are limited by the budgetary cap of 1.27% of Union GDP.[15] The EU has thus famously been characterized as a "regulatory state."[16] In addition, in the EU's cybersecurity policy, regulatory policies are predominant. Consequently, this study characterizes the EU's approach to cybersecurity as "regulatory." The legal analysis allows us to assess regulatory instruments on their merit, i.e. the extent to which they provide supranational harmonization and build toward an actual EU-wide policy. It has further been instrumental to the constitutional analysis and the interpretation of legal cases.[17] In legal terms, "regulation" is taken to refer not only to

---

[14] This distinction was coined by Theodore Lowi. See Lowi, T. (1964). "American business, public policy, case studies, and political theory," *World Politics*, 16(1964): 677–715.

[15] Laffan, B. (1997). *The Finances of the European Union* (New York: St. Martin's Press), p. 127; Pollack, M. (1994). "Creeping competence: The expanding agenda of the European Community," *Journal of Public Policy*, 14(2): 95–145.

[16] Majone, G. (1994). "The rise of the regulatory State in Europe," *West European Politics*, 77; Majone, G. (ed.) (1996). *Regulating Europe* (New York: Routledge); Eberlein, B. and E. Grande (1994). "Beyond delegation: Transnational regulatory regimes and the EU regulatory state," *Journal of European Public Policy*, 12(1): 89–112; Pollack, M. (1994). "Creeping competence: The expanding agenda of the European Community," *Journal of Public Policy*, 14(2): 95–145. The development of the EU as a regulatory state has been related to the "negative integration" of European markets following liberalization, after which the state is no longer seen as the primary distributive actor taking care of the public good, but rather as a regulatory agent providing the regulatory conditions for a smoothly functioning market (see Scharpf, F. (1996). "Politische Optionen im vollendeten Binnenmarkt," in M. Jachtenfuchs and B. Kohler-Koch (eds.), *Europäische Integration* (Opladen: Leske+Budrich)); Scharpf, F. (1999). *Governing in Europe. Effective and Democratic?* (Oxford: OUP). Moreover, the EU as a regulatory state has been linked to the process of agencification, i.e. the delegation of powers to centralized EU agencies (see Chamon, M. (2011). "EU agencies between Meroni and Romano or the devil and the deep blue sea," *Common Market Law Review*, 48(4): 1055–1107); Bast, J. (2006). "Book Review: *Dilemmas of European Integration: The Ambiguities & Pitfalls of Integration by Stealth*," by Giandomenico Majone. (Oxford: Oxford University Press, 2005)," *Common Market Law Review*, 43(2): 597–599.

[17] This study takes the European law as its legal framework and does not aim to include a comparative perspective, including international or national law in this framework. Reference to international law is only made when necessary to complement the European law perspective.

legislation following Article 288 of the TFEU but also to the adoption of soft law, guidelines, and standards, with or without the involvement of EU agencies. In response to the problem statement, this study answers the following questions: (1) what comprises the EU's current cybersecurity policy; (2) how the EU's cybersecurity policy has come into being; (3) what strategy the EU pursues with this policy in the context of international cyber governance; and (4) how the EU's regulatory approach to the strongly interrelated digital policy issue of data protection was created.

In this chapter, we introduce the role of resilience in the EU's approach to cybersecurity and discuss the EU's norm-pushing role on data protection. Then we pursue an orderly analysis of the EU's approach to cybersecurity in full, which is categorized by the policy domains of the internal market; the Area of Freedom, Security and Justice (AFSJ); the Common Security and Defence Policy (CSDP); and the Common Foreign and Security Policy (CFSP).

2.2. The EU's Cybersecurity Policy

The EU has been primarily driven by an internal market rationale in the creation of its cybersecurity policy, which entails that the EU deploy its competence for the regulation of the internal market to issue common (regulatory) policy on cybersecurity. This choice of competence is partly pragmatic. Internal market regulation has been at the core of the European project since its inception, and the corresponding Treaty basis, Article 114 TFEU, is still the most versatile and widely used legal basis. However, the choice has also been engrained in European policymaking by the argumentation which introduced digital policy as a whole within the EU's mandate. This argumentation can be traced back to the completion of the internal market in 1985.[18] The economic opportunities of the emerging global market for digital services and goods led the Commission to identify information and communications technology (ICT) and the digital domain as a potential area of Union action.[19] In the decades that followed, the economic opportunities of the digital market continued to serve as the impetus for the EU's digital policymaking and prevailed when it became apparent

---

[18] Dewar, R. S. (2017). "Cyber security in the European Union: An historical institutionalist analysis of a 21st century security concern," PhD Dissertation, University of Glasgow, p. 125.
[19] *COM* (85) 310 final (Milan, June 14, 1985).

that digitalization brought risks as well as benefits.[20] These risks are interpreted in an economic rather than a security discourse: cyberthreats undermine citizens' trust in online services and negatively impact the economy.[21] In turn, the EU is legitimized to take measures to improve cybersecurity to protect the internal market. This idea is the core of the internal market rationale. Three decades and some later, the internal market rationale still functions as the primary rationale in the EU's approach to cybersecurity and determines the legislative, political, and industrial agenda on cybersecurity. The internal market rationale is characteristic for the EU's cybersecurity policy and clearly distinguishes the EU from other actors on the global stage, which generally take a much more security- and defence-oriented approach to cybersecurity.

The EU's cybersecurity policy is delineated by the foundational Treaties, which define and restrict the EU's competences. When compared to regional and international organizations in global cyber governance with narrow, clearly formulated mandates specifically devoted to cybersecurity,[22] the EU's mandate for cybersecurity is muddled. The foundational Treaties do not provide a specific, unifying legal basis for the EU to issue legislation on cybersecurity, which consequently remains a legal competence of the Member States.[23] The EU's role is therefore primarily coordinative. In this role, the EU aims to create coherence in Member States' approaches and regulate the policy domains affected by cyberthreats in which the Treaties do confer powers upon the EU. These domains include (1) the internal market; (2) AFSJ; (3) CSDP; and (4) CFSP.[24] The EU has broad competences to regulate the single market.[25] In contrast, the EU's competences in the AFSJ

---

[20]Dewar, R.S. (2017). "Cyber security in the European Union: An historical institutionalist analysis of a 21st century security concern," PhD Dissertation, University of Glasgow.

[21]*COM* (2015) 192 final (Brussels, May 6, 2015), pp. 12–13.

[22]Pawlak, P. (2019). "The EU's role on shaping the cyber regime complex," *European Foreign Affairs Review*, **24**(2): 167–186, 169.

[23]Article 43(1) TFEU does allow for the adoption of Council Decisions. Following the principle of subsidiarity, codified in Article 5 TEU, any competences not conferred upon the EU remain with the Member States, Article 5(2) TEU.

[24]This categorization is in line with the 2013 Cyber Security Strategy and, in a different order, was presented in Bendiek, A. (2018). "The EU as a force for peace in international cyber diplomacy," *SWP Comment*, No. 19, April.

[25]Article 4(2)(a) of the TFEU provides the EU with shared competences in the area of the internal market. Article 114 (TFEU) has long proven a fruitful legal basis for legislative development, making the internal market into the most full-bodied area of European policy and law.

are mainly restricted to matters of law enforcement.[26] Moreover, although the EU's moderate mandate to formulate cyber defence projects within the CSDP has recently gained somewhat of a political momentum, the CFSP and CSDP are still mostly nationally governed.[27] Interestingly, cybersecurity as a new policy field has proven able to yield relatively broad political support for common action. Cybersecurity has functioned as a tool for the EU legislator to expand the range of Union action in domains outside of the internal market, particularly stretching the Treaty provisions for security and foreign policy goals. The constitutional restrictions to the EU's cybersecurity approach have hence also triggered a deepening of European integration.

2.2.1. *The EU's cybersecurity strategy*

The EU's cybersecurity policy has only been been provided with an overarching strategy in 2013, with the adoption of the Cyber Security Strategy (CSS).[28] The CSS not only reflects the internal market rationale but also attests to a spillover of cybersecurity policy into domains other than the internal market. The policy priorities set out in 2013, confirmed by the 2017 review and renewal of the CSS,[29] entail: (1) achieving cyber resilience; (2) reducing cybercrime; (3) developing cyber defence policy and capabilities related to the CSDP; (4) developing industrial and technological resources necessary for cybersecurity; and (5) establishing a coherent cyberspace policy.

At the core of the EU's cybersecurity strategy lies the pursuit of cyber resilience. Resilience is a common thread through all domains of the EU's cybersecurity policy as well the 2016 Global Strategy.[30] The concept, therefore, deserves special attention. In foreign policy and defence, resilience is a means of deterring potential attacks. Deterrence-by-resilience is an approach within deterrence-by-denial, and can as such be contrasted with

---

[26] See Section 2.4 for more on the constitutional construction of the AFSJ.

[27] See Sections 2.5 and 2.6 for more on the constitutional construction of the CFSP and CSDP.

[28] *JOIN* (2013) 1 final (Brussels, February 7, 2013).

[29] *JOIN* (2013) 1 final (Brussels, February 7, 2013); *SWD* (2017) 295 final (Brussels, September 13, 2017); *JOIN* (2017) 450 final (Brussels, September 13, 2017).

[30] European External Action Service (2016). "Shared vision, common action: A stronger Europe, a global strategy for the European Union's foreign and security policy," June. Available at: http://eeas.europa.eu/archives/docs/top_stories/pdf/eugs_review_web.pdf (accessed on August 14, 2019).

deterrence-by-retaliation. Deterrence-by-retaliation entails ensuring that any attack will be met with offensive countermeasures so intolerable that they will deter future attacks by the same or other attackers.[31] Deterrence-by-denial, in contrast, focuses on defensive rather than offensive means, on protecting rather than avenging. Resilience can be defined as the ability to "resist and regenerate" or "quickly restore the original shape after an attack."[32] Deterrence-by-resilience in cyberspace thus entails ensuring that ICT infrastructures have high levels of in-built security measures and are able to recover quickly from attacks. ICT infrastructures of public authorities, providers of essential services, and operators of critical infrastructures deserve special attention in this regard. However, to the EU, the resilience of the private sector is primordial, as decreasing the potential financial gains of cyberattacks logically decreases their economic risks. To the EU, resilience implies "security begins internally."[33] In the EU's cybersecurity policy, the core strategy is to achieve "resilience through regulation."[34] The regulatory agenda essentially aims to increase the standards for the security of the EU's ICT structures and their capacity to recover from cyberattacks.[35] The regulatory agenda is complemented, first, by an industrial agenda that aims to improve the competitiveness of the EU's ICT and cybersecurity sectors and decrease the dependence on non-EU suppliers, which is of strategic importance because dependence is a security risk, and second, with foreign policy efforts aimed at trust-building, creating global interdependence, and advocating common norms.[36]

The CSS is being implemented in a piecemeal fashion. Two recent major policy projects have been instrumental to this implementation.

---

[31] Bendiek, A. and T. Metzger (2015). "Deterrence theory in the cyber-century. Lessons from a state-of-the-art literature review," *SWP Working Paper* No. 2, May, p. 6.

[32] Bendiek, A. (2017). "A paradigm shift in the EU's common foreign and security policy: From transformation to resilience," SWP Research Paper No. 11, October, p. 6; Bendiek, A. and T. Metzger (2015). "Deterrence theory in the cyber-century. Lessons from a state-of-the-art literature review," *SWP Working Paper* No. 2, May, p. 6.

[33] Bendiek, A. (2017). "A paradigm shift in the EU's common foreign and security policy: From transformation to resilience," *SWP Research Paper* No. 11, October, p. 14.

[34] Wessel, R. A. (2019). "Cybersecurity in the European Union: Resilience through regulation?" in E. C. Pérez (ed.) *Routledge Handbook of EU Security Law and Policy* (London/ New York: Routledge).

[35] Bendiek, A. (2017). "A paradigm shift in the EU's common foreign and security policy: From transformation to resilience," *SWP Research Paper* No. 11, October, p. 14.

[36] *Ibid.*

First, in 2014, the Juncker Commission announced that a Digital Single Market (DSM) strategy would be at the top of its political agenda.[37] Cybersecurity forms an integral part of the DSM as an essential tool for averting economic damage to and conserving consumer trust in the European markets. Second, in 2015, the Commission employed the constitutional bases of the AFSJ for the construction of the so-called Security Union.[38] Where the Security Union serves to protect the European market, cybersecurity — an integral part of the Security Union — serves to protect the European digital market. The key elements of the EU's cybersecurity approach today stem from either one of these two projects, notwithstanding frequent mutual overlaps which illustrate the cross-sectional nature of cybersecurity as a policy field. In sum, however, regulatory and policy developments stretch across policy domains at varying speeds. Harmonization has been achieved in some fields, such as the protection of information systems and certification, and has lagged behind in others, such as substantive and procedural criminal law. Investments in digital infrastructure and technology have steadily increased but are as of yet insufficient to compensate for the deficient competitiveness of the EU's ICT market. As a consequence, the institutional and policy cohesion of the EU's approach to cybersecurity is subject to criticism.[39]

Cybersecurity efforts in all domains are eventually accessory or complementary to the internal market and serve to protect the resilience of the internal market rather than the EU's territory as such. The most concrete legislative and political efforts follow the internal market rationale: the Union is legitimized to formulate a common policy and promote

---

[37] Juncker, J.-C. (2014). "A new start for Europe: My agenda for jobs, growth, fairness and democratic change. Political guidelines for the next European Commission. Opening statement in the European Parliament plenary session," *European Commission*, July 15. Available at: https://ec.europa.eu/commission/sites/beta-political/files/juncker-political-guidelines-speech_en.pdf (accessed on August 19, 2019).

[38] European Political Strategy Centre (2016). "Towards a 'Security Union': Bolstering the EU's counter-terrorism response," *European Commission*, April 20. Available at: https://ec.europa.eu/epsc/publications/strategic-notes/towards-%E2%80%98security-union%E2%80%99_en (accessed on August 22, 2019).

[39] Carrapico, H. and A. Barrinha (2017). "The EU as a coherent (cyber)security actor?" *JCMS* **55**(6): 1254–1272; A. Bendiek, A. (2017). "Europe's patchwork approach to cyber defence needs a complete overhaul," *Council on Foreign Relations*, August 30. Available at: https://www.cfr.org/blog/europes-patchwork-approach-cyber-defense-needs-complete-overhaul (accessed on September 4, 2019).

harmonized standards on cybersecurity because the regulation of the internal market requires it.

2.2.2. *Data protection regulation*

The European Court of Justice (ECJ, the Court) oversees the application of the Treaties in line with the law.[40] The Court is therefore essential to the effectiveness and resilience of the EU as a regulatory power. It has not issued any rulings on cybersecurity specifically, which is not surprising given the novelty of the most substantial regulatory instruments on cybersecurity.[41] Nevertheless, its case law on data protection set a clear precedent. Data protection and cybersecurity are closely interrelated. In cases on data protection, the Court confirmed internal market regulation as a legal basis for regulating cyberspace, introduced data security into the EU's regulatory framework, entrenched the fundamental right to data protection, and reinforced the extraterritorial scope of the EU's data protection law.

The Court in the Digital Rights Ireland case assessed the Data Retention Directive by the fundamental rights to private life and privacy.[42] It set strict minimum standards for data security and went so far as to invalidate the Data Retention Directive because the general obligation to retain traffic data and location data did not meet those standards.[43] Notably, the Court focused on the Directive's secondary objective: that of security.[44] This focus suggests that the suitability of Article 114 as a legal basis for data protection legislation can be questioned,[45] but not as such

---

[40] Article 19 TEU.

[41] The Cybersecurity Act and the NIS Directive are discussed in Section 2.3.2.

[42] Articles 7, 8, and 11 of the Charter of Fundamental Rights of the European Union. European Court of Justice, Joined Cases C-293/12 and C-594/12 "Digital Rights Ireland," April 8, 2014, para. 23.

[43] European Court of Justice, Joined Cases C-293/12 and C-594/12 "Digital Rights Ireland," April 8, 2014.

[44] European Court of Justice, Joined Cases C-293/12 and C-594/12 "Digital Rights Ireland," April 8, 2014.

[45] Lynskey, O. (2014). "The Data Retention Directive is incompatible with the rights to privacy and data protection and is invalid in its entirety: Digital Rights Ireland," *Common Market Law Review*, **51**(2014): 1789–1812.

by the Court.[46] The decision made explicit that the EU legal community provides a high level of security in cyberspace, even if the constitutional basis to do so stems from the internal market, thereby emphasizing the interrelation of internal market regulation and security. Although data security refers specifically to the security measures needed to protect personal data from cyberthreats, the introduction of security requirements on all data processors — i.e. public as well as private actors — set a clear precedent on the EU's forward regulatory policy on digital issues. In the Tele2 and Watson case, the Court assessed the general obligation for providers of electronic communications services to retain data. The Court confirmed that the standards it set out in Digital Rights Ireland are mandatory and that it is indeed competent to review not only the retention, but also the access to data.[47] The requirements have since been codified in the General Data Protection Regulation (GDPR).[48]

In the Google Spain case, then, the Court famously established the "right to be forgotten."[49] This case buttressed the prevalence of the fundamental right to data protection in the EU, which in the Google Spain case was weighed against the right to information and Google's economic interests.[50] The Google Spain case confirms that the EU takes the perspective of the data subject, i.e. the customer or individual, rather than that of the data processor, i.e. businesses or governments. This rights-oriented perspective is diametrically opposite to the market-oriented perspective,

---

[46]The early regulatory instruments on data protection were also based on Article 114 TFEU. See Directive 95/46/EC of the European Parliament and of the Council of October 24, 1995, on the protection of individuals with regard to the processing of personal data and on the free movement of such data, Recitals 2 and 3.

[47]European Court of Justice, Joined Cases C-203/15 and C-698/15 "Tele2 and Watson," December 21, 2016.

[48]See in particular Article 5(1)(f) and Section 2 Regulation (EU) 2016/679 of the European Parliament and of the Council of 27 April 2016 on the protection of natural persons with regard to the processing of personal data and on the free movement of such data, and repealing Directive 95/46/EC (General Data Protection Regulation).

[49]European Court of Justice, Case C131/12 "Google Spain SL and Google Inc. v Agencia Española de Protección de Datos (AEPD) and Mario Costeja González," May 13, 2014.

[50]European Court of Justice, Case C131/12 "Google Spain SL and Google Inc. v Agencia Española de Protección de Datos (AEPD) and Mario Costeja González," May 13, 2014, para. 97.

which is predominant in the US.[51] The Google Spain case has helped create a strong fundamental right to data protection,[52] which may well obstruct free data flows. Following a recurrent pattern in EU law, the Court's rights-oriented interpretation has now been codified in Article 16 TFEU, which provides an express legal basis for the EU to protect the fundamental right to data protection.[53] Article 16 TFEU, in addition to the internal market rationale and the security dimension of data protection, functioned as the legal basis for the GDPR.[54]

The ECJ case law has also reinforced the extraterritorial effect of the EU's data protection law. This effect has both two dimensions. By means of the so-called Brussels effect, EU data protection law is adopted by businesses outside of the EU's physical borders because of the economic incentive to access the internal market. This extrajudicial effect is remarkably strong and credited to the comprehensive nature of the EU's regulatory frameworks.[55] In addition to the Brussels effect, third countries are incentivized to adopt EU-level data protection standards by adequacy decisions and data protection standards in bilateral agreements. Data transfers to a third country are only categorically allowed if an "adequate level of protection" is ensured. An adequacy decision exempts data controllers or processors established in or processing personal data belonging to data subjects in the EU from referring to any

---

[51]Rosen, J. (2012). "The right to be forgotten," *Stanford Law Review Online*, **64**: 88; Steinke, G. (2002). "Data privacy approaches from US and EU perspectives," *Telematics and Informatics*, **19**(2): 193; Farrel, H. (2002). "Negotiating privacy across arenas: The EU-US," in H. Farrell and A. Newman (eds.), *Of Privacy and Power: The Transatlantic Struggle over Freedom and Security* (Princeton, NJ: Princeton University Press), p. 105.

[52]The fundamental right to data protection is not only codified in Article 8 of the Charter of Fundamental Rights of the European Union but also provided with a constitutional basis in Article 16 TFEU.

[53]Cunningham, M. (2013). "Diminishing sovereignty: How European privacy law became international norm," *Santa Clara Journal of International Law*, **11**(2): 421–453, 440.

[54]Regulation (EU) 2016/679 of the European Parliament and of the Council of 27 April 2016 on the protection of natural persons with regard to the processing of personal data and on the free movement of such data, and repealing Directive 95/46/EC (General Data Protection Regulation). The right to be forgotten is also codified in Article 17 of the GDPR.

[55]Bradford, A. (2019). "The Brussels Effect," *Northwestern University Law Review*, **107**(1); Bendiek, A. and M. Römer (2019). "Externalizing Europe: The global effects of European data protection," *Digital Policy, Regulation and Governance*, **21**(1): 32–43.

specific authorization for data transfers.[56] In the Schrems case, the Court heightened the standards for adequacy decisions by establishing that third countries need a level of protection which is "essentially equivalent" to that in the EU.[57] Again, these heightened standards are now codified in the GDPR.[58] In its opinion on the bilateral agreement between the EU and Canada on a Passenger Name Record (PNR), the Court obliged the EU to renegotiate the agreement because it did not provide sufficient rights protection for data subjects. The Court thereby reaffirmed that it does not hesitate to impose high data protection standards in questions concerning the EU's external relations. In the recent Google v. CNIL case, the Court ruled on the territorial scope of the right to be forgotten. In line with the Advocate-General,[59] the Court does not go so far as to order the global application of the right to be forgotten.[60] To do so would have been very bold indeed. Nevertheless, the Court refrains from addressing or acknowledging the much-cited arguments that a global application of the right to be forgotten would create serious extraterritorial enforcement issues and lead to the global imposition of the EU's view on the fundamental right to privacy.[61] Moreover, the Court emphasizes that European law does not exclude the global application of the right to be forgotten and specifically enables national courts to judge per individual case whether the balance between the right

---

[56]Article 3, Article 13(1)(f), Article 45(1) Regulation (EU) 2016/679.

[57]European Court of Justice, Case C-362/14, "Maximillian Schrems v Data Protection Commissioner," October 6, 2015.

[58]Article 45(1) Regulation (EU) 2016/679.

[59]Opinion of Advocate-General Szpunar, January 10, 2019.

[60]European Court of Justice, Case C507/17, "Google LLC v Commission nationale de l'informatique et des libertés (CNIL)," September 24, 2019, para. 64.

[61]Taylor, M. (2017). "Google Spain Revisited," *European Data Protection Law Review*, **3**: 195; Nunziato, D. C. (2018). "The fourth year of forgetting: The troubling expansion of the right to be forgotten," *University of Pennsylvania Journal of International Law*, **39**: 1032–1034, 1011; Kuner, C. (2016). "The Court of Justice of the EU Judgment on data protection and Internet search engines: Current issues and future challenges," in B. Hess and C. Marionotty (eds.), *Protecting Privacy in Private International and Procedural Law and by Data Protection* (Abingdon: Routledge); van Alsenoy, B. and M. Koekkoek (2015). "Internet and jurisdiction after Google Spain: The extra-territorial reach of the EU's 'Right to be forgotten'," *KU Leuven and Leuven Centre for Global Governance Studies Working Paper* No. 152, March, p. 5.

to privacy and the right to information requires a global scope.[62] The overt extraterritorial application of EU data protection law thus remains an option.

The ECJ's case law on data protection demonstrates how the EU's regulatory power lies in consistently pushing for minimum standards both internally and externally. Responding to and entrenching this case law, the GDPR is currently the clearest and most comprehensive legislative framework on data protection globally, and the EU a global norm-setting power. The EU has the ambition to play a similar role in cybersecurity. It thus consistently pushes for international norms on cybersecurity at the GGE level at the United Nations. However, with EU being the largest internal market in the world, the core strength of the EU regulatory policy lies with the externalization of internal market-related standards. The example of data protection regulation suggests that adhering to high minimum standards in a clear and comprehensive regulatory framework compatible with norms and values enshrined in the Treaties and the Charter might enable the EU to act as a global norm-builder on cybersecurity as well.[63]

2.3. Single Market

The internal market rationale and its persistence in the EU's approach to cybersecurity has led to a situation in which the core of the EU's cybersecurity policy is founded upon the EU's mandate for internal market regulation, i.e. Article 114 TFEU. This mandate is also the source of most of the vast body of European law to date. As noted by Wessel, the extensive competences of the Union in the internal market have provided several "hooks" to harmonize or approximate legislation relating to cybersecurity with the aim of smoothening the functioning of the internal market.[64] As the foundational cornerstone of the EU, internal market regulation generally also enjoys the most widely shared political support. Moreover, the sheer size of EU as the largest single market in the world has been

---

[62] European Court of Justice, Case C507/17, "Google LLC v Commission nationale de l'informatique et des libertés (CNIL)," September 24, 2019, para. 72. Again, the Court in so ruling followed the Opinion of Advocate-General Szpunar, January 10, 2019, para. 62.

[63] The Charter of Fundamental Rights of the European Union.

[64] Wessel, R. A. (2019). "Cybersecurity in the European Union: Resilience through regulation?" in E. C. Pérez (ed.), *Routledge Handbook of EU Security Law and Policy* (London/ New York: Routledge).

identified as a main cause of the external effects of European law.[65] The global regulatory potential of internal market regulation is thus considerable. Moreover, internal market regulation is the path to increase the cyber resilience of the EU's internal — which lies at the heart of the EU's cybersecurity strategy.

A central role in the coordination and governance of EU cybersecurity regulation has been reserved for the European Union Agency for Cybersecurity (ENISA). ENISA supports the EU's market-coordinating role. It was founded in 2005 on temporary mandates, but its position is significantly solidified in 2019. Its mandate now includes providing cybersecurity certification, supporting capacity-building and drafting of cybersecurity policies, and helping implement vulnerability disclosure policies.[66]

2.3.1. *DSM*

The DSM was presented in 2015 as a key priority of the Juncker Commission's political agenda.[67] A DSM is defined as "one in which the free movement of goods, persons, services and capital is ensured and where individuals and businesses can seamlessly access and exercise online activities under conditions of fair competition, and a high level of consumer and personal data protection, irrespective of their nationality or place of residence."[68] Essentially, the DSM entails achieving the elimination of internal borders in the digital economy by means of regulatory convergence. Despite the cross-border nature of the Internet itself, digital economic activity in the EU is still highly compartmentalized across national borders.[69] The DSM strategy includes no less than 30 legislative

---

[65]Bradford, A. (2013). "The Brussels effect," *Northwestern University Law Review*, **107**(1).

[66]Regulation (EU) 2019/881 of the European Parliament and of the Council of 17 April 2019 on ENISA (the European Union Agency for Cybersecurity) and on information and communications technology cybersecurity certification and repealing Regulation (EU) No 526/2013 (Cybersecurity Act).

[67]*COM* (2015) 192 final (Brussels, May 6, 2015).

[68]*COM* (2015) 192 final (Brussels, May 6, 2015), p. 3.

[69]Adamski, D. (2018). "Lost on the digital platform: Europe's legal travails with the Digital Single Market," *Common Market Law Review*, **55**: 719–752.

initiatives, 28 of which have been concluded.[70] Core initiatives have addressed the obstacles formed by geoblocking[71]; online payments[72]; the portability of online content[73]; and diverging regulatory frameworks regarding data protection,[74] copyright,[75] and electronic communication.[76] Strategic investments complement these regulatory efforts.

Cybersecurity is instrumental to the DSM strategy. The more connected the European digital economy, the more vulnerable it is to cyberthreats — a network is only as strong as its weakest link.[77] The EU aims to increase the resilience of internal market as a whole as well as vitalize the single market for cybersecurity products and services. These objectives are mutually complementary: a reinforced European market for cybersecurity products will help facilitate greater resilience, whilst businesses abiding by higher cybersecurity standards will rely more heavily on the European cybersecurity market. Resilience in the CSS refers to

---

[70] European Commission, "Shaping the Digital Single Market," *European Commission.* Available at: https://ec.europa.eu/digital-single-market/en/policies/shaping-digital-single-market (accessed on August 16, 2019).

[71] Regulation (EU) 2018/302 of the European Parliament and of the Council of 28 February 2018 on addressing unjustified geoblocking and other forms of discrimination based on customers' nationality, place of residence or place of establishment within the internal market and amending Regulations (EC) No 2006/2004 and (EU) 2017/2394 and Directive 2009/22/EC (Text with EEA relevance.).

[72] Directive 2015/2366 of the European Parliament and of the Council of 25 Nov. 2015 on payment services in the internal market, amending Directives 2002/65/EC, 2009/110/EC and 2013/36/EU and Regulation (EU) 1093/2010, and repealing Directive 2007/64/EC, O.J. 2015, L 337/35.

[73] Regulation (EU) 2017/1128 of the European Parliament and of the Council of 14 June 2017 on cross-border portability of online content services in the internal market.

[74] Regulation (EU) 2016/679 of the European Parliament and of the Council of 27 April 2016 on the protection of natural persons with regard to the processing of personal data and on the free movement of such data, and repealing Directive 95/46/EC (General Data Protection Regulation).

[75] Directive (EU) 2019/790 of the European Parliament and of the Council of 17 April 2019 on copyright and related rights in the Digital Single Market and amending Directives 96/9/EC and 2001/29/EC.

[76] Directive (EU) 2018/1972 of the European Parliament and of the Council of 11 December 2018 establishing the European Electronic Communications Code (Recast).

[77] *COM* (2017) 0228 final (Brussels, May 10, 2017).

"the capacities of any technical or natural system to regulate itself."[78] In the DSM, a resilient regulatory network entails creating minimum standards for net security, e.g. by means of cybersecurity standards and mandatory cyber hygiene measures for businesses and service operators.[79] Moreover, the EU aims to create a "level playing field" necessary for a single market for cybersecurity and increase the competitiveness of the EU's ICT and cybersecurity sectors. It must be stressed in this regard that relying on non-European suppliers in ICT has not only economic but also important security implications.

2.3.2. *Regulation*

The 2016 NIS Directive,[80] based on Article 114 TFEU, was the first piece of horizontal EU legislation on cybersecurity and aims to install a minimum level of security with network and information systems to smoothen the functioning of the internal market.[81] The NIS directive prescribes security and notification requirements for operators of essential services and digital service providers.[82] Adherence to these requirements is to be supervised by the competent authorities in Member States.[83] While the societal function of essential services is rather obvious, the prescription of security norms and obligations for digital service providers is justified by the internal market rationale, i.e. the dependence of businesses and, in extension, the functioning of the internal market on digital services.[84]

---

[78]*JOIN* (2013) 1 final (Brussels, February 7, 2013).

[79]Bendiek, A., R. Bossong and M. Schulze (2017). "The EU's revised cybersecurity strategy: Half-hearted progress on far-reaching challenges," *SWP Comment* No. 47, November, p. 3.

[80]Directive (EU) 2016/1148 of the European Parliament and of the Council of 6 July 2016 concerning measures for a high common level of security of network and information systems across the Union.

[81]Article 1 Directive (EU) 2016/1148. A very tentative predecessor of the NIS Directive could be seen in the European Critical Infrastructure Protection Directive (Council Directive 2008/114/EC) of which the effectiveness has recently been reviewed by the Commission.

[82]Recitals 49–54 Directive (EU) 2016/1148.

[83]Recitals 19 and 59–61 Directive (EU) 2016/1148.

[84]Recital 48 explains that: "The security, continuity and reliability of the type of digital services referred to in this Directive are of the essence for the smooth functioning of many

The Directive is, however, less rigid in its approach to the much broader category of digital service providers than in its approach to operators of essential services,[85] the identification of which is entrusted to the Member States.[86] This difference can be justified by the societal function of essential services but becomes more nuanced when essential services or public administration are heavily dependent upon digital services, in which case the Directive suggests further contractual security obligations.[87] In addition, Member States must develop a national cybersecurity strategy.[88] The implementation deadline of the NIS Directive passed in May 2018. At the time of writing, the NIS Directive has not yet been (fully) transposed in Belgium, Bulgaria, Hungary, and Luxembourg.[89] This is despite considerable efforts of the Commission to aid Member States in the implementation.[90]

A core obligation introduced by the NIS Directive which deserves special attention is the obligation to create national Computer Security Incident Response Teams (CSIRTs).[91] A network of CSIRTs is created at the Union level.[92] National CSIRTs voluntarily exchange information on cyberincidents which are serious but fall below the level of a

---

businesses. A disruption of such a digital service could prevent the provision of other services which rely on it and could thus have an impact on key economic and societal activities in the Union. Such digital services might therefore be of crucial importance for the smooth functioning of businesses that depend on them and, moreover, for the participation of such businesses in the internal market and cross-border trade across the Union."

[85] Recital 49, for example, makes explicit that "the security requirements for digital service providers should be lighter"; Recital 57 sets out that "this Directive should take a differentiated approach with respect to the level of harmonisation in relation to those two groups of entities. For operators of essential services, Member States should be able to identify the relevant operators and impose stricter requirements than those laid down in this Directive. Member States should not identify digital service providers, as this Directive should apply to all digital service providers within its scope."

[86] Recitals 19–25, article 5 Directive (EU) 2016/1148.

[87] Recital 54 Directive (EU) 2016/1148.

[88] Article 7 Directive (EU) 2016/1148.

[89] European Commission, "State-of-play of the transposition of the NIS Directive." Available at: https://ec.europa.eu/digital-single-market/en/state-play-transposition-nis-directive (accessed on August 28, 2019).

[90] *COM* (2017) 0476 final (Brussels, October 10, 2017).

[91] Article 9 Directive (EU) 2016/1148.

[92] Article 12 Directive (EU) 2016/1148.

national crisis. The CSIRTs play a central role in the Commission's Communication on a coordinated EU response in case of a large-scale cybersecurity incident.[93] In the accompanying Blueprint, the Commission sets out in detail the cooperation between the EU institutions and mechanisms in case of a large-scale cybersecurity incident.[94] At the political level, the Interinstitutional Policy for Crises Response (IPCR) may now also be activated for cyberincidents. The IPCR enables the Council Presidency to call roundtable meetings for the Permanent Representatives Committee (COREPER) or Political and Security Committee (PSC) and bring in relevant stakeholders from Member States, EU institutions, EU agencies, and third parties such as non-EU countries and international organizations.[95] These are crisis meetings to identify bottlenecks and produce proposals for action for cross-cutting issues. The IPCR is also closely connected to the activation of the solidarity clause.[96] At the technical level, the CSIRTS are central and cooperate with, amongst others, CERT-EU (the Computer Emergency Response Team of the EU institutions) and ENISA. In case of a major incident, the CSIRT Network Chair presents an EU Cybersecurity Incident Situation Report to the Council Presidency, the Commission, and the CFSP's High Representative (HRVP).[97] The CSIRTs are thus instrumental for the situational awareness required for further strategic deliberation at the political level. The instrumental position of the CSIRTs, an internal market-based information sharing network, for essentially intergovernmental security deliberations at the Council is characteristic for the EU's regulatory cybersecurity policy.

The Cybersecurity Act was adopted in 2019 and presents a significant step toward coherence in the EU's regulatory framework for cybersecurity.[98] The Act renewed and expanded ENISA's now-permanent

---

[93] COM (2017) 6100 final (Brussels, September 13, 2017).

[94] Annex 1 to COM (2017) 6100 final (Brussels, September 13, 2017).

[95] Following Article 240 TFEU and Article 38, respectively, COREPER is responsible for preparing the work of the Council of the European Union and PSC is a Committee of the Council of the European Union dealing with the CFSP.

[96] The solidarity clause (Article 222, TFEU) is discussed at length in paragraph 6.2. See Annex 1 to COM (2017) 6100 final (Brussels, September 13, 2017), p. 15.

[97] Annex 1 to COM (2017) 6100 final (Brussels, September 13, 2017).

[98] Regulation (EU) 2019/881 of the European Parliament and of the Council of 17 April 2019 on ENISA (the European Union Agency for Cybersecurity) and on information and communications technology cybersecurity certification and repealing Regulation (EU) No 526/2013 (Cybersecurity Act).

mandate and increased its budget and capacity.[99] Most importantly, the regulation finally introduced the legal basis to adopt an EU-wide cybersecurity certification scheme for ICT products.[100] Rather detailed provisions on the adoption of such a scheme and provisions that should be included are provided.[101] ENISA will play a central role and prepare a candidate certification scheme, for which an ad hoc working group is currently being assembled.[102] The relevance of an EU-wide certification scheme is important. Certification is not legislation but rather to be regarded as harmonized standard setting of which the legal status is still ambiguous. Such standard setting is an increasingly important co-regulatory instrument.[103] As is habitual with standard setting, the certification schemes will not be mandatory, although the option of mandatory standards is set out to be explored.[104] It has been noted that mandatory standards have much greater potential to be externalized to non-EU markets.[105] Indeed, a clear, comprehensive, bold, and mandatory cybersecurity certification scheme would be a core asset of the EU's norm-pushing power. However, it can be questioned whether the EU has a sufficient legal mandate for adopting mandatory standards for cybersecurity. Co-regulation might be the highest attainable strategy and a clear, comprehensive, and bold certification scheme still has significant policy clout. Internally, certification schemes can significantly increase the security of IT products and services and allow customers to make informed decisions, boosting market trust and decreasing costs — disparities in national certification schemes have so far led to fragmentation and higher costs.[106] Externally, a voluntary EU-wide certification scheme would still put the EU in a stronger position

---

[99] Recitals 18–64 and articles 9–12 Regulation (EU) 2019/881.

[100] Article 46 Regulation (EU) 2019/881.

[101] Articles 47–49 and article 54(1)(a)–(v) Regulation (EU) 2019/881.

[102] ENISA (2019). "Call for expression of interest for the first ad hoc working group on cybersecurity certification," August 6. Available at: https://www.enisa.europa.eu/news/enisa-news/call-for-expression-of-interest-for-the-first-ad-hoc-working-group-on-cybersecurity-certification (accessed on August 30, 2019).

[103] Tovo, C. (2018). "Judicial review of harmonized standards: Changing the paradigms of legality and legitimacy of private rulemaking under EU law," *Common Market Law Review*, **55**(4): 1187–1216.

[104] Recital 92 Regulation (EU) 2019/881.

[105] Bendiek, A., R. Bossong and M. Schulze (2017). "The EU's revised cybersecurity strategy: Half-hearted progress on far-reaching challenges," *SWP Comment* No. 47, November, p. 4.

[106] Recital 67 Regulation (EU) 2019/881.

to push for global norms on the security of ICT products.[107] Moreover, increased regulatory convergence on the EU's ICT market will increase its competitiveness.

In 2018, the Commission put forward a proposal for a Regulation on preventing the dissemination of terrorist content online.[108] The Regulation would establish a responsibility with Internet platforms to take down terrorist content within one hour and establish a positive obligation to detect content and prevent its reappearance.[109] The EU Fundamental Rights Agency (FRA) expressed concern that the definition of terrorist content in the Proposal is broader than the definition in the Framework Decision on terrorism and is at odds with the freedom of expression.[110] The Regulation statedly aims to "guarantee the smooth functioning of the Digital Single Market,"[111] but was also presented as a legislative priority of the Security Union in the 2018 State of the Union speech by Juncker.[112] The Regulation thereby illustrates how cybersecurity as a cross-sectional policy concern has extended from internal market regulation into the security domain.

2.3.3. *Soft law*

The Commission aims to increase the coherence of Member States' approaches to cybersecurity via Recommendations. One example is the sector-specific Recommendations on cybersecurity in the energy sector.[113] The Commission also started to aim for an EU-wide approach to the

---

[107]Bendiek, A., R. Bossong and M. Schulze (2017). "The EU's revised cybersecurity strategy: Half-hearted progress on far-reaching challenges," *SWP Comment* No. 47, November, p. 4.

[108]*COM* (2018) 640 final (Brussels, September 12, 2018).

[109]*Ibid.*

[110]European Parliament (2018). "Preventing the dissemination of terrorist content online," *European Parliament Legislative train schedule: Area of justice and fundamental rights*, September 2018. Available at: http://www.europarl.europa.eu/legislative-train/theme-area-of-justice-and-fundamental-rights/file-preventing-the-dissemination-of-terrorist-content-online (accessed on August 27, 2019).

[111]*COM* (2018) 640 final (Brussels, September 12, 2018).

[112]Juncker, J-C. (2018). "State of the Union 2018: The hour of European sovereignty, Authorised version of the State of the Union Address 2018," *European Commission*, September. Available at: https://ec.europa.eu/commission/sites/beta-political/files/soteu2018-speech_en_0.pdf (accessed on September 10, 2019).

[113]*SWD* (2019) 1240 final (Brussels, April 3, 2019).

cybersecurity of 5G networks. Following its 2016 Action Plan[114] and the ensuing heated debate in the European Parliament[115] and concern in the European Council,[116] the Commission published a Recommendation on the cybersecurity of 5G networks.[117] Although 5G networks will act as the building blocks of much of the Union's digital infrastructure of the coming decade, EU ICT businesses are not the strongest competitors on the market for 5G technology. The EU has defied US requests for a blanket ban on Chinese companies from participating in the auction to establish 5G structures, which would stand at odds with its consistent commitment to a free and open trade policy. The Commission's Recommendation is clear in stating that not only technical but also other factors can influence cybersecurity risks of 5G networks, amongst which "the overall risk of influence by a third country, notably in relation to its model of governance, the absence of cooperation agreements on security, or similar arrangements, such as adequacy decisions, as regards data protection,"[118] hinting at the US and China. The Commission aims to assemble a common EU Toolbox to address the cybersecurity risks connected to 5G networks before December 31, 2019, based on risk assessments by Member States and ENISA's threat landscape mapping.[119] The extent to which Member States succeed in developing a common approach to the 5G question will prove an important test for the strategic autonomy of the EU on the global digital stage.[120] For the EU to fulfill its norm-setting ambitions in global cyberpolicy issues, it would be best if the common EU Toolbox is as clear and bold as possible.

2.3.4. *Industrial policy*

Strategic investments under the EU's industrial policy form an important addition to the EU's regulatory approach to cybersecurity. This policy sets out to help develop the industrial and technological resources necessary

---

[114]*COM* (2016) 588 final (Brussels, September 14, 2016).

[115]European Parliament, Resolution 2019/2575 (RSP) (Strasbourg, March 12, 2019).

[116]Council of the European Union (2019). "European Council conclusions of 21 and 22 March 2019," 1/19 (Brussels, March 22, 2019).

[117]*COM* (2019) 2335 final (Brussels, March 26, 2019).

[118]Recital 20 *COM* (2019) 2335 final (Brussels, March 26, 2019).

[119]*COM* (2019) 2335 final (Brussels, March 26, 2019).

[120]Lippert, B., N. von Ondarza and V. Perthes (2019)., "European strategic autonomy: Actors, issues, conflicts of interests," *SWP Research Paper* No. 04, March.

for cybersecurity by strategically investing in the competitiveness of the EU's digital and cybersecurity industry and pooling training and expertise.[121] The urgency thereof was recently addressed by ENISA in the policy paper announcing a policy consultation with the pressing title "EU ICT Industrial Policy: Breaking the Cycle of Failure."[122] ENISA emphasizes the interlinkage of the ICT industry and cybersecurity and notes that the EU is an "ICT taker rather than an ICT maker," "sandwiched" between the US and China.[123] The same diagnosis accounts for the European market for cybersecurity products: the EU is a net importer of cybersecurity products and largely dependent upon non-European suppliers.[124]

The digital market and cybersecurity are prominently featured in the Digital Europe and Horizon Europe programs. Both programs have been provisionally agreed upon as part of the EU's long-term (2021–2027) Multiannual Financial Framework, which is still being negotiated. The first ever Digital Europe program will invest in digital capacity and infrastructure building and lists cybersecurity and trust as one of its five priorities. About €2 billion is reserved for "boosting cyber defence and the EU's cybersecurity industry, financing state-of-the-art cybersecurity equipment and infrastructure as well as supporting the development of the necessary skills and knowledge."[125] Horizon Europe is a renewal of Horizon 2020, the broader research and innovation program within the EU budget. Cybersecurity is not listed as such in the Horizon Europe proposal, but the program does set out to reinforce technological and industrial capacities under the Global Challenges and Industrial Competitiveness pillar, for which €52.7 billion is reserved.[126] Recently, the Commission declared that

---

[121] *JOIN* (2013) 1 final (Brussels, February 7, 2013), p. 12.

[122] ENISA (2019). "ENISA puts out EU ICT Industrial Policy paper for consultation," *European Agency on Cybersecurity*, July 10. Available at: https://www.enisa.europa.eu/news/enisa-news/enisa-puts-out-eu-ict-industrial-policy-paper-for-consultation (accessed on September 25, 2019).

[123] ENISA (2019). "Consultation Paper — EU ICT industrial policy: Breaking the cycle of failure," *European Agency on Cybersecurity*, July, pp. 1–2.

[124] *COM* (2018) 630 final (Brussels, September 12, 2018), p. 1.

[125] European Commission (2018). "Press release: EU budget: Commission proposes €9.2 billion investment in first ever digital programme," *European Commission*, June 6. Available at: https://europa.eu/rapid/press-release_IP-18-4043_en.htm (accessed on September 16, 2019).

[126] European Commission (2019). "Press release: EU budget for 2021-2027: Commission welcomes provisional agreement on Horizon Europe, the future EU research and

€135 million will be made available under Horizon Europe for cybersecurity projects by citizens and small- and medium-sized enterprises (SMEs).[127]

The Commission also proposed the establishment of a European Cybersecurity Industrial, Technology and Research Competence Centre and a Network of National Coordination Centers to more specifically steer the efforts to rejuvenate the European cybersecurity sector.[128] The Centre would implement the allocation of funding for cybersecurity provided under the Horizon Europe and Digital Europe programs by taking into account the whole cybersecurity value chain. It will focus on the cooperation between cybersecurity supply and demand chains, civilian and military efforts, Member States and research and industrial communities, and strive for the deployment of the latest cybersecurity technology.[129]

The lacking human capital of the EU's ICT market is a key concern to the EU's competitiveness in cybersecurity markets. A substantial increase in human development is desired and could be facilitated by harmonized training and curricula, but the EU's lack of competences in the field of education makes this challenging.[130] A tentative first step has been made within the European Cybersecurity Industrial, Technology and Research Competence Centre, which sets out to support education policymakers to create the expertise necessary for a European cybersecurity market.[131] Moreover, based on CSDP provisions, a European Security and Defence College brings together, on a voluntary basis, Member States and academic expertise to train CSDP employees on, amongst other areas, cybersecurity.[132]

innovation programme," *European Commission*, March 20. Available at: https://europa.eu/rapid/press-release_IP-19-1676_en.htm (accessed on September 16, 2019).

[127] *COM* (2019) 353 final (Brussels, July 24, 2019).

[128] The legal bases for the establishment of the Centre are the EU's competences for research and innovation and competitiveness (Articles 187 and 173, TFEU); *COM* (2018) 630 final (Brussels, September 12, 2018).

[129] *COM* (2018) 630 final (Brussels, September 12, 2018), pp. 4–5.

[130] Bendiek, A., R. Bossong and M. Schulze (2017). "The EU's revised cybersecurity strategy: Half-hearted progress on far-reaching challenges," *SWP Comment* No. 47, November, pp. 3–4.

[131] *COM* (2018) 630 final (Brussels, September 12, 2018), p. 4.

[132] Council Joint Action 2005/575/CFSP (Brussels, July 18, 2005).

2.4. AFSJ

Cybercrime is an economic risk to the EU.[133] Cybersecurity is a measure to avert this risk and increase the trust of investors and consumers in the internal market.[134] This economic perspective, which follows from the internal market rationale, is characteristic of the EU's prioritization of cybercrime as a threat to be addressed by cybersecurity. Drastically reducing cybercrime is the second policy aim in the CSS and has been an objective since 2005.[135] The effective EU-wide investigation and prosecution of cybercrime is primordial to the concept of resilience. However, this aim is ambitious for the EU as a supranational organization with limited competences for criminal law in a scattered landscape of national jurisdictions.

The EU's competences for cybercrime fall within the AFSJ.[136] Most, but not all[137] Member States have joined the AFSJ, and it provides no

---

[133]Cybercrime is not comprehensively defined in European law, but only in the Cyber Security Strategy, as criminal activity using information systems or computers as a primary means and/or a target. Proxies, i.e. private criminal actors without reported ties to state actors (non-state actors) are reportedly used by states. See: *JOIN* (2013) 1 final (Brussels, February 7, 2013), p. 3.

[134]Under the challenge "Security" for a Single European Information Space, the Commission listed "making internet safer from fraudsters, harmful content and technology failures to increase trust amongst investors and consumers." See: *COM* (2005) 229 (Brussels, June 1, 2005), p. 5; also quoted in Dewar, R. S. (2017), "Cyber security in the European Union: an historical institutionalist analysis of a 21st century security concern," PhD Dissertation, University of Glasgow, p. 152.

[135]*JOIN* (2013) 1 final (Brussels, February 7, 2013), p. 4; the first legislative instrument on cybercrime was Council Framework Decision 2005/222/JHA of 24 February 2005 on attacks against information systems.

[136]The creation of an AFSJ was one of the objectives of the EU as noted in Article 3(2) TEU and was realized by the 1999 Tampere Council. The AFSJ is regulated in Title V, Chapters 2–5 of the TFEU and became fully effective on December 1, 2014. The AFSJ encompasses the Schengen *acquis*, i.e. the elimination of all internal borders, and includes the establishment of common policies on border checks, asylum, immigration, judicial cooperation in civil and criminal matters, and police cooperation. The AFSJ is an area of shared competence following Article 4(2)(j) TFEU and is subject to the regular legislative procedure, save for some exceptions which require unanimity in the Council. The requirement of unanimity applies to modifications of Article 77(3) TFEU; Article 81(3) TFEU; Article 82(2)(d) TFEU; the identification of the areas of serious crime prescribed in Article 83(1) TFEU; Article 86(1) TFEU; Article 87(3) TFEU, and Article 89 TFEU.

[137]The AFSJ accommodates opt-out possibilities for the UK, Ireland, and Denmark, and opt-in possibilities for non-Member States that are part of the Schengen area (Norway, Iceland, Switzerland, and Lichtenstein).

basis for the harmonization of criminal law, merely for the approximation of national law by prescribing minimum rules on certain areas of serious crime, including cybercrime.[138] Consequently, the center of gravity in the AFSJ lies with judicial and law enforcement cooperation.[139] The establishment of Europol and EC3, Eurojust, OLAF and, since recently,[140] EPPO have helped facilitate this cooperation. Europol, in particular, has matured into an important point of coordination for law enforcement in the EU and has functioned as the platform for several cooperative initiatives on cybercrime.[141] Recent legislative proposals expand upon the legal basis for judicial and law enforcement cooperation by harmonizing matters of procedural criminal law.

2.4.1. *The Security Union*

The Security Union is a policy agenda which fortified the security narrative in the EU. Alongside the reinforced economic imperative to combat cybercrime presented by the DSM strategy, the Security Union has boosted regulatory developments on cybersecurity within the AFSJ. The Juncker Commission, in 2015, first presented a European Agenda on Security (EAS), which frames cross-border threats, primary amongst which is cybercrime, as a European task that must be responded to by the deepening of European cooperation.[142] In 2016, the Commission followed up on the EAS by announcing the creation of "an effective and genuine" Security Union on the legal basis of the AFSJ.[143] The Security Union illustrates the political momentum for European security cooperation after the terror attacks in Brussels, Madrid, London, Copenhagen, and Paris. The Security Union advanced the implementation of the EAS

---

[138] These areas are identified in Article 83(1) TFEU. The Treaty refers to computer crime.

[139] The legal basis for this cooperation are the provisions on mutual recognition and judicial cooperation (Articles 81–84 TFEU).

[140] The establishment of an EPPO is fairly recent. It is based on Article 86 TFEU and has been realized by means of Council Regulation (EU) 2017/1939 of 12 October 2017 implementing enhanced cooperation on the establishment of the European Public Prosecutor's Office (the EPPO).

[141] Fahey, E. (2014). "The EU's cybercrime and cyber-security rulemaking: Mapping the internal and external dimensions of EU security," *European Journal of Risk Regulation*, 5(1): 46–60.

[142] *COM* (2015) 185 final (Strasbourg, April 28, 2015).

[143] Article 67(3) TFEU.

and drew particular attention to its cohesion, identifying and addressing implementation gaps.[144] Speedy and significant process has been made on the Security Union agenda so far, primary amongst which has been the appointment of a European Commissioner for Security specifically tasked with the implementation of the EAS. The Security Union thus demonstrates how cybersecurity policy has recently spilled over into the security domain and has been an important driver of European integration.

The Security Union explicitly interweaves domestic and foreign policies and the internal and external dimensions of security.[145] This fits the distinctly hybrid nature of the threats addressed by the Security Union agenda (alongside cybercrime, also counter-terrorism and organized crime) (see COM (2015) 185, https://www.cepol.europa.eu/sites/default/files/european-agenda-security.pdf). By significantly expanding the external dimension of security in the AFSJ, the EU is effectively equating the term "Security" in "Security and Defence" with that in "Freedom, Security and Justice," thereby circumventing the constitutional obstacles to moving forward on the CSDP. The AFSJ was transformed from an isolated domestic policy area on justice and home affairs to the legal basis for a European narrative on security in the comprehensive sense of the word.[146] The Security Union as a political agenda thereby also signals the growing approval of European cooperation on security issues.[147]

---

[144]COM (2016) 230 final (Brussels, April 20, 2016). A notable novelty of the Security Union is also the consistent reporting on its implementation, which draws particular attention to implementation gaps and inconsistencies. Progress reports and a track record of legislative efforts can be consulted at European Commission, "European Agenda on Security — Legislative Documents," *European Commission*. Available at: https://ec.europa.eu/home-affairs/what-we-do/policies/european-agenda-security/legislative-documents_en (accessed on August 23, 2019).

[145]COM (2015) 185 final (Strasbourg, April 28, 2015), p. 4; Sperling, J. and M. Webber (2019). "The European Union, security governance and collective securitization," *West European Politics*, **42**(2): 228–260.

[146]Herlin-Karnell, E. (2019). *The Constitutional Structure of Europe's Area of 'Freedom, Security and Justice' and the Right to Justification* (London: Bloomsbury Publishing), p. 4; Hegemann, H. and U. Schneckener (2019). "Politicising European security: From technocratic to contentious politics?" *European Security*, **28**(2): 133–152, 140.

[147]Bendiek, A. (2017). "A paradigm shift in the EU's common foreign and security policy: From transformation to resilience," *SWP Research Paper* No. 11, October, pp. 16–17.

2.4.2. *Regulation*

The Council of Europe Convention on Cybercrime (also termed Budapest Convention) is the main point of reference for the EU's efforts toward combating cybercrime. The Convention continues to serve as the primary source of norms the Commission promotes internally and externally.[148]

The Treaty provision to prescribe minimum rules has been employed a number of times for cybersecurity offenses. In principle, the Treaty only allows for the adoption of Directives, which prescribe minimum rules and require subsequent adoption into national law.[149] The concern of disparities between Member States and delayed implementation is therefore inevitable, and further harmonization is desired.[150] First, a Directive on the sexual exploitation of children online has been in place for some time.[151] Second, the 2013 Directive on Attacks against Information Systems[152] explicitly builds on and largely reproduces the norms and definitions in the Budapest Convention[153] and criminalizes a sparse number of basic cyber offences[154] and minimum penalties.[155] More advanced cybercrimes such as identity theft and, interestingly, attacks against information systems, are excluded. The Directive enables sanctions against natural and legal persons.[156] The EU has, with the Directive, effectively bypassed the hesitance of some Member States to ratify the Convention.[157] Third, the 2014

---

[148]Pawlak, P. (2019). "The EU's role on shaping the cyber regime complex," *European Foreign Affairs Review*, **24**(2): 167–186.

[149]Article 288 TFEU.

[150]Bendiek, A., R. Bossong and M. Schulze (2017). "The EU's revised cybersecurity strategy: Half-hearted progress on far-reaching challenges," *SWP Comment* No. 47, November, p. 5.

[151]Directive 2011/93/EU replacing Council Framework decision 2004/68/JHA.

[152]Directive 2013/40/EU of the European Parliament and of the Council of 12 August 2013 on attacks against information systems and replacing Council Framework Decision 2005/222/JHA.

[153]Recital 15 Directive 2013/40/EU.

[154]Included offences are illegal access to information systems, system interference, and data interference and interception.

[155]Directive 2013/40/EU of the European Parliament and of the Council of 12 August 2013 on attacks against information systems and replacing Council Framework Decision 2005/222/JHA.

[156]Article 2(c) Directive 2013/40/EU.

[157]Ireland and Sweden have as of yet not ratified the Convention.

Directive on European Investigative Orders (EIO Directive)[158] regulates the legislative and technical obstacles to effective investigations to some extent but does not eliminate all problems.[159] For example, a provision on e-evidence is lacking.

In April 2018, the Commission therefore put forward a proposal for an "e-evidence" Regulation.[160] Interestingly, the Council had urged the Commission to do so — a novelty in the field of criminal justice, signalling increasing willingness on the part of Member States to give in on sovereignty concerns in the face of cyberthreats. Another novelty is the choice for a Regulation, which is a more tangible legal instrument than a Directive.[161] In addition to the aforementioned Regulation, the Commission is pushing for EU participation in the multilateral negotiations on a Protocol on e-evidence to the Budapest Convention as well as preparing for the formal launch of a bilateral EU–US agreement on cross-border access to electronic evidence under the auspices of the Council of Europe Convention on Cybercrime.[162] Finally, legislative progress has been made on criminal provisions on fraud and forgery in cashless media. The Commission in 2017 proposed a Directive which would establish minimum rules on the fraudulent use of ((non-)corporeal) non-cash payment instruments, which includes virtual currencies such as bitcoin.[163]

---

[158] Directive 2014/41/EU of the European Parliament and of the Council of 3 April 2014 regarding the European Investigation Order in criminal matters.

[159] Christou, G. (2018). "The challenges of cybercrime governance in the European Union," *European Politics and Society*, **19**(3): 355–375.

[160] *COM* (2018) 225 final (Brussels, April 17, 2018).

[161] The legal basis for the Regulation is Article 82(1) TFEU, which has not previously been used for the proposal of Regulations. See also Franssen, V. (2018). "The European Commission's e-evidence proposal: Toward an EU-wide obligation for service providers to cooperate with law enforcement?" *European Law Blog*, October 12. Available at: https://europeanlawblog.eu/2018/10/12/the-european-commissions-e-evidence-proposal-toward-an-eu-wide-obligation-for-service-providers-to-cooperate-with-law-enforcement/ (accessed on October 10, 2019).

[162] European Commission (2019). "Factsheet: Questions and answers: Mandate for the second additional protocol to the Budapest Convention," *European Commission*, February 5. Available at: https://europa.eu/rapid/press-release_MEMO-19-865_en.htm (accessed on October 7, 2019).

[163] *COM* (2017) 0489 final — 2017/0226 (COD) (Brussels, September 13, 2017).

The Directive would also improve the exchange of information and cooperation between criminal justice authorities.[164]

2.4.3. *Law enforcement cooperation*

Cooperation between national law enforcement authorities is currently the most effective answer to tackling cross-border cybercrime in a borderless digital market. The effective EU-wide investigation and prosecution of cybercrime builds is instrumental to cyber resilience because it provides the strategic insight necessary to design in-built security measures and recover quickly from attacks. Moreover, it is vital to the thorny question of attributing serious cyberattacks.[165] Europol, since 2013, composes of a Cybercrime Centre (EC3) specifically dedicated to the investigation of cyber offences. EC3 aims to be the focal point for the criminal investigation of cyber offences in the EU. However, the secondary role of EC3 in the IPCR, which was introduced in Section 2.3.2, calls the success of this ambition into question. EC3 faces challenges in the legislative and institutional conditions under which it operates. First, it has to align its operations with other institutional cybersecurity actors such as Eurojust and ENISA.[166] Second, and more importantly, several legislative and technical obstacles formed by the patchwork of national jurisdictions continue to obstruct digital forensic opportunities. EC3 highlights the fact that investigative leads are lost because joint investigations lack timely access to communication data and other e-evidence, despite the EIO Directive.[167] Within EC3, however, the Member-States–led Joint Cybercrime Action Taskforce (J-CAT) has been praised for effectively enabling joint cross-jurisdictional investigations under flexible administrative conditions.[168]

---

[164]Recital 24–27 and Article 15 COM (2017) 0489 final — 2017/0226 (COD) (Brussels, September 13, 2017).

[165]Bendiek, A. (2018). "The EU as a force for peace in international cyber diplomacy," *SWP Comment* No. 19, April, p. 8.

[166]Bendiek, A., R. Bossong and M. Schulze (2017). "The EU's revised cybersecurity strategy: Half-hearted progress on far-reaching challenges," *SWP Comment* No. 47, November, p. 3.

[167]IOCTA 2017, p. 13.

[168]Christou, G. (2019). "The collective securitisation of cyberspace in the European Union," *West European Politics*, **42**(2): 278–301, 292–293; Christou, G. (2018). "The

2.5. CFSP

The CFSP includes all matters of foreign policy except for trade, which falls under the Common Commercial Policy.[169] The European Council, acting unanimously, is the primary actor in the CFSP. In tandem with the Council, it identifies strategic interests, assembles common policies, and takes concrete decisions.[170] The option to adopt legislation based on the CFSP is legally excluded, making Council decisions the Union's most tangible instrument on foreign affairs.[171] However, foreign policy concerns have increasingly permeated other domains of Union legislation, which has led to the adoption of legislative proposals which are in effect instrumental toward the CFSP. The implementation of the CFSP is overseen by the HRVP and in practice realized by the European External Action Service (EEAS), which includes 139 European delegations in third states.[172]

Following its declared commitment to multilateralism,[173] the EU has consistently participated in UNGGE (United Nations Group of Governmental Experts) on Advancing responsible State behaviour in cyberspace in the context of international security talks, pushing forward the standards adopted under the Budapest Convention.[174] Since UNGGE negotiations were halted without results in 2017, some signal a move toward "coalitions of the willing," i.e. the acceptance of a more scattered approach in which willing international partners enhance cyber cooperation.[175] Nevertheless, several Member States remain heavily invested in

---

challenges of cybercrime governance in the European Union," *European Politics and Society*, **19**(3): 355–375; Reitano, T., T. Oerting and M. Hunter (2015). "Innovations in international cooperation to counter cybercrime: The joint cybercrime action taskforce." *The European Review of Organised Crime*, **2**(2): 142–154.

[169] Article 3(1)(e) and Part V, Title II TFEU.

[170] Article 22(1), Article 24(1) TEU, and Article 26 TEU.

[171] Article 24(1) TEU, Article 25 TEU, and Article 31 TEU.

[172] Article 26 TEU.

[173] Articles 21(1) and 21(2)(h) set out that the Union shall seek multilateral solutions to common problems and promote an international system based on multilateral cooperation.

[174] Bendiek, A. (2018). "The EU as a force for peace in international cyber diplomacy," *SWP Comment* No. 19, April.

[175] Pawlak, P. (2019). "The EU's role on shaping the cyber regime complex," *European Foreign Affairs Review*, **24**(2): 167–186.

UNGGE talks, providing a counterweight against the "Open-Ended Working Group" initiated by Russia.[176] Like global counterparts, the EU has also maintained bilateral cyber dialogues with countries such as the US, Canada, China, Japan, and South Korea.

2.5.1. *Cyber Diplomacy Toolbox*

The EU's approach to cybersecurity under the CFSP has, in 2017, been streamlined by the adoption of the Cyber Diplomacy Toolbox.[177] The Toolbox has the potential to function as a model for diplomatic responses to cybersecurity issues. The EU distinguishes four categories of responses: preventative, cooperative, stabilizing, and restrictive. These responses are complementary to the lawful responses for Member States' self-defence based on national constitutions and the NATO legal framework.

Part of the Cyber Diplomacy Toolbox is the Council Regulation on a sanctions regime adopted in May 2019, which prescribes the freezing of funds and economic resources of any natural or legal person, entity, or body responsible for (attempted) cyberattacks with a (potentially) significant effect.[178] The sanctions regime also codifies the principle of due diligence, by making explicit the Member State's positive obligation to take the necessary measures to prevent the passing of natural persons involved in cyberattacks through their territories.[179]

---

[176]The OEWG will report back to the UN General Assembly in 2020; the UNGGE's agenda is planned for the period 2019–2021. See Resolution adopted by the General Assembly on 5 December 2018 [on the report of the First Committee (A/73/505)], United Nations General Assembly. Available at: https://undocs.org/en/A/RES/73/27; Resolution adopted by the General Assembly on 22 December 2018 [on the report of the First Committee (A/73/505)], United Nations General Assembly. Available at: https://undocs. org/en/A/RES/73/266 (accessed on August 22, 2019).

[177]Council of the European Union (2017). "Council Conclusions on a Framework for a Joint EU Diplomatic Response to Malicious Cyber Activities ("Cyber Diplomacy Toolbox")," 10474/17 (Brussels, June 19).

[178]Council Regulation (EU) 2019/796 of 17 May 2019 concerning restrictive measures against cyber-attacks threatening the Union or its Member States. The sanctions regime is based on Article 215 TFEU, which allows for the adoption of restrictive measures.

[179]Article 4 Council Regulation (EU) 2019/796.

2.5.2. *Disinformation*

Disinformation has become a key concern within the CFSP after the European Council in 2015 asked the HRVP for a common approach. In the run-up to the European Parliament elections of May 2019, several initiatives were set up. The HRVP led an Action Plan against Disinformation.[180] The Code of Practice against Disinformation is a joint commitment of the Commission, online platforms, and other signatories.[181] The Rapid Alert System, which was set up to coordinate the responses to disinformation in the EU election campaigns, will be evaluated in Autumn 2019. A European Cooperation Network on Elections, with participation by the relevant national authorities, will contribute to this evaluation. The establishment of a cooperative EU Internet Forum aims to further complement the cooperation between Member States and online platforms by enabling dialogue between Home Affairs ministers, the Internet industry, and other stakeholders.

2.5.3. *Dual-use policy*

Other than for the CFSP, the EU has an exclusive competence for a Common Commercial Policy (CCP). The CCP is thus an opportune area of common action with the potential to complement efforts under the CFSP. The comprehensiveness of the EU's approach to cybersecurity has hence been enhanced by introducing cybersecurity considerations in trade. The recently adopted Foreign Direct Investment (FDI) Regulation provides a first step toward EU cooperation on investment screening.[182] It allows the Commission to issue opinions on the security or public order implications of certain investments and promotes coordination on FDI between Member States.[183] Cybersecurity is one of the factors suggested to help determine whether FDI is likely to affect security or the public

---

[180] *JOIN* (2018) 36 final (Brussels, December 5, 2018).

[181] *COM* (2018) 236 final (Brussels, April 26, 2018).

[182] Regulation 2019/452 of the European Parliament and of the Council of 19 March 2019 establishing a framework for the screening of foreign direct investments into the Union.

[183] European Commission (2019). "Press release: EU foreign investments screening regulation enters into force," *European Commission*, April 10. Available at: https://europa.eu/rapid/press-release_IP-19-2088_en.htm (accessed on October 14, 2019).

order.[184] In addition, increased awareness of the strategic importance of dual-use goods to cyberthreats has led the Commission to update the Regulation on expert controls for dual-use goods in 2018.[185]

2.6. CSDP

The CSDP is a subcategory of the CFSP. CSDP initiatives have to navigate several constitutional limitations and political reluctance due to national sovereignty concerns. The Treaties only provide for the "progressive framing" of a CSDP which "might lead" to a common defence.[186] Consequently, the EU's abilities in the defence domain have so far remained limited to "exhorting, facilitating, and incentivizing."[187] There are no standing European military forces or headquarters, and NATO remains the main focal point for European defence cooperation.[188] A full-fledged political Defence Union can only be established unanimously by the European Council.[189] This decision has not been taken, although it has notably been called for by the European Parliament in 2016.[190] The European Defence Agency (EDA) merely plays a coordinating role.[191] In extension, cyber defence is not the primary component of cybersecurity to most Member States or the EU.

---

[184] Article 4(1)(b) Regulation 2019/452.

[185] *SWD* (2017) 295 final (Brussels, September 13, 2017), p. 45; *JOIN* (2017) 450 final (Brussels, September 13, 2017), p. 10, 13, 17; Commission Delegated Regulation (EU) 2018/1922 of 10 October 2018 amending Council Regulation (EC) No 428/2009 setting up a Community regime for the control of exports, transfer, brokering, and transit of dual-use items.

[186] Article 24(1) and Article 42(1) TEU. The CFSP was very carefully introduced in the 1992 Treaty of Maastricht and gradually developed with subsequent treaty revisions. The basis for the CFSP and the CDSP is Article 4(2) TFEU and the areas are regulated in Title V (Articles 21-46) of the TEU. The Treaties keep foreign policy matters relatively separate from other policy areas and EU institutions and only tentatively provides for a CSDP.

[187] Biscop, S. (2017). "Oratio pro pesco," *Egmont Paper* No. 91, January, p. 3.

[188] Bendiek, A. (2017). "A paradigm shift in the EU's Common Foreign and Security Policy: From transformation to resilience," *SWP Research Paper* No. 11, October, p. 6. See also Article 41(2) TEU.

[189] Article 41(2) TEU.

[190] Resolution 2016/2067 (INI), European Parliament (Strasbourg, November 23, 2016).

[191] Article 42(3) TEU and Article 45 TEU.

Nevertheless, the development of a cyber defence policy and capabilities related to the CSDP is one of the strategic aims in the CSS. The Commission has partly circumvented the constitutional limitations of the CSDP by progressing the Security Union based on AFSJ provisions and proposing the European Defence Fund based on internal market-related provisions. The support for the Defence Union has, in recent years, caused an increase in initiatives in the cyber defence domain. In turn, cybersecurity has been one of the drivers of the current political momentum for security and defence integration in the EU.[192] At their core, however, cyber defence initiatives are mostly focused on the industrial development of the European defence market.

2.6.1. *Solidarity clause*

One key development for cyber defence has been the renewed interpretation of the EU "solidarity clause" (Article 222 TFEU). The solidarity clause legitimizes a joint EU response based on classical justice and Home Affairs policies in case of severe cyberattacks. The solidarity clause legitimizes action by both the Union and Member States. The latter means, following the adoption of rules and procedures to enable the operation of the solidarity clause, "any situation which may have a severe impact on people, the environment or property."[193] The solidarity clause is therefore different than the "Mutual Defence Clause" (Article 42(7) TEU). The latter strongly resembles and is complementary to Article 5 of the NATO Treaty, which legitimizes military action on behalf of all signatories in the case of an armed attack against just one. The Mutual Defence Clause and Article 5 of the NATO Treaty refer only to national military action in the case of physical, armed attacks. The suitability of the solidarity clause for cyberincidents pleads for the relevance of EU defence cooperation alongside NATO. Following the Commission's Blueprint, activation of the solidarity clause in case of a large-scale cybersecurity incident is linked to IPCR, which in turn is based upon the CSIRTs network.[194]

---

[192]Bendiek, A. (2017). "A paradigm shift in the EU's Common Foreign and Security Policy: From transformation to resilience," *SWP Research Paper* No. 11, October.

[193]Article 3(a) of Council Decision 2014/415/EU.

[194]Annex 1 to COM (2017) 6100 final (Brussels, September 13, 2017), 15.

2.6.2. *Common defence cooperation*

A common cyber defence policy has, in recent years, been called for by the European Council,[195] EU military staff, EDA, HRVP,[196] the European Parliament[197] and jointly by the EU and NATO.[198] In 2014, the European Council agreed on a Cyber Defence Policy Framework,[199] which was updated in 2018.[200] The framework prioritizes capacity-building. It focuses on building cyber defence capacities in Member States and providing steering principles for cooperation with the private sector, as well as enhancing the protection of CSDP communication networks.[201] Within the EDA, a plethora of smaller projects have been set up to improve cyber defence, including a Collaboration Database (CoDaBa) and a Capability Development Plan (CDP).[202] Following the 2016 Joint Framework on countering hybrid threats,[203] several scenario-based policy discussions have taken place under the Finnish Council Presidency.

Only in December 2017, 25 Member States finally made use of the permanent structured cooperation (PESCO) Treaty provision, which allows for a flexible integration under the CDSP.[204] The establishment of

---

[195] Council of the European Union, "EU Cyber Defence Policy Framework 15585/14," *Council of the European Union*, November 18, 2014.

[196] The adoption of a Cyber Defence Policy Framework was, in fact, proposed by the EDA, the High Commissioner, and the Commission jointly.

[197] European Parliament, Resolution 2016/2067 (INI) (Strasbourg, November 23, 2016).

[198] NATO, Cyber Defence Pledge (Warsaw, July 8, 2016).

[199] Council of the European Union (2014). "EU Cyber Defence Policy Framework 15585/14," *Council of the European Union*, November 18.

[200] Council of the European Union (2018). "EU Cyber Defence Policy Framework (14413/18m 2018 update)," *Council of the European Union*, November 19.

[201] Council of the European Union (2014). "EU Cyber Defence Policy Framework 15585/14," *Council of the European Union*, November 18.

[202] Other projects by EDA include the Deployable Cyber Evidence Collection and Evaluation Capacity (DCEC²), the Cyber Situation Awareness Package (CySAP), the Cyber Defence Training & Exercises Coordination Platform (CD TEXP), and the "Demand Pooling for the Cyber Defence Training and Exercise support by the Private Sector" (DePoCyTE).

[203] *JOIN* (2016) 018 final (Brussels, April 6, 2019).

[204] PESCO is based on Article 46(2) TEU.

PESCO is a remarkable development[205] and seen by some as the most opportune pathway to promote EU defence integration.[206] Within PESCO, Member States can initiate joint defence cooperation projects, which may then voluntarily be joined by interested Member States.[207] There are currently 34 PESCO projects, out of which 12 have specifically been dedicated to cyber defence. At the same time, NATO remains the main focal point for European cyber defence cooperation in Europe.[208] Cooperation between the EU and NATO has intensified, by introducing a Cyber Defence Pledge[209] and resulting in joint projects on early-warning capabilities for headquarters and a Multi-Agent System for Advanced Persistent Threat detection (MASFAD).[210]

2.6.3. *Common defence investment*

The Commission in 2017 proposed a European Defence Fund. Interestingly, the legal basis for the EDF were the Treaty articles for industry and development, illustrating the close interrelationship of cyber defence and the internal market — a conclusion which is underlined by the fact that the proposal was marked a "text with EEA relevance."[211] Under the EDF, the Commission intends to allocate annual budget to joint research in defence technologies, as well as enable the joint procurement

---

[205]Blockmans, S. (2018). "The EU's modular approach to defence integration: An inclusive, ambitious and legally binding PESCO?" *Common Market Law Review*, **55**: 1785–1826; Editorial Comments, "A stronger Common Foreign and Security Policy for a self-reliant Union?" *Common Market Law Review*, **55**(2018): 1675–1684.

[206]Koehnig, N. and M. Walter-Franke (2017). "France and Germany: Spearheading a European Security and Defence Union?" *Policy Paper Jacques Delors Institut*, No. 202, July.

[207]Council Decision 2017/2315 (Brussels, December 8, 2017).

[208]Annegret Bendiek, "A Paradigm Shift in the EU's Common Foreign and Security Policy: From Transformation to Resilience," *SWP Research Paper* No. 11, October, 2017, p. 6. See also article 41(2) TEU.

[209]NATO, Cyber Defence Pledge (Warsaw, July 8, 2016).

[210]Annegret Bendiek, "A Paradigm Shift in the EU's Common Foreign and Security Policy: From Transformation to Resilience," *SWP Research Paper* No. 11, October, 2017, p. 20.

[211]Articles 173(3), 182(4), 183 and 188(2) TFEU. Editorial Comments, "A stronger Common Foreign and Security Policy for a self-reliant Union?" *Common Market Law Review*, **55**(2018): 1675–1684.

of military materials, of which the Commission estimates that it would save around €100 billion per year.[212] Under the 2021–2027 Multiannual Financial Framework, the EDF is set out to amount to €500 million per year.[213] Within this budget, which is still being negotiated, the most recent Commission proposals include a €182 million investment in cyber situational awareness and a €27 million investment in AI, virtual reality, and cyber technologies.[214] In addition, EDA has started cooperating with the European Investment Bank.[215] The EDF and other initiatives to stimulate investment in defence measures present a much-needed impulse to the EU's cybersecurity defence industry. However, again, these initiatives are economic at heart. Rather than unifying 28 diverging strategic cultures into a common defence policy, the EU's strength lies in the regulation and stimulation of the defence industry.

2.7. Conclusion

The creation of the EU's cybersecurity policy has been driven by an internal market rationale. Cyberthreats were mainly regarded as an economic risk — EU action was needed to protect the common market. This rationale has driven the most substantial elements of the EU's approach to cybersecurity (the Cybersecurity Act and the NIS Directive), which are foremost instruments of internal market regulation. Despite the lack of an express legal basis for EU cybersecurity policy, it has become a view widely shared that "Member States or individual companies cannot cope with this challenge alone. There is need for coordination and strategic

---

[212] European Commission, "Factsheet: The European Defence Action Plan — FAQs," *European Commission*, November 30, 2016, Available at: https://europa.eu/rapid/press-release_MEMO-16-4101_en.htm (accessed on September 13, 2019).

[213] Annegret Bendiek, "A Paradigm Shift in the EU's Common Foreign and Security Policy: From Transformation to Resilience," *SWP Research Paper* No. 11, October, 2017, p. 18.

[214] European Commission, "Press Release: European Defence Fund," *European Commission*, March 19, 2019, Available at: https://ec.europa.eu/commission/news/european-defence-fund-2019-mar-19_en (accessed on September 13, 2019).

[215] European Defence Agency, "Press Release: European Defence Agency and European Investment Bank Sign Cooperation Agreement," *European Defence Agency*, February 28, 2018, Available at: https://www.eda.europa.eu/info-hub/press-centre/latest-press-releases/2018/02/28/ (accessed on September 20, 2019).

vision."[216] Surging cyberthreats and the curtailing competitiveness of the EU's digital economy have indeed increased the urgency of cybersecurity as a policy concern to EU institutions. "If current trends continue unmitigated, the EU may end up being entirely dependent on third countries for key technologies. This would leave our economy, security and society exposed and vulnerable on an unprecedented scale. [...] Importantly, it can also threaten our democracies."[217] Therefore, internal market regulation and industrial policies are now complemented with increased law enforcement cooperation on cybercrime (EC3), a proposal for harmonized standards on information sharing (e-evidence), tentative steps toward formulating a common foreign policy on cyberthreats (the Cyber Diplomacy Toolbox), and common defence projects (PESCO). Cybersecurity has hence helped to deepen European integration in the politically sensitive areas of security and defence.

Nevertheless, in spite of the increase in the policy domains in which cybersecurity is addressed, the locus of the EU's approach to cybersecurity remains with the internal market. Even in the defence domain, the most impactful innovation is a stimulus for the European defence market (EDF). The EU's cybersecurity policy aims to regulate and protect the internal market. A resilient regulatory framework on cybersecurity is a double-edged sword. Internally, it serves to protect European citizens with the high level of fundamental rights protection that the EU prides itself on. It is also an imperative requirement for the European single market to benefit from the transition to the digital age — as fragmented regulatory frameworks obstruct intra-EU, cross-border economic activity. Externally, regulation helps secure the public and private sectors to achieve the cyber resilience the EU counts on to create deterrence against cyberthreats. Moreover, as demonstrated by the case of data protection, a large share of the EU's geostrategic strength lies in its regulatory power and the externalization of its norms and values.

---

[216]Directorate General for Communications Networks, Content and Technology. The leaked document was obtained by Politico. See Cerulus, L. and B. Smith-Meyer (2019). "Commission pitched 'leadership package' for digital autonomy," *Politico Pro*, August 22. Available at: https://www.politico.eu/pro/commission-pitched-leadership-package-for-digital-autonomy/?utm_source=POLITICO.EU&utm_campaign=d6d644f016-EMAIL_CAMPAIGN_2019_08_22_10_54&utm_medium=email&utm_term=0_10959edeb5-d6d644f016-190421257 (accessed on October 24, 2019).
[217]*Ibid.*

Regulatory frameworks are the EU's forte. It remains to be seen exactly how the incoming Von der Leyen Commission will follow up on digital and cybersecurity policy. The European Commission's digital department has in any case given clear directions in its proposal for a Digital Leadership Package in a leaked internal Commission document dated July 2019.[218] This Package with a "strong geostrategic aspect" would revamp the EU's industrial policy and build toward the much-cited, elusive term "strategic autonomy."[219] It would fix investment priorities such as European high-level computing capacities and processor technologies, a research and investment roadmap for technologies such as 5G and 6G, a blockchain infrastructure for public services, as well as a European Cybersecurity Shield based on quantum technologies. The package is proposed alongside an Action plan to make the ICT sector more sustainable and an AI regulatory framework, including a single market legal instrument that "should set a world-standard for AI regulation." Moreover, the Digital Services Act, which is expected to replace the e-Commerce Directive, could serve as an important regulatory tool for the ICT sector. The leaked documents as well as the new Commissioner's portfolios clearly indicate that digital competitiveness and cyber resilience will be top priorities in 2019–2024. A bold regulatory strategy on cybersecurity could thus very well turn out to be the success story of the "geopolitical Commission."

---

[218] *Ibid.*

[219] Lippert, B., N. von Ondarza and V. Perthes (2019). "European strategic autonomy: Actors, issues, conflicts of interests," *SWP Research Paper* No. 04, March; Franke, U. and T. Varma (2019). "Independence play: Europe's pursuit of strategic autonomy," *European Council on Foreign Relations*, July.

Annex I

Cybersecurity in the EU: Areas of Responsibility

	Single market	AFSJ: Area of Freedom, Security and Justice	CSDP: Cyber Defence	CFSP: Cyber Diplomacy
EU	ENISA CSIRT network CERT-EU	Europol (EC3) Eurojust EU-LISA	EDA GSA ESDC	EEAS SIAC (EU INTCEN, EUMS INT) EU SITROOM EU Hybrid Fusion Cell ERCC
National	Authorities in charge of NIS National CSIRTs	Executive and data-protection authorities	Defence, military, and security agencies	Foreign ministries

Notes: *EC3*: European Cybercrime Centre; *CSIRT*: Computer Security Incident Response Team; *CERT*: Computer Emergency Response Team; *EDA*: European Defence Agency; *ESDC*: European Security and Defence College; *EEAS*: European External Action Service; *ENISA*: European Union Agency for Network and Information Security; *ERCC*: Emergency Response Coordination Centre; *EU INTCEN*: European Union Intelligence and Situation Centre; *EU-LISA*: European Agency for the Operational Management of Large-scale IT Systems in the Area of Freedom, Security and Justice; *EU SITROOM*: European Union Situation Room; *EUMS INT*: European Union Military Staff, Intelligence Directorate Mission; *GSA*: European Global Navigation Satellite Systems Agency; *NIS*: Network and Information Security; *SIAC*: Single Intelligence Analysis Capacity.

Chapter 3

Regulations in Cyberspace in Latin America and the Caribbean: Challenges and Opportunities

Boris Saavedra* and Emma Corcodilos†

*William J. Perry Center for Hemispheric Defense Studies — WJPC,
National Defense University, Washington, DC, USA*

**Saavedrab@ndu.edu
†Emmaecor@gmail.com*

If we continue to develop our technology without wisdom or prudence, our servant may prove to be our executioner.

Omar Bradley

Abstract

Cyberspace vulnerabilities constitute a major challenge to decision-makers in Latin America and the Caribbean. There is a growing concern in the region on the lack of an effective legal framework to control this limitless environment. All legal systems used in the region present their own challenges, but within each one is a lack of capacity to efficiently

---

§Disclaimer: The views expressed in this testimony are the authors' own and do not necessarily reflect the views of WJPC, National Defense University, or the Department of Defense.

regulate cyberspace. Additionally, while the public sector focuses on the common good and the private sector focuses on profit, both must be united under a common regulatory framework that facilitates the objectives of security for society. This chapter addresses the current status of cyberspace regulations in Latin America and the Caribbean (LAC) and the challenges faced in implementing them.

3.1. Introduction

The growing speed of cyber capabilities resulted in a vast increase in global security risks. Countries, therefore, struggle to implement regulations to protect their societies quickly enough to keep up with cyberthreats that emerge daily. While many other areas of security and defense are more easily regulated, cyberspace has one distinct characteristic: it is not constrained by boundaries. This limitless environment of cybersecurity also poses a challenge to the international community in containing and controlling such threats.

This chapter aims to provide the current status of cyberspace regulations in Latin America and the Caribbean (LAC) and the challenges faced in implementing them. This is done by examining the historical developments of regulations in various countries focusing on the three legal systems used in the region. Because all the countries discussed either utilize a civil legal system, a common legal system, or a mixture of both, the contrast in efforts and systematic challenges for all three systems will also be discussed as possible results of lacking regulatory abilities.

Above all, the resilience of the public and private sectors is essential to upholding national security worldwide, especially regarding cyberspace. With the public sector focused on protecting the common good, and the private sector focused on strong business profits, both must come together under one regulatory framework in order to fulfill their security goals. This is seen most successfully through the efforts of the European Union (EU), specifically in the area of privacy, which is one of the many critical areas of cybersecurity that require an effective regulation for the security of cyberspace. The EU model is often followed by countries around the world, including those in LAC. For a general sense of cybersecurity regulations in LAC, Table A (available in the Appendix) outlines each country in the region with cybersecurity legislation or frameworks (such as those for data protection, cybercrime, e-government, information technology [IT], and critical infrastructure) as well as their legal system and the date of implementation.

3.2. Legal Systems and Public–Private Partnerships

Most countries in the world utilize a civil law system, a common law system, or a mixture of both. Much of Central and South America utilizes civil law, which finds its roots in the Roman legal system. There is almost always a written constitution in these countries based on specific legal codes (i.e. civil codes, constitutional law, etc.). Civil law systems only recognize laws passed through the legislative system to be binding law. Common law systems, on the other hand, are influenced by case law. While many of these countries utilize a constitutional and legislative process, they also consider judicial decisions to be binding law. Although many of these countries find a legal foundation in the doctrine of *stare decisis*,[1] courts have the ability to create new interpretations of the law when given different facts in a new case.[2] This allows for common law systems to be more malleable, as they do not always have to go through the lengthy legislative process in order to implement new regulations.

Regardless of the legal system, Public–Private Partnerships (PPPs) are an essential element of cybersecurity, as the public and private sectors are the two most important actors in the race against cyberthreats. Their resilience depends on cooperation, as practiced through PPPs. Before analyzing each country's challenges and regulations individually, it is first important to understand the challenges of creating PPPs through contracts given a country's legal system. Civil law countries do not have much freedom of contract, as parties to the contract are often unable to decide which provisions they want to contract out of, and many provisions are not expressly included, but rather implied through other underlying laws that make it unnecessary to repeat them contractually. This can be problematic because of the ambiguity of the contract rules. Contracts in civil law

---

[1] *Stare decisis* is the principle that current cases should be decided in congruence with past precedent.

[2] PPLRC (2006). "Key features of common law or civil law systems," World Bank Group, September 6. Available at: https://ppp.worldbank.org/public-private-partnership/legislation-regulation/framework-assessment/legal-systems/common-vs-civil-law#Common_Law_System (accessed on February 4, 2019).

systems are shorter due to their omission of specific language, leaving disputes between parties to be resolved by operation of law after the creation of the contract. Regarding cybersecurity regulations, PPPs in a civil law system leave much room for error due to debatable language. For instance, legal language regarding the protection of "critical infrastructure" lacks clarity, as the definition of "critical infrastructure" may change through different legislation over time at the context of the state.[3] In addition, because civil law systems are set in codified law, many PPP agreements will be unenforceable if they are not in exact congruence with the country's laws. This will set PPPs back, as contracts often need to be rearranged in order to adapt to a country's laws. Common law systems, on the other hand, have much more freedom of contract. Unlike civil law systems, very few provisions are implied. While this requires a longer contract, it leaves less room for dispute in the long run. In addition, common law allows PPP contracts to be much more flexible because most provisions are permitted if they are not expressly prohibited by a country's laws or regulations. This allows for PPPs to be more easily established, and any question of legality is decided by the courts rather than by already established laws.[4]

To illustrate this, Brazil has been a constant target of cyberattacks for several years now. Brazil was a victim of Anonymous in 2013; the group successfully attacked the country's largest media group, Grupo Globo, the Brazilian intelligence agency, and the Ministry of Justice. Brazil's 2016 cyberattacks, however, posed a unique set of challenges as they faced the threat of cyberattacks on all 36 of Banrisul's online banking domains; it is likely that these hackers obtained access to users' ATM transactions, thus, being able to access their credit information. The prevalence of these attacks against Brazil's government agencies, financial institutions, and citizens has served as a wakeup call for the Brazilian government to increase its security and reduce the risks of these attacks. Being a common law country, Brazil has addressed their cybersecurity issues, and the Brazilian Congress has since been working on cybercrime and surveillance legislation. This includes a

---

[3] Weaver, Y. (2016). "Basic differences between a common law system and a civil law system in terms of contracts and business," *LSL*, May 31. Available at: lslcpas.com/basic-differences-common-law-system-civil-law-system-terms-contracts-business/ (accessed on February 4, 2019).

[4] PPLRC (2016). "Legal and regulatory issues concerning public-private partnerships," World Bank Group, July 13. Available at: https://ppp.worldbank.org/public-private-partnership/legislation-regulation (accessed on February 7, 2019).

series of proposed bills which, if approved, will make it easier for prosecutors and police to access personal data without a judicial order.

3.3. Cyberspace Regulations in Countries using Civil Law Systems

For the analysis of the LAC countries that use the civil legal system, we have selected Brazil and Colombia as the countries that have made the most progress in establishing legislation for cyberspace activities. Among various countries within the LAC region, Brazil is one of the most economically advanced that utilizes civil law. Given its mass adoption of information communications technology (ICT), Brazil is a top target for cyberattacks.[5] The Brazilian Federal Constitution first guarantees privacy protection as a fundamental right of all people. Brazil's most recent piece of legislation dealing with cybersecurity issues is the Brazilian General Data Protection Law (LGPD, when translated to Portuguese), which focuses on regulating the use and protection of personal data by the public and private sectors.[6] The LGPD followed the EU's implementation of their General Data Protection Regulation (GDPR) and contains many similar provisions. The implementation within the Brazilian system, however, has been challenging and ongoing. Taking six years to be passed by Congress, the LGPD has been partially delayed by President Jair Bolsonaro due to the COVID-19 pandemic. Although the LGPD will be implemented by September 16, 2020, the enforcement of its administrative sanctions upon breaches of the law will not be permitted until August 1, 2021." (*source*: Law No. 14.010/2020, accessible at the following link: https://www.in. gov.br/en/web/dou/-/lei-n-14.010-de-10-de-junho-%20de-2020-261279456 accessed on September 25, 2020). In this case, regulations run the risk of being outdated due to the dynamic pace of cyber risks. This is one of multiple laws that has been and will continue to be adopted through a bill that

---

[5]Muggah, R. (2017). "Brazil struggles with effective cyber-crime response," Jane's Military & Security Assessments Intelligence Centre. Available at: https://www.janes.com/ images/assets/518/73518/Brazil_struggles_with_effective_cyber-crime_response.pdf (accessed on February 5, 2019).

[6]Thomaz, A. C. E. and F. F. Kujawski (2018). "The privacy, data protection and cybersecurity law review — Brazil," *The Law Reviews,* October. Available at: https://thelawreviews.co.uk/edition/the-privacy-data-protection-and-cybersecurity-law-review-edition-5/1175622/brazil (accessed on February 5, 2019).

was designed to regulate issues from years before its implementation.[7] In addition to privacy concerns, Brazil faces cyberthreats toward their supervisory control and data acquisition (SCADA) devices, which control most of the country's critical infrastructure.[8] The Brazilian government has taken steps to define its critical infrastructure as early as 2010 and recognizes the nexus between protecting that infrastructure and cyber risks.[9] Most recently, the Central Bank of Brazil has followed Resolution No. 4658 as a cybersecurity policy framework to protect infrastructure related to cyber.[10] Brazil also works with the Organization of American States (OAS), which is a body that helps to facilitate projects with participation from both the public and private sectors. Although Brazil has taken small steps to protect and regulate its critical infrastructure through technical review and national guidelines for inspection by the National Telecommunications Agency (ANATEL), many efforts lack resources and capacity. ANATEL has even been criticized by Brazil's Federal Accountability Office for its inability to meet oversight commitments sufficiently.[11] Brazil is also lacking the necessary amount of coordination between all stakeholders deploying SCADA devices, both public and private. Additionally, because Brazil utilizes a system that allows for both the Federal Police of Brazil and the state police in the country to handle ICT offenses, there is often a risk of competing competencies and a lack of communication between the two.[12] This makes the utilization of a centralized task force helpful in coordinating information and identifying critical cyberthreats in relation to national security and critical

---

[7]De Souza, D. P. B. (2018). "Brazil: Cybersecurity 2019," Global Legal Group Limited, October 16. Available at: https://iclg.com/practice-areas/cybersecurity-laws-and-regulations/brazil (accessed on February 20, 2019).

[8]"Brazil's Critical Infrastructure Faces a Growing Risk of Cyberattacks," Council on Foreign Relations, April 10. Available at: https://www.cfr.org/blog/brazils-critical-infrastructure-faces-growing-risk-cyberattacks (accessed on March 5, 2019).

[9]Meyer, A. (2010). "Brazil infrastructure," *Brazil*. Available at: https://www.brazil.org.za/brazil-infrastructure.html (accessed on April 2, 2019).

[10]Banco Central Do Brazil (2018). "Resolution CMN 4,658," April 26. Available at: https://www.bcb.gov.br/ingles/norms/Resolution%204658.pdf (accessed on March 20, 2019).

[11]ANATEL (2015). "Ordinance No. 50640," December 22. Available at: http://www.anatel.gov.br/legislacao/procedimentos-de-fiscalizacao/887-portaria-50640 (accessed on March 11, 2019).

[12]"Specialized Cybercrime Unites: Good Practice Study," *CryberCrime@IPA,* November 9, 2011. Available at: https://rm.coe.int/2467-htcu-study-v30-9nov11/16802f6a33 (accessed on March 11, 2019).

infrastructure issues. Although Brazil is lacking this entity, they utilize the Computer Forensic Unit of the Federal Police to inform their Congress during policymaking processes, as recommended by the REMJA Working Group on Cybercrime.[13] Adding to the challenges of Brazil's ability to regulate cybersecurity, the country's oversight structure allows for a long list of ministries and government entities to have influence over cybersecurity issues.[14] No single agency is tasked with the overall coordination among over seven different ministries and departments that control aspects of privacy and security in the cyber sector. In terms of legislation to combat cybercrime, Brazil's Congress has been faced with many bills that, if passed, would allow for access to personal data without a judicial order, prolonging public opposition due to privacy concerns.

Much like Brazil, Colombia's civil law groundings guarantee the right to privacy in its Constitution and includes a "habeas data" right, allowing citizens the right to know about and control personal information that has been collected in public or private databases. Colombia's cybersecurity legislation focus has been on data protection. There are two main data protection laws in Colombia, the most recent being Law 1581 of 2012, which deals with reporting requirements and general regulations; however, instances of security breaches often go unreported despite this regulation.[15] This law, among others, is inspired by European data regulations with a focus on consent. The law designates the Superintendence of Industry and Commerce (SIC) as the main data protection authority with the responsibility to enforce regulations by conducting unannounced audits, raids, and investigations, as well as the ability to penalize for non-compliance to the law.[16] Additionally, laws have been created that further promote adherence

[13] Inter-American Development Bank and Organization of American States (2016). "Cybersecurity: Are we ready in Latin America and the Caribbean?" *IADB*, March. Available at: https://publications.iadb.org/en/cybersecurity-are-we-ready-latin-america-and-caribbean (accessed on February 10, 2019).

[14] Muggah, R. (2017). "Brazil struggles with effective cyber-crime response," *Jane's*. Available at: https://www.janes.com/images/assets/518/73518/Brazil_struggles_with_effective_cyber-crime_response.pdf (accessed on March 21, 2019).

[15] Inter-American Development Bank and Organization of American States (2016). "Cybersecurity: Are we ready in Latin America and the Caribbean?" *IADB*, March. Available at: https://publications.iadb.org/en/cybersecurity-are-we-ready-latin-america-and-caribbean (accessed on February 10, 2019).

[16] Barrera Silva, N. (2018). "Colombia," *The Law Reviews*, October. Available at: https://thelawreviews.co.uk/edition/the-privacy-data-protection-and-cybersecurity-law-review-edition-5/1175627/colombia (accessed on March 1, 2019).

to Colombia's cyber regulations, such as Law 1273 of 2009 that hands out penalties of as much as four years in prison.[17] In regards to Colombia's fight against cybercrime, their National Council for Economic and Social Policy (CONPES) directs cybersecurity and cyber defense policy in the country, releasing CONPES 3701 in 2011.[18] This document acted as a guide for the government in forming cybersecurity and cyber defense policy, and its recommendations pushed Colombia to set up a cyber defense system that aimed to protect state institutions and government information.[19] In addition, the new CONPES document established working groups consisting of government entities and private organizations to protect the country's critical infrastructure.[20] Colombia is projected to release a National Defense Strategy for Critical Infrastructure based on the groups' work. Following a scandal involving wiretapping abuses by heads of the military and of the Administrative Security Department (DAS) in early 2014, President Santos sought help from the OAS, resulting in the creation of the National Mission of Technical Assistance on Cyber Security.[21] The objective was to generate further recommendations that would give the government a more solid base when implementing its systems. The mission also included international perspectives from government officials of various countries, as well as representatives from the Council of Europe (COE), Interpol, the UN, and the Organization for Economic Cooperation and Development (OECD). Its main recommendation of the mission was to harmonize the new system with the international Convention on Cybercrime, otherwise known as the Budapest Convention, to allow for the country to consider best practices on digital crime legislation. In 2016, CONPES 3854 was drafted, replacing CONPES 3701, focusing more on risk management and the promotion of public awareness

---

[17]"Colombia cuenta con una política nacional de seguridad digital," *Mintic*, April 15, 2016. Available at: https://www.mintic.gov.co/portal/604/w3-article-15033.html (accessed on March 20, 2019).

[18]Cáceres García, J. A. (2016). "Cyberdefense and cybersecurity in Colombia," *Dialogo*, September 22.

[19]*Ibid.*

[20]Organization of American States (2015). "Report on cybersecurity and critical infrastructure in the Americas," *OAS*. Available at: https://www.sites.oas.org/cyber/Documents/2015%20-%20OAS%20Trend%20Micro%20Report%20on%20Cybersecurity%20and%20CIP%20in%20the%20Americas.pdf (accessed on May 4, 2019).

[21]*Freedomhouse* (2018). "Colombia Country Report." Available at: https://freedomhouse.org/country/colombia (accessed on November 2020).

campaigns. While Colombia sets a good example for being the first LAC country to fully recognize recommendations of the OECD, both CONPES reports failed to produce hard policy upfront. CONPES 3854 evaluated the aftermath of goals made in 3701, one of which being to "strengthen legislation on cybersecurity and cyber defense," but the document admitted to only developing binding regulation aimed at the protection of personal rights and data. Although the document mentions a National Digital Security Policy, the document itself is only projecting the construction of a "plan" that will be executed sometime between 2016 and 2019 to form their policy, with the hope of its implementation, using CONPES 3854 as a guideline, by 2020. So, while CONPES 3854 acknowledges the need to adapt legislation to fast-moving threats in cyberspace, Colombia's policies still lag behind new threats. Both CONPES reports defined cyber critical infrastructure but protective regulations have yet to be implemented. The Emergency Security Response Team of Colombia (COLCERT) is mainly responsible for protecting national infrastructure against cyber incidents that threaten national security, but they do not have any PPPs to help bolster this protection. Despite the country's utilization of international cooperation and guidelines from the Budapest Convention, a policy has not yet been implemented for the country regarding cybersecurity and defense, and there is much backlash from civil society groups regarding CONPES 8354's focus on military and economic issues at the expense of broader social and human rights concerns, such as privacy.[22]

Taking into consideration the cybercrime trends in Colombia, the current dynamic of these cybersecurity issues reflect the steady growth of incidents in the country. Business Email Compromise attacks (BEC) are some of the most predominant cyberattacks that compromise the safety of private information and of the overall integrity of everyone involved. In Colombia, the estimated figure of losses is between 300 and 5,000 million Colombian pesos, depending on the size of the individuals affected by the attack. It is estimated that, in 2020, cybercrime will continue to become more sophisticated and, consequently, more difficult to counterattack; it is for this reason that Colombia ought to take needed measures to protect the information and telecommunication technology of its country. By recognizing and targeting the issue effectively, we can expect fewer violations of information security and a safer cyber community for all.

---

[22]*Ibid.*

3.4. Cyberspace Regulations in Countries using Common Law Systems

When analyzing countries with common legal systems, we have chosen Belize and Trinidad and Tobago as examples of countries exerting the most effort to combat cyber issues. To date, electronic transaction legislation is the closest Belize has come to cyber legislation, as seen in the Interception of Communications Act of 2010 (provisions relating to interception and when it is allowed), the Electronic Transactions Act of 2003 (facilitates the appropriate use and protection of transactions), and the Telecommunications Act of 2002 (protects telecommunications and outlines offences and penalties of non-compliance).[23] Belize is one of the only countries in the LAC region that does not have any regulations pertaining to data protection or overall cybersecurity or crime. Belize has a Freedom of Information Act (2000), which protects personal information of citizens, but does not mention electronic data.[24] Belize's Medium Term Development Strategy 2010–2013 serves as a framework to the government for the creation of legislation to, among other things, address issues of "data protection and privacy, cybercrime, and network security." The strategy also highlights the appointment of an ICT Task Force that is to create and update the National ICT Policy; however, there only seems to be a National ICT Strategy (2011), and it neither mentions cyber issues nor data protection.[25] The National e-Government Strategy and Work Plan 2015–2018 is another framework created by Belize to guide its Central Information Technology Office (CITO) to produce further e-government frameworks. Although the strategy does not focus much on cybersecurity, one of its pillars is to enhance national security, with one of the many objectives aimed at "build[ing] technical and legislative capacity to respond to, mitigate, and protect against cybercrime and offences within the public sector." The strategy also recommends the creation of a Computer Security Incident Response Team (CSIRT) to produce cybersecurity information, support in the event of a cyber incident, and collaboration. However, no CSIRT has been created, though the national police

---

[23]"Repository Cybercrime, Database of Legislation," *UNODC*. Available at: https://sherloc.unodc.org/ (accessed on February 10, 2019).

[24]Freedom of Information Act, December 31, 2000.

[25]Belize National ICT Strategy, 2011. Available at: http://lincompany.kz/pdf/Africa/Beliz2011.pdf (accessed on June 1, 2019).

often collaborate with international CSIRTs when dealing with cyber issues. While Belize does not have any cybersecurity legislation on the topic, they do mention in their strategy the importance of protecting critical infrastructure and the need to secure information networks, though they do not define what critical infrastructure is in their own country. Lastly, the strategy claims that the CITO will work with the agency responsible for cybercrime and cybersecurity in order to produce a cybersecurity national policy, strategy, and action plan and ensures the government of Belize will focus more on creating policies and legislation that supports the strategy overall, one of which being data protection regulations.[26] In 2017, Belize hosted a Cyber Security Symposium with the goal of collaboration and development, among both the public and private sectors, of a national framework dealing with cybersecurity issues. Although Belize conducts helpful collaborative events such as their symposium and has created various strategies dealing with future cybersecurity regulations, the country has failed to fully implement any of the guidelines dealing with cyber issues and lacks the cooperation of PPPs.

Like many other LAC countries, the focus of Trinidad and Tobago regarding cybersecurity has been on data protection. The country's most recent regulation is the Data Protection Act (DPA) of 2011, which provides protections to personal privacy and information that is collected by private and public bodies; however, the DPA functions as if it is not implemented, as the enforcement body of the act, The Office of the Information Commissioner, has not yet been established, and many of the DPA's provisions have not yet been enacted.[27] The Information Commissioner, if established, would have the ability to enter premises and question citizens, as well as to search for and collect their data without a court order or warrant.[28] This, along with the fact that certain provisions of the bill have not yet been enacted into law (such as those protecting the rights of journalists), has raised concerns over the correct balance of privacy and constitutional rights to freedom. In 2016, the Public Administration and Communications

---

[26]Belize National E-Government Strategy, 2015.

[27]*DLA Piper* (2019). "Data protection laws of the world: Trinidad and Tobago," January 28. Available at: https://www.dlapiperdataprotection.com/index.html?t=law&c=TT (accessed on June 2, 2019).

[28]Lyndersay, M. (2016). "The challenges of the Data Protection Bill," *Trinidad and Tobago Guardian,* October 24. Available at: http://www.guardian.co.tt/lifestyle/challenges-data-protection-bill-6.2.359349.b246c2daff (accessed on April 1, 2019).

Ministry agreed to review and potentially amend the act, but to date, no changes have been implemented. The government has also created a PPP between Trinidad and Tobago and public and private operators and owners of critical energy infrastructure, which focuses on preventing, anticipating, and responding to all threats to the country's energy sector.[29] With regards to cybercrime, Trinidad and Tobago produced a National Cyber Security Strategy of 2012, which is meant to provide guidelines for all legislation that follows.[30] Some of the most important areas this document addresses is defining critical infrastructure in the nation, pledging to focus on the interdependence of critical information infrastructure protection (CIIP) and critical infrastructure protection (CIP), using international frameworks and partnerships to guide legislation, and implementing education awareness and training.[31] While the framework lays out good ideas, it has not yet delivered on all of its promises. The Cybercrime Bill of 2017 has not yet been enacted into law and faces much social backlash. Like the DPA, the bill criminalizes journalists and whistleblowers who leak illegally obtained data, including government documents. This is an issue for the public because these types of leaks are some of the only ways that many actors can hold their government accountable, and the lack of set law impedes Trinidad and Tobago's ability to move forward. Additionally, there is a lag in cybersecurity awareness and advancements due to a lack of financial and human resources.

3.5. Cyberspace Regulations in Countries Using a Mixture of Common and Civil Law Systems

Regarding countries in the LAC region utilizing a mixture of both legal systems, we have chosen to analyze the legislative efforts of Guyana and Puerto Rico. Guyana currently has no legislation or framework

---

[29]Inter-American Development Bank and Organization of American States (2015). "Report on cybersecurity and critical infrastructure in the Americas." Available at: https://www.sites.oas.org/cyber/Documents/2015%20-%20OAS%20Trend%20Micro%20Report%20on%20Cybersecurity%20and%20CIP%20in%20the%20Americas.pdf (accessed on March 10, 2019).

[30]ENISA (2015). "Trinidad and Tobago cyber security strategy," February 3. Available at: https://www.enisa.europa.eu/topics/national-cyber-security-strategies/ncss-map/strategies/trinidad-and-tobago-cyber-security-strategy (accessed on April 6, 2019).

[31]Organization of American States (2014). "Latin American and Caribbean cyber security trends," *Symantec*, June. Available at: https://www.symantec.com/content/en/us/enterprise/other_resources/b-cyber-security-trends-report-lamc.pdf (accessed on April 1, 2019).

regarding data protection. In 2015, the government amended its Financial Institutions Bill to allow the Guyana Revenue Authority (GRA) to access data of all citizens for various investigative purposes, which withdrew the previous bill's requirement for the GRA to make a lawful request before gaining access to such information.[32] This received criticism by the Private Sector Commission (PSC) due to the lack of legislation that protects confidential information in the country. Although the PSC recommended a short-term adoption of US frameworks to the Attorney General, nothing on this front has been accomplished.[33] Since then, the government has publicly stated that the need for such privacy regulation is not yet needed due to international treaty obligations to the US,[34] such as The Foreign Account Tax Compliance Act (FACTA) requiring those living outside of the US to produce yearly reports of their non-US financial accounts, which for Guyana comes from the GRA.[35] In terms of government entities, Guyana has a National Data Management Agency that does not focus on aspects of data protection. In 2018, the country passed a cybercrime bill that was originally criticized by the opposition People's Progressive Party (PPP) for clauses that restricted the rights of the press and threatened whistleblowers by criminalizing computer users who promote discontent toward the government. In response, the government produced amendments that removed obstacles to a free press and more rigidly defined the type of electronic data that was to be prohibited. Even with these amendments in place, the House continues to disagree on various provisions and refuses to take responsibility for inclusion of certain clauses, as the PPP either were not present to vote at certain times of the bill's amendment process or lacked the voting powers to do so without

---

[32]Paul, J. (2015). "No immediate need for data protection laws — Finance Minister," *iNewsGuyana*, November 18. Available at: https://www.inewsguyana.com/no-immediate-need-for-data-protection-laws-finance-minister/ (accessed on March 18, 2019).

[33]*Guyana Times* (2015). "Govt to address concerns on data protection laws," *Mola*, November 12, 2015. Available at: https://mola.gov.gy/15-news-/319-govt-to-address-concerns-on-data-protection-laws (accessed on March 10, 2019).

[34]Paul, J. (2015). "No immediate need for data protection laws — Finance Minister," *iNewsGuyana*, November 18. Available at: https://www.inewsguyana.com/no-immediate-need-for-data-protection-laws-finance-minister/ (accessed on March 10, 2019).

[35]*Ibid.*

major support of certain government members.[36] An upside of the bill is a requirement to expose law enforcement officials, including state prosecutors, to cybersecurity training; however, legal professionals have not yet undergone such training. In addition, many attorneys have argued that the bill is not in alignment with the Budapest Convention and lacks provisions allowing for international cooperation; however, Guyana has neither signed nor ratified the convention and is therefore not legally bound to it.[37] Additionally, Guyana is behind in assessing its Critical National Infrastructure (CNI) assets and vulnerabilities, and owners of CNI rarely adhere to security standards or report incidences due to a lack of legislation regarding and identifying CNI.[38] In 2015, Guyana collaborated with experts from the OAS' Inter-American Committee Against Terrorism (OAS/CICTE) in a two-day workshop to identify other countries' best practices in developing a National Cybersecurity Policy Framework, such as that in Trinidad and Tobago.[39] Another goal of the workshop was to establish a National Task Force to address the country's cyber needs, which has not yet been accomplished. Although the country has established a National CIRT to provide analysis and incident response to cybersecurity issues, its capabilities are limited due to the absence of a national cybersecurity strategy or policy and a lack of awareness of cyber-related issues in the government. The CIRT is also not governed by legislation, but rather by cabinet approval, and there is currently no legal requirement for private-sector entities to report cyber incidents to the government. The main challenges to the future of Guyana's cybersecurity advancement and regulation is a lack of personnel with required skill sets, the absence of national regulations or frameworks, inadequate training,

---

[36] Staff Reporter (2018). "Cybercrime Bill passed," *Guyana Chronicle*, July 21. Available at: http://guyanachronicle.com/2018/07/21/cybercrime-bill-passed (accessed on March 18, 2019).

[37] Cybercrime Programme Office of the Council of Europe (C-PROC) (2018). "Cybercrime digest," *COE*, May 1. Available at: https://www.coe.int/documents/9252320/19115368/CPROC+Digest+2018-05-01.pdf/bcef7798-011b-92b4-def8-4ed13dd03b4c (accessed on March 5, 2019).

[38] Inter-American Development Bank and Organization of American States (2016). "Cybersecurity: Are we ready in Latin America and the Caribbean?" *IADB*, March. Available at: https://publications.iadb.org/en/cybersecurity-are-we-ready-latin-america-and-caribbean (accessed on March 10, 2019).

[39] Staff Writer (2015). "Gov't to hold cyber security workshop," *Stabroek News*, August 5. Available at: https://www.stabroeknews.com/2015/news/guyana/08/05/govt-to-hold-cyber-security-workshop/ (accessed on March 5, 2019).

and the fact that cybersecurity threats are not currently viewed by the government as a top priority.[40]

Before explaining regulatory efforts in Puerto Rico, it is first important to understand Puerto Rico's legal system. Although Puerto Rico is a US unincorporated territory, the LAC region, as well as a majority of Puerto Ricans, view the territory as a part of Latin America. Before its affiliation with the US, Puerto Rico utilized the Spanish civil code. Because the US uses a common law system based on the doctrine of judicial precedent, Puerto Rico adopted a mixed legal system that incorporated both common and civil law aspects.[41] Although Puerto Rico has the ability to create and amend its own constitution, US Code Title 48, "Territories and Insular Possessions" requires Puerto Rico to adopt all US statutory laws that are not "locally inapplicable."[42] Puerto Rico has its own Supreme Court and applies new laws based on case law precedent[43]; however, the US Supreme Court, although independent of that in Puerto Rico, can review Puerto Rico's Supreme Court decisions on a *writ of certiorari.*[44]

Although Puerto Rico adopts cybersecurity legislation from the US, the territory has implemented its own regulations, namely dealing with data protection. Puerto Rico currently has no overarching authority or single law that outlines broad protective regulations of citizens' data.[45] There are, however, a few individual laws that regulate aspects of a citizen's personally identifiable information.[46] One of the first pieces of legislation regarding the protection of personal data is Act No. 111 of 2005 (Citizen Information of Data Banks Security Act), which provides requirements for commercial entities to protect personal information of consumers who are customers of said entities of said entities. Because

---

[40] Organization of American States (2014). "Latin American and Caribbean cyber security trends," *Symantec*, June. Available at: https://www.symantec.com/content/en/us/enterprise/other_resources/b-cyber-security-trends-report-lamc.pdf (accessed on March 7, 2019).

[41] Zorilla and Silverstrini Attorneys at Law (2019). "Puerto Rico legal system," *Zspalaw*. Available at: https://www.zspalaw.com/puerto-rico-legal-system.html (accessed on April 2, 2019).

[42] 48 USC 734, *Cornell Law*, January 4, 2012. Available at: https://www.law.cornell.edu/uscode/pdf/uscode48/lii_usc_TI_48_CH_4_SC_I_SE_734.pdf (accessed on April 8, 2019).

[43] 28 US Code, Section 1258, *Cornell Law*. Available at: https://www.law.cornell.edu/uscode/text/28/1258 (accessed on March 8, 2019).

[44] In other words, the US can review decisions when it deems necessary.

[45] Seda-Fernandez, E. J. and M. Y. Haack (2019). "Data Privacy Law," March 8.

[46] *Ibid.*

this act does not address the handling of such information after the termination of that customer relationship, Act No. 234 was implemented in 2014 to require commercial entities to discard all data in a way that protects consumer privacy, such as by "shredding, deleting, or modifying" it to render the personal information unreadable or indecipherable by any method.[47] As of present, Puerto Rico has produced House Bill 607 amending Act No. 234 to require the holders of personally identifiable information to notify consumers of violations, compromises, or unauthorized access to their personal information within 24 hours of becoming aware of a breach.[48] This amendment is meant to further protect citizens' personal data and expand protections against privacy violations such as identity theft. Recognizing the lack of legislation establishing parameters to protect growing accumulations of personal data by companies, Puerto Rico has also proposed Senate Bill 1231, which would create the Digital Privacy Protection Act in order to guarantee rights to privacy by including protective regulations for information held in automated databases and private-sector business manuals. The main goal of the bill is to allow for citizens to demand a company to refrain from selling their personal information to third parties, which is currently not restricted in Puerto Rico. Additionally, citizens would be able to request a company to terminate their personal information from its databases or records and advise third parties who the data had been shared with to do the same.[49] So far, Puerto Rico's attempts to reform outdated laws show their commitment to addressing new threats that emerge from enhanced access to personal information. The main issue Puerto Rico faces is a lack of an overarching data protection or cybersecurity authority to deal with both privacy and security issues. In addition, there is a lack of a data protection law that encompasses all aspects of citizens' security issues, as well as an absence of any cybersecurity regulation, specifically regarding Puerto Rican critical infrastructure, which is not often discussed by the government.

---

[47]Medida P C1484, *OSLPR,* May 7, 2019. Available at: oslpr.org/legislatura/tl2013/tl_busca_avanzada.asp?rcs=P%20C1484 (accessed on April 1, 2019).

[48]Open States (2017). "Puerto Rico House Bill 607," *Open States,* January 14. Available at: https://info.digitalguardian.com/rs/768-OQW-145/images/the-definitive-guide-to-us-state-data-breach-laws.pdf (accessed on April 12, 2019).

[49]Miranda, M. (2019). "Bill introduced to protect, regulate, personal data in Puerto Rico," *Caribbean Business,* March 25. Available at: https://caribbeanbusiness.com/bill-introduced-to-protect-regulate-personal-data-in-puerto-rico/ (accessed on June 1, 2019).

3.6. Conclusion

Countries in the LAC region face many cybersecurity challenges, given the rapidly evolving pace of cyberthreats. Most obstacles for these countries come from a lack of coordination between the public and private sectors, minimal resources and capacity, the absence of a legal framework, and the inability for many countries to implement regulations quickly enough to keep up with new threats, which is especially true for countries utilizing civil law systems. Countries that focus on data protection and privacy often neglect defining and protecting their critical infrastructure, and countries forming cybercrime legislation focus on accessing citizen's information and have received public backlash due to privacy concerns. Many civil law countries may also struggle with establishing helpful PPPs due to a lack of freedom of contract. Although many LAC countries utilizing common law have not yet created case law on these issues, the fluid nature of such a system in regions such as the US has proven to allow for a more flexible legal environment, especially when regarding issues of privacy. For instance, in 2018, Carpenter v. United States created precedent declaring a lawful warrant requirement in order to obtain cell phone data of US citizens.[50] While case law in the US is helpful, the EU serves as a frontrunner in cyber efforts and often influences the actions of both the US and LAC regions. The EU likely has an easier time dealing with cybersecurity issues because they utilize a mixed legal system, incorporating aspects of both civil and common law. Their judicial system allows for them to rule over certain aspects of the law, they have a non-political interest in market competition, and they have grown their capacities due to their freedom of contract through PPPs and international cooperation to implement their overall commitment to cybersecurity. The EU also focuses on some of the most important aspects of cybersecurity: data privacy, critical infrastructure, and cybercrime.

In 2018, the EU passed a General Data Protection Regulation (GDPR) with the goal of updating laws that protect citizens' personal information. GDPR not only gives control to citizens over their data but also regulates how public and private actors handle personal information.[51] In addition,

---

[50]Wessler, N. F. (2018). "The Supreme Court's groundbreaking privacy victory for the digital age," *ACLU*, June 22. Available at: https://www.aclu.org/blog/privacy-technology/location-tracking/supreme-courts-groundbreaking-privacy-victory-digital-age (accessed on May 25, 2019).

[51]EU GDPR (2018). "GDPR Key Changes." Available at: https://eugdpr.org/the-regulation/ (accessed on May 25, 2019).

unlike the US, the EU takes market competition and data protection very seriously. The region is currently looking to combine the two in a set of constraints that would promote the market value of smaller companies while regulating companies with large market power that have unlimited access to user data. In the US, online market power is measured by how much data a user is willing to give up to a company, and those accessing the most data, such as Facebook and Twitter, often swallow competitors' values. Courts often only view online business monopolies as an issue if they are clearly harming consumers. In this sense, the EU has an easier time regulating these companies, as antitrust debates in the US are usually prosecuted in front of a judge, while in the EU, the European Commission itself has the power to decide cases without approval of national governments. In the US, only federal agencies can impose these types of federal laws.[52] In addition, privacy is a fundamental right in the EU Charter the way that freedom of speech is in the US Constitution. Because of the EU's hard stance on privacy, US regulations are often discussed by EU courts to determine whether American laws are protective enough as to allow for European data to flow through the US. If regulations are not up to par with those in the EU, the functioning of other country's Internet companies, such as those in the US, could be compromised.[53] In addition to privacy concerns, the European Parliament approved a Cybersecurity Act this year, which focuses on the expertise of the European Union Agency for Cybersecurity (ENISA) in developing legislation, considering best practices, enhancing capacity-building in Member States, providing education and training, and enhancing cooperation with PPPs to combat cybersecurity issues and protect critical infrastructure.[54] While cybercrime is incorporated into the act, there are also other bodies that work to combat attacks against critical infrastructure, such as Europol's European Cybercrime Center, along with efforts of ENISA.[55]

In line with EU standards, many LAC countries have followed suite and adopted regulations in congruence with the GDPR. Brazil, for instance, based its data privacy law off of that in the EU, and many

---

[52] *The Economist* (2019). "The power of privacy," March 23–29, pp. 19–20.

[53] *The Economist* (2019). "The Cambridge Analytica Bill," March 2–8, p. 22.

[54] *Hunton Security Blog* (2019). "EU Parliament approves the proposal for Cybersecurity Act," March 28. Available at: https://www.huntonprivacyblog.com/2019/03/28/eu-parliament-approves-the-proposal-for-cybersecurity-act/ (accessed on February 18, 2019). (magazine).

[55] *Eur-Lex* (2013). Directive 2013/40/EU, August 12. Available at: https://eur-lex.europa.eu/LexUriServ/LexUriServ.do?uri=OJ:L:2013:218:0008:0014:EN:PDF (accessed on May 10, 2019).

Ibero-American Member States, which are mostly from LAC countries, have agreed to the Standards for Data Protection, which uses the GDPR as a policy guideline.[56] In addition, many LAC countries have agreed to adhere to the Budapest Convention, which is an international agreement laying out cybersecurity framework requirements for each member. Agreements on the international level, however, continue to be lacking. Many countries that have signed and ratified the Budapest Convention have not yet implemented its recommendations, and the convention will not have enough effect without ratification by larger members of the community, such as Russia and China. In addition, because cyberspace has no boundaries, a binding international law is too difficult to pass. While the United Nations (UN) has attempted to work toward alleviating international cybersecurity threats, not much has been done on the front of international adherence. Acts of cybercrime are nearly impossible to identify, and no court in the international community hears cases regarding international cybercrimes, as there is no set international law prohibiting them that is binding on all UN Member States, and there is no agreed upon definition of what constitutes a "cybercrime."[57] Conducting investigations to prove an attack is also difficult without infringing on another nation's sovereignty.[58] The United Nations Security Council will not likely produce a resolution dealing with cybercrime due to its current makeup, which includes Russia and China, two countries that would not benefit from such a resolution. Due to these issues, as well as those aforementioned, the LAC region is likely to continue to follow the EU in setting up their own regulations, and the utilization of international cooperation and the establishment of PPPs are the most feasible mechanisms to boost their chances of implementing strong legislation to combat cybersecurity issues. Unfortunately, the United Nations has not made any real effort to advance cybersecurity efforts that assist the international community in regards to the issue. It is for this reason that Latin American countries have

[56] Day, J. (2018). "Privacy and cybersecurity developments in Latin America," *JDSUPRA*, June 25. Available at: https://www.jdsupra.com/legalnews/privacy-and-cybersecurity-developments-13277/ (accessed on May 12, 2019).

[57] Chang, W., W. Chung, H. Chen and S. Chou (2003). "An international perspective on fighting cybercrime," *Intelligence and Security Informatics*, **2665**: 379–384.

[58] United Nations Office on Drugs and Crime (UNODC) (2013). "Comprehensive study on cybercrime," February, pp. 185. Available at: https://www.unodc.org/documents/commissions/CCPCJ/CCPCJ_Sessions/CCPCJ_22/_E-CN15-2013-CRP05/Comprehensive_study_on_cybercrime.pdf (accessed on May 4, 2019).

focused on the efforts made by the EU and the US; these two entities have served as a model for countries in Latin America to follow for their own cybersecurity legislation and regulations. Several countries in Latin America continue to face recurrent cybersecurity challenges that have allowed for the development and implementation of comprehensive data protection legislation. Consequently, the approaches taken by both the EU and the US have served as a guideline for countries in Latin America; e.g. the EU's GDPR was used as a ground rule for the publication of the Standards for Data Protection for the Ibero-American States by the Red Iberoamericana in June 2017. It is by following the already established obligations in the US and the EU that Latin American nations are able to craft, structure, and implement an effective and efficient cybersecurity legal system.

Appendix

Table A: LAC countries and their legal systems, legislation, and implementation dates.

Country	Legal System	Cyberspace Legislation Title	Date
Antigua & Barbuda	Common Law	Electronic Crimes Act	2013
		Data Protection Act	2013
Argentina	Civil Law	Personal Data Protection Law	2000
		Computer Crimes Law	2008
Bahamas	Common Law	Computer Misuse Act	2003
		Data Protection Act	2003
Barbados	Common Law	Computer Misuse Act	2005
Belize	Common Law	Telecommunications Act	2002
		Electronic Transactions Act	2003
		Interception of Communications Act	2010
		National ICT Strategy	2010
		National E-Government Policy	2015
Bolivia	Civil Law	General Law on Telecommunications, Information and Communication Technologies	2011
		E-Government Implementation Plan	2017
Brazil	Civil Law	Information and Communications Security and Cyber Security Strategy	2015
		General Data Protection Law	2020

Table A: *(Continued)*

Country	Legal System	Cyberspace Legislation Title	Date
Cayman Islands	Common Law	Data Protection Law	2019
Chile	Civil Law	General Telecommunications Act	1982
		Personal Data Protection Law	1999
		National Cybersecurity Policy	2017
Colombia	Civil Law	Protection Information and Data Law	2009
		Policy Guidelines on Cybersecurity and Cyberdefense	2011
		Personal Data Protection Act	2011
		Data Protection Law	2012
		National Digital Security Policy	2016
Costa Rica	Civil Law	National Cybersecurity Strategy	2017
Cuba	Civil Law	Safety Regulations for Information Technologies	2007
Dominican Republic	Civil Law	Law Against Crimes and High Technology Offenses	2007
		Protection of Personal Data Law	2013
		Establishing and Regulating the National Cybersecurity Strategy Decree	2018
Ecuador	Civil Law	E-commerce, Electronic Signatures and Data Messages Law	2002
		National Plan for Electronic Governance	2017
El Salvador	Civil Law	Special Law Against Cybercrime and Related Offenses	2016
French Guiana	Civil Law	Information Systems Defense Strategy: France's Strategy	2011
		Cyber Defense Pact	2014
		National Digital Security Strategy	2015
		Transportation of the EU The Security of Network and Information Systems Directive	2018
Grenada	Common Law	ICT National Strategic Plan	2006
		Electronic Crimes Act	2013
Guatemala	Civil Law	National Cybersecurity Strategy	2018

(Continued)

Table A: (*Continued*)

Country	Legal System	Cyberspace Legislation Title	Date
Guyana	Mixed Law	Cybercrime Bill	2018
Honduras	Civil Law	Electronic Transactions Act	2006
		Cybercrimes Act	2010
		Digital Agenda of Honduras	2013
Jamaica	Common Law	National Cyber Security Strategy	2015
Mexico	Civil Law	Protection of Private Personal Data	2010
		National Cybersecurity Strategy	2017
Nicaragua	Civil Law	Data Protection Law	2012
Panama	Civil Law	National Strategy for Cyber Security and Critical Infrastructure	2013
Paraguay	Civil Law	Law Amending the Penal Code	2011
		Data Protection Law	2015
		National Cybersecurity Plan	2017
Perú	Civil Law	Personal Data Protection Law	2011
		National Policy on E-Government and Information Technology	2013
		Computer Crimes Act	2014
Puerto Rico	Mixed Law	Citizen Information of Data Banks Security Act	2005
		Consumer's Confidential Personal Identifiers Protection Act	2014
St. Kitts & Nevis	Common Law	National ICT Strategic Plan	2006
		Electronic Crimes Act	2009
St. Lucia	Mixed Law	Computer Misuse Act	2011
		National ICT Policy and Strategy	2013
		Data Protection (Amendment) Act	2015
St. Vincent and the Grenadines	Common Law	Privacy Act	2003
		Electronic Evidence Act	2004
		Electronic Transactions Act	2007
		National ICT Strategy and Action Plan	2010
Suriname	Civil Law	Telecommunications Facilities Act	2004

Table A: (*Continued*)

Country	Legal System	Cyberspace Legislation Title	Date
Trinidad and Tobago	Common Law	Data Protection Act	2011
		National Cyber Security Strategy	2012
Uruguay	Civil Law	Protection of Personal Data Law	2008
		Decreto de Seguridad de la Información para Organismos de la Administración Pública	2009
		Estandarización de los Nombres de Dominio de la Administración Central	2014
		Agenda Digital 2020	2017
Venezuela	Civil Law	Special Law on Computer Crimes	2001
		Law on Electronic Signatures and Data Messages	2001
		Info-Government Act	2014

Chapter 4

Cybersecurity and Legislation: The Case Study of Singapore

Benjamin Ang

*Cyber and Homeland Defence Centre of Excellence
for National Security — CENS RSIS,
Nanyang Technological University, Singapore*

isbang@ntu.edu.sg

Abstract

Many South-East Asian Nations member states lack a legislative or regulatory framework. This is in the context of the view that cyberspace is global and thus local sovereignty principles are less to be applied. the South-East Asian Nations member states have appointed Singapore in 2018 to propose a mechanism to enhance cyber coordination and agreed in principle to certain voluntary norms of behavior in cyberspace. Singapore was one of the earliest Southeast Asian states to enact its Computer Misuse Act in 1993, and later to publish its national Cybersecurity Strategy in 2016, and to enact its Cybersecurity Act in 2018. This chapter looks at the evolution of cybersecurity legislation in Singapore and examines Singapore as a case study of how a small state in Asia has approached cybersecurity legislation.

4.1. Introduction

Cybersecurity legislation varies from nation to nation because different nations have different conceptions of what "cyberspace" is and how "cybersecurity" is defined. For example, some states, like the US, view cyberspace as a "global commons," where sovereignty principles derived from physical territory do not apply, such that it is beyond the authority or control of the state. Their concept of cybersecurity focuses on the confidential, integrity, and availability of the computer systems that form cyberspace, but not the content flowing through those systems. Other states, like China, believe in Internet sovereignty in cyberspace, and the "right of individual countries to independently choose their own path of cyber development and model of cyber regulation."[1] Their concept of cybersecurity considers not only protection of computer systems, but also regulating the content that flows through the computer systems.

4.2. Computer Misuse Act

Combating cybercrime is a high priority for Asian nations, and Singapore enacted its Computer Misuse Act (CMA) in 1993 to address computer crimes in Singapore. The CMA has been amended several times since then, as recently as 2017. It extends to acts committed by persons located outside Singapore, if the effects take place in Singapore.

CMA covers "computer crime" (acts usually referred to as "hacking" where the computer is the target of the crime) as compared with "cyber-crime" (crimes committed in cyberspace where the computer is used as an instrument of committing the crime, such as fraud, theft, and extortion, which are covered under the Penal Code). Penalties are severe, ranging from heavy fines to imprisonment. The main criminal offences under the CMA are:

- Section 3: Unauthorized access to computer material — this includes accessing, viewing, or copying data without authorization;
- Section 4: Access with intent to commit or facilitate commission of offence — this applies when a Section 3 offence is committed in order to facilitate a further offence against persons or property, such as unauthorized access to a bank's computer server to steal money[2];

---

[1] Zeng, J. T. Stevens and Y. Chen (2017). "China's solution to global cyber governance: Unpacking the domestic discourse of 'internet sovereignty.'" *Politics and Policy*, **45**(3): 432–464. Available at: https://www.researchgate.net/publication/317834062_China's_Solution_to_Global_Cyber_Governance_Unpacking_the_Domestic_Discourse_of_Internet_Sovereignty (accessed February 4, 2020).
[2] PP v Ho Poh Leong Nelson DAC 8535–8537/2002.

- Section 5: Unauthorized modification of computer material — this includes deletion, amendment, and tampering with data without authorization; it also includes website defacement[3];
- Section 6: Unauthorized use or interception of computer service — this includes using a network without authorization, also cloning of mobile phones for foreigners to make international calls[4];
- Section 7: Unauthorized obstruction of use of computer — this includes preventing persons from using computer systems through Distributed Denial of Service (DDoS)[5] or ransomware;
- Section 8: Unauthorized disclosure of access code — this includes disclosing PIN or passwords without authorization;
- Section 8A: Supplying, etc., personal information obtained in contravention of certain provisions — this includes selling data which has been stolen, e.g. in a data breach, which would contravene Section 3;
- Section 8B: Obtaining, etc., items for use in certain offences — this includes obtaining hacking tools or malware, which could be used to commit an offence under any of the Sections 3 to 7.

Sections 8A and 8B were enacted in 2017 in recognition of the evolution of computer crime tactics and techniques. The provisions contain exceptions for investigators and researchers who acquire the data or tools without the intention to commit crimes. This illustrates the necessity to review cybercrime or computer crime legislation regularly, to identify the rapid developments that accompany the rapid changes in technology and society, and to respond with amendments where necessary.

Prior to the enactment of the CMA, there were no offences under the Penal Code which could be used effectively to prosecute persons who committed the acts listed above. As a common law jurisdiction, where the courts interpret legislation according to precedents, there were no good precedents to handle, e.g. unauthorized access to data or tampering with data, thus it was necessary for CMA to create a new body of law in Singapore.

---

[3] PP v Lim Zhaoming Edwin MA 339/99/02.
[4] Chang Yiak Hua v PP MA 157/97/01.
[5] PP v Tan Cheng Kang DAC 8409–8411/2000.

This is in line with the approaches adopted by Singapore in combating computer crime[6]:

(1) Passing new legislation that creates crimes where activity warrants it;
(2) Imposing severe penalties as punishment and as deterrents;
(3) Providing law enforcement agencies with additional powers, granting them extra-territorial jurisdiction, and creating new agencies with specially trained experts to deal with this technological crimes; and
(4) Making it a crime to abet or even to attempt to perpetrate computer crimes.

The CMA has been actively used since its enactment for prosecuting ATM card skimmers and persons who gain unauthorized access to data. In one high profile case in 2001, two lawyers were charged for unauthorized copying of computer files from their employer's computer systems after they had tendered their resignations.[7]

More recently, seven former Citibank private bankers faced 1,223 charges under CMA and bank secrecy laws for allegedly accessing Citibank's computer network without authority and downloading or printing client data, to take to rival bank UBS in 2006.

Singapore Police Force (SPF) statistics show that cases under the CMA increased by 40.3%, from 858 cases in 2017 to 1,204 cases in 2018. Such cases included unauthorized access or transaction of an individual's online accounts, unauthorized purchases using credit/debit cards, and phishing emails that obtained sensitive personal information such as passwords and credit card details. It is unknown whether these statistics are due to an actual increase in CMA offences committed, or due to increased effectiveness of the SPF.

Besides computer crimes (CMA offences), the SPF pursues cybercrime (computer-enabled fraud, extortion) under the Penal Code. Internet

---

[6]Chik, W. (2006). "Computer crime, cyber crime and challenges to law making: A critical comparative study of the adequacies of computer crime and cyber crime legislation in the United States, the United Kingdom and Singapore." Paper presented at the *VI Computer Law World Conference*, Edinburgh, Scotland, UK. Available at: http://www.law.ed.ac.uk/ahrb/complaw (accessed January 5, 2007).

[7]PP v (1) Eddee Ng Ka Luon; (2) Tan Su Ean DAC 1788/2001 & Ors.

love scams[8] decreased by 20.1% to 660 cases in 2018, from 826 cases in 2017. The total amount cheated fell to around S$27.5 million in 2018, from around S$37 million in 2017. SPF credits the Transnational Commercial Crime Task Force (TCTF) that was set up in October 2017 to investigate transnational scams, including Internet love scams, as the TCTF has closed over 600 bank accounts and recovered more than S$1.4 million since starting operations. Unfortunately, there has been a 36.1% increase in e-commerce scams, loan scams, credit-for-sex scams, and China official impersonation scams[9] to 3,954 cases in 2018, from 2,905 cases in 2017.

Up to 2018, Section 15A of the CMA gave the Minister power to authorize or direct any person or organization to take emergency cybersecurity measures and comply with necessary requirements, for the purposes of preventing, detecting, or countering any serious and imminent threat to the provision of any essential service, or to the national security, defense, foreign relations, economy, public health, public safety, or public order of Singapore. This section was repealed in 2018 when the Cybersecurity Act 2018 came into force and has been reenacted in that Act instead.

4.3. Singapore's Cybersecurity Strategy

While the CMA deals with computer crimes and the Penal Code deals with cybercrimes, Singapore also recognized that transnational cyberattacks were (and are) increasing in frequency, sophistication, and impact. The nation became particularly concerned about cyberattacks on essential services such as power and banking services, which could cause significant disruptions to the economy and society. Cyberattacks on Estonia's banks, government, and media in 2007, on the Iranian nuclear power plant in 2010, and on the Ukrainian power grid in 2015, all highlighted the risks to states. Singapore itself suffered a series of high-profile website defacements in 2013 by a hacker called "The Messiah," who was

---

[8] In Internet love scams, the criminal, using a fake identity, seduces the victim online and persuades the love-struck victim to transfer money to the criminal for various fictitious reasons.

[9] In credit-for-sex scams, the victims transfer money in the hope of obtaining sexual favors; in "China official impersonation scams," the criminal impersonates a PRC official and extorts payment of a fictitious fine from the victim, who is often a PRC national working in Singapore.

arrested in Malaysia later that year with the help of Malaysian police. Singapore is particularly vulnerable because it is an open economy and highly connected to the rest of the world.

Recognizing the need for a comprehensive approach, Singapore launched its Cybersecurity Strategy in 2016, which sets out Singapore's vision, goals, and priorities for cybersecurity. Under its four pillars, the state will:

(1) **Strengthen the resilience of our Critical Information Infrastructure (CII)** — placing responsibility on owners of CII (that provide essential services) to protect their systems.
(2) **Mobilize businesses and the community to make cyberspace safer, by countering cyber threats, combating cybercrime and protecting personal data** — recognizing the work done by SPF under the National Cybercrime Action Plan, and the Personal Data Protection Commission under the Personal Data Protection Act.
(3) **Develop a vibrant cybersecurity ecosystem comprising a skilled workforce, technologically advanced companies, and strong research collaborations** — allocating resources for education, retraining, and capacity building, and also to give incentives for top cybersecurity companies and researchers to come to Singapore.
(4) **Step up efforts to forge strong international partnerships** — allocating resources to building regional and international relationships, including capacity building for ASEAN member states to help them develop their own cybersecurity strategies, policies, and legislation.

The Strategy is implemented by the Cyber Security Agency of Singapore (CSA), which is the Singaporean government agency, under the Prime Minister's Office but administratively managed by the Ministry of Communications and Information. CSA provides centralized oversight of national cybersecurity functions and works with public and private sector leads to protect Singapore's critical services. As part of the Strategy, CSA prepared the Cybersecurity Act, which was enacted in 2018.

4.4. Singapore Cybersecurity Act 2018

The Cybersecurity Act was passed in 2018 and establishes a legal framework for the oversight and maintenance of national cybersecurity in Singapore. Its four key objectives are to:

(1) Strengthen the protection of CII against cyber-attacks.
Part 3 of the Act provides that CSA can designate organizations as CII and regulates the owners of CII with regard to their cybersecurity. CII are computer systems necessary for continuous delivery of essential services (including national security, defense, foreign relations, economy, public health, public safety, or public order of Singapore). The Act provides a framework for the designation of CII and establishes the obligations on CII owners to proactively protect the CII from cyberattacks. The CII owner is required:

(a) to provide the Commissioner with information relating to the CII (Section 10);
(b) to comply with codes of practice, standards of performance, or written directions in relation to the CII as may be issued by the Commissioner (Sections 11 and 12);
(c) to notify the Commissioner of any change in ownership of the CII (Section 13);
(d) to notify the Commissioner of any prescribed cybersecurity incidents relating to the CII (Section 14);
(e) to cause regular audits of the compliance of the CII with the Act, codes of practice, and standards of performance, to be carried out by an auditor approved or appointed by the Commissioner (Section 15);
(f) to carry out regular cybersecurity risk assessments of the CII (Section 15); and
(g) to participate in cybersecurity exercises as required by the Commissioner (Section 16).

Section 11 empowers the Commissioner to issue or approve one or more codes of practice or standards of performance for the regulation of owners of CII.

(2) Authorize CSA to prevent and respond to cybersecurity threats and incidents.
Part 4 of the Act provides measures to prevent, manage, and respond to cybersecurity threats and incidents in Singapore.

A "cybersecurity threat" is defined "as an act or activity (known or suspected) carried out on or through a computer or computer system, that may imminently jeopardize or affect adversely, without lawful authority, the cybersecurity of a computer or computer system. An example of a cybersecurity threat is a phishing email, or an email that is infected with a malicious computer program."

A "cybersecurity incident" is defined as "an act or activity carried out without lawful authority on or through a computer or computer system that jeopardises or adversely affects its cybersecurity or the cybersecurity of another computer or computer system. A cybersecurity incident is essentially a cybersecurity threat that has been realised. An example of a cybersecurity incident is the unauthorised hacking of a computer by a hacker, the accessing of a hyperlink in a phishing email by the recipient resulting in the installation of a malicious computer program on the recipient's computer, or the opening of an infected document in an email by the recipient resulting in the execution of a malicious computer program on the recipient's computer."

Under the Act, the Commissioner of Cybersecurity (the head of the CSA) can investigate the above-mentioned cybersecurity threats and incidents to determine their impact and prevent further harm, depending on the severity of the cybersecurity threat or incident. For lower-impact incidents, the Commissioner would only gather information. But in more serious incidents, the Commissioner has more intrusive powers, for the purpose of assessing the impact, eliminating the cybersecurity threat, or otherwise preventing harm arising from the cybersecurity threat or incident or preventing a further cybersecurity incident from arising. A cybersecurity threat or incident satisfies the severity threshold if:

(a) it creates a risk of significant harm being caused to a CII (even if the harm may not be of a nature that creates a risk of disruption to the provision of that essential service related to that CII);
(b) it creates a risk of disruption to the provision of an essential service;
(c) it creates a threat to the national security, defense, foreign relations, economy, public health, public safety, or public order of Singapore; or
(d) the cybersecurity threat or incident is of a severe nature, in terms of the severity of the harm that may be caused to persons in Singapore or the number of computers or value of the information put at risk, whether or not the computers or computer systems put at risk are themselves CII.

If this severity threshold is met, the Commissioner can

(a) direct any person to provide information about the incident or threat;
(b) direct the person to carry out such remedial measures, or to cease carrying on such activities, in relation to the affected computer or computer system, in order to minimize cybersecurity vulnerabilities;
(c) require the person to take any action to assist with the investigation, including but not limited to:
    (i) preserving the state of the affected computer or computer system by not using it;
    (ii) monitoring the affected computer or computer system;
    (iii) performing a scan of the affected computer or computer system to detect cybersecurity vulnerabilities and to assess the impact of the cybersecurity incident; and
    (iv) allowing the incident response officer to connect any equipment to, or install any computer program on, the affected computer or computer system as necessary;
(d) after giving reasonable notice, enter premises where the affected computer or computer system is reasonably suspected to be located;
(e) access, inspect, and check the operation of the affected computer or computer system, or use the computer or computer system to search any data contained in or available to such computer or computer system;
(f) perform a scan of the affected computer or computer system to detect cybersecurity vulnerabilities;
(g) take a copy of or extracts from, any electronic record or computer program affected by the cybersecurity incident;
(h) with the consent of the owner, take possession of any computer or other equipment for the purpose of carrying out further examination or analysis.

In the event of much more serious incidents, the Act gives the Minister a further and broader level of powers under Section 23. Where it is necessary for the purposes of preventing, detecting, or countering any serious and imminent threat to the provision of any essential service, or to the national security, defense, foreign relations, economy, public health, public safety, or public order of Singapore, the Minister can authorize or direct any person or organization to take emergency cybersecurity measures and comply with necessary requirements. The text was adopted from Section 15A of CMA and is reproduced verbatim below to illustrate the wide scope of the powers:

Emergency cybersecurity measures and requirements

(1) The Minister may, if satisfied that it is necessary for the purposes of preventing, detecting or countering any serious and imminent threat to —

   (a) the provision of any essential service; or

   (b) the national security, defence, foreign relations, economy, public health, public safety or public order of Singapore, by a certificate under the Minister's hand, authorise or direct any person or organisation specified in the certificate (called in this section the specified person) to take such measures or comply with such requirements as may be necessary to prevent, detect or counter any threat to a computer or computer system or any class of computers or computer systems.

(2) The measures and requirements mentioned in subsection (1) may include, without limitation —

   (a) the exercise by the specified person of the powers in sections 39(1)(a) and (b) and (2)(a) and (b) and 40(2)(a), (b) and (c) of the Criminal Procedure Code (Cap. 68);

   (b) requiring or authorizing the specified person to direct another person to provide any information that is necessary to identify, detect or counter any such threat, including —

      (i) information relating to the design, configuration or operation of any computer, computer program or computer system; and

      (ii) information relating to the cybersecurity of any computer, computer program or computer system;

   (c) providing to the Minister or the Commissioner any information (including real-time information) obtained from any computer controlled or operated by the specified person, or obtained by the specified person from another person pursuant to a measure or requirement under paragraph (b), that is necessary to identify, detect or counter any such threat, including —

      (i) information relating to the design, configuration or operation of any computer, computer program or computer system; and

      (ii) information relating to the cybersecurity of any computer, computer program or computer system; and

   (d) providing to the Minister or the Commissioner a report of a breach or an attempted breach of cybersecurity of a description specified in the certificate under subsection (1), relating to any computer controlled or operated by the specified person.

(3) **Establish a framework for sharing cybersecurity information.**
Since information sharing between government and owners of computer systems is essential to identify vulnerabilities and prevent cyber incidents, Part 4 of the Act provides a framework for CSA to request information, and for the protection and sharing of such information. The Act does not make it mandatory for non-CII organizations to share information.

(4) **Establish a light-touch licensing framework for cybersecurity service providers.**
Part 5 provides for the licensing of providers of certain cybersecurity services — penetration testing and managed security operations center (SOC) monitoring.

4.5. Consultation Process

Some lessons can be learned from the process by which the Cybersecurity Act was enacted. The Ministry of Communications and Information (MCI) and the CSA held a public consultation exercise on the draft Cybersecurity Bill[10] from July 10 to August 24, 2017. They received so much feedback that they extended the consultation period for more time to provide feedback. Respondents included members of the public, local and international organizations, and academia, industry and professional associations, resulting in 92 written submissions. CSA also participated in dialogues with industry organizations and professional associations to address queries regarding the Bill. Even before the public consultation exercise, MCI and CSA had held closed-door consultations with key stakeholders, including those from the 11 CII sectors, industry associations, and cybersecurity professionals.

Much of this feedback was positive, including support for the comprehensiveness of the Bill in dealing with protection of CII, but others, including local business owners and regional law firms, raised concerns about the powers granted to the CSA to take information when responding to cyber breach incidents, which they feared would conflict with banking secrecy and data privacy requirements, and could in turn harm the competitiveness of businesses in Singapore. For example, if CSA exercised

---

[10]Statutes are "Bills" before they come into force; when they come into force they become "Acts."

their power to access servers during a cyber incident, they could, in the process, access sensitive information such as banking data, trade secrets, and other data covered by international regulations such as the European Union's General Data Protection Regulation (GDPR).

In response, the Minister and CSA had to clarify in Parliament and in the media that any exercise of powers to deal with a cyber incident would focus on technical information, not personal data. CSA also stated that it would appoint assistant commissioners for each sector, to take into account existing sector-specific requirements, including international ones. These assistant commissioners would be involved in any incident response activity, to coordinate with the computer system owners and to help monitor any regulatory or compliance requirements. This clarification helped to assuage some concerns and to improve confidence in the final Act.

There were other significant areas of concern in the original Bill that was proposed, which were subsequently changed or clarified after the public consultation. For example, there was concern that suppliers and third-party vendors of CII would be subject to the Act, but the report clarified that only systems that have been officially designated as CIIs will be subject to the legal duties of compliance, thus excluding suppliers and third-party vendors. There was also concern that a company that has been officially designated as a CII would be subject to the Official Secrets Act, and therefore unable to disclose to suppliers or vendors that it was CII — this section was removed from the final Act. The greatest concern was raised about the proposed licensing regime for almost all individuals and companies in the provision of cybersecurity services, as this would have been deeply onerous for the cybersecurity industry, not to mention difficult to implement given the limited resources of the regulators. The final Act only covers penetration testing and managed SOC monitoring, which appears to be a reasonable compromise.

This type of consultation may therefore be a key to developing "future-proof legislation" that can adapt to rapid developments in the scientific, technical, and technological field and formulating laws that can be dynamic and evolve to meet the changing threats. The report has recognized that it would be unwieldy to legislate a distinction between "investigative" and "non-investigative" types of licensable services. Future-proofing sometimes requires stepping away from the very natural tendency to try to define every possible scenario in detail, because new situations will emerge that defy prediction. Instead, it can be more effective to be flexible and to review the landscape on a regular basis.

Legislation can be considered future-proof if it is proactive, provides legal clarity and certainty, and if citizens consider it to be legitimate because of their participation in bringing outcomes or solutions to collective problems. Public consultation is, therefore, a good way to help make legislation future-proof, especially in fields like cybersecurity where the issues affect every aspect of society. This has been recognized by government — e.g. the Monetary Authority of Singapore (MAS) has shared that despite its drawbacks — it lengthens the policymaking process and requires resources — public consultation improves the policymaking process by tapping practitioners' market knowledge to validate and refine policies, identifying implementation issues in advance, providing an avenue to explain and garner support for legislation, and ensuring greater certainty for affected parties.

These are all benefits that are deeply relevant to cybersecurity legislation. A healthy level of public–private partnership and participation by industry, civil society, experts, academics, and business owners can provide the Government with the breadth and depth of up-to-date expertise that is required for policymaking in this field, especially in response to developments in international regulations, quantum computing, big data, machine learning, and artificial intelligence.

For example, businesses here may accept the CSA's powers for incident response for now, because of a high level of trust in the authorities. However, if international regulations like the European Union's GDPR impose more requirements on Singapore companies dealing with European customers, the private sector may then have to step forward to form an independent industry body for oversight and to safeguard businesses.

A successful public–private partnership will require the active participation of all parties. Since the report mentions further public consultation, it should follow the best practices of this round, which include allowing the public contributions to influence decisions, recognizing and communicating the needs and interests of all participants, and communicating to participants how their input affected the decisions. While it would be unrealistic to expect the authority to implement every input, all contributions should be recognized to encourage participation in future processes.

On the other hand, industry, civil society, experts, academics, and business owners should continue to contribute frankly and vigorously to the discussion. The healthy dialogue that has arisen from this public consultation is a good start and will be essential in the years to come as cybersecurity develops in ways we cannot imagine today, and legislation has to evolve in response.

Chapter 5

Hacking Back under International Law: Toward Effective Remedies against Cyberattacks for Non-State Actors

Deborah Housen-Couriel*

*Hebrew University Cyber Security Research
Center — Cyber Law Program and Konfidas Digital Ltd., Israel*

deb.hc@konfidas.com

Abstract

The unilateral response by non-state actors such as private companies to unauthorized, hostile breach of their computer systems and data — "hacking back" — poses knotty problems under national and international law. National laws have so far fallen short of providing effective remedies for targeted companies that suffer financial and reputational losses, and the applicable international law is complex and underutilized. This chapter explores two possible avenues of effective remedy for such non-state actors: (1) reparations via the doctrine of diplomatic protection when attacks originate outside of national borders; and (2) state authorization for hackbacks under defined parameters for cyberattacks, without reference to their point of origin. Further study is needed to develop more effective remedies under both national and international

---

*I am indebted to Assaf Harel, Herb Lin, Pnina Sharvit-Baruch, and Amit Sheniak for their valuable comments on early drafts; and to Mirit Sharabi for her research assistance. All errors are my own.

law for private sector actors, especially operators of critical infrastructure, as their influence as key stakeholders in global cybersecurity escalate. Such remedies should leverage the commonality of cybersecurity interests shared by them and their nation-state.

5.1. Introduction to the Problem and Present Analysis

The unilateral response on the part of non-state actors such as private companies through cyber means to unauthorized, hostile breach of their computer systems and data — "hacking back" — poses knotty problems under both national and international law. Such entities have, in recent years, suffered financial damages to the tune of billions of dollars, as well as experienced impact on their reputations, functionality, and business continuity, as targets of hostile cyber operations (see Figure 5.1).[1] On the one hand, domestic criminal and civil law frameworks, ostensibly the primary source of amelioration for private-sector actors, have not so far provided effective remedies for the negative consequences of cyberattacks.[2] On the other hand, the international law on hacking back by non-state actors is complex and still being fully elucidated.[3]

---

[1]MIT Technology Review Insights (2019). "An innovation war: Cybersecurity vs. cybercrime." *MIT Technology Review*, October 18.

[2]See Corcoran, B. (2020). "A comparative study of domestic laws constraining private sector active defense measures in cyberspace," *Harvard National Security Journal*, **1**. For example, consider the US$5 million reward offered by the US government in December 2019 for information leading to the arrest of a member of the Russian-based hacking group Evil Corp. The group was accused of targeting banks, manufacturers, and other private-sector actors since 2011 and defrauding them of over US$100 million. In turning to the public, the US government offered "the largest reward ever offered for an accused cybercriminal." See Barret, B. (2019). "Alleged Russian Hacker Evil Corp. indicted," *Wired*, December 12. Available at: https://www.wired.com/story/alleged-russian-hacker-evil-corp-indicted/. Although the Russian government initially provided some assistance to the FBI, this cooperation ceased and there are no applicable extradition treaties between the two countries that might now serve as a formal basis for cooperation.

[3]Macak, K. (2016). "Decoding Article 8 of the International Law Commission's articles on state responsibility: Attribution of cyber operations by non-state actors," *Journal of Conflict and Security Law*, **14**: 405.

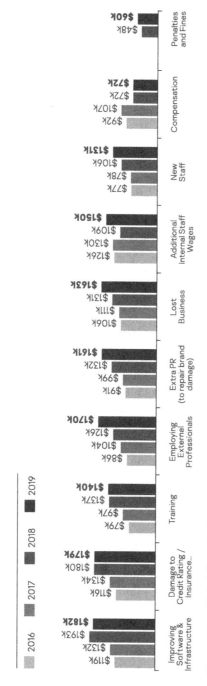

Figure 5.1. Global financial impacts on private sector actors of breaches.

Source: Kaspersky, IT security economics, 2019. https://go.kaspersky.com/rs/802-IJN-240/images/GL_Kaspersky_Report-IT-Security-Economics_report_2019.pdf.

Specifically, when both the perpetrator and the target of cyberattacks are states, a hostile cyberattack may be recognized by international law as coercive, and cross the threshold of legality to constitute an internationally wrongful act.[4] Such categorization under international law gives rise to a number of state-to-state options, depending on the nature of the act: *realis tempus* options in response to coercive acts, such as countermeasures, and ultimately, self-defense; and *post-facto* forms of reparation under the law of state responsibility.[5] The present scope does not permit review of these state-to-state options, which have been extensively analyzed in the literature.[6] Yet such remedies for hostile, transborder cyber breaches are not directly available to non-state actors under international law, although these entities are currently targeted on an ongoing basis and suffer significant financial, reputational, and operational damages. The June 2017 NotPetya attack is one example of the deep global impact such cyberattacks may have on private corporations; the damages it caused are already estimated in the billions of dollars and are still being assessed.

Given the urgent need for effective remedies for private actors in such situations as a matter of global cybersecurity, especially when these actors own, operate, and defend critical infrastructure, this chapter focuses on an initial analysis of two possible effective remedies for non-state actors: *post-facto* reparation measures under international law, when the origin of attacks is extra-territorial; and the more controversial real-time state authorization of private-actor hackbacks under national law. Both of these courses of action require close cooperation between the private sector actor and its host state. We propose herein that such cooperation is increasingly critical to leveraging the commonality of cybersecurity interests between the two, especially as the status and influence of private sector actors as key stakeholders in global cybersecurity escalate — and national cyber defense capabilities continue to be limited in their capacity

---

[4] See: Report of the International Law Commission on the Work of its Fifty-Third Session, *33 UN GAOR Supplement No. 10*, Article 3, UN Doc. A/56/10 (2001). Reprinted in *Yearbook of the International Law Commission 26*, UN Doc. A/CN.4/SER.A/2001/Add.1 (Part 2) [hereinafter ILC Draft Articles].

[5] *Ibid.* Article 34 (enumerating three types of reparation for the injury caused by a wrongful international act: restitution, compensation, and satisfaction). See also: *infra* Section 5.5.

[6] See, e.g., Delarue, F. (2020). Cyber Operations and International Law (UK: Cambridge University Press); and Lahmann, H. (2020). *Unilateral Remedies to Cyber Operations* (MA, USA: Cambridge University Press)

to defend such actors. The context for this analysis is the ongoing evolution of international norms with respect to activity of all actors in cyberspace, and the policy implications of these developments.[7]

This chapter is structured as follows. In Section 5.2, hackbacks are defined and the *sui generis* nature of private sector activity in cyberspace characterized. Section 5.3 reviews some of the current challenges under both national laws and international law for non-state actors suffering hostile cyber activity. Section 5.4 establishes the concept of "effective remedy" for such actors, and Section 5.5 explores two avenues of effective remedy with respect to for a specific type of private-sector actor — an entity operating critical infrastructure — one in the aftermath of a cyberattack on the non-state actor under international law (reparation via diplomatic protection), and the other in real time (state authorization of private-actor response). Finally, possible directions for development of international law with respect to a wider palette of effective remedies for private actors in responding to hostile cyber events are proposed, as well as the policy ramifications of closer identification of the interests of state and non-state actors for stability in cyberspace.[8] We conclude by noting hacking-back–related issues that require further work and additional state practice and, for that matter, non-state practice.

5.2. Defining Hackbacks: What is the Problem?

5.2.1. *The thresholds of incident response*

Hackbacks encompass a broad typology of measures to defend computer networks and their data once a hostile infiltration has taken place. Here, the

---

[7]See: Efrony, D. and Y. Shany (2018). "A rule book on the shelf? Tallinn Manual 2.0 on cyber operations and subsequent state practice," *American Journal of International Law*, 112(4): 583; Hollis, D. and M. Finnemore (2016). "Constructing norms for global cybersecurity," *American Journal of International Law*, **425**: 110.

[8]These ramifications have controversial implications, which require a critical public policy discussion. See e.g., Merrigan, E. (2019). "Blurred lines between state and non-state actors," Council on Foreign Relations, December 5. Available at: https://www.cfr.org/blog/blurred-lines-between-state-and-non-state-actors (accessed on October 2020). It is important to note that for the purpose of the analysis, we have set aside important international law issues relating to attribution of cyberattacks, the doctrine of diplomatic protection, and the quantification of damages. These central issues are treated extensively in the scholarly literature, and their integration into the following analysis awaits further work.

term "hacking back" describes the initiative taken by a non-state entity such as a private company in response to a hostile cyber operation that has impacted its computer networks, electronic data stored on those networks, or both. Alternative terms such as "active cyber defense" and "mitigative counterstriking" are sometimes used to describe this type of cyber operation.[9]

Hacking back includes activities on the part of the targeted non-state actor that go beyond its own computer network and may include intrusion into the attacker's network in order to stem an ongoing cyberattack and mitigate damages to the targeted actor. The impetus for network self-protection stems from an approach of incident response, which may also be mandated by national law to promote cybersecurity of national critical infrastructure, as will be discussed later.[10] It is a measure that is implemented, almost inevitably, on the international level since cyber-enabled networks are transboundary in nature and utilize cyber infrastructures such as cloud-based computing with distributed servers, undersea cable systems, and satellite networks. Moreover, hacking back is anything but a theoretical self-help measure. It is utilized by private sector actors as a *de facto* solution to hostile cyber events, albeit non-transparently and with frequency and scope that is not easily measurable:

---

[9]For example, the US draft bill introduced in June 2019, the Active Cyber Defense Certainty Act (ACDC), defines the term "active cyber defense measure" as "any measure undertaken by, or at the direction of a defender and consisting of accessing without authorization the computer of the attacker to the defender's own network to gather information in order to … establish attribution of criminal activity … disrupt continued unauthorized activity against the defenders own network; or … monitor the behavior of an attacker." See: Active Cyber Defense Security Act, H.R. 3270, 116th Cong. (2019). By way of contrast, the UK uses the term "active cyber defense" to describe activities undertaken exclusively by its National Cyber Security Centre to bolster cybersecurity in private organizations. See: National Cyber Security Centre (2019). "Cyber Defence Program — The Second Year." Available at: https://www.ncsc.gov.uk/report/active-cyber-defence-report-2019 (accessed on October 2020). The term "mitigative counterstriking" is another term in use. See: Kesan, J. and C. Hayes (2012). "Mitigative counterstriking: Self-defense and deterrence in cyberspace," *Harvard Law and Technology Journal*, **429**: 25.

[10]On the relationship between hacking back and incident response, including a practitioner's view of the difficulty of establishing clear boundaries between the two, see Braverman, J. and G. Evron, "Sounding a call to arms: Using "hack-back" techniques as part of incident response." [unpublished draft manuscript]; and F. Rashid (2017), "Legal hack back lets you go after attackers in your network." Available at: https://www.csoonline.com/article/3234661/legal-hack-back-lets-you-go-after-attackers-in-your-network.html (accessed on November 9, 2020).

We know that a significant number of cyber security professionals, at least a third, claim to have already engaged in retaliatory hacking (according to a survey taken at Black Hat).... a CEO of a power company [has] talked about retaliating if anyone attacked the electric grid. There have been many rumors and anecdotes of banks hiring hackers abroad to disrupt or retaliate against attackers. A Dutch scholar recently spoke about the growing practice in the Dutch financial industry of hiring ... firms for server takedown services.[11]

Irrespective of the actual intensity of contemporary hackback operations on the part of private-sector actors at present, our analysis proceeds on the assumption that hackbacks are part and parcel of the cyber defense strategy of private-sector actors.[12]

A key threshold for determining the legality of a hackback under both international and domestic law is that of penetration into the network perimeter of the initiator of the hostile cyber attacker, whether it is a state or non-state entity. The spectrum of hackback activities, once a hostile attack has taken place (or strong indications that it will take place are evident), includes actions on both the targeted systems and the attacker's systems: the gathering of information about the attacker and its system and data; using a variety of tools that include "canary trap" markings on data sent into attacker's system in order to identify vulnerabilities; penetrating vulnerabilities that have been identified, either transparently or surreptitiously; broadening and maintaining access privileges within the system; and causing functional or physical impact on the attacker's system or data.[13]

Three legal and policy approaches to this spectrum of hackbacking operations are relevant to our analysis. The *minimalist approach* to hackbacking permissibility condones it up until the point of entry into the

---

[11]Hoffman, W. (2018). "The future of cyber defence," Carnegie Endowment for International Peace, July.

[12]On the scope of private actor hackbacks, see also Messerschmidt, J. (2013). "Hackback: Permitting retaliatory hacking by non-state actors as proportionate countermeasures to transboundary cyberharm," *Columbia Journal of Transnational Law*, **275**: 52; Schmidle, N. (2018). "The digital vigilantes who hack back," *New Yorker*, April 30. Available at: https://www.newyorker.com/magazine/2018/05/07/the-digital-vigilantes-who-hack-back (accessed on October 2020).

[13]See also: Kesan & Hayes, *supra* note 9, 474–488 (noting the spectrum of modes of hackbacks).

attacker's network perimeter; an approach of *deep access* allows for intentional damage to the attacker's data or network; and the *moderate approach* lies in the middle: access into the attacker's system in order to mitigate the attack, which will probably impact system functionality and data even if actual damage to the attacker's network does not occur.

5.2.2. The sui generis nature of private actors' activity in cyberspace

Examples of high-profile attacks on non-state actors over the past few years include breaches suffered by Sony Pictures, Target, and JP Morgan (2014); Ashley Madison and the Ukrainian Prykarpattyaoblenergo power grid (2015); Deutsche Bahn, Renault, Telefonica, Equifax, Maersk, and the SWIFT electronic funds transfer system (2017); Facebook, Marriot, Westinghouse, Boeing, and Saudi Aramco (2018); and the 2019 breaches of British Airways, CapitalOne, Siemens, Bayer, Airbus, and Pitney Bowes.[14] Such breaches, which are carried out against companies targeted by hostile state and non-state actors using ransomware, data extraction and publication, denial of service and distributed denial of service, phishing, and industrial espionage, have an ongoing global impact that is deepening in terms of the frequency of breaches, their sophistication, and their financial costs, as shown in Figure 5.1.[15] Moreover, when hostile cyber activities affect privately-owned critical infrastructures, they not only impact private sector interests such as data loss, personnel downtime, reputational damages, and business and operational disruption but also, by definition, affect critical national interests, whether financial, administrative, or security-related.

---

[14]Center for Strategic and International Studies, "Significant cyber incidents." Available at: https://www.csis.org/programs/technology-policy-program/significant-cyber-incidents (accessed on October 2020) (timeline); and CheckPoint (2019). "Cyber Attack Trends Analysis, 2019 Security Report 01." http://www.snt.hr/boxcontent/CheckPointSecurity-Report2019_vol01.pdf (accessed on October 2020).

[15]CheckPoint, *Ibid.*; World Economic Forum (2019). "Global risks report 2019," pp. 15–16. Cyber insurance policies may mitigate some financial losses, although it is still developing. See: Levite, A., S. Kannry and W. Hoffman (2018). "Addressing the private sector cybersecurity predicament: The indispensable role of insurance," Carnegie Endowment for International Peace, November 7.

We argue here that the time is ripe for the confluence of interest among private-sector actors operating critical infrastructure such as power grids, water supply systems, banks, stock exchanges, financial transfer systems, and transportation systems[16] to drive the leverage of both international law and domestic law measures of two types: (1) increased use of state-to-state reparations for damages to non-state actors caused by hostile cyber operations as well as (2) the real-time authorization on the part of the state to permit the targeted private entity to conduct operations on its behalf and as its agent when critical infrastructure operability is at risk. Moreover, we propose that a close analysis of the law of state responsibility provides a basis for the identification of a core nexus of interests between private entities and their host states that can serve to develop these two remedies and increase their effectiveness. Certain private actors that are targeted by hostile cyber breaches such as those described earlier may in fact have recourse to newly emerging domestic law remedies, as we shall discuss later.[17] Yet overwhelmingly, domestic law remedies have, up until now, proven largely ineffective.[18] Hostile cyber activities are often trans-jurisdictional and throw up considerable barriers to enforcement of domestic laws, even across the borders of like-minded states sharing an interest in prosecution of cybercrimes.[19]

---

[16]For categorization of entities as cyber-enabled critical infrastructure, see, e.g., US Cybersecurity & Infrastructure Security Agency (2020). "Critical infrastructure sectors," March 24. Available at: https://www.cisa.gov/critical-infrastructure-sectors; Directive 2016/1148 (accessed on October 2020), of the European Parliament and of the Council of 6 July 2016 Concerning Measures for a High Common Level of Security of Network and Information Systems Across the Union, 2016 O.J. (L 194), Annex 2 [hereinafter NIS Directive]; National Security Ministerial Committee Resolution No. 84/B of December 11, 2002 (Isr.).

[17]See also: Crootof, R. (2018). "International cybertorts: Expanding state accountability in cyberspace," *Cornell Law Review*, **565**: 103 (discussing development of state accountability for "cybertorts").

[18]There is currently a lack of reliable data on the attribution of hostile cyber activities to state and non-state actors alike — and on the attribution to state versus non-state actors, specifically. But see: Buchan, R. (2016). "Cyberspace, non-state actors and the obligation to prevent transboundary harm," *Journal of Conflict and Security Law*, **429**: 21 ("[I]t is likely that malicious transboundary cyber conduct committed by non-state actors now exceeds that committed by states."). The reasons for this lack of transparency have been widely discussed. See, e.g., Efrony & Shany, *supra* note 7.

[19]On the ineffectiveness of the US Computer Fraud and Abuse Act prohibiting unauthorized access to computer systems, see Wu, T. (2013). "Fixing the worst law in technology,"

In brief, due to the combination of their ongoing exposure to cyberattacks and the dearth of effective remedies in the face of such exposure, non-state actors operating critical infrastructure occupy a *sui generis* position with respect to their ability to ensure cybersecurity for these operations. Effective remedies under both domestic and international law are a critical issue for global cybersecurity, as the risk of attacks on critical infrastructure increases.[20]

5.3. Lack of Clear Legal Recourse Beyond the First Threshold under National Legislation and International Law

5.3.1. *The risks of hacking back beyond the first threshold*

The legality of private-sector hackbacks, as described earlier, has been reviewed extensively in the academic and policy literature, under both international and domestic law.[21] The primary risks of hacking back along this spectrum, as well as the opposition to it as a legal and policy measure, include the mistaken identity of attackers as a result of incorrect attribution on the part of the actor hacking back; collateral damage to third-party

New Yorker, March 18. Available at: https://www.newyorker.com/news/news-desk/fixing-the-worst-law-in-technology (accessed on October 2020); Schneier, B. (2020). "Clarifying the computer fraud and abuse act," Schneier on Security, *Cryptogram*, April 15. Available at: https://www.schneier.com/crypto-gram/archives/2020/0415.html (accessed on October 2020).

[20]Braue, D. (2020). "Infrastructure cyberattacks pose a clear and present danger in 2020 and beyond," *CSO*, January 16. ("76.1 percent of respondents to the [World Economic Forum's] Global Risk Report 2020 agreed that the risk of cyberattacks against infrastructure would increase this year — slightly ahead of cyberattacks that steal money or data.").

[21]See, e.g., Global Commission for the Stability of Cyberspace (2018). "Additional note to the norm against offensive cyber operations by non-state actors"; Blair, D., M. Chertoff, F. Cilluffo and N. O'Connor (eds.) 2016). *Into the Gray Zone: The Private Sector and Active Defense against Cyber Threats*; Rosenzweig, P. (2014). "International law and private actor defensive measures," *Stanford Journal of International Law*, **103**: 50; Eichensehr, K. E. (2017). "Would the United States be responsible for private hacking?" *Just Security*, October 17. Available at: https://www.justsecurity.org/46013/united-states-responsible-private-hacking/ (accessed on October 2020).

entities; "domino effects"; and fears of escalation of cyber conflict.[22] In general, hackbacks that remain below the first access threshold — i.e., they refrain from penetration into the attacker's network — are treated as legitimate and within the bounds of legality on both the national and international planes.

Beyond the first threshold, at the point of entry into the attacker's computer systems, hackbacks are viewed as less legitimate and problematic from the point of national and international law. Many national legal systems are thus ambivalent with respect to hackbacks. The Global Commission for the Stability of Cyberspace summarized this lack of clarity in its November 2019 report:

> Some states do not control or may actively ignore these practices, despite the risk they impose upon the stability and security of cyberspace. However, in many states such practices would be unlawful, if not criminalized, while in other states they appear to be neither prohibited nor explicitly authorized. A few states are, nevertheless, considering legitimizing non-state actors' offensive cyber operations. Indeed, some have decided or proposed domestic legislation to allow offensive operations by nonstate actors.[23]

We now review several examples of domestic laws that address the issue of hackbacks on the part of private-sector commercial entities by permitting the second access threshold, i.e. a deep access or moderate approach. While these examples are too sparse to represent a trend toward effective remedies for private-sector actors under national laws, they do indicate some states' engagement with the need to permit private-sector hackbacks under national laws, even when these require some prior authorization on the part of the state.

5.3.2. *Review of selected domestic law remedies*

The first, most prominent example of the "proposed domestic legislation" referred to in the Global Commission's Report is the US Active Cyber

---

[22] Global Commission for the Stability of Cyberspace (2019). "A call to action on advancing cyberstability: Global Commission launches final report." Available at: https://cyberstability. org/news/a-call-to-action-on-advancing-cyberstability-global-commission-launches-final-report/ (accessed on October 2020); Additional Note, *supra* note 22.
[23] A Call to Action.

Defense Certainty Act (ACDC) aiming to amend Title 18 of the US Code, and currently receiving public comment.[24] The bill aims to amend federal criminal law in order to provide a defense for private organizations engaging in hackbacks to defend against unauthorized intrusions into their computer systems. The defense hinges upon the requirement that the FBI be notified before any measures are undertaken by the organization. Section 5 of ACDC, entitled "Notification Requirement for the Use of Active Cyber Defense Measures," states:

> A defender who uses an active cyber defense measure under the preceding section must notify the FBI National Cyber Investigative Joint Task Force and receive a response from the FBI acknowledging receipt of the notification prior to using the measure.[25]

While controversial, the ACDC is currently still under discussion in the Judiciary Committee's Subcommittee on Crime, Terrorism and Homeland Security.[26]

A second example is Singapore's Cybersecurity Act of 2018, which authorizes private actors to take action "in relation to a cybersecurity threat" within Singapore's territory or outside of it and provides exemption from criminal and civil liability for all persons "when carrying out such an order issued by the Commissioner of Cybersecurity."[27] Private sector actors may, conceivably, request such a directive as part of their exchange of information with the Commissioner. Similarly, operators of "critical information infrastructure" may be directed by the Commissioner to take action "in relation to a cybersecurity threat," which encompasses any "act or activity (whether known or suspected) carried out on or

---

[24] Active Cyber Defense Security Act, H.R. 3270, 116th Cong. (2019).

[25] See: H.R. 3270. The required notification "must include the type of cyber breach that the person or entity was a victim of, the intended target of the active cyber defense measure, the steps the defender plans to take to preserve evidence of the attacker's criminal cyber intrusion, as well as the steps they plan to prevent damage to intermediary computers not under the ownership of the attacker and other information requested by the FBI to assist with oversight." (Section 5.2).

[26] Chesney, R. (2019). "Hackback is back: Assessing the Active Cyber Defense Certainty Act," *Lawfare*, June 14.

[27] Act No. 9 of 2018, Cybersecurity Act of 2018, Articles 12(2)(a), 20(3), 23 (March 16, 2018). Available at: https://sso.agc.gov.sg/Acts-Supp/9-2018/Published/20180312?DocDate=20180312 (accessed on October 2020) (Sing.)

through a computer or computer system, that may imminently jeopardise or affect adversely, without lawful authority..." computer systems of the critical information infrastructure operator.[28] Moreover, operators of may receive ministerial authorization in order to counter "any serious and imminent threat to the provision of an essential service or the national security, defence, foreign relations, economy, public health, public safety or public order of Singapore."[29]

The Singaporean approach has been characterized by Craig, Shackelford, and Hiller as an interesting development because of its more permissive approach to the private sector hackbacks: "...whereas it does not fully legalize private active defense, it does create a mechanism for state-sanctioned active defense to protect critical national infrastructure."[30]

Corcoran, in his survey of 20 national laws addressing "active cyber defense,"[31] identifies three other examples of the permissibility of specific types of hackbacks: Australia's Telecommunications Act, Canada's Criminal Code, and South Korea's Network Act. He also specifies four states which explicitly reserve the right to hack back to agencies of the state (Estonia, the Netherlands, Taiwan, and the UK)[32]; and notes the proposed Israeli legislative initiative, currently in draft, to allow the National Cyber Directorate to direct private organizations actions in order to "detect, withstand and prevent" cyberattacks.[33] While these few examples of national laws that permit non-state actors to hack back under state supervision or permission are notable and move toward the provision of an effective remedy for such actors, they are rare at present. Moreover, transparency with respect to the actual implementation of these laws

---

[28] *Ibid.* Articles 2 & 12(2)(a).

[29] *Ibid.* Article 23. The extent of the limitations of such ministerial authorization is ambiguous. See *Ibid.* Article 23(3).

[30] Craig, A., S. Shackelford and J. Hiller (2015). "Proactive cybersecurity: A comparative industry and regulatory analysis," *American Business Law Journal*, **52**: 721–723.

[31] Corcoran, *supra* note 2, at 23–24, Tables 1 and 7, app.

[32] *Ibid.*

[33] Proposed Draft Bill, Cybersecurity and National Cyber Directorate Law, Article 26 (2018) (unofficial version). Available at: https://www.gov.il/he/departments/news/cyberlawpublic (accessed on November 9, 2020) [in Hebrew]. See also: Ministry of Justice, Policy on Prosecution and Sentencing for the Crime of Illegal Access to Computer Materials, Guideline 2.38 [in Hebrew], Article 30(d) (August 27, 2018).

is lacking, as with other aspects of state and non-state activity in cyberspace.[34]

Corcoran's survey concludes that most of the 20 countries he reviewed do not permit non-state actors to undertake any actions that constitute unauthorized access into the computer systems of another entity, in effect restricting incident response to activities under the first access threshold mentioned above.[35] Craig, Shackelford and Hiller agree with this assessment,[36] further emphasizing the need for effective remedies for private-sector actors. This current restrictive approach also characterizes international law and policy trends, as we shall see in Section 5.3.3.

5.3.3. *International law with respect to hackbacks by non-state actors*

In the international law and policy context, a similar reluctance to allow private actors to move beyond the first threshold obtains, in contrast to the legal authority supporting state responses to hostile cyber activity. While a full analysis of the international law applicable to self-help measures available to states in response to hostile cyber activity is beyond the scope of this chapter, a brief summary will set out the thresholds for state responses that come under the international law of self-defense and extend to deep access into computer systems outside of the state's jurisdiction. We will also briefly outline the parameters of the attacking state's responsibility for its internationally wrongful acts, should the cyberattack not constitute a use of force yet still incur state responsibility.[37]

---

[34] On the lack of transparency of state activity in cyberspace in general, see Efrony & Shany, *supra* note 7, at 583.

[35] Corcoran, *supra* note 2, at 49 ("With the exception of the draft laws in the U.S. and Israel already discussed, states are generally silent on active defense authorities outside the limited exception for ISPs. But they can and do prohibit computer crimes when carried out under the authority of a group or corporation. Unsurprisingly, every state surveyed has some general provision pertaining to corporate liability in its penal or procedural code.").

[36] Craig, Shackelford and Hiller, *supra* note 30, at 55 ("[P]roactive cybersecurity programs have become mainstream [yet they] decidedly do not promote 'hack back' approaches.").

[37] See: Schmitt, M. (ed.) (2017). *Tallinn Manual 2.0 on the International Law Applicable to Cyber Operations* (MA, USA: Cambridge University Press) pp. 301–372 (hereinafter Tallinn Manual 2.0).

5.3.3.1. *State-to-state hackbacks*

As a general rule, a state that has been impacted by hostile cyber activity, including such activity impacting critical infrastructure, which is attributable to another state must first determine whether the hostile activity constitutes an internationally wrongful act, including a use of force in violation of international law.[38] This determination establishes the responsibility of the state from which the hostile attack has emanated, i.e. whether the attack has been initiated by governmental agencies or non-governmental actors.[39] Should a state identify a hostile cyber operation as constituting an armed attack against it under Article 51 of the UN Charter[40] — and assuming credible attribution for such an internationally wrongful act[41] — it may undertake countermeasures[42] or exercise its inherent right of self-defense against the attack.[43] Such a response will be subject to the usual constraints of necessity, proportionality, imminence,

---

[38] *Ibid.* at 9–167. In any event, states must attempt to settle their international disputes, including those involving cyber activities, the continuance of which is likely to endanger the maintenance of international peace and security, by peaceful means. See: UN Charter Articles 2(3) and 33(1). Rule 65 of the Tallinn Manual also clarifies that the obligation to attempt to settle international disputes peacefully is, in the view of the International Group of Experts, only obligatory when the dispute is likely to endanger international peace and security.

[39] See: Buchan, R. and N. Tsagourias (2016). "Special Issue: Non-state actors and responsibility in cyberspace: State responsibility, individual criminal responsibility and issues of evidence," *Journal of Conflict and Security Law*, **377**: 21.

[40] UN Charter Article 51 ("Nothing in the Charter shall impair the inherent right of individual or collective self-defence if an armed attack occurs against a State"). Collective self-defense against a cyber operation amounting to an armed attack may only be exercised at the request of the victim State and within the scope of the request. See: Tallinn Manual 2.0, *supra* note 37, at Rule 74.

[41] Macak, *supra* note 3.

[42] Tallinn Manual 2.0, *supra* note 37, at Rules 20–26. The ILC Draft Articles define countermeasures as "measures that would otherwise be contrary to the international obligations of the international obligations of the injured state vis-à-vis the responsible state, if they were not taken by the former in response to an internationally wrongful act by the latter in order to procure cessation and reparation." (ILC Draft Articles, Article 22, para.1).

[43] Military and Paramilitary Activities in and Against Nicaragua (Nicar. v. U.S.), Judgment, 1986 I.C.J. Rep. 14, Section 228 (June 27). The US has adopted a different approach, stating that any cyber operation that constitutes an illegal use of force against a State potentially gives rise to a right to take necessary and proportionate action in self-defense,

and immediacy.[44] Additional aspects of the traditional right to self-defense are applicable to state activity in cyberspace as well. Thus, anticipatory self-defense[45] and collective self-defense[46] are available options for targeted states. Nonetheless, the determination of the threshold for a state's self-defense response is still unsettled and will depend upon the targeted state's assessment of the situation, including the scale and effect of the cyberattack.[47] For example, it is unclear whether a cyberattack that significantly disrupts essential governmental services without causing physical damage (thus falling short of the UN Charter's Article 51 "armed attack" requirement, as it is presently understood[48]) will justify an act of self-defense on the part of the targeted state, or a resort on its part to a request for collective self-defense.[49] When such a state-to-state response occurs exclusively through cyber means, it essentially constitutes a deep-access hackback.[50]

---

meaning there is no gravity threshold distinguishing uses of force from armed attacks. See: US Department of Defense, *Law of War Manual*, Section 16.3.31 (2016).

[44] Tallinn Manual 2.0, *supra* note 37, at Rules 71–75.

[45] Tallinn Manual 2.0, *supra* note 37, at Rule 73; see also: Schmitt, M. N. (1999). "Computer network attack and the use of force in international law: Thoughts on a normative framework," *Columbia Journal of Transnational Law*, **885**: 37, 914–915.

[46] Tallinn Manual 2.0, *supra* note 37, at 301–372. The Security Council may act under UN Charter Chapter VII in response to hostile cyber events (but refer to UN Charter Article 41 for Security Council measures in cyberspace not involving the use of armed force are to be employed to give effect to its decisions). See also: Stoltenberg, J. (2019). "NATO will defend itself," *NATO*, August 27. Available at: https://www.nato.int/cps/en/natohq/news_168435.htm?selectedLocale=en (accessed on October 2020) (discussing NATO policy on the applicability of NATO Charter's Article 5).

[47] Tallinn Manual 2.0, *supra* note 37, at Rule 71.

[48] UN Charter Article 51 ("Nothing in the present Charter shall impair the inherent right of individual or collective self-defence if an armed attack occurs against a Member of the United Nations, until the Security Council has taken measures necessary to maintain international peace and security. Measures taken by Members in the exercise of this right of self-defence shall be immediately reported to the Security Council and shall not in any way affect the authority and responsibility of the Security Council under the present Charter to take at any time such action as it deems necessary in order to maintain or restore international peace and security.").

[49] Efrony & Shany, *supra* note 7.

[50] Although international law does not require that the response be "in kind," and it may include both cyber and physical means.

There has been extensive scholarly analysis over the past several years with respect to the thresholds and scope of the exercise of the above-mentioned measures on the part of states, which is beyond our current purview; and state practice is still evolving in this context.[51] Notably, several states have recently taken steps to make the criteria for their self-help assessments more transparent, including the UK, US, the Netherlands, France, and Estonia. For example, in May 2019, Estonia's President Kersti Kaljulaid stated a position advocating collective countermeasures:

> [W]e already know that cyber operations, which cause injury or death to persons or damage or destruction of objects, could amount to use of force or armed attack under the UN Charter.[…]. Such harmful effects could be caused by a cyber operation, which for example, targets digital infrastructure or services necessary for the functioning of society. And let's not forget — growing digitalization of our societies and services can also lower the threshold for harmful effects. In order to prevent such effects, states maintain all rights, in accordance with international law, to respond to harmful cyber operations either individually or in a collective manner. Among other options for collective response, Estonia is furthering the position that states which are not directly injured may apply countermeasures to support the state directly affected by the malicious cyber operation. It is therefore important that states may respond collectively to unlawful cyber operations where diplomatic action is insufficient, but no lawful recourse to use of force exists.[52]

---

[51] See Tallinn Manual 2.0 and Efrony & Shany, *supra* note 7. For recent developments toward a sharper resolution of the scope of self-defense in response to cyber operations, see Schmitt, M. N. (2009). "The Netherlands releases a tour de force on international law in cyberspace: An analysis," *Just Security*, October 14. Available at: https://www.justsecurity.org/66562/the-netherlands-releases-a-tour-de-force-on-international-law-in-cyberspace-analysis/ (accessed on October 2020); Schmitt, M. N. (2019). "France's major statement on international law and cyber: An assessment," *Just Security*, September 16. Available at: https://www.justsecurity.org/66194/frances-major-statement-on-international-law-and-cyber-an-assessment/ (accessed on October 2020). See also International Committee of the Red Cross (2019). "International humanitarian law and cyber operations during armed conflicts," Position Paper, p. 7.

[52] Address of President Kersti Kaljulaid, *CyCon Conference*, Tallinn, May 2019 (emphasis added).

Legal analysis of this "collective countermeasures" option under international law, as well as the less-recognized option of retorsion as a legitimate response to hostile cyber operations, is also the subject of recent scholarly review.[53]

To summarize, transparent evidence of the utilization by states of the remedy of self-defense response to hostile cyberattacks is at present lacking, even where attribution has been established, characterizing this remedy as marked by a "prevailing ambivalence."[54] However, the present gap between state responses to hostile cyber activity and the effective remedies permitted under international law to states is not the result of any lack of such remedies. The relatively clear parameters of international law with respect to state responsibility for hostile cyber activity originating in its territory as an internationally wrongful act is not at issue; rather the state practice with respect to the application of these effective remedies is still evolving. Moreover, as we shall show below, international law also provides several well-established modes of *post-facto* redress under the general heading of reparations, when the actors, both perpetrator and target, are states. Thus, reparations in the form of restitution, compensation, and/or satisfaction provide several avenues of effective remedy for nation-state actors.[55] This situation sharply differs from that applying to private-sector actors that are targeted by hostile cyberattacks.

---

[53]Kosseff, J. (2020) "Retorsion as a response to ongoing malign cyber operations," Chapter 1, pp. 17–24; Roguski, P. (2020). "Countermeasures in cyberspace: Lex lata, progressive development, or a bad idea?" Chapter 2, pp. 25–42, in T. Jancarkova, L. Lindstrom, M. Signoretti, I. Tolga and G. Visky (eds.), *20/20 Vision: The Next Decade* (Tallin: CCDCOE).

[54]Johns, F. (2019). "War without words," *AJIL Unbound*, **113**: 67, 69.

[55]The academic literature on the normative status of such state-to-state cyber hostilities is extensive; although a comprehensive review is beyond the scope of this chapter, we will refer to aspects of the current parameters of the law as it is relevant to the remedies available to non-state actors via the states through which they can establish modes of recourse. See, e.g., Efrony & Shany, *supra* note 7 (2019). "A rule book on the shelf? Tallinn Manual 2.0 on cyberoperations and subsequent state practice," *AJIL Unbound*, **67**: 13; Hollis, D. and M. Finnemore (2016). "Constructing norms for global cybersecurity," *American Journal of International Law*, **425**: 110.

5.3.3.2. *Non-state actor hackbacks under international law*

The self-help options available to states for responding to hostile cyber activity are not directly available to non-state actors under international law.[56] Since the latter are not directly subject to the collective security regime (and the relevant aspects of international customary law) under which these remedies apply, only states and international organizations may exercise these measures directly. Non-state actors must rely upon the international legal personality of the state with which they have a sufficient nexus of identity, such as a corporate registration or a license for operation; as well as that state's political readiness and initiative, in order to respond under international law.[57] Moreover, international law specifically proscribes self-help measures on their part.[58] For example, the Council of Europe's Budapest Convention on Cybercrime, ratified by 65 countries, requires signatory countries to define as illegal "access to the whole or any part of a computer system without right," thus criminalizing hackbacks beyond the first threshold under their respective national laws.[59] Significantly, the Convention also requires state parties to impose corporate liability for violation of activities defined as criminal by its provisions.[60] Additional examples of adoption of a first threshold approach at the international level include the 2018 Paris Call for Trust and Security in Cyberspace, which advocates "No private hack

---

[56]Buchan & Tsagourias, *supra* note 39.

[57]Johns, F. (2010). International Legal Personality; Nijman, J. (2010). "Non-state actors and the international rule of law," in Math, N. and C. Ryngaert (eds.), *Non-State Actor Dynamics in International Law* (Abingdon, UK: Routledge).

[58]Tallinn 2.0 notes a hypothetical situation in which a private company has experienced a cyberattack by a foreign state. The Group of Experts conclude that, as a matter of *lex lata*, the "corporation does not violate the sovereignty of that State if it hacks back," since only states are obligated to respect each other's sovereignty. But see also the commentary under Rule 24, at 130–131. This conclusion, however, begs the question of attribution of the private company's hackback to its own state, and the subsequent state responsibility that the latter would bear. The issue at hand is whether a legally permissible resolution of the situation can be contemplated by international law.

[59]Council of Europe, Convention on Cybercrime, Article 2, July 1, 2004, ETS No. 185. Available at: https://www.coe.int/en/web/conventions/full-list/-/conventions/treaty/185 (accessed on October 2020). Its provisions of the 2001 Convention on Cybercrime are also reflected in domestic laws such as the US Computer Fraud and Abuse Act (CFAA) and Israel's 1995 Computer Law.

[60]*Ibid.*

back" in its Principle 8;[61] and the Global Commission on the Stability of Cyberspace (GCSC) proposed norm against non-state actors engaging in "offensive" cyber operations and state actors' prevention of such activities.[62] It is worth noting, as well, that the UN Group of Governmental Experts (GGE) process has so far limited the scope of its work to "responsible behaviour of States," relating to non-state actors only peripherally[63]; as has the Shanghai Cooperation Organization's International Code of Conduct for Information Security.[64] Thus, while states have a relatively well-recognized and well-trodden path available for the development of international legal norms in cyberspace through acknowledged sources of law such as treaties, custom (state practice and *opinio juris*), and general principles[65] — as plagued as this path may currently be by geopolitical difficulties, jurisdictional challenges, and other substantive legal issues — it is much less clear how private sector actors "enter the game" of permissible response to hostile cyber activities on the international plane.[66]

---

[61] Paris Call (2018). "Paris Call for trust and security in cyberspace," Principle 8, November 12. Available at: https://pariscall.international/en/ (accessed on October 2020) ("No private hack back — Take steps to prevent non-State actors, including the private sector, from hacking-back, for their own purposes or those of other non-State actors."). The Paris Call is currently supported by 75 states, 26 public authorities and local governments, 341 organizations and members of civil society, and 624 companies and private sector entities.

[62] A Call to Action, *supra* note 22 ("Non-state actors should not engage in offensive cyber operations and state actors should prevent such activities and respond if they occur.").

[63] UN Secretary-General (2019). Developments in the Field of Information and Telecommunications in the Context of International Security, June 24, UN Document A/74/120, at 28(e) ("States must not use proxies to commit internationally wrongful acts using ICTs, and should seek to ensure that their territory is not used by non-State actors to commit such acts.").

[64] UN (2015). "Letter Dated 9 January 2015 from the Permanent Representatives of China, Kazakhstan, Kyrgyzstan, the Russian Federation, Tajikistan and Uzbekistan to the United Nations addressed to the Secretary-General," January 13, Article 9, UN Document A/69/723 ("All States must cooperate fully with other interested parties in encouraging a deeper understanding by all elements in society, including the private sector and civil-society institutions, of their responsibility to ensure information security, by means including the creation of a culture of information security and the provision of support for efforts to protect critical information infrastructure.").

[65] See: Statute of the International Court of Justice (1945). Article 38(1)(d), October 24, 33 UNTS 993 (referencing sources of international law).

[66] See: Schmitt, M. N. & S. Watts (2016). "Beyond state-centrism: International law and non-state actors in cyberspace," *Journal of Conflict and Security Law*, **595**: 21.

Their situation is *sui generis* for three reasons. First, non-state actors act in cyberspace with technical capabilities that are, in many cases, at least as extensive and impactful as those of states. In particular, multinational corporations carry out their cyber activities in a fully global context that is already impacting the development of cyberspace and its normative governance: it is difficult to bring to mind precedents for this type of non-state actor influence and impact on the international regulation of human activity worldwide.

Second, while national laws may be the primary legal and regulatory framework for private actors because of their physical location and corporate registration, the trans-jurisdictional nature of organizations' cyber activity — and obviously that of multinationals — requires a transnational approach to their activities.[67] Several global norm-formation initiatives on the part of multinationals attest to their awareness of their roles as key stakeholders and influencers in the international arena in which they operate and their interest in establishing relevant norms on the international plane.[68] Examples include the governance initiatives of Facebook, Microsoft, Twitter, and YouTube in the framework of the Global Internet Forum to Counter Terrorism (GIFCT), established in July 2017 "as a group of companies dedicated to disrupting terrorist abuse of members' digital platforms"[69]; Microsoft's International Cybersecurity Norms Overview and its plan for an independent cyber attribution body[70]; the RAND Corporation's development of the plan in the form of a Global Cyber Attribution Consortium based on non-state actors[71]; Facebook's security program

---

[67]This aspect implicates the concept of remedies for transboundary harm, which is beyond the scope of this chapter. See: Messerschmidt, *supra* note 12.

[68]Setting aside the obvious commercial value of such initiatives.

[69]Members now include Dropbox, Amazon, LinkedIn, and WhatsApp. Following the terrorist attack in Christchurch, New Zealand, in March 2019, GIFCT expanded its mandate to include extremist content. Members have created a shared industry database of "hashes," or digital identifiers, for violent terrorist imagery and recruitment videos that they remove from their services. See: Global Internet Forum to Counter Terrorism. Available at: https://gifct.org/leadership/ (accessed on October 2020).

[70]See: Microsoft, "International Cybersecurity Norms" at: https://www.microsoft.com/en-us/cybersecurity/content-hub/international-cybersecurity-norms-overview (accessed on October 2020).

[71]Mueller, M.(2017). A global attribution organization — Thinking it through," *The Internet Governance Project*, June 4. Available at: https://www.internetgovernance.org/2017/06/04/a-global-cyber-attribution-org/ (accessed on October 2020).

for the accounts of presidential campaigns and election officials in anticipation of foreign interference in the 2020 US election[72]; the CyberPeace Institute founded in 2019 by Microsoft, MasterCard, and the Hewlett Foundation[73]; and the Cybersecurity Tech Accord.[74]

Finally, as noted above, non-state actors do in fact prosecute responses to cyberattacks along the hackback spectrum described earlier, even beyond the second threshold, on a regular basis.[75] Indeed, the establishment of cybersecurity capabilities that allow them the technical capacity to do so, in the context of pro-active defensive cyber safeguards, may be mandated by domestic law, particularly in the financial and health sectors.[76] Thus, private-sector organizations that have been breached may carry out incident response measures that include information-gathering about the attacker and its capabilities, identification of the attacker's mode of operation and vulnerabilities, and the use of digital forensics processes and tools that are capable of impacting the attacker's computer systems and data. In the view of two practitioners, for many private actors:

---

[72] See: Rosen, G. *et al.* (2019). "Helping to protect the 2020 US Elections," *Facebook*, October 21. Available at: https://newsroom.fb.com/news/2019/10/update-on-election-integrity-efforts/ (accessed on October 2020).

[73] See: CyberPeace Institute at https://cyberpeaceinstitute.org/ (accessed on October 2020).

[74] See: Tech Accord at https://cybertechaccord.org/ (accessed on October 2020).

[75] Harris, S. (2014). "The mercenaries," *Slate*, November 12. ("To date, no American company has been willing to say that it engages in offensive cyber operations designed to steal information or destroy an adversary's system. But former intelligence officials say "hack-backs" — that is, breaking into the intruder's computer, which is illegal in the United States — are occurring, even if they're not advertised. "It is illegal. It is going on," says a former senior NSA official, now a corporate consultant."). See also: Braverman & Evron, *supra* note 10; Schmidle, *supra* note 12; Rich, W.(2018). "The US leans on private firms to expose foreign hackers," *Wired*, November 29. Available at: https://www.wired.com/story/private-firms-do-government-dirty-work/ (accessed on October 2020).

[76] For example, owners of critical infrastructure are required to implement proactive cybersecurity measures that include incident response under the Bank of Israel's Directive 361 (Supervisor of Banks, Proper Conduct of Banking Business Directive 361, Cyber Defense Management, Articles 15, 16, 18, 25–26.) and Singapore's Act No. 9 of 2018, Cybersecurity Act of 2018, pt. III (March 16, 2018). Available at: https://sso.agc.gov.sg/Act/CA2018 (accessed on November 9, 2020).

...."hack-back" techniques are not inherently different from incident response techniques [....] In fact, it is possible to consider the two things are not separated by a divide, but rather that they're both located on a single spectrum. This would imply that "hack-back" is simply a form of extreme incident response....[77]

It is argued here that as we move toward the development of critical effective remedies for private-sector actors, especially critical infrastructure operators, their present technical and operational capacities for hacking back cannot be ignored and should be understood in the context of their current status and influence as key stakeholders in global cybersecurity.

5.4. The Concept of Effective Remedy under International Law

"Effective remedy" is a concept applied by various regimes of international law, without specifically defined common parameters across these regimes. For instance, the ILC Draft Articles defines the term as "the desired outcome of cooperation among states in response to the gravest breaches of a peremptory norm of general international law," including aggression.[78] The Universal Declaration of Rights and the International Covenant on Civil and Political Rights apply the term to those measures undertaken by State parties to ensure that the safeguarding of rights and freedoms, including their enforcement, be provided to individuals.[79] International Environmental Law, International Arbitration Law, and the Law of the Sea each define the term in a slightly different way, having in common their ensuring of appropriate, feasible and acceptable remedies to non-state actors on the international plane.[80]

---

[77] Braverman & Evron, *supra* note 10, at 2.

[78] ILC Draft Articles, *supra* note 4, commentary to Article 41, Section 3 & commentary to Articles 40 and 41. The obligation rests upon states that have violated peremptory norms "to make an appropriate response" to said serious breaches of the law.

[79] G.A. Res. 217 (III) A, Article 8, Universal Declaration of Human Rights (December 10, 1948); International Covenant on Civil and Political Rights, Article 2(2)(a) (March 23, 1976), 999 UNTS 171.

[80] See: McArthur, J. (2018). "International Environmental Law: Can it overcome its weaknesses to create an effective remedy for global warming?" *Santa Clara Journal of*

For present purposes, an "effective remedy" refers to any international-law–based measure that provides a non-state actor, especially a private corporation operating critical infrastructure, with the means to respond in real time to a hostile cyber event, by blocking or mitigating a transboundary cyberattack; as well as reparatory measures that allow a return to the *status quo ante* to the extent possible.

5.5. Toward Effective Remedies for Non-State Entities Targeted by Hostile Cyber Operations

In 2012, while discussing hacking back as an option for private-sector actors, Kesan and Hayes observed that "there is an urgent need for dialog on this topic....[n]ew discussions and analyses are needed to ensure that responsive actions can be grounded in sound policy."[81] Discussions and analyses have in fact taken place — yet sound policy, and law, still remains beyond our grasp. In this section, we explore two possible directions toward effective remedies for private entities, especially operators of critical infrastructure that provide essential services to the public: *post-facto* remedies under international law and duly-supervised domestic law authorization of private-actor hackbacks.

5.5.1. *Post-facto remedies under international law*

The first type of measure that may serve as an effective remedy is **reparation via the doctrine of diplomatic protection under international law.** Reparations constitute a *post-facto* measure[82] that may become available after a cyberattack which constitutes an internationally wrongful act (a) has taken place, (b) has negatively impacted the private sector actor,

---

International Law, **253**: 10; Yiannibas, K. (2018). "The adaptability of international arbitration: Reforming the arbitration mechanism to provide effective remedy for business-related human rights abuses," *Netherlands Quarterly Human Rights*, **214**: 36. See also: Convention on the Law of the Sea, Article 235, November 16, 1994, 1833 UNTS 3 (prescribing State responsibility for protecting and preserving the marine environment and "recourse ... for prompt and adequate compensation or other relief in respect of damage caused by pollution of the marine environment by natural or juridical persons under their jurisdiction").

[81] Kesan & Hayes, *supra* note 9, at 433.

[82] ILC Draft Articles, *supra* note 4, Articles 31–34.

(c) has been duly attributed, and (d) the damage it has caused has been quantified, at least to at least an initial extent. Reparation takes on the three forms of restitution, compensation, and satisfaction.[83] For any of these three reparation remedies to become relevant for a non-state actor, a state must adopt that actor's claim under the doctrine of diplomatic protection.[84] Such adoption requires a substantive nexus between the private actor and the state, as well as the readiness of the state to so engage with both that actor and the second state that is to be held responsible for the internationally wrongful act. There is an additional requirement under diplomatic protection that the non-state actor exhaust local remedies in the offending state, which we set aside for the moment and return to below.

ILC Draft Article 31 defines and describes the obligation of the State which is responsible for an internationally wrongful act "to make full reparation for the injury caused" by said act, where "injury" may be either physical or non-physical the latter type being especially appropriate to the cyber context.[85] ILC Article 34 determines that the State may carry out this obligation in any of the three aforementioned ways: restitution, compensation, or satisfaction, either singly or in combination. Assuming adoption of the private actor's claim by its host state, the usual ramifications of state responsibility ensue.

Although the scholarly literature on each of these remedies is extensive, their application to reparation for cyber operations that constitute an internationally wrongful act is still developing.[86] The issue is not one of applicability, as international law does extend the requirement of reparation for internationally wrongful acts into cyber space. The Tallinn Manual addressed this in its Rule 28: "A responsible State must make full reparation for injury suffered by an injured State as the result of an internationally wrongful act committed by cyber means."[87] Moreover,

---

[83] ILC Draft Articles, *supra* note 4, Article 31.

[84] International Law Commission, Articles of Diplomatic Protection, 2006. Available at: https://legal.un.org/ilc/texts/instruments/english/draft_articles/9_8_2006.pdf (accessed on November 9, 2020); *Yearbook of the International Law Commission* (2001). "Diplomatic protection," Chapter VII.

[85] ILC Draft Articles, *supra* note 4, Article 31. The non-physical aspects are defined as "moral" injuries.

[86] See Delarue, *supra* note 6, 399–416; and (on the relevance of insurance policies for the transfer of cyber risk) Levite, Kannry & Hoffman, *supra* note 15.

[87] Tallinn Manual 2.0, at 144.

when such cyber-enabled injuries are suffered by individuals or other entities within the state, the *lex lata* allows for the State of their nationality to claim reparations on their behalf. Examples given in the commentary to Rule 28 include compensation for lost advertising revenue because of a DDoS operation against a commercial website; "permanent diminished value of national companies caused by a cyber operation against economic targets"; and costs associated with incident response.[88] Thus, in principle, once the host state duly agrees to adopt the claims of private sector actors, there is no substantive barrier under international law to the full exercise of the right to reparation for such non-state actors.

Procedural barriers under diplomatic protection are nevertheless significant, if they are not mitigated by treaty arrangements between the states involved. These barriers include the quantification of the damage caused by the cyberattack; credible attribution; and perhaps most significantly, the requirement that the non-state actor exhaust the domestic law remedies of the state that has allegedly carried out the internationally wrongful act. Amerasinghe discusses the evolution and practice of this last requirement (which flows from the sovereignty of that state), and notes that some flexibility in its application do exist. For example, exceptions and limitations may come into play when domestic remedies "...although available, are not in the circumstances applicable to the particular injury of which the alien complains." He further notes that limitations of the requirement to exhaust remedies may be based on their ineffectiveness or futility in a given situation, including circumstances in which they "clearly will not satisfy the object sought by the claimant."[89] Both of these situations exemplify the lack of an effective remedy that must be exhausted under the damaging state's domestic law. Deeper study of the implementation of diplomatic protection in a contemporary context in general, and the cyber context in particular, is needed, building on the implicit flexibility of the customary law.

We argue here that this is a significant, under-explored path to effective remedy for non-state actors targeted by hostile cyber operations. It does require the active involvement of the host state in taking on the claims of private sector actors, a more active engagement than is currently

---

[88] *Ibid.*, at 150–151. See as well "Capacity of Government to Espouse Claims of Shareholders of a Foreign Corporation within the Jurisdiction of the Offending State," 1 Cal.W.Intn'l.L.J. 141 (1970).

[89] Amerasinghe, C. (2008). *Diplomatic Protection*, Oxford University Press, pp. 150–155.

common (although notably seen in the US government involvement in the response to the 2014 hack of Sony Pictures[90]). Two points possible paths forward are salient in this context. The first is the development of a similar route to effective cyber remedies for private-sector actors as that developed in the context of the adoption of regimes for direct financial compensation to private entities for internationally wrongful acts of states, in the financial and commercial contexts, such as bilateral and regional agreements for the protection of investments.[91] Other examples under international law include the development of rights protections for private-sector actors under the Law of the Sea Convention[92] and environmental protection regimes.

Second, when the target of hostile cyber activity is a private-sector entity, an additional *lex lata* concept strengthens this path to effective remedy and may ease the requirement of a host state's adoption of a private actor's claim. This is the crucial determination made in Article 33(2) of the ILC Draft Articles, which provides that the scope of international obligations of state responsibility is "without prejudice to any right, arising from the international responsibility of a State, **which may accrue directly to any person or entity other than a State**."[93] The commentary expands upon the independent status of such a person or entity, as follows:

> [Article 33(2)] deals with the secondary obligation of States in relation to cessation and reparation, and these obligations may be owed, inter alia, to one or several States or to the international community as a whole. In cases where the primary obligation is owed to a non-State entity, it may be that some procedure is available whereby that entity can invoke the responsibility on its own and without the intermediation of any State.[94]

---

[90]BBC (2014). "Sony hack: White House views attack as security issue," December 19. Available at: https://www.bbc.com/news/world-us-canada-30538154 (accessed on October 2020).

[91]See Amerasinghe, C. (2008). *Diplomatic Protection*, Oxford University Press, esp. Chapter 17, "The Effect of Investment Treaties and of International Investment Law."

[92]Law of the Sea Convention *supra* note 80. Article 235: "Responsibility and liability."

[93]ILC Draft Articles, *supra* note 4, Article 33(2).

[94]*Ibid.*

The instances cited in the commentary are human rights treaties that directly benefit individuals, and the above-mentioned investment protection agreements. Development of similar regimes for direct compensation of private-sector actors for injuries caused by hostile cyber operations will bring a significant contribution to providing them with effective remedies. One direction might be the establishment of claims tribunals for cyber damages under bilateral or multilateral treaties, similar to those established for recovery regimes within investment treaties.[95]

An additional challenge and task for further elucidation of effective remedy for private-sector actors, is the development of cyber-specific forms of restitution, compensation, and satisfaction within the obligation to provide reparations for internationally wrongful acts. A chief difficulty is the quantification of the injury caused by a cyberattack, even assuming credible attribution. Delarue describes this challenge, in the context of the 2017 NotPetya malware attack, estimated to have caused more than US$1 billion in damage worldwide.[96] Insurance coverage of the losses of several private companies are still in the process of being determined and recovered, and at present, the quantification of damages is one of several barriers to these settlements.[97]

Finally, it is reiterated here that effective remedies for private-sector actors are best advanced with respect to critical infrastructures, which may be targeted with the aim of crippling national functionality even in countries where such infrastructures are operated as private businesses, independently of government control.

5.5.2. *State authorization of private-actor response under domestic law*

The second type of measure, which is more legally controversial, is the **real-time authorization** on the part of the state, under national law, to permit the

---

[95] See: Gaukrodger, D. (2014). *Investment Treaties and Shareholder Claims: Analysis of Treaty Practice*, (Paris: OECD).

[96] ILC Draft Articles, *supra* note 4, at 414–416.

[97] There is also disagreement around the issue of exclusion of acts of war in cyber insurance policies. See The Council of Insurance Agents and Brokers (2019). "NotPetya: A war-like exclusion?" May 2. Available at: https://www.ciab.com/resources/notpetya-a-war-like-exclusion/ (accessed on October 2020).

targeted private entity to conduct operations on its behalf and as its agent — including the option of undertaking countermeasures and self-defense by means of hacking back — within certain defined parameters. This measure entwines the self-help measure of the private entity with that of the state, on the basis of a commonality of interest between the two. Several examples have been reviewed in Section 5.3.2, and will not be reiterated here.

5.6. Directions for Development of International Law and Policy

This chapter has aimed to bring to the fore some existing remedies under international law for non-state actors which are targeted by hostile cyber-attacks on the part of both states and other non-state actors and to explore the possibilities of expanding domestic law remedies for the same situations. In particular, we have emphasized the need for greater utilization of the three forms of state-to-state reparations under international law, which may be proactively leveraged to benefit private actors where (a) attribution has been established; (b) a shared interest in cybersecurity between the private actor and the state exists; and (c) the state is willing to take on the private actor's claim as its own under the doctrine of diplomatic protection and/or the situations that obtain under ILC Draft Article 33(2); and (d) the damage inflicted by the cyberattack is quantifiable. We have proposed that this is most likely when the private actor is an operator of critical infrastructure, a situation under which the nexus between the state and the private actor is relatively robust, and thus a state may be more likely to adopt such an actor's claim of injury and demand for reparation.

The second path explored as an effective remedy for non-state actors is legally sanctioned, transparent state authorization of the private entity to conduct hackbacks that are self-help operations as a response on behalf of the state and as its agent, especially with regard to privately owned critical infrastructure. As shown earlier, the call for overall transparency with respect to state and non-state actors' activities in cyberspace is amplifying on the part of legal scholars, policymakers, and some state actors. Our analysis echoes these entreaties.

Undoubtedly, non-state actors are already full players in cyberspace at the level of contemporary cyber activities, policy, and governance. Yet since classic international law does not provide such actors with effective remedies on their own for internationally wrongful acts but, as we have seen, requires states to serve, in a manner, as their proxies at the international level, we have argued that such remedies should be leveraged to the extent possible until such time as autonomous effective remedies are developed for non-state actors under international law. An externality of such a development might be increased accountability for the activities of non-state actors in cyberspace as well, reducing the current non-transparency that obtains with "Wild West" hackbacks on their part.

Kesan and Hayes have put forward the case for a governmental agency that might be take on the task of hackbacks on behalf of private-sector entities, subject to transparent criteria and judicial review — and assuming the necessary rapidity of response and availability of optimal technology.[98] This may provide an effective remedy at the level of domestic law, but leaves open the international law legality, as well as the issue of reparations for any damages suffered by the private company as a result of the hostile cyber activity. There, the establishment of tribunals for the settlement of cyber-specific disputes would contribute to the development of effective remedies.

We conclude with Delarue's observation of the role of non-state actors in the current transitions in international cyber law:

> Alongside the traditional subjects of international law, numerous non-state actors — such as nongovernmental organisations (NGOs), multinational enterprises, national liberation movements and other types of group — are increasingly involved in, and influencing, international relations as well as, to some extent, processes of international law norm-building. This is also true regarding cyber norms. [...T]hese various norms have not yet been endorsed by states and should not be regarded as soft law. However, they constitute proposals and initiatives that contribute to the dynamism and evolution of the discussions of these issues.[99]

As to the further development of effective remedies for non-state actors for financial, reputational, and operational damages caused by

---

[98] Kesan & Hayes, *supra* note 9, at 534, 537.

[99] Delarue, *supra* note 6, at 313. See also: Noortmann, M. and C. Ryngaert, "Introduction: Non-state actors: International law's problematic case," in *Non-State Actor Dynamics, supra* note 58, at 1 ("[Non-state actors] have ... acquired enforceable and less enforceable international legal entitlements.").

cyberattacks, it seems inevitable that the *lex feranda* will, eventually, explicitly incorporate states' acknowledgment of the critical role that non-state actors are accruing in the development of norms for activity in cyber-space. In particular, multinational enterprises which are incorporated under domestic law regimes in a number of states — sometimes in the tens — constitute a global presence, influence, and impact that we cannot afford to discount in the formation of binding cyberspace norms that aim to advance global cybersecurity. Continuing to disallow effective reme-dies for such important cyberspace stakeholders, such as bolstering avenues for financial and other types of reparations and permitting state-authorized or autonomous hackbacks within recognized parameters, damages the credibility of international law as it evolves to meet the chal-lenges and the threats to stability posed by new types of activity in cyberspace.

Chapter 6

Maritime Cyber: Threats and Challenges

Eyal Pinko

*International Institute for Migration and Security Research,
Bulgaria, Sofia*

eyal.pinko@gmail.com

Abstract

The world of shipping and maritime transportation has experienced a major transformation in recent years, with the growth in connectivity, communication, digitization, automation, and integration of information systems and logistics systems of the seaports, vessels, and the shipping companies. The technological transformation of the vessels and the seaports is occurring simultaneously with major upward trends in the quantity of maritime cargo transportation and the increasing number of vessels and their size. This is as a result of globalization processes and the growth in global trade and the global economy, the increasing demand for energy, and the growth in economic activity in exclusive economic zones (EEZs) all over the world. Cyberattackers view the seaports and the shipping companies as quality targets, because the amount of information they possess, the high turnover in the industry, and the technological vulnerability of the systems. Cyberattackers see high value in attacking the maritime industry. The goals of cyberattacks on the maritime industry and on maritime assets and infrastructure may include financial profits, influence on public opinion, reputation damage, political gain, or military purposes, such as disruption or shutdown of a nation's critical assets as part of hybrid warfare strategy. This chapter will describe the threats and challenges faced by the maritime industry.

6.1. The Threat

In 2011, a cyberattack was carried out against the port of Anvers, Belgium.[1] The attackers were a drug cartel that penetrated the cargo management systems and changed bills of lading in order to conceal the smuggling of drugs. Attacks with similar objectives have been carried out in the port of Antwerp, Belgium, and against various authorities in Australia between the years 2011 and 2013.

In 2011, the Iranian national shipping company, IRISL, came under cyberattack by unknown entities.[2] During the cyberattack, the company's entire database was erased, including information on cargo, ships, and containers.

In October 2013, a cyberattack was carried out against a cruise ship through the Automatic Identification System (AIS).[3] As a result of this cyberattack, the identity and location of the ship were changed. The attack was carried out by an Italian academic as a demonstration only and was intended as a warning signal. During the same year, there were cyberattacks on two oil drilling rigs, one off the coast of Africa, which caused it to tilt on its side and sink, and the other on a South Korean rig that shut it down for 19 days.[4]

In June 2017, a cyberattack increased the level of cyber awareness in the maritime domain. This cyberattack was carried out against MAERSK, the largest shipping company in the world. The attack continued for about a week and shut down tens of thousands of computer terminals in the company's branches worldwide and, as a result, disrupted customer services. The losses to the company due to the cyberattack were estimated

---

[1] Sea Trade Maritime News (2013). "Antwerp incident highlights maritime IT security," October 21. Available at: https://www.seatrade-maritime.com/news/europe/antwerp-incident-highlights-maritime-it-security-risk/ (accessed on March 2019).

[2] Hutchins, R. (2015). "Carriers threatened by cyberattacks, experts warn," March 3. Available at: https://www.joc.com/maritime-news/container-lines/carriers-threatened-cyber-attacks-experts-warn_20150303.html (accessed on March 2019).

[3] San Simon and Duch (2014). "Weaknesses in ship tracking systems," 11 April. Available at: http://www.lsansimon.com/en/weaknesses-in-ship-tracking-systems/ (accessed on March 2019).

[4] Wagstaff, J. (2014). "All at sea: Global shipping fleet exposed to hacking threat," *Reuters*, 24 April. Available at: https://www.reuters.com/article/us-cybersecurity-shipping/all-at-sea-global-shipping-fleet-exposed-to-hacking-threat-idUSBREA3M20820140423 (accessed on March 2019).

to be more than US$400 million.[5] Following the MAERSK attack, there were other attacks against ports and shipping companies all over the world.

In July 2019, the US Coast Guard revealed[6] that a cyberattack took place in February 2019 on a merchant vessel heading to the Port of New York. The attacked vessel could not keep on its sail to the port, and the crew reported that their shipboard network had been "totally debilitated" by malware. The issue could not be resolved either by those onboard or by the shipping company's system administrators working onshore. The US Coast Guard sent a response team onboard the vessel that solved the problem and let the vessel sail to its destiny at the port of New York.

It is not the first time that a vessel was under a cyberattack. During August 2017, a US Navy guided-missile destroyer collided with a merchant ship in waters east of Singapore and the Straits of Malacca. At first, the US Navy said that the incident occurred due to a cyberattack on the navigation systems of the ships, which forced the ship to deviate from its course. But after a while, the Navy stated that the collision was caused by a human navigation error. Maritime cyber experts do believe that this incident caused by a cyberattack.[7]

In most cases of cyberattacks, the attackers are not identified, and the damage caused by them includes disruption or shutdown of services provided by ports and shipping companies and is manifested as economic, ecological, or reputational damage and even security threats.

The world of shipping and maritime transportation has experienced a major transformation in recent years, in particular with growing connectivity, communication, digitization, automation and integration of information systems and logistics systems of the seaports, vessels, and the shipping companies and their customers. Ports operate numerous computerized systems for port management, loading and unloading of containers

---

[5]Greenberg, A. (2018). "The untold story of NotPetya, the most devastating cyber attack in history," August 22. Available at: https://www.wired.com/story/notpetya-cyberattack-ukraine-russia-code-crashed-the-world/ (accessed on March 2019).

[6]Rundle, J. (2019). "Coast guard details February cyber attack on ship," July 26. Available at: https://www.wsj.com/articles/coast-guard-details-february-cyberattack-on-ship-11564133401 (accessed on March 2019).

[7]Demchak, C. *et al.* (2018). "Navy collisions: Competence, overload and cyber factors," August 29. Available at: https://www.maritime-executive.com/editorials/navy-collisions-competence-overload-and-cyber-factors (accessed on March 2019).

and cargo, movement and storage within the port, billing and customer's services systems, physical security systems, and maritime control systems (Vessel Traffic Management System [VTMS]), etc.

All of the systems are connected by means of the Internet and satellite communication systems and are also connected to the vessels.

Vessels are equipped with numerous systems, such as detection and navigation satellite systems (Global Navigation Satellite System [GNSS]), identification and monitoring of ships (AIS[8]), loading of navigation maps (Electronic Chart Display and Information Systems [ECDIS]), control of the engines and steering, control of various sensors (such as monitoring of fuel, oil, water flow, fire/smoke, etc.), and control of cargo and transshipment. The various systems onboard a vessel are interconnected and integrated as well as connected to the port and the shipping companies by means of satellite communication and other channels of communication.

The technological transformation of the vessels, the shipping companies, and the seaports is occurring simultaneously with major upward trends in the quantity of maritime cargo transportation and the increasing number of vessels and their size. As a result of globalization and the growth in global trade and the economy, there is increasing demand for energy and growth in economic activity in exclusive economic zones (EEZs) all over the world.

The global economy processes are based primarily on maritime trade and transport, and there are already about 8,300 seaports in more than 210 countries and more than 52,000 cargo ships at the time of writing. It is expected that by 2023, there will be about 68,000 such ships.[9]

The annual rate of growth in the volume of maritime trade and transportation is expected to reach about 3.2% during the next five years, and already at present, more than 80% of global trade by volume occurs in the maritime arena.

Global economic changes, increasing importance of the ports and shipping to the world's economies, integration of technological advances, multiplicity of seaport and ship systems, and the connectivity between them are increasingly exposing ports and ships to cyberthreats.

---

[8]Lo, C. (2019). "GPS spoofing: What is the risk for ship navigation," April 15. Available at: https://www.ship-technology.com/features/ship-navigation-risks/ (accessed on March 2019).
[9]UNCTAD (2018). "Merchant fleet." Available at: https://stats.unctad.org/handbook/MaritimeTransport/MerchantFleet.html (accessed on March 2019).

With the growth of global economy and maritime transportation, there is still no world regulation concerning cybersecurity and the measures should be taken in order to prevent cyberattack on the maritime industry. In June 2017,[10] the International Maritime Organization (IMO), which sets rules for security and safety for the maritime industry, published short code of practice to the maritime industry. The IMO is working on cyber-security regulation, which is to be published as a draft in the first quarter of 2021 and expected to be mandatory for every vessel from the first quarter of 2022.

Cyberattackers view the ports and the shipping companies as quality targets, in view of the huge amount of information they possess, the high turnover in the industry, and the technological vulnerability of the systems.

Cyberattackers, who are being supported and used by criminal organizations, terror organizations, activists, or nation-states, are searching for ways and methods to exploit technological advances and systems in order to carry out cyberattacks on the seaports, on shipping companies, and even on vessels.

The goals of cyberattacks on the maritime industry and on maritime assets and national infrastructure might be financial profits, influence on public opinion, reputation damage, political gain or for military purposes, such as to disrupt or shut down a nation's critical assets and national infrastructure as part of a hybrid warfare strategy.

6.2. Cyber Threats to Seaports and Shipping Companies

Seaports use many different systems in order to operate offshore and onshore logistics. Figure 6.1 shows the main systems used by the ports.

The following types of cyberthreats are faced by seaports and shipping companies:

(1) The partial or complete shutdown of a port for a long period of time, which will affect imports and exports to and from the country and the services provided by the port, as well as the country's chain of supply

---

[10] IMO, "Maritime cyber risk." Available at: https://www.imo.org/en/OurWork/Security/Pages/Cyber-security.aspx (accessed on November 2020).

Figure 6.1.   A port's main systems.

Source: https://homeport.uscg.mil/Lists/Content/Attachments/2203/OCIA_Consequences%20to%20
Seaport%20Operations%20from%20Malicious%20Cyber%20Activity.pdf

(such as the country's ability to provide for the energy and food supply needs of its citizens). **The shutdown of a port** can be accomplished by several means:

(a) The shutdown/disruption of the port management system (Terminal Operation System [TOS]).

(b) The shutdown or disruption of the cranes and transportation systems (loading/unloading and storage of containers).

(2) Economic damage caused by the disruption of port's information systems and the alteration of identity records of containers, including their location at the port's yard and their destination (the customer and his location).

(3) Mass destruction caused by hazardous substances that are found in large quantities in the ports and on ships being loaded and unloaded.

(4) The overturning of a ship in the port, which is liable to partially or completely close the port, by means of a change in the loading plans of containers in the TOS system and a change in a ship's center of gravity, which will affect its stability in the water, especially at the open sea. Undesirable intervention and a change in the loading plans within the TOS may even lead to the sinking of a ship at sea.

(5) Inability to monitor the port's traffic in order to control entry and exit of ships by penetrating the VTMS systems which control the seaborne activity in the port and in the sea routes to the port.

(6) Physical penetration of terrorists or criminals into the port (from land or from sea) using manipulation or shutdown of the security systems, including sensors, cameras, and command and control sites in the port.

(7) Smuggling good by changing and manipulating the vessel manifest, by penetrating the information systems of the ports or the shipping company.

(8) Ecological damage by damaging the port's systems or ships' systems in the port.

(9) Damage to the public image and reputation of the port or the shipping company.

(10) Gathering of sensitive national and organizational information from the port's information systems.

A cyberattack on a seaport or shipping companies can be carried out by means of the Internet (e.g. Denial of Service attacks, ransom attack, brute force attack, etc.), disruption of satellite navigation systems, physical penetration, or attack on the organizational supply chain or suppliers working for the port or shipping companies to gain vital information or control of the port's systems.

6.3. Cyberthreats to Vessels

The main operational systems onboard a ship can be divided as follows:

(1) Navigation and identification
(2) Chief engineering — Engines and power
(3) Information systems (IT) and management systems
(4) Communication
(5) Crew's personal systems.

The critical systems that might be exposed to cyberattacks onboard vessels are:

(1) **Communications systems**: e.g. satellite connections, Wi-Fi networks, and public address and alarm systems;
(2) **Bridge and navigation systems**: e.g. GPS and other positioning and charting systems, the AIS system, and the Global Maritime Distress and Safety System;

(3) **Propulsion and machinery power control systems**: e.g. the engine governor and integrated ship controls;

(4) **Access control systems**: e.g. the closed-circuit cameras, shipboard security alarms, and bridge navigation alarms;

(5) **Passenger information systems**: e.g. financial and billing systems and electronic health records for those who visit the doctor;

(6) **Passenger-facing networks**: e.g. public Wi-Fi and guest entertainment systems;

(7) **Core infrastructure systems**: e.g. routers, switches, firewalls, intrusion prevention systems, and security event logging;

(8) **Administrative systems**: e.g. crew tracking and personnel systems and crew-facing Wi-Fi or networks.

The risk of a cyberattack on vessels (whether the vessel is in the port or at the open seas) can be of the following types:

(1) Overturning or sinking of a ship in the port or at sea, which can be achieved by penetrating and changing the ship's loading planning program, thereby changing the center of mass of the ship. By overturning or sinking of a ship, a cyberattacker can create a partial or complete closing and disruption of the port or a shipping lane.

(2) Taking control remotely of a ship's steering and navigation systems, which will enable the attacker to inflict the following types of damage:

(a) To navigate the ship to an undesirable route or cause a collision with another ship or some other object (e.g. a port, a pier, an oil drilling rig).

(b) To paralyze a ship at sea by penetrating and overcoming its navigation systems or its engines and power generators.

(c) To eliminate the ability to build a maritime picture for navigation at sea by attacking the radar systems, command and control or other computerized navigation means, and systems such as the automatic updating map service (which is being downloaded from the Internet by satellite communication, for example).

(d) To hijack a ship for purposes of terror or piracy by taking control of its systems and stopping it in the middle of the ocean.[11]

---

[11]An interesting event occurred in February 2019 when a container vessel was stopped about 200 nm from the shore of New York, without being able to resume sailing, after it

(3) To carry out a mass terror attack using hazardous materials that are to be found in large quantities on ships while they are loading/unloading or at sea.
(4) To cause ecological damage through the release of fuel or other polluting substances.
(5) Smuggling by means of altering or fabricating the ship's bills of lading (manifest).
(6) Damage to public image or reputation that will cause economic losses to shipping companies.

A cyberattack on a vessel can be accomplished through penetration by the vessel's communication channels (such as satellite, RF, or AIS) to the vessel's control and navigation system, GNSS disruption, or attack on the chain of supply of the vessel.

For example, cyberattackers might attack a vessel using the AIS channel as a penetration point[12] and can:

(1) Modify all ship details, including position, course, cargo, flag state, name, Mobile Maritime Service Identity (MMSI) status, etc.
(2) Create fake vessels with identical details e.g. an Iranian vessel with nuclear cargo could appear off the US coast.
(3) Create and modify Aid to Navigations (AToN) entries, such as buoys and lighthouses. This leads to scenarios such as blocking the entrance to a harbor, causing a ship to wreck, etc.
(4) Create and modify marine search and rescue aircraft such as helicopters and light aircraft, e.g. make a Coast Guard helicopter carry out a search and take off on a reconnaissance trip.
(5) Fake a "man-in-the-water" distress beacon at any location that will also trigger alarms on all vessels within approximately 50 km radius.

---

suffered from massive cyberattack. The US Coast Guard sent a intimidate team onboard the vessel that solved the problem and let the vessel sail to its destiny at the port of New York. Not many details were revealed about that incident. Five month later, the US Coast Guard revealed the incident and along with it published recommendations and code of practice to ship owners, in order to implement cybersecurity measures onboard ships.

[12]San Simon and Duch (2014). "Weaknesses in ship tracking systems," April 11. Available at: http://www.lsansimon.com/en/weaknesses-in-ship-tracking-systems/ (accessed on March 2019).

(6) Fake a Closest Point of Approach (CPA) alert and trigger a collision warning alert. In some cases, this can even cause software on the vessel to calculate an alternative course to avoid the collision, allowing an attacker to physically direct the vessel in a certain direction.
(7) Send false weather information to a vessel, e.g. to advise of storms approaching its course.
(8) Force all ships to send AIS traffic more frequently than normal, resulting in a flooding attack on all vessels and marine authorities in the area.

Such types of cyberattacks are possible because the AIS protocol was designed without taking into account, apparently, security considerations.

More than 400,000 ships are using the AIS tracking system, obligatory for all commercial (non-fishing) vessels over 300 metric tons, as well as all passenger ships, regardless of their size and tonnage.

In the last few years, there have been several reports of GPS spoofing in the Black Sea by at least 20 ships through the GNSS systems.[13] GPS spoofing might cause ships to report their location incorrectly and thereby cause wrong navigation to their destination.

Another form of damage can be caused by manipulating the GPS synchronized time (1 PPS), which can disrupt the integration with information systems at the shipping companies or at the ports via the satellite communication link.

6.4. Challenges in Providing Cyber Protection to Ports and Vessels

Protecting ports and shipping against cyberthreats is a complex task. Some of the challenges are:

(1) Development of an organizational/security culture in the ports and in the shipping companies, which will ensure secure behavior and personal responsibility among the employees and the management

---

[13]Jones, M. (2017). "Spoofing in the Black Sea: What really happened?" October 11. Available at: https://www.gpsworld.com/spoofing-in-the-black-sea-what-really-happened/ (accessed on March 2019).

levels, in addition to the assimilation of procedures, awareness, and work methods for the improvement of organizational preparedness against cyberattacks.

(2) Shipping companies manage ports, goods, and cargo in many countries, with a wide geographical dispersion. This makes it difficult to create a unified defense strategy that will provide protection to all of the ports and the connectivity between them.

(3) There are many ports, shipping companies, and ships operating worldwide without a unified configuration of information systems, detection and navigation systems, communication and control, etc.

(4) There are various crews of different nationalities operating on the ships, very often with little security awareness and no control or supervision by an information security professional.

(5) Supervision and monitoring of threats around the clock and throughout the year, including real-time monitoring and warning and the ability to deal with a threat within the shortest time possible.

Therefore, it is necessary to create cyber protection and security solutions that are, on one hand, as generic and economically feasible as possible and, on the other hand, provide solutions for the heterogeneous configurations of the various systems on ships and in ports and against the large number and variety of threats.

6.5. Conclusion

In an increasingly globalized world, the world economy derives growth in maritime shipping and transportation. Therefore, maritime trade is crucial for the economy, energy, security and sovereignty of countries worldwide.

Concurrent to the growth of shipping, the vessels themselves and the seaports are becoming increasingly sophisticated, advanced, and controlled by computerized and automated systems. The computerized systems running the ports and the vessels are connected by satellite communication and other means of communication, thus seaports, vessels, and shipping companies thrive in one big ecosystem.

While the growth of maritime trade and technology within maritime shipping is rapid, cyberattackers are targeting the maritime industry for financial profits, influence on public opinion, reputation damage, political gain, or for military purposes. Maritime cyberattackers, in the new age of piracy, can be crime organizations (or lone criminals), terror outfits, amateur attackers, and even nation states, willing to collect information on their adversary's infrastructure or gain access and control on their systems as part of "under the radar" military acts.

Most of the maritime industry companies (from seaports to ship owners and shipping companies) are not ready and protected enough against cyberattacks. Furthermore, there is no unified regulation for the maritime industry yet, although the International Maritime Organization (IMO) is working on regulation that will fit the maritime industry, focusing on vessels. The IMO regulation is expecting to be published during 2021, and it will take years in order to implement the upcoming regulations.

The challenges of implementing cybersecurity measures, procedures, and infrastructure in the maritime industry companies are complicated, yet they should be completed with utmost priority in order to be more prepared, secure, and resilient in the face of cyberattacks.

Chapter 7

Class Action against Cyberattackers

*Chagai Vinizky**

The Academic Center for Law and Science, Hod Hasharon
Begin Institute of Law and Zionism, Jerusalem, Israel

Chagai@mishpat.ac.il

Abstract

The world of information security has been working for many years to protect against cyberattacks, but the use of legal tools to prevent them is only now developing at a rapid pace. This chapter examines the ability to use the class action mechanism to deter cyberattackers. The article presents the mechanism of class action and its various characteristics in several countries. Next, it reviews the use made to date of class actions against service providers who were the victims of cyberattacks, and proposes a new mechanism that would encourage plaintiffs in class actions to sue also the cyberattackers themselves to deter them.

7.1. Introduction

Cyberattacks occur daily, causing extensive economic and security damage. The objective of the attack may be theft of personal or financial data, causing damage without any benefit to the attacker or it may be to

---

*The author wishes to thank Attorney Aviel Flint for useful comments and Adi Shiman for excellent research assistance.

inflict security damages. The world of information security has been working for many years to protect against these attacks, but the use of legal tools to prevent them is only now developing. This chapter examines the ability to use the class action mechanism to deter cyberattackers. To date, this mechanism has been used in cases of cyberattacks primarily to sue service providers affected by such attacks, which have caused harm to their customers. Customers have sued service providers for various reasons, primarily for security failure, but these claims do not serve to deter the cyberattackers themselves. This chapter describes the mechanism of class action, as it developed in various legal systems, and discusses the differences between these systems. Next, it discusses the deterrent purpose of class action suits, including their ability to achieve public and national goals, as a basis for justifying their use to deter cyberattackers and to reduce the prevalence of these attacks.

7.2. The Class Action Mechanism: A Comparative View

The class action mechanism allows the filing of a class action suit in the name of all potential claimants (hereinafter, "group members"), so that the judicial ruling applies proportionally to all group members. States may be classified based on four criteria with respect to how they implement class action suits:

(1) some states allow a private party to be the representative plaintiff, alongside public entities, and some states allow only public entities to file class action suits[1];

---

[1] In Israel, a private individual who has a personal cause of action can file a claim on behalf of the group, and it is possible for public entities to file a class action, according to Section 4 of the Class Actions Law, 2006. In France, group claims can be filed by organizations but not by private individuals (see Code de la Santé Publique, Art. L.1143-1 et seq). In Italy, a class action can be filed by a private individual or by a consumer organization (Codice del Consumo, Art — 140 Decreto Legislativo 6 settembre 2005, n. 206). In Portugal, a class action can be filed by a private person or organizations and by public authorities (Lei n.º 83/95, 31 de Agosto, Art 1-2). In Belgium, only consumer organizations and associations can file a class action (Loi Portant Insertion d'un Titre 2 "De l'action en réparation collective' au livre XVII 'Procédures juridictionnelles particulières" du Code de droit économique et portant insertion des définitions propres au livre XVII dans le livre 1er du Code de droit économique of 28 March 2014, Moniteur Belge of 29 April, p. 35201). In Sweden, a private person, a consumer organization, or a public

(2) some states have a two-stage mechanism: in the first stage, the claim is approved as a class action suit, and in the second stage it is conducted, whereas other states have a one-stage mechanism, in which the suit is conducted without the need for prior approval[2];

(3) some states restrict class action suits to certain grounds, others do not impose such limitations[3];

---

authority can file a class action (SFS 2002: 599 Lagen om Grupprättegång). In Poland, only a public entity can file a class action (Ustawa o dochodzeniu roszczeń w postępowa niu grupowym, Dziennik Ustaw 2010, no 7; item. 44 p. 1). In Lithuania, a private person, an association, or a professional union can file a class action [Lietuvos Respublikos civilinio proceso kodksas. Valstybės ţinios, 2000, Nr. 74-2262; 2002, Nr. 36 — 1340 (Rule 441 (4))]. In Russia, a private person can file a class action [Arbitrazhnyy Protsessualnyy Kodeks Rossiyskoy Federatsii ot 24 iyulya 2002 no. 95-FZ (http://www.wipo.int/edocs/lexdocs/ laws/en/ru/ru072en.pdf)]. (accessed on October 12, 2020). In Mexico, private individuals, public entities, associations, and the Attorney General can file a class action (Código Federal de Procedimientos Civiles, Art. 585). In Chile, public entities that or a group of at least 50 people can file a class action [Ley N ° 19.555, 14 de Julio de 2004, Diario Oficial [D.O.] (Chile)]. In Japan, only consumer organizations that have been approved can file class action lawsuits (Act on Special Provisions of Civil Court Procedures for Collective Recovery of Property Damage of Consumers, No. 96 of 2013). For more details, see: Flint, A. and Vinizky, C. (2017). *Class Actions* (Zafririm: Nevo), 23–64, 108–109.

[2] A two-stage mechanism exists in the US under Regulation 23 of the Federal Rules of Civil Procedure; in Italy, Italian Consumer Protection Law, *supra* note 1; in Belgium, Belgian Law, *supra* note 1; in Sweden, Swedish Law, *supra* note 1; in Lithuania, Lithuanian Law, *supra* note 1; in South Korea, see: http://elaw.klri.re.kr/kor_service/ lawView.do?hseq=28408&lang=ENG1; (accessed on October 12, 2020) in South Africa, the judicial mechanism is two-stage, Trustees for the Time Being of the Children's Resource Center Trust v. Pioneer Food (Pty) Ltd, 2013 1 All SA 648, para. 23–26 (SCA). See also Mukaddam v. Pioneer Foods (Pty) Ltd, 2013 2 SA 213. In Canada, there is a two-stage mechanism in the Ontario District, Class Proceedings Act, 1992, S.O. 1992, c. 5 (1) (e), in the Province of Quebec, Code of Civil Procedure, R.S.Q. c. C-25, Book IX, art. 999, and in the District of British Columbia, Class Proceedings Act, R.S.B.C. 1996, c. 4 (2). In Israel, there is a two-stage mechanism, paras. 8–9 of the Class Actions Law, 2006, but in suits filed under the 1992 Law on Environmental Hazards Prevention (Civil Claims), the mechanism is one-stage (para. 10). A one-stage mechanism exists in Australia, see: Mulheron, R. P. (2004). *The Class Action In Common Law Legal Systems: A Comparative Perspective* (Oxford: Hart), p. 24; and in Portugal, Article 13 of the Portuguese Law, *supra* note 1. For more details, see Flint & Vinizky. *supra* note 1.

[3] In England, suits can be file only on antitrust-related grounds, under Section 47B of the Competition Act 1998. In Israel, there are 14 matters in which class action can be filed, section 3 (a) and the Second Schedule to the Class Action Law, 2006, and a group claim

(4) some states have an opt-in mechanism, so that potential claimants must join the group explicitly, making it difficult to form a large group, whereas other states have an opt-out mechanism, so that group membership is defined by the court, and members must explicitly withdraw if they do not wish to be part of the suit, which greatly facilitates the forming of a large group.[4]

---

can also be filed under Law on Environmental Hazards Prevention (Civil Claims), 1992. In New Zealand, there is no restriction on issues in which class action suits can be filed. In India, class action can be filed only in the securities area, The Companies Act, 2013 (No. 18 of 2013). In France, a group claim can be filed only in consumer, antitrust, and health issues (see: Loi n° 2014-344 sur la consummation; Loi n° 2016-41 de modernisation du système de santé); in Italy, only in consumer issues (see: Italian Consumer Protection Law, *supra* note 1); in Portugal, claims can be filed in the areas of environmental protection, health, quality of life, and consumer rights (see Portuguese Law *supra* note 1); in Belgium, claims can filed only in consumer protection issues (see Belgian Law, *supra* note 1); in Poland, claims can be filed only in consumer protection and tort issues (Polish Law, *supra* note 1); in Lithuania, there is no restriction on issues in which class action suits can be filed (Lithuanian Law, *supra* note 1); in Russia, a class action can be filed in any area (Russian law, *supra* note 1); in Mexico, a class action can be filed only in the field of consumer protection law and environmental protection law (Article 578 of Mexican Law, *supra* note 1); in Japan, the only claims that can be filed are illegal profiteering and consumer claims based on contractual obligations (see: Madderra, M. J. (2014). "The new class actions in Japan," *Pacific Rim Law & Policy Journal Association*, **23**: 795, 810); in South Korea, a class action can be filed only in securities (see South Korean Law, *supra* note 2). For more detail, see Flint & Vinizky, *supra* note 1. In the US, according to the federal model, in Canada, and in Australia, there is no restriction on the grounds on which a class action can be filed, *ibid.*, p. 107.

[4]In the US, an opt-out mechanism exists under Regulation 23 of the Federal Rules of Civil Procedure. An exception to this rule is found in claims filed for violation of the Fair Labor Standards Act 1938. These claims include only those who chose to join the claim. See: Alexander, C. (2010). "Would an opt in requirement fix the class action settlement? Evidence from the Fair Labor Standards Act," *Mississippi Law Journal*, **80**: 443, 459. In Canada, the mechanism in place in Quebec and Ontario is opt-out, whereas in British Columbia the mechanism is opt-out only in respect of British Columbia residents, and residents of other regions can join only by way of opt-in (Quebec Law, *supra* note 2, Article 1005; in Ontario, *supra* note 2, Article 9; in British Columbia Law, *supra* note 2, Section 16 (1)). An opt-out mechanism exists also in Australia (Dorajay Pty Ltd v. Aristocrat Leisure Ltd, (2005) 147 FCR 394, 425-426, 431 (Stone J.)). In India, The Companies Act, 2013 Article 245 (6) (No. 18 of 2013); in Portugal, Portuguese law, *supra* note 1; in South Korea, the South Korean law, *supra* note 2. In Israel, there is an opt-out mechanism under

7.3. Class Action as a Deterrent Device

Class action suits have many goals, including exercising the right of access to the court[5]; providing appropriate relief to the victims in the group[6]; effective, fair, and exhaustive management of the claims[7];

Section 11 of the Class Actions Law, 2006. At the same time, for claims under the Environmental Hazards (Civil Claims) Law, 1992, there is an opt-in mechanism (Section 12 of the law). In the Netherlands, a representative settlement agreement can be approved through an opt-out mechanism (see: De Wet Collectieve Afwikkeling Massaschade (TK 31.762 no. 1)). In Argentina, the Supreme Court recognized the possibility of filing a class action, in effect applying the opt-out mechanism (Halabi, Ernesto c/PEN ley 25.873 y decreto 1563/04 s/amparo). An opt-in mechanism exists in Italy (Italian Consumer Protection Law, *supra* note 1); in Sweden, Swedish Law, *supra* note 1; in Poland, Polish Law, *supra* note 1; in Lithuania, Lithuanian Law, *supra* note 1; in Russia, Russian Law, *supra* note 1; in Mexico, Mexican Law, *supra* note 1; in Japan, Madderra, *supra* note 3, p. 808; in Malaysia, the possibility of filing a claim through a representative is a form of opt-in (Order 15, rule 6, ROC); in New Zealand, the usual approach in the case law is opt-in (Houghton v. Saunders, (2008) 19 PRNZ 173, para. 68 (HC)). In England, the court determines whether to apply opt-in or opt-out under Section 47B (10), (11) of the Competition Act 1998. A similar arrangement exists in Belgium (Belgian Law, *supra* note 1); for more details, see Flint & Vinizky, *supra* note 1.

[5]The class action is justified mainly when the amount of each group member's personal claim does not justify independent trial management, or when filing a claim in certain cases, such as in the area of securities, entails significant financing costs for procuring an economic opinion, so that, in the absence of the class action mechanism, group members cannot exercise their right to sue in court (see Flint & Vinizky, *supra* note 1, at 69–70). See also: Article 1 (1) of the Class Actions Law, 2006 (Israel).

[6]Emphasizing this purpose is especially important in cases when the court prefers to instruct the defendant, in its verdict against him, to make a contribution to public nonprofits, instead of providing relief to members of the group, when the latter is impractical. In view of this purpose, such possibility should exist only when there is a threshold that makes compensation for group members "impractical under the circumstances," otherwise the preferred option is to compensate group members (Flint & Vinizky, *supra* note 1, at 77–80; Articles 1(3), 20 (c) of the Class Actions Law, 2006 (Israel)).

[7]This objective fulfills the public interest of effectively managing similar claims. Efficiency is not everything, however, and the process must also be fair to the defendant. Therefore, a class action should not be approved if it were to prejudice the defendant's constitutional right to due process. See: Amchem Products, Inc. v. Windsor, 521 U.S. 591, 613, 615 (1997); Flint & Vinizky, *supra* note 1, at 80–81, 226–244; Articles 1 (4), 8 (a) (2) of the Class Actions Law, 2006 (Israel).

denial of profit to the violator, that is, preventing unjust enrichment[8]; advancement of norms of fairness and probity[9]; advancement of the principle of equity[10]; advancement of the value of freedom[11];

---

[8] This purpose is intended to fulfill the basic rule in the sources of Hebrew law "that no sinner shall profit [from his sin]." See in this context: HaCohen (2005). "One may do anybody a favor without his knowledge, but no one may act to another's disadvantage without his awareness"; "Studies on the issue of class action in light of the principles of Jewish law," *Shaarei Mishpat*, **4**: 153, 177–179, 188–189. The principle of denying unjust enrichment is also mentioned in the writings of Aristotle and Cicero, and it has echoes in Roman law; see: Friedman, D. and E. Shapira Bar-Or (2015). *The Laws of Unjust Enrichment*, Vol. 1, Third Edition, p. 26 and the references therein. This purpose is important in cases in which it can be assumed that deterrence has been achieved, but nevertheless the offender should not be allowed to keep his bounty (Flint & Vinizky, *supra* note 1, 82–83).

[9] This is based on the principle of Hebrew law "do what is right and good," Deuteronomy 18. For using this principle to justify class actions, see Adm. Pet. App. 2978/13 Water Galilee Corporation and Regional Sewage Ltd. v. Younes, Section 15 (published in Nevo, 2015). This principle is of particular importance in the context of arranging compromise regarding the future conduct of the defendant (Flint & Vinizky, *supra* note 1, at 83–84).

[10] One of the most important rulings in modern history is undoubtedly Brown v. Board of Education, 347 U.S. 483 (1954). The ruling was based, among others, on a class action in relation to racial segregation in the American education system. In this suit, it was not claimed that there was a disadvantage in segregated schools *per se*, but rather that the very separation was discriminatory. Indeed, the Supreme Court unanimously ruled in 1953 that separate education is inherently discriminatory, so that segregation promotes inequality and is contrary to the 14th Amendment to the US Constitution. Another example of a class action that succeeded in significantly advancing the value of equality is the class action in which Coca-Cola Company agreed to pay US$192.5 million in compensation for systematic discrimination against African Americans, and to appoint a public overseer to review discrimination complaints in the future (Ingram v. Coca-Cola Co., FRD 200 (ND GA 2001); Abdallah v. Coca-Cola Co., 133 F. Supp. 2d 1364 (ND Ga. 2001)). For the possibility of filing a class action aimed at preventing discrimination, as regulated in Israel, see *supra* note 3. For additional rulings and other options for advancing equality through the institution of class action, see Flint & Vinizky, *supra* note 1, 30–31, 84–87.

[11] This goal is reflected in the possibility offered by the class action to allow individual claimants to defend their property and their freedom from harm to their property and the property of members of the group, not only to allow a public authority to do so, as is the case in some states; see *supra* note 1. See also: Flint & Vinizky, *supra* note 1, at 87–88.

encouragement of community participation[12]; advancement of the value of distributive justice[13]; and protection of the environment.[14]

There is no doubt that one of the most important goals, if not the most important one, is deterrence against violating the law. When a potential tortfeasor intends to harm many entities to a degree that does not justify an individual claim on the part of each injured party, without the mechanism of the class action, no civil deterrent is in place. Therefore, an argument can be made that this is the foremost goal that class action suits are intended to achieve, even more important than other goals. In support of this argument, note that various legal systems allow public authorities and organizations to file class action suits, attesting to the fact that the legislature sought to give precedence to the principle of law enforcement, and therefore allowed also entities that have no direct cause to take legal

---

[12]This goal is furthered by the fact that a group member represents the community of people who sustained harm. In addition, in cases when the compensation to the members of the group is not feasible, the court may order any kind of relief for the benefit of the group as a whole or for the benefit of the public. See Article 20 (c) (1) of the Class Actions Law, 2006 (Israel). Promoting the value of community would favor compensation for the group over compensation for the public (Flint & Vinizky, *supra* note 1, at 88–90).

[13]The advancement of distributive justice is reflected in Hebrew law and in the writings of Aristotle. For these sources, see Flint & Vinizky, *supra* note 1, at 91. In class actions, this principle can be expressed by taking into account the defendant's financial position in awarding the compensation and specifying manner in which it is paid (see Section 20 (4) (2) of the Class Actions Law, 2006 (Israel)) as well as by awarding compensation for the benefit of the public, which may be allocated to populations in need (see CA 10085/08 Tnuva Agricultural Cooperative Marketing Center Ltd. v. Estate of Ravi P.S. 60 (published in Nevo, 2011)). See also Flint & Vinizky, *ibid.*, at 77–78, 90–94.

[14]Class actions can also protect the environment. For example, Erin Brockovich's well-known lawsuit, which was the subject of a Hollywood movie, ended in a US$333 million compensation to residents of a California town, whose drinking water was polluted by a gas and electricity company (amounting to about US$268,000 per resident), Anderson v. Pacific Gas & Electric Company (Superior Court of the County of San Bernardino, File BCV 00300, 1993). Although only the immediate victims received the compensation, the judgment also contributed to environmental protection. See also the settlement reached in a class action lawsuit in Israel against Europe Asia Pipeline Co. for its liability for oil spill damage in the Arava, amounting to NIS 100 million, of which NIS 20 million will be allocated for the rehabilitation of the damaged nature reserve, and NIS 10 million for monitoring and preventing future oil leakages. To advance this value, certain countries have restricted the range of issues that can be claimed in a class action, but include in it the prevention of environmental damage, as is the case in Israel (see *supra* note 3).

action, to file class action suits. Furthermore, in some legal systems, especially in countries where the continental system is in force, individual citizens do not have the right to file class action suits, only certain organizations do.[15] Therefore, to achieve the objective of deterrence, when it comes to class action lawsuits against cyberattackers, it is of great importance that this instrument target the cyberattackers directly, and not only against companies whose service to customers has been impaired because of the cyberattack.

7.4. Class Action Suits as a Means of Achieving National Policy Goals

Class action suits can also assist national policy goals. A recent example of this is the request to approve a class action lawsuit filed against Airbnb.[16] This company operates a website where short-term rental apartments are offered. It is considered to be the largest of its kind in the world, listing, among others, rental apartments located in Judea and Samaria. Yet, after pressure exerted by various entities, including a corporation called Kerem Navot, which urged and advised Airbnb to stop listing properties located in Israeli communities in Judea and Samaria, on November 19, 2018, Airbnb announced that it intended to remove from its site apartments located in Israeli communities in Judea and Samaria.[17] Following this announcement, a motion for class action was filed in the name of Ms. Maanit Rabinowitz, who lives in Kida, Samaria, claiming

---

[15]See Flint & Vinizky, *supra* note 1 at 70–77.

[16]Class action 54132-11-18 Rabinowitz v. Airbnb, Inc. (Published in Nebo 18.7.2019). For the sake of disclosure, this claim was filed by the author of this chapter and by Attorney Aviel Flint.

[17]For the Airbnb decision, see; Airbnb (2018). "Listings in disputed regions by Airbnb," November 19. Available at: https://news.airbnb.com/listings-in-disputed-regions/. (accessed on October 13, 2020). For Kerem Navot, see https://www.keremnavot.org/heairbnb, (accessed on October 13, 2020). which includes the Kerem Navot report that recommended Airbnb to "cease providing services in or around the West Bank settlements, including the publication of properties in the territories or any other assistance in renting settlement assets," p. 5. See also pp. 3–4 of the report. The report was published a day after the Airbnb decision, but on page 35 of the report, it says that "Human Rights Watch and Kerem Navot wrote to Airbnb companies ... regarding their human rights policies and procedures and contacted them regarding their settlement operations."

that Airbnb violated the provisions of the Prohibition of Discrimination Act on products, services, and entrance to entertainment venues and public places, 2000 (Israel, henceforth "Prohibition of Discrimination Act"), which prohibits a public service provider, including tourist services, from discriminating in the supply of a product or service, among others, because of place of residence. In view of the fact that the discrimination specifically targeted Israeli settlers, it was claimed that discrimination is based on country of origin and worldview, which is also prohibited in accordance with the Prohibition of Discrimination Act. The law also prohibits the publication of an announcement that contains such prohibited discrimination. Both the discrimination and discriminatory announcement are considered a tort.[18] The possibility of filing a class action suit in this matter was the result of the fact that, in accordance with Israeli legislation, a class action can be filed in relation to 14 matters listed in the Second Schedule to the Class Action Law, 2006,[19] and the above ground of prohibition against discrimination is one of them.[20]

As noted, the Kerem Navot organization called for boycotting the vacation accommodations in Judea and Samaria. It is possible to argue that by doing so, it committed a tort according to Section 2 of the Law on the Prevention of Injury to the State of Israel through a Boycott, 2011 (hereinafter, "Boycott Prevention Law"). Section 1 of the Law defines "Boycott of the State of Israel," among others, as intentional refusal to associate economically with a person only because of that person's affiliation with an area under Israeli control, which is liable to cause economic harm, and Judea and Samaria are areas under Israeli control. Yet, it was not possible to file a class action suit for this tort, because it is not listed in the Second Schedule to the Class Actions Law. Therefore, in the application for approval of the above-mentioned class action claim, it was argued that Kerem Navot advised and coaxed Airbnb to announce the above policy statement, and therefore committed the tort jointly with Airbnb, according to Israeli law,[21] which states that anyone who advises or induces an entity to commit an act is liable for the tort being committed, as if they had committed it themselves. Because Kerem Navot advised Airbnb to immediately stop listing advertisements for rentals in

---

[18] Articles 5-2 of the Prohibition of Discrimination Act 2000 (Israel).
[19] See *supra* note 3.
[20] See Section 3 (1) and the Second Schedule (Item 7) of the Class Actions Law, 2006 (Israel).
[21] Section 12 of the Tort Ordinance (new version) (Israel).

communities in Judea and Samaria, it was argued that it enticed and advised Airbnb, and it was therefore equally responsible for the tort committed by Airbnb, as specified under the Prohibition of Discrimination Act. In accordance with Israeli law, when two defendants are jointly responsible for the tort, they are liable jointly and separately. In other words, the plaintiff can claim the full amount awarded by the court from each of the tortfeasors, and the tortfeasor who paid more than its share can file a claim against the other for the relative part for which it is liable.[22]

The process ended when Ms. Rabinowitz and Airbnb agreed to withdraw the application for approval of the class action, in light of the fact that Airbnb decided to cancel the above policy announcement before it was implemented in practice, and agreed to post on its website a statement stating that it will not delist the hosting assets located in the Judea and Samaria settlements. Subsequently, the two parties agreed not to continue the process, and Airbnb refrained from admitting to the allegations against it. The parties also agreed that Ms. Rabinowitz should be compensated, and the court approved a fee for her attorneys.[23]

This case demonstrates that the class action mechanism may also be used to accomplish national political goals, such as the prevention of boycott against Israel or the territories of Judea and Samaria. To refine the possibility of using class action suits for this purpose, the Israeli Minister of Justice was asked to add this ground, in accordance with the Boycott Prevention Law, as an independent ground that allows the filing of class action suits. This was required, because previously in many cases of calls for a boycott not followed by an actual boycott, it was not possible to file a class action suit against the initiators of such calls. Another reason justifying an independent ground in accordance with the Boycott Prevention Law has to do with cases where a call for a boycott has led to the cancellation of a cultural event in Israel, as it has happened in the past. In these cases, it is even more difficult to rely on the grounds of discrimination based on residence, which is intended primarily for discrimination on the basis of specific residence, and it is therefore desirable to allow class action suits against the initiator of the boycott based on the Boycott Prevention Law, on behalf of all those affected by the boycott. Moreover, when there is a call for boycotting products from Judea and Samaria, there is a problem in relying on the Prohibition on Discrimination Act, because

---

[22] Section 11 of the Tort Ordinance (new version) (Israel).

[23] Rabinovitz, *supra* note 16.

it concerns discrimination in the provision of a product or public service rather than discrimination in the purchase of goods. Therefore, it is desirable, in these cases as well, to allow class action suits based on the Boycott Prevention Law against the initiator of the boycott on behalf of all those affected by it.[24]

When a person calls for a boycott, the potential boycott is usually aimed at a certain public that may be harmed by it. A class action based on this ground naturally raises substantive questions of fact or law that are common to all group members, and therefore, making it appropriate to be settled as a class action. Advancing the value of equality, which is designed to prevent discrimination and boycotts, is one of the goals of the class action mechanism in the US and Israel.[25] Furthermore, allowing the filing of a class action suit based on the Boycott Prevention Law will make it possible to enforce it through civil lawyers. In the case of calls for cultural, academic, or economic boycott of Israel or of entities operating in Judea and Samaria, it will be possible to consider the filing of a class action suit against the initiator of the boycott on behalf of those who are harmed by it. Filing of class action suits that would economically harm those who initiate the boycott and cause them to defend themselves each time they initiate a boycott can be a significant deterrent in this matter, which is one of the important goals of the class action mechanism.[26]

7.5. Class Action Suits against Companies Affected by Cyberattacks: Literature Review

In the past, trade secrets were referred to as "the new gold of the market place."[27] These days, personal data are called "the new oil," a valuable

---

[24]"Proposal to add a ground to class action lawsuit deriving from the Boycott Prevention Law, 2011." For the sake of disclosure, the proposal was submitted by the author of this chapter. In accordance with Article 30 of the Class Actions Law (2006), the Minister of Justice in Israel may, in consultation with the Minister of Finance and with the approval of the Constitution and Law Committee of the Knesset, add a ground to the Second Schedule.

[25]See *supra* note 10.

[26]See *supra* note 15 and adjacent text.

[27]Epstein, M. A. and S. D. Levi (1988). "Protecting trade secret information: A plan for proactive strategy," *The Business Lawyer*, **43**(1): 887; Epstein and Levi cite: Miles, G. L.

resource that has evolved into a uniquely coveted asset.[28] In a study conducted by Romanosky, Hoffman, and Acquisti on 230 US Federal actions for breach of data security between the years 2000–2010, there is an estimation that since 2005, 543 million records were lost as a result of 2,800 data breaches, and that in 2010, identity theft caused consumers US$13.3 billion in losses.[29] Since then, these numbers have increased every year. Marcus has shown that, between 2005 and 2018, 9,395 breaches of information have been documented, exposing more than a billion records. These breaches are not limited to certain industries. They include attacks on banks, retailers, entertainment companies, healthcare providers, and even federal agencies.[30]

In the Convention on Cybercrime, two sections prohibit causing computer damage. The first section defines "data interference" as causing damage and deleting or modifying data without authorization. The second section defines "system interference" as significant prevention of the proper functioning of a computer system by inserting, damaging, deleting, or altering computer data.[31] For the purposes of the research conducted by Romanosky and colleagues, a data security breach has been defined broadly as unauthorized exposure of personal information by an organization.[32] The empirical study the article describes shows that federal action for information security breach usually has several characteristics:

(1986). "Information thieves are now corporate enemy," *Business Week*, May 5, p. 120 (citing D. B. Parker of S.R.I. International).

[28] Marcus, D. J. (2018). "The data breach dilemma: Proactive solutions for protecting consumers' personal information," *Duke Law Journal*, **68**: 555, 562. The value of information regarding the personal data in the possession of companies is estimated in billions, *ibid*, p. 563.

[29] Romanosky, S., D. Hoffman and A. Acquisti (2014). "Empirical analysis of data breach litigation," *Journal of Empirical and Legal Studies*, **11**: 74–75.

[30] Marcus, *supra* note 28, 561–562. The data are from the Identity Theft Resource Center.

[31] Vasiu, I. and L. Vasiu (2014). "Break on through: An analysis of computer damage cases," *Pittsburgh Journal of Technology, Law & Policy*, **14**: 158, 162. See: Council of Europe (2014). *Convention on Cybercrime*, January 18. Available at: http://conventions.coe.int/Treaty/Commun/ChercheSig.asp?NT=185&CM=&DF=&CL=ENG (accessed on October 13, 2020).

[32] Romanosky *et al.*, *supra* note 29, at 79. Another definition appears in Marcus' article, *supra* note 28 at 561: "Data breaches occur when an individual name plus a social security number, driver's license number, medical record or financial record (credit/debit cards included) are potentially put at risk because of exposure through either electronic or paper means," Data Breaches, Identity Theft Resource Center. Available

(1) the plaintiffs seek compensation for one or more of the following: actual loss as a result of identity theft, for example, financial or medical fraud, emotional distress, the cost of prevention of additional damage in the future, such as credit monitoring and identity theft insurance, and increased risk of future harm;

(2) the claims are usually private class action lawsuits, although some of the claims for breach of information security are filed by public entities;

(3) the defendants are generally large firms, such as banks, insurance companies, companies that provide medical services, retailers, or other private businesses;

(4) the range of grounds used by the plaintiffs is broad and includes grounds from common law, tort law, contract law, as well as statutory grounds;

(5) the vast majority of claims are settled by a compromise, or rejected for reasons having to do with the law or because the plaintiff failed to prove actual damages.[33]

To prove actual damages, most courts require showing that the stolen information has been put to use or that it may be used in the near future. Given the difficulty of tracking stolen information after a security breach, plaintiffs have great difficulty complying with this requirement.[34]

According to Romanosky and colleagues, analysis indicates that the chances of defendants settling are 30% higher when the plaintiffs claim financial harm as a result of information leakage, or when they face a class action that has been approved (76% of information security breaches are being filed as class actions).[35] These claims are suitable for class action,

---

at: http://www.idtheftcenter.org/Data-Breaches/data-breaches (accessed on October 13, 2020). [https://perma.cc/M6AG-RXBQ] (accessed on October 13, 2020).

[33] *Ibid.*, p. 76.

[34] Marcus, *supra* note 28, at 566–567. In light of this, federal courts have become an obstacle to plaintiffs suing for information security breaches. The reluctance of courts to extend the scope for plaintiffs' legal claims overshadows the few cases that succeeded in overcoming this hurdle. It also prevents victims from receiving financial compensation and hinders significant change in cybersecurity practices, *ibid.* p. 569.

[35] Romanosky *et al.*, *supra* note 29, at 76, 83, 92, 98, 102. The study also found that the chances of a firm to be sued were 3.5 times greater if the individuals sustained economic damage, and if the breach exposed medical information, the probability of a plea bargain

because group members are homogeneous and have shared questions regarding the facts and the law, therefore they are more likely to be approved as class actions.[36] About two decades ago, concern was raised that class actions may be an ineffective tool for claims in Internet disputes over virus damage, because approval requests were expected to be rejected for failure to comply with the administrative and priority requirements of the law. In accordance with these requirements, the court must ensure that the group can manage the claim effectively, and that the use of class action is preferable to any other instrument in the case at hand.[37] Yet, given the number of class actions filed and approved in the US in this area, this concern seems to have been unfounded.

Lawyers have an incentive to file class action suits: their fees are affected by the amount awarded — the larger the security breach, the greater are the fees of the attorney handling the lawsuit, and the higher the incentive to bring the lawsuit to court. Thus, the first hypothesis of the study was that there is a positive correlation between the chances of a claim being filed and the number of records lost.[38] Indeed, according to the data collected, an average of 98,000 records were damaged in lawsuits that did not reach the federal courts, whereas the cases that were heard in federal courts dealt with an average of 5.3 million damaged records.[39]

Regarding the characteristics of the breaches themselves, it was found that claims were not more likely to be filed for breaches resulting from a cyberattack than for breaches resulting from stolen or lost data. Nevertheless, the likelihood of firms that exposed without authorization or lost personal information to be sued was three times greater than the likelihood of suits being filed for breaches caused by data theft.[40] This

---

increased by 31%, *ibid.*, pp. 76–77. For a discussion of shareholders' securities fraud class actions against their companies for losses incurred as a result of a data breach, see Marcus, *supra* note 28, at 570–574. For restrictions on class action lawsuits in the area of securities in the US, see Flint & Vinizky, *supra* note 1, at 32–33, 107.

[36] Brooks, R. A. (1998). "Deterring the spread of viruses online: Can tort law tighten the "net"?" *The Review of Litigation*, **17**: 343, 384. See also Cesare, K. (2001). "Prosecuting computer virus authors: The need for an adequate and immediate international solution," *Transnational Law*, **14**: 135, 163.

[37] *Ibid*, p. 391.

[38] Romanosky *et al.*, *supra* note 29, at 83.

[39] *Ibid.*, p. 86.

[40] *Ibid.*, p. 102.

indicates that claimants tend to penalize far more (and lawyers are more confident in filing suits against) companies that have been negligent in protecting their consumers' information than companies that were themselves the unfortunate victims of computer hardware theft.[41] Yet, only breaches caused by cyberattacks showed a positive and strong correlation with reaching a compromise, which in this case was 10 times higher than in the case when the breach was due to theft or loss of hardware.[42] The authors believe these data may help assess the risk of companies and help price insurance contracts against cyber vulnerability.[43] By contrast, claims for statutory damages show no correlation with compromise settlements.[44] In Israel, statutory damages cannot be claimed in a class action.[45]

With regard to compromise arrangements, the study found that the vast majority of claims for breach of information security were rejected by the courts or reached a compromise settlement. Of the 230 cases investigated, only two cases could be cited in which the plaintiff received a favorable verdict by a judge or a jury. Therefore, the plaintiffs and their attorneys tend to settle if the profits from the settlement outweigh the costs associated with continuing the trial. One of the reasons for dismissing numerous lawsuits for information security breaches is the plaintiffs' inability to show that they sustained concrete damages that justify continuing the lawsuit. Plaintiffs who sustained real damage could eventually overcome this obstacle and reach compromise settlements.[46] A similar

---

[41] *Ibid.*, p. 91. Similarly, security breaches involving financial information and credit cards are more likely to reach federal courts. As far as breaches involving medical information are concerned, it seems that the ratios of cases that reach federal courts and of those that do not are about the same, *ibid.*, p. 87.

[42] *Ibid.*, pp. 76–77, 102.

[43] *Ibid.*, p. 102.

[44] *Ibid.*, p. 98.

[45] Section 20 (e) of the Class Actions Law (2006) states that: "The court shall not award an exemplary compensation in a class action suit, nor will it award compensation without proof of damages, except in a claim as specified in Part 9 of the Second Schedule, but this shall not prevent awarding compensation for non-financial damage." Item 9 concerns claims regarding people with disabilities.

[46] *Ibid*, p. 92. Although harm to financial information has led to more litigation, it does not appear to have increased a plaintiff's chances of reaching a settlement. By contrast, the risk posed to medical information showed a stronger correlation with reaching a compromise settlement, *ibid.*, p. 102

phenomenon can be found in Israel. Only 0.07% of approval requests reach a final decision in the class action suit itself.[47]

7.6. Class Action against Cyberattackers

Class action suits against cyberattackers are subject to several significant failures:

(1) inability to discover the identity of the cyberattacker[48];
(2) the assumption that in most cases the pockets of the cyberattackers are not deep enough to pay the amount ordered by the court, and they may not even have the means to cover the legal expenses that may be charged against them[49];
(3) lack of recognized grounds for taking action against a cyberattacker based on which it is possible file a class action. As noted in Section 7.2, in a large part of the states where a class action can be brought, the grounds are limited to specific ones, and do not include a ground that allows a claim against cyberattackers[50];
(4) problems in private international law: even if the perpetrators are caught, it may be difficult to prosecute them because of challenges

---

[47]Flint & Vinizky, *supra* note 1 at 597.

[48]Capturing the violators and bringing them to trial is becoming increasingly difficult, Marcus, *supra* note 28, at 565; Chalfant, M. (2017). "Feds find some foreign hackers are out of reach," November 29. Available at: http://thehill.com/business-a-lobbying/362458-feds-find-some-foreign-hackers-are-out-of-reach (accessed on October 13, 2020). [https://perma.cc/ZKK8-V9QU] (accessed on October 13, 2020). (discussing the challenges of attributing these attacks to specific individuals and then extraditing them to the US to face criminal charges). See also: Ena, M. (2008). "Securing online transactions: Crime prevention is the key," *Fordham Urban Law Journal*, **35**: 147, 170, 175, emphasizing that to reduce the risk of being caught and to thwart criminal investigations, cyberattackers have developed anti-forensic software designed to remove all traces of the break-in, further complicating the investigations. See also Paige, C. (2017). "Anderson Cyber Attack Exception to the Foreign Sovereign Immunities Act," *Cornell Law Review*, **102**: 1087, 1089, stressing that one of the problems in identifying cyberattackers is that its identification information is classified government information.

[49]Brooks, *supra* note 36, at 346: "Because individuals who release viruses may be judgment proof, software distributors and on-line service providers present more lucrative targets."

[50]*Supra* note 3.

related to international jurisdiction; it may be difficult to ascribe the offense to an offender who is a citizen of a foreign country,[51] including determining the place where the tort was committed and the appropriate judicial authority that can hear the claim.[52]

Despite the global nature of the Internet, claimants must file their class actions under the laws of a particular state, with differences in substantive law creating dilemmas concerning the available legal choices.[53] The likelihood of enforcing a judgment against cyberattackers in a foreign country raises another difficulty.[54] A recent example is the case of Alexei Burkov, a Russian citizen, suspected of selling credit card data of US citizens. Burkov was arrested in 2015 in Israel, in response to a US request, which demanded his extradition. At the same time, Burkov claimed that Russia had also applied to Israel for extradition. This case has received wide media attention because of the claim that Russia has sentenced Naama Issachar, an Israeli woman who was caught in a light drug offense, to 7.5 years of imprisonment (a sentence entirely disproportionate to the offense committed), to induce Israel to extradite Burkov to Russia in return for a reduced sentence to Issachar.[55] Burkov was extradited to the US after the Israeli Supreme Court ruling, on November 10, 2019.[56] This case, which dragged on for four years, shows that the issue of jurisdiction to try cyberattackers can take a long time, and involve a struggle between sovereign states.

These four failures deter cyber victims or thwart the possibility of suing cyberattackers directly in a class action. Therefore, as we noted in

---

[51] *Supra* note 48.

[52] Brooks *supra* note 36, at 345, 392.

[53] Ena, *supra* note 48, at 178.

[54] Anderson, *supra* note 48, p. 1089.

[55] Keinon, H. (2019). "Naama Issachar and others: Problem solving through hostage taking," *The Jerusalem Post*, October 31. Available at: https://www.jpost.com/Israel-News/Naama-Issachar-and-others-problem-solving-through-hostage-taking-606467 (accessed on October 13, 2020). If indeed Russia did impose an exceedingly strict punishment on Naama Issachar because she is Israeli, Israel has an obligation to assist her by virtue of Section 6 (a) of the Basic Law: Israel the Nation State of the Jewish People, which provides that "The state will strive to ensure the safety of the members of the Jewish people and of its citizens in trouble or in captivity due to the fact of their Jewishness or their citizenship."

[56] HCJ 7272/19, Alexei Burkov v. Minister of Justice (published in Nevo, 10.11.19).

Section 7.5, victims of cyberattacks prefer to sue the company that provided them with a particular service, causing damage to its customers because of a cyberattack that the company has experienced. These are the cases of banks whose information security was breached, of Internet or software providers responsible for spreading a virus, and of security software providers of the anti-virus programs that were defective or did not properly warn the plaintiffs.[57] At times, the defendants are the employers of the tortfeasors who spread the virus, such as software companies, Internet Service Providers, or databases. Corporations and service or software providers are responsible for the negligent acts of their employees, to the extent that the acts were undertaken as part of their employment, even if the employer did not approve them.[58] This situation results in a serious legal failure, with no civil deterrent against the cyberattackers themselves.[59]

There are two main solutions to these failures. The first solution covers several aspects:

(1) A statutory rule provides that any lawsuit against companies that have been the victims of a cyberattack and whose clients were harmed must also be filed against the cyberattackers. The ground against the cyber-attackers must be an independent one, if a grounds exists that allows filing a class action; alternatively, the cyberattacker is considered to be a joint offender, similarly to the procedure described in Section 7.4, in the case of Airbnb.[60] With respect to cyberattackers, the ground

---

[57]Brooks, *supra* note 36, at 385–386: "Class defendants would likely include software or service providers liable for the virus infection, rather than judgment-proof individuals who create and distribute viruses. They likely also would include security software providers liable for anti-viral software that may have been defective or that failed to warn the plaintiffs." See also *supra* note 49; Anderson, *supra* note 48, at 1089; Cesare, *supra* note 36, at 163. For companies that may be sued, Cesare suggests purchasing insurance and developing a secure computing strategy.

[58]Brooks, *supra* note 36, at 359: "In most cases, target defendants will ultimately be employers of the tortfeasors who distribute the virus, such as software companies, ISPs, bulletin board systems ("BBS") operators, or data repositories, as individuals responsible for releasing a virus are likely to be judgment proof. Corporations and service or software providers will be held liable for their employees' negligent acts where the acts are within the scope of employment, even if the employer has not authorized them."

[59]Cesare, *supra* note 36, at 163–164, also emphasizes the importance of criminal deterrence.

[60]For possible grounds against cyberattackers, see Brooks, *supra* note 36, at 366–379.

would be a violation of the company's service, which is not as enticing as in the Airbnb case. It requires a wider rule, allowing to consider as joint offenders the cyberattacker and the company that was harmed by the attack because it did not properly defend against it. Naturally, it is desirable for states that recognize class actions on certain grounds to add an independent ground against cyberattackers, so that class action claimants do not have to rely on the rules of joint offenders.[61]

(2) A public class action fund should be created to finance the search for cyberattackers.[62] If the cyberattackers are located, a claim is filed against the company that provided the affected service and against the cyberattackers, jointly and severally, so that the compensation granted by the court and the legal expenses can be collected in full from the company, which can then continue to pursue the cyberattackers legally to pay their share. This would solve both the deep pocket problem and the need to deter cyberattackers from attacking companies that provide services to customers. If the attacker is not found, the claim is allowed against the affected company alone. This can achieve deterrence against the cyberattacker and at the same time provide an incentive for the class action claimant to sue the attacker as well. Such a rule is justified, because the company is also among the victims of the cyberattack. Admittedly, such a fund would be effective in the search for attackers who were not careful to disguise their identities, but it may also deter attackers who know how to disguise their identities, because they cannot know with any certainty that they would not be discovered in a financially supported effort. In light of the need to enforce the verdicts in the various countries, cooperation between countries that recognize the importance of the matter is required.

---

[61] Similar to the proposal in Israel to add the grounds of the Boycott Prevention Law, see *supra* note 24 and the adjacent text. For the call to countries to cooperate with regard to cybersecurity events through domestic criminal and civil legislation, including support of criminal investigations and obtaining evidence, see: Gross, O. (2015) "Cyber responsibility to protect: Legal obligations of states directly affected by cyber-incidents," *Cornell International Law Journal*, **48**: 481, 510–511. See also Ena, *supra* note 48 at 175, calling on law enforcement agencies to rely on the cooperation of the private sector and of foreign governments in their fight against cybercrime.

[62] For the creation of a fund to finance class action lawsuits, see, for example, Section 27 of the Class Action Law 2006 (Israel).

A second solution is to allow public entities to undertake class action against cyberattackers. As noted in Section 7.2, in many of the states that recognize class action suits, public entities have the option of filing such suits.[63] As far as government entities are concerned, as opposed to NGOs, there is no need to create an incentive to sue, but what is needed is a public decision that this is an important public interest. This would make it possible to use public funds for identifying cyberattackers. It would naturally require recognition of the ability of public entities to engage in this activity, because in some countries, the ability of public organizations to file class action suits is limited to organizations whose objectives include the filing of such suits.[64]

These solutions emphasize the fact that the purposes of a class action against cyberattackers are not limited to the exercise of the plaintiffs' right of access the court, the provision of adequate relief to the victims, and the effective and fair management of the claims, because these objectives can be achieved even when only the company whose service has been harmed in a cyberattack is being sued. Class actions also against the cyberattackers themselves serve the purpose of deterring these attacks,[65] and when the cyberattacks are intended to damage the national infrastructure or security, they also serve national goals.[66]

---

[63] *Supra* note 1.

[64] *Ibid.* See, for example, Section 4(a)(2), (3) of the Class Action Law 2006 (Israel).

[65] *Supra* note 15 and the adjacent text. See also Brooks, *supra* note 36 at 345. The claim that criminal prosecution for online fraud as well as private legal actions serve as deterrents contributes to the security of online transactions, and is an integral part of an effective program to prevent cybercrime on the Web. See Ena, *supra* note 48. For the importance of deterrence of cyberattackers, see Cesare, *supra* note 36, at 163–164.

[66] See Section 7.4. For a discussion of US government efforts to prevent large-scale security breaches in collaboration with several authorities, as a matter of national security, see Marcus, *supra* note 28, at 575–579; for a discussion of the Computer Fraud and Abuse Act (CFAA), which includes US federal law provisions relating to computer damage related to unauthorized access to national security information, see Vasiu & Vasiu, *supra* note 31. On this and other laws that enable criminal legislation to protect computer data from harm, destruction, modification, or gaining access, and on allowing civil damages to be claimed for these damages, see Brooks, *supra* note 36, at 351–357. In this context, note another solution proposed for cases in which the cyberattack was carried out under the auspices of a foreign government. The proposed solution, given the difficulty in locating the cyberattackers themselves, is to sue the foreign state. To this end, an exception was proposed to

7.7. Summary

This chapter reviewed the mechanism of class action from a comparative standpoint, and the objectives of this mechanism, with emphasis on the deterrence aspect. The class action mechanism may also serve national policy goals, aiming to initiate a discussion regarding whether such mechanism could deter cyberattackers who are liable to harm the public and the national infrastructure. The bulk of class actions in case of cyberattacks was filed against companies whose service to their customers was compromised because of the cyberattack. These include Internet and software vendors responsible for spreading the virus, and vendors of security software that failed. At the same time, the option of filing class action suits against the cyberattackers themselves has not been realized. The chapter discussed the failures in filing a class action against the cyberattackers themselves and offered solutions to correct these failures, so that class actions may be filed against the cyberattackers themselves, thereby fulfilling the deterrent objective of class actions, as well as the objective of protecting national infrastructures from such attacks.

---

the Foreign Sovereign Immunities Act (FSIA), so that the foreign state can be sued for damages if a cyberattack conducted under its auspices; see Anderson, *supra* note 48.

Chapter 8

The Role of Non-State Actors in Cybersecurity International Cooperation

*Naomi Elimelech Shamra**

*International Treaties Department,
Ministry of Foreign Affairs, Jerusalem, Israel*

Naomi.ElimelechShamra@mfa.gov.il, Naomie@mfa.gov.il

Abstract

The evolution of communication technologies, while bringing unprecedented benefits, has created challenges in criminal justice and rule of law in the cyberspace. Internet technology has emerged as a facilitator for existing crimes and provided a new space for a new type of crimes that are computer and data related, such as crimes against infrastructures of cyberspace or crimes committed using cyberspace as a platform. Since in this field of cyberspace, many private companies, NGO's and other non-state actors play a major role and share various interests, it is crucial to examine the abilities and responsibilities of such actors under International Law.

* This chapter was originally written as part of the work at the International Treaties Department in the field of Cybercrime. The author would like to thank Adv. Maya Freund and David Padwa for their assistance in writing the chapter and Prof. Boaz Sanjero, Dr. Haim Vismonsky, Adv. Keren Shahar, Senior Deputy Legal Adviser in the MFA and Superintendent Elad (Bili) Blibaum, Head of Cyber Fusion Center, National Cyber Crime Unit at Israel Police, and Adv. Omry Levin for their insightful comments.

8.1. Introduction

The evolution of communication technologies, while bringing unprecedented benefits, created challenges in criminal justice and rule of law in the cyberspace. Internet technology has emerged as a facilitator for existing crimes and provided a new space for a new type of crimes that is computer and data related. Cybercrimes include using the Internet and other cyber systems to commit fraud, steal, and sell child pornography and other banned materials.[1]

Cybercrimes present many challenges. First, they are not confined by national boundaries, and digital evidence relating to one crime can be dispersed in multiple states. Second, the Internet allows the perpetrators to launch attacks anonymously and quickly disappear. Third, even when the perpetrator is located, the prosecution is not without challenges as there are jurisdictional issues to confront, given the multiplicity of countries potentially involved in cybercrimes.[2]

Tackling these challenges can only be achieved by international cooperation to conduct digital investigations and to locate and prosecute the perpetrator. Thus numerous international initiatives attempt to address the problems posed by the spread of criminal activity on computer networks and build a secure cyberspace, by facilitating a straightforward process to conduct digital cross-border investigations and attempting to eliminate "patches of the world where a cybercriminal is beyond the reach of the national laws."[3]

However, the differences in states' interests and their approaches on the protection of personal data raise obstacles to the conclusion of a global agreement. This situation led to the emergence of private actors' norm-shaping initiatives in an attempt to fill the gap between the need for a secure cyberspace and the absence of agreed international norms. This chapter attempts to examine the question of what role private companies should play in the development of cybersecurity norms.

---

[1] For an overview of cybercrimes, see: Moore, R. (2015). *Cybercrime: Investigating High-Technology Computer Crime*, 2nd Edition (London and New York: Routledge), pp. 4–12.
[2] For an overview of the challenges of cybercrime see Clough, J. (2015). *Principles of Cybercrime*, 2nd Edition (Cambridge: Cambridge University Press), pp. 5–9.
[3] Cerezo, A. I., J. Lopez and A. Patel (2007). "International cooperation to fight transnational cybercrime," in *Proceedings of the International 2nd Annual Workshop on Digital Forensics & Incident Analysis*, Samos, Greece, August 27, p. 13.

The chapter will first present the main convention on cybercrimes — the Convention on Cybercrime of the Council of Europe (hereinafter "the Budapest Convention") — and other selected initiatives on the state level. After presenting an overview of the obstacles to reach a global agreement, it will focus on the emergence of non-state actors in cybersecurity cooperation. Finally, it will discuss the role non-state actors should play in the development of cybersecurity norms by examining the role of private companies in international law, the predominance of non-state actors in cybersecurity that obliges States to take them into consideration, and the gain and limits of their integration into cybersecurity international cooperation. The main argument presented here is that non-state actors need to be part of the cybersecurity international cooperation but states should not lose sight that cybersecurity cooperation lies within their responsibility and should limit the influence of private companies to its benefits.

As a preliminary remark, it is important to distinguish between several key terms: the term "cybersecurity" refers to both "cyberattacks" and "cybercrimes." The term "cyberattacks" refers to attacks launched against the infrastructure of cyberspace. The term "cybercrimes" refers to crimes committed via cyberspace. This chapter focuses mainly on cybercrimes. Despite the fact that these terms are not interchangeable, similar methods and instruments may be used at times to combat both cybercrimes and cyberattacks.

8.2. The Budapest Convention and Other Selected States' Initiatives

The most comprehensive and the first multilateral instrument drafted to answer the challenges of cybercrimes is the Budapest Convention, which was opened for signature in Budapest in November 2001 to both member states of the Council of Europe and non-members. Sixty-three states are currently parties to the Convention. In addition to most EU countries, the US, Japan, Australia, Canada, Israel (since September 2016), and others have ratified the convention.[4]

The Budapest Convention is a criminal justice treaty which provides the states with three tools to fight cybercrimes: (1) the criminalization of several listed types of attacks against and by means of computers;

---

[4]Council of Europe Portal (2019). "Chart of signatures and ratification of Treaty 185 — Convention on Cybercrime." Available at: https://www.coe.int/en/web/conventions/full-list/-/conventions/treaty/185/signatures?p_auth=T3VZMbSZ (accessed on October 2020).

(2) procedural law tools to make the investigation of cybercrime and the securing of electronic evidence in relation to any crime more effective and subject to rule of law safeguards; and (3) international police and judicial cooperation on cybercrime and e-evidence.[5] The Convention does not create substantive criminal law offenses or legal procedures but requires parties to ensure that their domestic laws criminalize the offenses defined in the Convention, to ensure the states have the necessary procedural authorities to investigate and prosecute cybercrime offences effectively, and to provide international police and judicial cooperation to fight against cybercrime. The Convention also improves the cooperation between law enforcement agencies and Internet Service Providers (ISPs) by clarifying the situations in which government agents can request information from ISPs.[6]

The Budapest Convention defines nine offences: illegal access, illegal interception, data interference, system interference, misuse of devices, computer-related forgery, offences related to child pornography, and offences related to copyright and neighboring rights. Those offenses are grouped in four different categories: (1) offences against the confidentiality, integrity, and availability of computer data and systems; (2) computer-related forgery and fraud; (3) child pornography; (4) offences related to infringements of copyright and related rights.

In addition, the Budapest Convention sets out the procedural powers each party shall adopt — expedited preservation of stored data, expedited preservation and partial disclosure of traffic data, production order, search and seizure of stored computer data, real-time collection of traffic data, and interception of content data.

Furthermore, the Budapest Convention contains a jurisdiction provision and sets out the provisions concerning general principles relating to international cooperation, extradition, general principles and procedures pertaining to mutual assistance requests in the absence of applicable international agreements, and specific provisions on mutual assistance regarding provisional measures and regarding investigative powers. Article 35 provides for the setting up of a 24/7 network for ensuring the immediate

---

[5] Segev, A. (2016). "The Budapest Convention on Cybercrime: A framework for capacity building," *Global Forum on Cyber Expertise*, December 7.

[6] Moore, R. (2015). Cybercrime: *Investigating High-Technology Computer Crime*, 2nd Edition (London and New York: Routledge), p. 261.

assistance for the purpose of investigations of cybercrimes and the electronic collection of evidence of a criminal offence.

In June 2017, the Cybercrime Convention Committee (T-CY) approved the Terms of Reference for the preparation of the Second Additional Protocol during the period from September 2017 to December 2019 for more effective mutual legal assistance, direct cooperation between investigating teams and judicial authorities, and direct cooperation with service providers in other jurisdictions.[7]

As presented earlier, the Convention offers a number of significant tools for international cooperation against cybercrimes and allows States that do not have diplomatic relations to cooperate in the fight against cybercrimes. Every nation was invited to join the Budapest Convention, but as mentioned earlier, only 63 states have ratified it. Notable Council of Europe States — Ireland, the Russian Federation, and Sweden — have not ratified the Convention and only 19 non-members of Council of Europe have accessed the Convention. Therefore, the number of ratifications would need to increase significantly in order to prevent safe havens for cybercriminals.[8]

The Budapest Convention was followed by regional instruments promoting international cooperation and harmonization of national legislation, such as the African Union, the Arab League, and the Shanghai Cooperation Organization (SCO).[9] The Shanghai Code of Conduct was signed in 2009, following the repercussion of cyberattacks in Estonia in 2007 and prepared during the conflict in Georgia in 2008. It focuses on fighting terrorism, separatism, and extremism and identifies the following threats: (1) development and use of weapons of information and preparation to undertake information warfare; (2) information terrorism

---

[7]Recommendation for a Council Decision authorizing the participation in negotiations on a second Additional Protocol to the Council of Europe Convention on Cybercrime (CETS No. 185) (Brussels, 5/2/2019 *COM* (2019) 71 Final), p. 2. Available at: https://eur-lex.europa.eu/legal-content/EN/TXT/?uri=CELLAR:8d1e03fe-2939-11e9-8d04-01aa75ed71a1 (accessed on October 2020).

[8]On data safe havens see Geltzer, J. N. (2004). "The new Pirates of the Caribbean: How data havens can provide safe harbors on the internet beyond governmental reach," *Southwestern Journal of Law and Trade in the Americas*, 443–434.

[9]UNIDR (2017). "The United Nations, cyberspace and international peace and security: Responding to complexity in the 21st century," UNIDIR Resources, pp. 44–45. Available at: http://www.unidir.org/files/publications/pdfs/the-united-nations-cyberspace-and-international-peace-and-security-en-691.pdf (accessed on October 2020).

and information crime; (3) use of dominant position in cyberspace to the detriment of interests and security of other states; (4) dissemination of information harmful to political systems; and (5) natural and/or human threats to safe and stable operations of the global and national information infrastructure.[10] In September 2011, China, Russia, Tajikistan, and Uzbekistan submitted the Shanghai Code of Conduct to the UN General Assembly for consideration. It was then revised and resubmitted in January 2015 by these states as well as Kazakhstan and Kyrgyzstan, but the new draft of the Code was also rejected by the UN General Assembly.[11]

Another initiative dates from March 10, 2016, when the Permanent Council of the Organization for Security and Co-operation in Europe (OSCE), in which is party to 57 states, adopted Decision No. 1202 on OSCE confidence-building measures to reduce the risks of conflict stemming from the use of information and communication technologies.[12] This decision focuses on cooperation between participating states to effectively mitigate cyberattacks that can have the potential to affect more than one participating state. The decision builds on transparency measures adopted by the participating states in 2013 which established, among others, contact points to ensure rapid communication and adds measures of cooperation such as sharing information on cyberthreats, reporting of vulnerabilities, and developing (where appropriate) shared responses.

On November 12, 2018, French President Emmanuel Macron initiated the Paris Call in order to bring together states, private-sector entities, and international organizations on a consensus statement related to growing concerns about cyberthreats. It has been signed by more than 60 states and many non-government entities. The Call is non-binding but the signatories agreed on key principles such as the importance of cooperation to prevent and recover form malicious cyberactivities, the need to strengthen international defense against criminals, promote digital cooperation, and

---

[10]de Alcantara, B. T. (2018). "SCO and cybersecurity: Eastern security vision for cyberspace," *International Relations and Diplomacy*, **6**(10) (October): 553.

[11]Gechlik, M. (2017). "Appropriate norms of state behavior in cyberspace: Governance in China and opportunities for US businesses," *Aegis Series Paper* No. 1706, p. 4.

[12]Decision No. 1202 OSCE Confidence-Building Measures to Reduce the Risks of Conflict Stemming from the Use of Information and Communication Technologies, PC.DEC/1202 (March 10, 2016). Available at: https://www.osce.org/pc/227281?download=true (accessed on October 2020).

increase capacity-building efforts.[13] Although the Paris Call is non-binding and does not provide practical tools for fighting cybercrimes, it illustrates the critical importance of international cooperation in the ongoing battle against cybercrimes.

The multiple national, regional, and international cybersecurity strategies over the last decade demonstrate the growing awareness of the need to a secure cyberspace and the need to set norms. However, the number of agreements or initiatives also demonstrates that a global agreement on how to govern cybersecurity is difficult to attain.

8.3. The Obstacles to a Global Agreement

The question of a global convention was discussed at the 12th United Nations Congress of the Commission on Crime Prevention and Criminal Justice (CCPCJ) in 2010. However, there was limited consensus among 45 states on the most appropriate way forward. Some states advocated for the use of current developed international law framework and globalizing the Budapest Convention with minor adaptation whereas others, which were not parts of the original drafting, including the Russian Federation and the BRICS, objected to signing a convention in which they had not been involved in the drafting. Another source of disagreement was the provisions relating to cross-border access to data to which those same states objected on procedural and substantive grounds.[14]

The 2010 CCPCJ resulted in a General Assembly Resolution that called for an intergovernmental group to study the problem of cybercrime and international response to it. Five sessions of the open-ended working group have been held in 2011, 2013, 2017, 2018, and 2019, and the reports from the second, third and fourth sessions of the CCPCJ Expert Group show that there are persistent disagreements among states.[15] According to the 2018 session of the CCPCJ Expert Group, some speakers were of the opinion that the Budapest Convention provides state parties with an effective legal and operational framework for addressing

---

[13] See: "Cybersecurity: Paris Call of 12 November 2018 for trust and security in cyberspace," *France Diplomatie*. Available at: https://pariscall.international/en/ (accessed on October 2020).

[14] UNIDR, *supra* note 9 at 44.

[15] *Ibid.*

cybercrime, while others viewed the Budapest Convention as a regional instrument that did not address the concerns of all member states.[16] States have their own particular interests and different concerns, especially with the emergence of cyberwarfare, which has given cybercrime a national security dimension that makes cooperation more difficult.[17] One of the main points of disagreement focus on the balance between security and the protection of personal data. For example, the European Union States seek to pursue strong safeguards for the protection of fundamental rights and freedoms of EU citizens. Those rights include privacy and personal data protection when personal data or electronic communications data is disclosed to law enforcement authorities in countries outside the European Union.[18]

Furthermore, states are protective of their domestic criminal law, and while some level of consensus may be achieved in respect of offences against the person and property, crimes against the state and against morality are more problematic.[19]

The Western notion of cybersecurity is also different from that of China and Russia. For example, the Shanghai Code of Conduct uses the concept of "information security" rather than "cybersecurity." The main points of divergence include the dominant position of some states in the cyberspace, the role of government in the management of cyberspace, citizens' privacy, and the application of international law to cyberwarfare.[20]

To sum up, although there is an understanding that a global convention would profit a secure cyberspace, the contrasting interests and perceptions of cybersecurity are evident obstacles to reaching a global agreement.

---

[16]Report on the meeting of the Expert Group to Conduct a Comprehensive Study on Cybercrime, held in Vienna from 3 to 5 April 2018, E/CN.15/2018/12. Available at: https://undocs.org/E/CN.15/2018/12 (accessed on October 2020).

[17]Jakobi, A. P. (2013). "Emergence and diffusion of global anti-crime regulations," in *Common Goods and Evils: The Formation of Global Crime Governance* p. 25.

[18]Recommendation for a Council Decision authorizing the participation in negotiations on a second Additional Protocol to the Council of Europe Convention on Cybercrime, *supra* note 7 at 6–7.

[19]Clough, *supra* note 2, at 24.

[20]https://carnegieendowment.org/2019/01/24/chinese-american-relations-in-cyberspace-toward-collaboration-or-confrontation-pub-78213 (accessed on October 2020).

8.4. The Emergence of Non-state Actors in Shaping Cybersecurity Norms

As states have not yet succeeded in reaching a global agreement, private-sectors actors, ISPs, and multinational information corporations (such as Microsoft, Google, Facebook) and private cybersecurity firms have begun to engage intensively with building cybersecurity norms. They have proposed at least eight initiatives in the years 2016–2017 and engaged with normative issues that traditionally are in the exclusive realm of states.[21] The prime examples of those initiatives are the Microsoft's "From Articulation to Implementation: Enabling Progress on Cybersecurity Norms" and the call for a Digital Geneva Convention (DGC).

In December 2014, Microsoft launched a report, "International Cybersecurity Norms — Reducing Conflict in an Internet-dependent World," proposing six initial cybersecurity norms to limit conflict in cyberspace. Microsoft declared that by publishing this paper, it "seeks to invigorate the debate" on cybersecurity. Microsoft stated that it attempts to put forward a framework for developing two types of norms: (1) for improving defenses by providing a foundation for national cybersecurity and international structures to increase understanding between states and (2) for limiting conflict or offensive operations to avoid conflicts in cyberspace.[22] In July 2016, Microsoft issued a follow-up paper: "From Articulation to Implementation: Enabling Progress on Cybersecurity Norms" on how the suggested norms should be implemented,[23] addressing the state and the Internet industry behaviors.[24]

---

[21] Housen-Couriel, D. (2017). "An analytical review and comparison of operative measures included in cyber diplomatic initiatives," in *Briefings from the Research Advisory Group* (New Delhi: Global Commission on the Stability of Cyberspace), p. 51. Available at: https://cyberstability.org/wp-content/uploads/2017/12/GCSC-Briefings-from-the-Research-Advisory-Group_New-Delhi-2017.pdf (accessed on October 2020).

[22] "International cybersecurity norms: Reducing conflict in an internet-dependent world," Microsoft. Available at: https://www.microsoft.com/en-us/cybersecurity/content-hub/reducing-conflict-in-Internet-dependent-world (accessed on October 2020).

[23] Microsoft (2016). "From articulation to implementation: Enabling progress on cybersecurity norms," June. Available at: https://www.microsoft.com/en-us/cybersecurity/content-hub/enabling-progress-on-cybersecurity-norms (accessed on October 2020).

[24] Henriksen, A. (2019). "The end of the road for the UN GGE process: The future regulation of cyberspace," *Journal of Cybersecurity*, **5**(1). Available at: https://doi.org/10.1093/cybsec/tyy009 (accessed on October 2020).

Furthermore, in February 2017, Microsoft initiated a call for DGC. The DGC encompasses three proposals: (1) an attribution organization that would analyze cybercrimes and cyberattacks and identify the perpetrators; (2) an industry agreement to create a shared set of principles and behaviors that would protect citizens; and (3) a mechanism to create binding rules for states.[25] The purpose of the Convention is to "commit government to implement the norms that have been developed to protect civilians on the internet in times of peace." Microsoft draws a parallel between the Fourth Geneva Convention, relying on the Red Cross to help protect civilians and the need for the "active assistance of the tech sector" in cybersecurity.[26]

In both initiatives, Microsoft perceives itself as the frontrunner in the field of cybersecurity. As such, it believes that the international community should attribute great importance to its views on cybersecurity-related issues. Microsoft acknowledges the role of states within the international system, but asks that they adopt a policy that would address the security concerns of users, as opposed to the states' economic interests.

The DGC was followed in 2018 by the publication of a "Practical guide — Cybersecurity Policy Framework" which according to its first chapter, is "designed for policy-makers involved in the development of cybersecurity regulations," and aspires "to provide a practical guide to the specific areas of cybersecurity regulation that policy-makers are currently most focused on." Microsoft claims that its guide has an "unrivaled vantage point on digital security" since its products are used by billions of people around the world, which means they often serve as the "first line of defense" against cybercrimes.[27] The Guide proposes, among other measures, the establishment and empowerment of a national cybersecurity agency, the development and update of cybercrime laws, and an international strategy for cybersecurity. The Guide suggests that a set of

---

[25] Vázquez Llorente, R. (2018). "A Digital Geneva Convention? The role of the private sector in cybersecurity," *LSE IDEAS*, May 20.

[26] Smith, B. (2017). "The need for a Digital Geneva Convention," *Microsoft*, February 14. Available at: https://blogs.microsoft.com/on-the-issues/2017/02/14/need-digital-geneva-convention/ (accessed on October 2020).

[27] "Cybersecurity Policy Framework," Microsoft, p. 7. Available at: https://www.microsoft.com/en-us/cybersecurity/content-hub/Cybersecurity-Policy-Framework (accessed on October 2020).

additional cybersecurity norms where existing rules are unclear or fall short in protecting civilians "should be informed not just by governments, but also by civil society and the private sector."[28] Namely, Microsoft demands that private companies be a significant partner in the development of cybersecurity norms.

Another example of non-state actors' initiative is the Cybersecurity Tech Accords, which is a public commitment shared by more than 100 companies to improve the security of cyberspace. As part of the Accords, the companies commit themselves to "support civil society, governments and international organizations in their efforts to advance security in cyberspace and to build cybersecurity capacity in developed and emerging economies alike."[29]

Furthermore, non-state actors take part in state initiatives such as the Paris Call described earlier and participate in international forums alongside states. As an example, the Global Conference on Cyber Space (GCCS), an annual Internet policy event where state representatives meet up with other actors to discuss various cyber issues, including norms for responsible behavior in cyberspace, has led to the launch of the Global Forum on Cyber Expertise (GFCE) in 2015. The GFCE is an informal platform for states, international organizations, and private companies to identify successful policies, practices, and ideas and multiply these on a global level, and the members must adhere to "The Hague Declaration on the GFCE." The GFCE focuses on cyber capacity-building in five different themes — cybersecurity policy and strategy, cyberincident management and critical infrastructure protection, cybercrime, cybersecurity culture and skills, and cybersecurity standards.[30]

Apart from acts with legislative character, there is a new tendency among the companies to attempt to gain semi-judicial authority. For example, Facebook has taken measures towards establishing a "supreme court" which will address cardinal issues regarding the platform it provides, mainly in prohibited content.[31] This, of course, provides an example

---

[28] "Cybersecurity Policy Framework," *supra* note 27, at 35.

[29] "Cybersecurity Tech Accord." Available at: https://cybertechaccord.org/accord/ (accessed on October 2020).

[30] See the Global Forum on Cyber Expertise website. Available at: https://thegfce.org/ (accessed on October 2020).

[31] https://csrcl.huji.ac.il/blog/facebooks-supreme-court (accessed on October 2020).

of the essential role the companies play in the international legal matter of cyberspace.

As the private sector is leading or participating in the development of international norms in the fight against cybercrime, it raises the question as to what should be the role for non-state actors in cybersecurity international cooperation.

8.5. What Role should Non-state Actors Play in Cybersecurity International Cooperation?

After stressing that private companies already participate to a certain extent in international law development, this section will attempt to demonstrate that the significant role of private companies in cybersecurity empowers them to play a certain role in the development of agreed international cybersecurity norms. Yet, the question of the extent of their involvement should be answered with respect to the gains and the limits of their participation.

8.5.1. *Private companies and treaty-making in international law*

Private companies exercise increasing influence in the creation of international norms, whereas classical international law and, specifically the law of treaties, only recognize the interaction of sovereign states. A party to a treaty, according to the 1969 Vienna Convention on the Law of Treaties,[32] is "a State which expressed its consent to be bound ... and for which the treaty is in force" (Article 2, para. 1). However, the role of international organizations has expanded as a result of the international community's need to attain the goals that states could not reach alone.[33] Treaty-making by international organization had become so widespread that in 1986, a second Vienna Convention on the Law of Treaties was drafted.[34] In the text

---

[32]Vienna Convention on the Law of Treaties, 1155 UNTS 331, 8 ILM 679, *entered into force* January 27, 1980.

[33]Charney, J. I. (1983). "Transnational corporations and developing public international law," *Duke Law Journal*, **1983**: 759.

[34]Vienna Convention on the Law of Treaties between States and International Organization, March 21, 1986, 25 ILM 543 (1986).

of the 1986 Vienna Convention, a party to a treaty is expressed as follows: "a party means a State or an international organization which has consented to be bound by a treaty and for which the treaty is in force" (Article 2, para. 1). Those definitions relate therefore only to a state or an international organization, in accordance with our concept of an international community made up of sovereign States.[35] This view was expressed in the Anglo-Iranian Oil Company case, where the International Court of Justice (ICJ) did not recognize an agreement between a corporation and a State as a treaty,[36] while it considered the question if the ICJ would have jurisdiction over an agreement between a private company and the State of Iran.[37]

However, there have been growing participation of non-state actors in international law. In the Libyan oil arbitrations of the 1970s, the arbitration tribunal determined that private actors who enter into relationships with states can choose to have those governed by international law (in place of or as a supplement to national law).[38] This found recognition in the establishment of the International Centre for the Settlement of Investment Disputes (ICSID), and in treaties providing for referral of private/states disputes to ICSID.[39] The growing participation of non-state actors also came to occur in the decision-making process leading to the conclusion of a treaty. Representatives of the private sectors are occasionally, at the request of a government, part to national delegations to conferences that negotiate and adopt treaties. In the International Labor Organization (ILO), national delegations include private representatives who may act independently of their governments. Furthermore, private actors have also come to be observers in multilateral treaty

---

[35] Schreuer, C. (1993). "The waning of the sovereign state: Towards a new paradigm for international law?" *European Journal of International Law*, **4**: 447–471.

[36] Anglo-Iranian Oil Co. (U.K. v. Iran), Judgment, 1952 ICJ Rep. 93, 112 (July 22).

[37] Some have argued that since a corporation cannot be a party to the ICJ Statute, the case was easily dismissed, but the dismissal of the case cannot necessarily be understood as a refusal to consider the Anglo-Iranian Oil Company as an international legal person. See: Worster, W. T. (2016). "Relative international legal personality of non-state actors," *Brooklyn Journal of International Law*, **42**(1): 244.

[38] Award on the Merits in Dispute Between Texaco Overseas Petroleum Company and the Government of the Libyan Arab Republic, 17 ILM 1 (1978).

[39] Brand, R. A. (1994). "External Sovereignty and International Law," *Fordham International Law Journal* **18**(5): 1692.

conferences, speaking, making proposals, and influencing the negotiation's outcome.[40]

Moreover, some entities, not constituted solely by States, have been responsible for the shaping of international norms and are considered to have some degree of functional international personality. For example, the World Anti-Doping Agency (WADA), is responsible for the World Anti-Doping Code harmonizing anti-doping standards across sports.[41] WADA was set up as a foundation under the initiative of the International Olympic Committee with the support and participation of intergovernmental organizations, governments, public authorities, and other public and private bodies fighting doping in sport. It consists of equal representatives from the Olympic Movement and public authorities.[42] Another example is the International Air Transport Association (IATA), which represents 290 airlines in 120 countries and has developed global commercial standards upon which the air transport industry is based.[43] Some have argued that the logical outcome of the increasing role of non-state actors in the treaty making would be an opening up of the treaty process for non-state actors to the extent that they assume the functions covered by the treaty, and that we need to substantively adjust our way of thinking about treaty law.[44]

In addition, the UN issued a number of reports and studies on the duties and responsibilities of business corporations under international law. Two notable reports are the "Norms on the Responsibility of Transnational Corporations and Other Business Enterprises with Regard to Human Rights" by the UN Sub-Commission on the Promotion and Protection of Human Rights on 13 August 2003,[45] and the "Promotion of All Human Rights, Civil, Political, Economic, Social and Cultural Rights, Including the Right to Development," released in 2009 by the UN

---

[40]Hollis, D. B. (2002). "Private actors in public international law: Amicus curiae and the case for the retention of state sovereignty," *Boston College International and Comparative Law Review*, **25**(2): 243–245.

[41]Worster, *supra* note 37, at 247.

[42]See World Anti-Doping Agency website. Available at: https://www.wada-ama.org/en/who-we-are (accessed on October 2020).

[43]Worster, *supra* note 37, at 247. See G.A. Res. 84 (1), annex A (Dec. 11, 1946).

[44]Schreuer, *supra* note 35, p. 458. See also Worster, *supra* note 37.

[45]UN Sub-Commission on the Promotion and Protection of Human Rights, "Norms on the Responsibilities of Transnational Corporations and other Business Enterprises with Regard to Human Rights," UN Doc E/CN.4/Sub.2/2003/12/Rev.2 (2003).

Secretary-General.[46] Both reports represented important steps in the process of considering whether and how to regulate the conduct of transnational corporations under international law.[47] Furthermore, in recent years, the International Law Commission (ILC) has started to address non-state actors due to their increasingly significant role in the international scene.[48] One of the main arguments to recognize private companies as international legal subjects is the need of international law to adapt itself to the changes on the international scene in order to preserve its relevance and effectiveness, and thus the need to set the relations between all the *de facto* powerful entities and not only between states and international organizations.[49]

Although the states are reluctant to accept private companies participation in international law, these developments demonstrate that private companies already participate to a certain extent in international law development[50] and contribute to the "inherent heterogeneity of modern partnerships in international law-making."[51]

8.5.2. *The predominance of private companies in cybersecurity*

Private companies play a crucial role in cybersecurity. First, cybercrimes are committed mostly on private companies' servers and infrastructure;

---

[46]UN Human Rights Council, Special Representative of the Secretary-General on the Issue of Human Rights and Transnational Corporations and other Business Enterprises, "promotion of all human rights, civil, political, economic, social and cultural rights, including the right to development," UN Doc A/HRC/11/13 (2009).

[47]Ku, J. G. (2012). "The limits of corporate rights under international law," *Chicago Journal of International Law* **12**: 736. Available at: https://scholarlycommons.law.hofstra. edu/faculty_scholarship/76 (accessed on October 2020).

[48]Zyberi, G. (2011). "Non-state actors from the perspective of the international law commission," in J. D'Aspremont (ed.), *Participants in the International Legal System: Multiple Perspectives on Non-State Actors in International Law* (New York and London: Routledge). Available at: https://www.researchgate.net/publication/256047923_Non-State_Actors_ from_the_Perspective_of_the_International_Law_Commission (accessed on October 2020).

[49]See Nowrot, K. (1993). "New approaches to the international legal personality of multinational corporations towards a rebuttal presumption of normative responsibilities," 8–10. Available at: http://esil-sedi.eu/wp-content/uploads/2018/04/Nowrot.pdf (accessed on October 2020).

[50]Charney, *supra* note 33, at 761–762.

[51]Dupuy, P.-M. (2005). "Proliferation of actors," in R. Wolfrum and V. Röben (eds.), *Developments of International Law in Treaty Making* (Heidelberg: Max Planck Institute), p. 541.

hence, it is their interest and ability to equip their tools with protection from cybercrimes. Consequently, protection from cybercrimes is primarily provided by private companies through defensive measures such as anti-virus and equipment design, immediate and effective response to the crime when identified, and the creation of firewalls around systems.[52] In addition to the private companies' technical ability to offer protection from cybercrimes, they play a bottom-up role in reaching international agreements, while private companies' needs for secure cyberspace lead to states' initiatives.

Furthermore, private companies play an essential role in law enforcement since they possess the digital evidence stored on their servers. This predominance of private companies in the fight against cybercrimes can be illustrated by the enactment of the American Clarifying Lawful Overseas Use of Data Act (the Cloud Act) which puts new obligations on American electronic communications providers to preserve and disclose customer data stored in foreign states with those providers or subsidiaries. The Cloud Act was enacted following the Microsoft–Ireland case,[53] which began in December 2013, when the US government asked Microsoft, in accordance with a court order, to provide the US government with the contents of the email box of a suspect of trafficking dangerous drugs. Upon receipt of the order, the company refused to comply with the order because the content of the electronic box was found in the company's servers that were stored outside of the US, in Ireland. The Federal Court of Appeals overturned the decision of the lower courts and ruled that the order was given without authority, since it was an extra-territorial act.

In response, the US has enacted the Cloud Act to confirm that the US government may obtain data stored abroad, even without an agreement between the states. In addition, the Cloud Act empowers the executive branch to enter into new executive agreements with foreign governments which will allow, under some circumstances, foreign governments to obtain data stored by American Internet companies. The Cloud Act highlights that companies are such important players in cybersecurity that in

---

[52] Sofaer, A. D., D. Clark and W. Diffie (2010). "Cyber security and international agreements," in *Proceedings of a Workshop on Deterring Cyberattacks: Informing Strategies and Developing Options for U.S. Policy* (Washington, D.C.: The National Academies Press), p. 183. Available at: http://cs.brown.edu/courses/cs180/sources/lec17/Sofaer.pdf (accessed on October 2020).

[53] United States v. Microsoft Corp., 584 US (2018).

order to obtain data stored abroad, they had to be addressed directly, and not the states where the data is stored.[54]

Moreover, there are many voices in recent years claiming that even companies that provides cybersecurity may have corporate social responsibility. Cybersecurity can be perceived as an "environmental condition" rather than a mere service that companies provide to their customers. One of the justifications for this position is that providing cybersecurity creates "herd immunity" that provides protection for non-customers too, and consequentially reduces sharply the number of vulnerable targets in the system.[55]

In light of their crucial position in cybersecurity, private companies' existence in cybersecurity cooperation cannot be disregarded. The question of the extent of their involvement should be answered in accordance with the gains and the limits of such participation.

8.5.3. *The benefits of private companies' participation in cybersecurity cooperation*

The tools and experience of private companies can greatly contribute to cybersecurity cooperation to prevent cybercrimes. First, private companies can facilitate the exchange of information to help reduce the number, diversity, duration, and impact of attacks, and coordinate vulnerability responses, thus improving practical cooperation within and among the states.

Second, private-sector entities have developed great expertise in cybercrimes, and their support and involvement can improve the prospect that policies and rules proposed internationally will reflect professional opinion rather than political objectives.[56] Furthermore, the participation by private companies can make the rule-making process more realistic and the result more acceptable to the parties, hence increasing the likelihood

---

[54]The Microsoft Case is not the first case to involve alleged claims for extra-territoriality on cyber issues. A similar claim was made, e.g. in La Ligue Contre Le Racisme et l'Antisemitisme v. Yahoo!, Inc., 379 F.3d 1120 (9th Cir., 2004). In the Yahoo! case, the court ruled that the French court cannot gain jurisdiction over the American Yahoo!, and therefore the American Yahoo! is not committed to its decision.

[55]Shackelford, S. (2017). "Exploring the 'shared responsibility' of cyber peace: Should cybersecurity be a human right?" *Indiana University Kelley School of Business Research Paper*, pp. 23–24.

[56]Sofaer, *supra* note 52, at 202.

that the rules will be successfully implemented.[57] More than three decades ago, Charney already called for more involvement of business groups in developing public international law, as "substantial business participation in the development of relevant international rule is both possible and desirable."[58] Among other examples, he referred to the Organization for Economic Cooperation and Development (OECD) as "another intergovernmental organization that can attribute part of its success to frequent consultation with business and labor groups."[59]

Third, private-sector involvement in cybersecurity cooperation can assist to fill the void in global consensus. Ideally, their involvement can increase their commitment to cybersecurity, resulting in promises to prevent from storing data in safe havens.

Finally, private companies' experience can contribute to the monitoring of norms. It has been suggested that an international treaty could establish a specialized agency to regulate cybersecurity in a manner that will preserve the private-sector influence over the development of cybersystem rules.[60]

8.5.4. *The limits of private companies' participation in cybersecurity cooperation*

The increasingly significant role of multinational corporations as actors on the international scene results in not only opportunities but also risks to the promotion of public interests.[61] As presented earlier, private companies could effectively contribute to cybersecurity international regulation, but on the other hand, they have the potential to promote their own interests at the expense of the general interests.

Unlike states whose primary interest is to provide protection for the citizens, private companies are motivated by their own incentives, the first being maximizing profit.[62] Therefore, private companies engage with partners in order to harvest the economic and other benefits of the engagement and not for the sake of providing security, even when they

---

[57]Charney, *supra* note 33, at 755.

[58]*Ibid.*, p.779.

[59]*Ibid.*, p. 778.

[60]Sofaer, *supra* note 52, at 202.

[61]Karsten Nowrot, *supra* note, at 2.

[62]Friedmann, W. (1962). "The changing dimensions of international law," *Columbia Law Review*, **62**: 13–14.

may act out of social responsibility. In this respect, citizens' security is a core task of the state and is too much of a delicate matter for the state to pass this responsibility to the private sector.[63]

Private companies fear that law enforcement considerations and government control of the information structure will affect and burden Internet businesses. They seek to prevent restrictions on Internet users, limitations on the use and sale of advanced encryption, and demands to record Internet traffic,[64] whereas those measures could sometimes be necessary for the prevention of cybercrimes and prosecuting perpetrators. For example, the enacting of the Cloud Act originated from the clash between the need of the US enforcement agencies to seize evidence stored by Microsoft, and Microsoft's refusal to hand in that data, despite Microsoft's attempts to lead the development of cybersecurity norms and initiated the Digital Geneva Convention for a secure cyberspace. While the Cloud Act highlights the crucial role of private companies in cybersecurity, it also emphasizes the need for states to preserve the role of providing security and leading the development of the norms in the fight against cybercrimes.

Furthermore, the role of non-private actors in cybersecurity cooperation cannot be examined in a void, but as part of the general discourse on whether the increasing influence of private companies' status in international cooperation erodes state sovereignty. This concern may be answered by the fact that states maintain the authority to determine who may participate in the process of adoption of treaty and the private-actor participation can only occur with the consent of the state.[65] Yet, as formulated by Duncan B. Hollis, "in admitting or expanding roles for private actors in public international law, one cannot lose sight of the need to ensure that the system maintains its legitimacy with respect to its existing actors–states."[66]

---

[63] Cavelty, M. D. and M. Suter (2009). "Public-private partnerships are no silver bullet: An expanded governance model for critical infrastructure protection," *International Journal of Critical Infrastructure Protection*, **2**(4): 181.

[64] Sofaer, A. D. and S. E. Goodman (2000). "A proposal for an international convention on cyber crime and terrorism [Draft]," Center for International Security and Cooperation (CISAC), Hoover Institution, p. 6. Available at: https://www.researchgate.net/publication/267551044_A_Proposal_for_an_International_Convention_on_Cyber_Crime_and_Terrorism (accessed on October 2020).

[65] See Hollis, *supra* note 40.

[66] *Ibid.*, p. 255.

In light of the above-mentioned example, the *de facto* influential position of private companies in cybersecurity should not result in their blind integration into the cybersecurity international cooperation and states should avoid giving them undue leverage.

8.6. Conclusion

In conclusion, non-state actors are among the most influential participants in cybersecurity, being endowed with a potential to not only contribute but also shape norms that do not promote public interests. In view of this ambivalent potential of multinational corporations in shaping norms, and taking into account their cardinal role in enforcing them, a balance should be found between the advantages and the shortcomings of the influence of the private companies in cybersecurity cooperation. On one hand, the preparatory work of a comprehensive cybersecurity agreement needs to involve private companies to benefit from their special expertise and their ability to effectively respond to cybercrimes. Member states at the 2018 meeting of the Expert Group to Conduct a Comprehensive study on Cybercrimes suggested that "Member States should foster strong and trustworthy public-private cooperation in the field of cybercrime, including cooperation between law enforcement authorities and communication service providers. Engaging in a dialogue with private industry, accompanied by public-private partnerships where possible and memorandums of understanding where needed, is also required to strengthen and facilitate cooperation."[67] On the other hand, while an increasing number of cybersecurity negotiations are initiated outside intergovernmental forums, it should be remembered that primary interest of private companies is not to provide security. Hence, states should be cautious and mitigate the influence of those companies on the cybersecurity norms by structuring their role in cybersecurity cooperation as part of states' initiatives, as opposed to adopting norms formulated in independent initiatives. Private companies' involvement is more appropriate in consultation to formulating the norms in international law regarding cybersecurity and assisting the states in the enforcement of these norms.

---

[67]Report on the meeting of the Expert Group to Conduct a Comprehensive Study on Cybercrime, *supra* note 67, p. 4.

Chapter 9

The INF Treaty and New START: Escalation Control, Strategic Fatalism, and the Role of Cyber

Stephen J. Cimbala

Political Science, Penn State Brandywine,
Media, Pennsylvania, USA

sjc2@psu.edu

Abstract

The fate of the Intermediate Nuclear Forces (Treaty) originally signed in 1987 between the US and the Soviet Union now appears sealed. US and Russian compliance with the INF Treaty ended in August 2019. INF withdrawal is significant not only for immediate force sizes and structures but also for the dynamics of nuclear deterrence in Europe and Asia. Nowadays and going forward, the assessment of nuclear forces will be based on their agility, flexibility, and responsiveness to diverse circumstances of nuclear crisis management or of limited deterrence failure. As such, the significance of "cyber" grows accordingly: the "smartness" of deterrent forces, including their suitability for escalation control and conflict termination, depends upon their information-dependent system integrity and resilience, especially if the template is complicated by the addition of missile defenses to the equation.

9.1. Introduction

Political leaders in Russia and the US have pronounced the Intermediate Nuclear Forces (INF) Treaty a dead letter.[1] The possibility of a slowdown or even retrenchment in US–Russian nuclear arms control cannot be excluded.[2] The decision to jettison the INF agreement, and the implications of that decision for the New START agreement, are often discussed in terms of alleged US or Russian violations of technical protocols. This perspective is important, but insufficient. In the following discussion, we first consider the assumption of a world without INF and its implications for deterrence stability and escalation control in Europe. Second, we discuss the New START treaty, which could be taken hostage by US–Russian confrontation in a post-INF world. Third, we assess the significance of US missile defenses as potential wildcards in determining the probable degree of US–Russian strategic nuclear stability with, or without, New START and INF agreements in place. Crossing over all these topics is the increasing future significance of military cyber technologies, including offensive and defensive exploitation of the electronic spectrum, and its implications for nuclear deterrence stability.

9.2. The INF Imbroglio

President Donald Trump and US Secretary of State Mike Pompeo announced that the US would withdraw from the INF Treaty in 2019. Signed in 1987 between the US and the Soviet Union, the agreement was

---

[1] The full name of the INF treaty is the Treaty Between the United States of America And The Union Of Soviet Socialist Republics On The Elimination of Their Intermediate-Range and Shorter-Range Missiles. The treaty includes ground-launched ballistic or cruise missiles with ranges from 500 to 5,500 km, whether nuclear or conventionally armed. The treaty was signed by the US President Ronald Reagan and Soviet General Secretary Mikhail Gorbachev on December 8, 1987.

[2] Expert assessments include: Tobey, W., P. S. Zolotarev, and U. Kuhn (2019). "The INF quandary: Preventing a nuclear arms race in Europe — Perspectives from the U.S., Russia and Germany," *Russia Matters*, Issue Brief, January, Belfer Center for Science and International Affairs, Harvard Kennedy School, https://www.russiamatters.org (accessed on October 2020).; and Pifer, S. (2018). "Is there a glimmer of hope for the INF Treaty?" Brookings, December 27, in *Johnson's Russia List* 2019 — #2 — January 3. Available at: davidjohnson@starpower.net

a milestone in nuclear arms control, requiring both NATO and the Soviet Union to remove from Europe all land-based ballistic and cruise missiles with estimated ranges between 500 and 5,500 km. The Trump announcement of US plans to withdraw from the INF agreement was preceded by US charges (by the Obama and Trump Administrations) that Russia was out of compliance with the terms of the treaty due to its deployment of the SSC-8 ground-launched cruise missile (Russian 9M729). Russia has denied violations and has accused the US of having deployed missile defense systems in Europe that could be repurposed as offensive strike systems within the treaty-prohibited ranges.[3]

Critics of Trump's decision to withdraw from the INF Treaty expressed concern not only about the agreement per se but also about the implications of US abrogation for the larger climate of US–Russian nuclear arms control. A deteriorating relationship as between the US and Russia over INF could spill over into disagreement over the extension of the New START agreement for strategic nuclear arms limitation signed in 2010. Failure to extend New START for five years in 2021 would leave

---

[3] For background and perspective, see: Korb, L. J. (2018). "Why it could (but shouldn't) be the end of the arms control era," *Bulletin of the Atomic Scientists*, October 23. Available at: https://thebulletin.org/2018/10/why-it-could-but-shouldnt-be-the-end-of-the-arms-control-era/ (accessed on October 2020). See also: Gordon, M. R. (2019). "Russia warns U.S. moves threaten 2011 nuclear pact," *Wall Street Journal, January* 15 in *Johnson's Russia List* 2019 — #9, January 15. Available at: davidjohnson@starpower.net; and Grove, T. (2018). "Putin threatens arms race as U.S. proposes to exit nuclear treaty," *Wall Street Journal*, December 6, in *Johnson's Russia List* 2018 — #212 — December 6; Podvig, P. (2018). "Russia insists it is in compliance with the INF Treaty," *Russian Strategic Nuclear Forces*, November 26, in *Johnson's Russia List* 2018 — #212 — December 6; Gladstone, R. (2018). "In bipartisan pleas, experts urge Trump to save nuclear treaty with Russia," *New York Times*, November 8, in *Johnson's Russia List* 2018 — #196 — November 8; Stefanovich, D. and M. Chalmers (2018). "Is this the end of nuclear arms control?" Russia International Affairs Council and Royal United Services Institute, November 12. Available at: https://rusi.org/publication/newsbrief/end-nuclear-arms-control (accessed on October 2020); Trenin, D. (2018). "Back to Pershings: What the U.S. withdrawal from the 1987 INF Treaty means," Carnegie Moscow Center, October 24, in *Johnson's Russia List* 2018 — #186 — October 24; Pifer, S. (2018). "The Trump administration is preparing a major mistake on the INF Treaty," Brookings Institution, October 19, in *Johnson's Russia List* 2018 — #185 — October 23; and Simmons, A. N., T. Grove and C. McBride (2018). "Russian officials slam trump's plans to exit nuclear treaty," *Wall Street Journal*, October 22, in *Johnson's Russia List* 2018 — #184 — October 22.

the world's two nuclear superpowers without a reliable regime for limiting the numbers of nuclear warheads deployed on missiles of intercontinental range and on heavy bombers. In addition, New START provides for inspections to verify the status of deployed warheads and launchers for each state, increasing the transparency of each state's deployments, and therefore contributing to mutual trust.

Another by-product of discarding New START and INF could be an open-ended nuclear arms race with respect to deployments of strategic and non-strategic nuclear weapons (NSNW) in Europe and Asia.[4] Russia has been skeptical of INF restrictions for many years, as China and other states increased their deployments of intermediate and shorter-range ballistic missiles, while Russia's arsenal remained a treaty-compliant nullity. Trump Administration officials have also noted China's growing inventory of ballistic missiles as one reason for their decision to withdraw from the INF treaty. According to experts, China views its land-based missiles armed with conventional warheads as "a pillar of their warfighting strategy" and useful across the spectrum of conflict.[5] As Jacob Stokes has noted:

> China plans to threaten or use its conventional missile arsenal against both regional countries and U.S. military assets and bases in Asia in the event of a future regional conflict, including one over Taiwan or islands in the East or South China seas. If such a conflict were to occur, experts assess China would use its conventional missiles to destroy its opponent's key military targets, starting with reconnaissance and early warning, command and control and air defenses, before moving on to missile sites, aircraft and ships.[6]

As a non-signatory to the INF treaty, China has no legal obligation to limit its development and deployment of ballistic missiles over any ranges. US foreign and defense strategy as well as nuclear posture

---

[4] Gorbachev, M. and G. P. Shultz (2018). "We participated in INF negotiations. Abandoning it threatens our very existence," *Washington Post*, December 5 in *Johnson's Russia List* 2018 — #212 — December 6.

[5] Stokes, J. and A. Blivas (2019). "China's missile program and potential U.S. withdrawal from the Intermediate-Range Nuclear Forces (INF) Treaty," U.S.-China Economic and Security Review Commission, January 28.

[6] *Ibid.*, p. 4.

statements are focused on Russia and China as the principal threats to US and allied security — along with Iran and North Korea as important but lesser threats.[7]

Possible side effects from removing the constraints of INF include not only an arms race in regional nuclear and missile deployments but also an unintentional blowback that reduces effective decision time for warning, crisis management, and nuclear response. One reason for signing the INF Treaty in 1987 was because of the short flight times to their intended targets that the Soviet SS-20 IRBMs and NATO's "572" deployments were presumably capable of achieving. Key cities in western Russia or in NATO Europe could be attacked with little warning compared to that provided by land- or sea-based intercontinental missiles of longer range. Reintroducing medium and intermediate ground-launched missiles into Europe could exacerbate a crisis by encouraging nations to place their respective nuclear attack warning and command-response systems on hair-trigger alert and prepared for prompt launch. Something like this happened in November 1983 when the NATO command post exercise Able Archer was in danger of being misconstrued by some Soviet observers as an actual alliance decision for nuclear release.[8] As Jon B. Wolfsthal has noted:

> In particular, the fear that misunderstandings could drive leaders on either side to make rash nuclear decisions for fear that decision time was short led to the negotiation of the 1987 Intermediate-Range Nuclear Forces Treaty, an agreement now on the chopping block.[9]

Other implications of the apparent US decision to depart the INF Treaty are more explicitly political in nature. One issue is the impact of dissolving the INF Treaty on the political cohesion of NATO. Many

---

[7]Grateful acknowledgment is made to Dr. Jacob W. Kipp for insights pertinent to this section. See also: Trenin, D. (2019). "Russian views of US nuclear modernization," *Bulletin of the Atomic Scientists*, January in *Johnson's Russia List* 2019 — #9 — January 15.

[8]Fischer, B. B. (2018). "Intelligence and disaster avoidance: The Soviet war scare and US-Soviet relations," Chapter 5 in S. J. Cimbala (ed.), *Mysteries of the Cold War* (London: Routledge Revivals), pp. 89–104.

[9]Wolfsthal, J. B. (2018). "With Russia and the U.S., nuclear risks never go out of vogue." Available at: http://www.russiamatters.org (accessed on October 2020). November 8 in *Johnson's Russia List* 2018 — #196 — November 8.

European members of NATO might prefer to have the INF remain in place even if either or both sides nibbled at the edges of non-compliance. From the standpoint of many Europeans, NATO's credibility as a deterrent to Russian aggression against a member state is less a matter of comparing numbers of deployed forces than it is about the reliability of the US nuclear guarantee for its allies. A wider spectrum of nuclear options for NATO and Russia, with respect to the yields of warheads and the diversity of launchers on each side, carries the risk of prioritizing the graduation of nuclear response to the certainty of it. From this perspective, Russia must not be permitted to believe that it can bite off an arm or leg of NATO territory and remain immune to high-end conventional or nuclear response directly on Russian territory.

The alternative perspective is offered in the Trump Administration's Nuclear Posture Review of 2018. From this standpoint, the US and NATO require a wider spectrum of nuclear options in order to have a credible deterrent against Russian provocations short of unlimited nuclear war.[10] Russia might believe that it could "escalate to de-escalate" a conventional war in Europe that was going badly for Russia by engaging in nuclear first use as a bargaining chip to deter further NATO resistance or escalation. This view holds that a wider spectrum of nuclear options creates a more believable message with respect to intra-war deterrence and escalation control than a narrower range of choices.[11]

In some sense we are back to the concept of limited war as a generator of risk, as Thomas Schelling has so expertly discussed it,[12] i.e. what is most important about a limited nuclear war is not the damage that has already taken place, but the relationship between that damage and the opponent's expectation about what further damage might ensue. This expectation will be based partly on the opponent's estimate of the first

---

[10]The case for nuclear flexibility is explained in Payne, K. B. (2018). "Nuclear deterrence in a new era: Applying 'tailored deterrence,'" National Institute for Public Policy Issue No. 431, May 21.

[11]Cimbala, S. J. (2018). "The Trump nuclear posture review: Three issues, nine implications," *Strategic Studies Quarterly*, 12(2): 9–16. See also: Payne, *supra* note 10; and Sokov, N. N. (2014). "Why Russia calls a limited nuclear strike 'de-escalation,'" *Bulletin of the Atomic Scientists*, March 13. Available at: https://thebulletin.org/2014/03/why-russia-calls-a-limited-nuclear-strike-de-escalation/ (accessed on October 2020).

[12]Schelling, T. C. (1966, repr. 2008). *Arms and Influence* (New Haven: Yale University Press).

side's capabilities, but also on its estimate of the first side's resolve in continuing up the ladder of escalation if its demands are not met. What is being tested in this instance is the capacity of both sides for risk management under conditions of uncertainty.[13]

9.3. The Priority of Risk Management

The significance of the preceding observation goes beyond the specific scenarios of escalation and limited nuclear war in Europe. In the second nuclear age, following the end of the Cold War and the demise of the Soviet Union, the major challenges to nuclear-strategic stability may occur in regions outside of Europe: the Middle East, South Asia, and East Asia.[14] In those settings, states and their leaders will be tested not only on their ability to practice deterrence per se. They will also be expected to rise to the demands of risk management under conditions of uncertainty. Insufficient thought has been given to this problem, even in scenarios relative to an outbreak of major war in Europe: even more so, with regard to Middle Eastern and Asian contretemps. What, for example, do we know reliably about the perspectives on risk management with respect to nuclear escalation that are held by the leaders in Iran, Pakistan, or North Korea? Precious little is the answer, based on what is available in the public domain.

The challenge of risk management in and outside of Europe is also related to the arguments for or against retaining the INF Treaty and/or New START. With respect to INF, a proliferation of medium- and intermediate-range missiles within Europe creates a Pandora's box of scenarios for which escalation management, including the problems of intra-war deterrence and war termination, have been thought through only superficially. War games at think tanks and war colleges may delve into these issues, but the analysis and discussions are confined largely to audiences of expert analysts, scholars, and former diplomats and military commanders. The diffusion of findings from these and other studies into the DNA

---

[13] Some experts doubt that any shooting war between the US and Russia could be contained below the nuclear threshold. See: Goble, P. (2018). "Any US-Russia military clash 'highly likely' to escalate into nuclear war, Arbatov says," in *Johnson's Russia List* 2018 — #212 — December 6.

[14] Bracken, P. (2012). *The Second Nuclear Age: Strategy, Danger, and the New World Politics* (New York: Henry Holt and Co./Times Books).

of policymakers is a more complicated problem. Harvard's JFK School emphasizes the importance of the difference between "policy formulation" and "policy implementation" for very good reasons. The implementation of policies requires a currency conversion: from good ideas and theoretical insights into procedures, routines, and standard operating procedures that organizations have rehearsed and practiced under realistic operational conditions.

The Cold War experience with nuclear crisis management is a reminder of the difficulty in getting policymakers and operators on the same page with respect to signaling determination and conciliation at the same time. There is all the difference in the world between policy formulation, customarily decided at the highest levels of government, and the operational implementation of those policies. During the Cuban missile crisis, for example, President Kennedy and members of the ExComm (his senior advisory group for crisis management) sought to convey to Soviet Premier Khrushchev US determination to have Soviet medium- and intermediate-range missiles removed from Cuba. But the US also sought to achieve this objective without military escalation that could lead to an outbreak of war between the US and the Soviet Union, including the possible expansion of that war into a nuclear conflict. Accordingly, the US instituted a blockade or quarantine against Soviet ships headed to Cuba. This decision was intended as a limited escalation in order to give the Soviets an option for a face-saving retreat without horizontal or vertical escalation.

Throughout the tense 13 days of the Cuban Missile Crisis, leaders were plagued by misperceptions of intentions and "normal" bureaucratic behavior that created dysfunctional speed bumps in the way of conflict resolution. In the US case, a U-2 reconnaissance plane on a routine mission wandered into Soviet air space, causing Soviet fighters to scramble; a scheduled test launch of a US intercontinental ballistic missile (ICBM) from California went ahead despite the heightened alert levels on both sides; and, an American U-2 was shot down over Cuba on the basis of a decision made by a local Soviet commander. On the Soviet side, in addition to the deployment of medium-range ballistic missiles (MRBMs) and intermediate-range ballistic missiles (IRBMs), the Soviets also deployed nuclear-capable tactical missiles with their ground forces in Cuba, with the understanding that ground-force commanders could use those missiles in the event of a US invasion of Cuba. As the crisis reached its denouement, Cuban leader Fidel Castro urged Khrushchev that the USSR should launch a preemptive nuclear first strike against the US. Castro claimed to have incontrovertible evidence that the US was preparing for an imminent attack on Cuba. As Khrushchev recalled:

> Only then did I realize that our friend Castro, whom I respect for his honesty and directness, had failed to understand us correctly. We had installed the missiles not for the purpose of attacking the United States, but to keep the United States from attacking Cuba. What does it mean to make a preemptive strike? We could deliver the first blow, but there would be an immediate counterblow — both against Cuba and against our own country.[15]

Of course, Khrushchev had additional motives for deploying nuclear missiles in Cuba, including an attempt to change the perceived balance of strategic nuclear-missile power as between the US and the Soviet Union. But he was able to climb down the ladder of escalation because US management of the crisis offered an option between provocation and conciliation. The US publicly accepted removal of the Soviet nuclear-capable missiles from Cuba in return for an American promise not to invade Cuba. In addition, the US also secretly agreed to eventual removal of Jupiter medium-range missiles from Turkey, about which the Soviets had previously complained.

These reflections on the Cuban missile crisis are not a distraction from our present endeavor, but a warning. As dangerous as the crisis was for humanity, it benefited from a simple structure of social action. There were two governments that shared responsibility for starting the crisis and for ending it. In the US and in the Soviet Union, political leadership exercised authoritative control over the armed forces. Although allies' needs and expectations figured into Soviet and American decision-making, the crisis was about the strategic nuclear relationship between two superpowers and the stealthy attempt by Khrushchev to adjust the perception of that balance.

In contrast, now consider a future crisis in Europe as between NATO and Russia. NATO has expanded to 29 countries from its Cold War membership of 16. In theory, a decision to invoke Article V in favor of collective military action requires unanimous consent of member states, as

---

[15] Schecter, J. L. and V. V. Vyacheslav (eds. and transl.) (1990). *Khrushchev Remembers: The Glasnost Tapes* (Boston, MA: Little, Brown, and Co.), p. 177.

represented in the NATO Council. In this large and heterogenous group of states, it will be sufficiently difficult to get a consensus in favor of any military action unless the Russians plump for an all-out invasion of Western Europe with the objective of dismantling NATO and occupying its remains. However, Russia lacks the military capability to impose such a *coup de main* on NATO. Therefore, it is more likely that Russia will seek to use its capacity for hybrid warfare, combining unconventional and conventional military steps, in order to divide NATO politically. Information operations can support both unconventional and conventional military deployments and tactics. For example, an infiltration of Estonia or Latvia by "little green men," (Russian or Russian-supported commandos outfitted in ways that conceal their real identities), combined with selective air and ground attacks into the Baltics and an extensive propaganda and disinformation campaign, could create a united NATO response. But such a campaign could also divide NATO political leaders, along a continuum of those in favor of steadfast resistance to those more unwilling to respond to military force, depending on who was threatened and to what extent.

Suppose, in the preceding case, NATO reacts with collective unity and begins to turn the military tide against Russia, with NATO's capabilities for conventional deep strike used against Russian forces engaged in fighting on NATO members' territory. Russian reinforcements from its western military districts come to the rescue of their besieged comrades in the Baltics, and NATO responds with air- and sea-launched strikes against Russian forces as they cross the border from Russia into Latvia. Russia interprets this last NATO move as an attack on its homeland and, in response, fires a warning shot in the form of an EMP burst that shorts out electronics throughout much of the battlespace and surrounding territories. The US places its strategic nuclear and theater nuclear forces on higher levels of alert while continuing its conventional deep strikes into Russian-occupied Latvia or Estonia and across the border into Russia. Russia also alerts its strategic and theater nuclear forces and both states' nuclear C3 (command, control, and communications) systems are now on the *qui vive*.

This situation would be complicated enough with the present deployments of theater nuclear and conventional weapons in Europe. Adding in unlimited numbers of ground-launched, medium- and intermediate-range missiles, per the demise of the INF Treaty, only complicates the challenge of nuclear risk management in this or any related scenario. Granted, the US and Russia also have sea- and air-launched weapons that could contribute to intra-theater deterrence (or escalation, depending on the case). However, ground-launched missiles have the special character that their prompt strike capabilities and locations invite preemptive attack on themselves. Their launchers are at known, easily detectable locations and could be destroyed with conventional as well as nuclear weapons. Once nuclear forces have been alerted and the possibility of escalation across the nuclear threshold cannot be excluded, military leaders will be pressing for the early destruction of MRBMs and IRBMs that are nuclear capable. Knowing this, Russian leaders may fear a situation in which they must "use them or lose them" and within a very small time for decision (shorter than the time assumed available for decision and response to a strategic nuclear attack by the US on Russia or vice versa).

With respect to this or other possible scenarios in the European theater of operations, the US and Russia might consider maintaining the INF Treaty in some revised form. Instead of banning all missiles of a certain range, they might agree to permit conventionally armed, but not nuclear-capable, ground-based delivery systems. An inspections regime could be established to verify that MRBMs and IRBMs deployed in Europe by either side are equipped with conventional warheads only. Russia would be free to deploy MRBMs and IRBMs (to an extent) and NATO could respond with symmetrical (more or less) deployments of its own. Verification of non-nuclear status would be more challenging for air-launched or sea-based systems, but not impossible. In any case, air-launched and sea-based weapons are less in need of verification, compared to ground-based systems, because they are less provocative from the standpoint of crisis stability. The known locations of ground-based systems make them potentially attractive targets for preemption.

One reason that the US is better off with, as opposed to without, the INF is that Russia has the advantage of being able to deploy intermediate- and shorter-range ground-based missiles on its own state territory. On the other hand, if the US sought to deploy ground-based missiles in Europe within range of Russia (or, for that matter, in Asia within range of China), consent of a willing ally to host those missiles and launchers would be needed. If those missiles were nuclear-capable, the burden of acceptance on the part of European or Asian allies of the US would be even greater. This is part of the reason why European government officials attempted to act as intermediaries between the US and Russia in order to preserve the present INF Treaty. In addition, European leaders urged the US to build a more persuasive case for withdrawing from the INF so that blame in the "public square" falls on Russia and not on the US or NATO. As noted by one (unidentified) European diplomat: "The US administration needs to take the Europeans with them. It's important that if the agreement fails it is clear to everyone that it is the Russians' fault. I think the administration gets this."[16]

Perhaps with the preceding points in mind, Russia steadfastly blamed the US for the probable demise of the INF, denies any accusation of cheating, and points to alleged US infractions of the treaty. Russian Deputy Foreign Minister Sergei Ryabkov reaffirmed Russia's refusal to accept responsibility for a failed treaty in November 2018:

> We believe that the US plans to withdraw from the INF Treaty, in case (this scenario) is implemented, will trigger a grave aftermath for European and global security. We deny any logic that tries to attribute to us actions, which allegedly pushed Washington to declare the plans to withdraw from the treaty.[17]

The US decision to withdraw from the INF treaty, first announced by President Trump in October 2018 and reiterated by Secretary of State Mike Pompeo in early February 2019, pointed to Russia's refusal to bring its development, testing, and deployment of the 9M729 missile into compliance with the requirements of the treaty. Instead of seeking to enforce the agreement by further negotiation and bargaining with Russia, the US closed the door on finding a mutually satisfactory solution and offered to Vladimir Putin a putative excuse for Russian INF-range missile modernization and deployment, including in Europe.[18] In addition, the apparent

---

[16]Borger, J. (2018). "European diplomats mount last-ditch effort to stop US scrapping INF treaty," *The Guardian*, November 18, in *Johnson's Russia List* 2018 — #202 —, November 19.

[17]TASS (2018). "Diplomat repudiates narrative that Russia's moves drive US into abandoning INF deal," November 19, in *Johnson's Russia List* 2018 — #202 —, November 19.

[18]US Aegis Ashore systems deployed in Eastern Europe could, from the Russian perspective, constitute a preparatory violation of the INF Treaty, given the potential capability of their launchers to fire conventional or nuclear-armed Tomahawk cruise missiles against Russia. The US retired its nuclear-armed Tomahawk cruise missiles between 2010 and 2013 but could quickly reinstate the nuclear option for Tomahawk if deemed necessary. See: Postol, T. (2019). "Russia may have violated the INF treaty. Here's how the United States appears to have done the same," *Bulletin of the Atomic Scientists*, February 7.

demise of the INF, amid a poisoned political atmosphere as between Washington and Moscow, increased the likelihood of a total collapse of the US–Russian nuclear arms control regime, including the future of the New START agreement.

The possible end to the INF Treaty is also connected to the durability of the entire Russian–American nuclear arms control regime, including the fate of the existing New START agreement on strategic nuclear arms limitation. New START expires in 2021 unless automatically extended by both sides for another five years. The agreement limits each state to a maximum number of 1,550 warheads on land-based ICBMs, submarine-launched ballistic missiles (SLBMs), and heavy bombers. New START also limits the numbers of operationally deployed and reserve delivery systems available to each state. Although some arms control experts might regard the automatic extension of New START until 2026 as a "no brainer," the present and foreseeable political climate as between the US and Russia does not guarantee such an outcome. One Russian author has warned:

> There is one more detail of fundamental importance. If the two leading military powers have failed to curb the race in strategic nuclear forces, there is no chance that hypersonic weapons, space-based systems, long-range conventional missiles, and cybersecurity warfare activities will ever be controlled. The arms race will spread to other domains.[19]

9.4. The Challenge of Cyber

Cyberspace activity is an example of the "domain spread" that may contribute to a weakening of deterrence and crisis stability.[20] Cyber war has the potential to undermine some of the basic premises upon which nuclear deterrence and crisis stability are based, in a number of ways.[21]

Available at: https://thebulletin.org/2019/02/russia-may-have-violated-the-inf-treaty-heres-how-the-united-states-appears-to-have-done-the-same/ (accessed on October 2020).

[19] Akulov, A. (2018). "Responding to US unleashing unfettered arms race: Russia's options," *Strategic Culture*, October 22, in *Johnson's Russia List* 2018 — #185 — October 23.

[20] The domains of warfare and/or deterrence include: land, sea, air, space, and cyberspace.

[21] Cyber war, like information war, is an inclusive term for the use of digital tools in support of military deterrence or defense objectives. For a sensible approach to terminology

First, nuclear crisis management assumes a certain degree of transparency about actors' intentions and capabilities. Cyberattacks could interfere with the clarity of communication between crisis-bound adversaries and lead them to doubt otherwise reassuring indicators of no enemy plan for preemptive or preventive strikes. Second, cyberattacks could be designed to directly compromise the performance of another state's warning, C3 (command, control, communications), intelligence, surveillance and reconnaissance systems, increasing fears of surprise attack and willingness to launch on warning with less than unimpeachable information. As David E. Sanger has noted:

> The implications of having our own command-and-control system compromised underscore why sabotaging similar systems in other nations is dangerous business. If American leaders — or Russian leaders — feared their missiles might not lift off when someone hit the button, or that they were programmed to go off-course, it could easily undermine the system of deterrence that has helped reduced the likelihood of nuclear war for the past several decades.[22]

Third, states actively engaged in peacetime computer network exploitation, including the mapping of enemy systems and procedures as well as the insertion of malware that may be activated "on the day," will find it difficult to resist the temptation to accelerate this exploitation as the onset of a crisis seems imminent. The result might be that, as a crisis moves from its early to its later stages, the information needed to resolve the crisis is ever more transient and unreliable. Fourth, cybersecurity issues have, in the case of Russia and the US, contributed to a toxic political atmosphere of mutual suspicion and doubt with respect to any larger and mutually agreeable enterprises. Alleged Russian interference in the American presidential elections of 2016, including Russian Internet Research Agency (IRA) and military intelligence (GRU) manipulation of social media in order to plant false narratives about American politics and

in these issues, see: Singer, P. W. and A. Friedman (2014). *Cybersecurity and Cyberwar: What Everyone Needs to Know* (Oxford: Oxford University Press); Futter, A. (2016). "Cyber threats and nuclear weapons: New questions for command and control, security and strategy," July 2016, RUSI Occasional Paper.
[22]Sanger, D. E. (2018). *The Perfect Weapon: War, Sabotage, and Fear in the Cyber Age* (New York: Crown Publishers), p. 299.

culture, has tied the hands of US leaders who might otherwise want détente and a more positive relationship with Russia.

Fifth, in addition to the corruption of information by means of attacks on computers and networks, cyberattacks have reportedly been used to disable nuclear infrastructure, including centrifuges and nuclear launch systems.[23] Sixth, in the future, smarter information systems and AI decision aids may appeal to policymakers or commanders as substitutes for the human factor in ensuring against nuclear vulnerability. For example, Russia's Cold War era "dead hand" system for post-attack launch of remaining ICBMs even after the national command authority had been paralyzed by nuclear strikes could inspire a 21st century equivalent that delegated the final decision to a truly automated "doomsday machine" even more relentless than its predecessor.[24] Seventh, cyber issues are central to the evolving relationship between anti-missile defenses and the offensive missile attacks that they are intended to defeat. Cold War era missile defenses were mainly a competition in physics and engineering. Although physics and engineering obviously still matter, the effectiveness of future US, Russian, or other national missile defenses will be increasingly dependent upon whether they are "state of the art" in information systems that support C4ISR (command, control, communications, computers, intelligence, surveillance, and reconnaissance).[25] In the case of national missile defenses, information systems must be able to provide accurate and timely warning and attack characterization; distinguish real threats from decoys; prioritize intercepts relative to the proximate threat posed by various attackers; and close the loop from sensor to decision-maker to shoot faster than the opposing force.

Eighth, related to this greater dependency upon cyber performance for missile defenses is the increased significance of space-based platforms

---

[23] *Ibid.*, pp. 41–47, 268–279.

[24] Lowther, A. and C. McGiffin (2019). "America needs a "dead hand," *War on the Rocks*, August 16. Available at: https://warontherocks.com/019/08/america-needs-a-dead-hand/ (accessed on October 2020). See also: Field, M. (2019). "Strangelove redux: US experts propose having AI control nuclear weapons," *Bulletin of the Atomic Scientists*, August 30. Available at: https://thebulletin.org/2019/08/strangelove-redux-us-experts-propose-having-ai-control-nuclear-weapons/ (accessed on October 2020).

[25] Slayton, R. (2013). *Arguments that Count: Physics, Computing, and Missile Defense, 1949–2012* (Cambridge, MA: The MIT Press), pp. 199–209 and passim.

and their growing requirements for improved cybersecurity.[26] Already the US and other spacefaring powers use space systems for reconnaissance, geolocation, communications, command-control, intelligence gathering, missile attack warning, and other vital functions in support of national defense and security.[27] The weaponization of space systems until now has been deflected by the Outer Space Treaty and by shared understandings that space is a "commons" that is available and necessary to all. However, future technology could make possible the basing of missile defenses or other weapons in space with space-to-earth or space-to-space strike capabilities. The latter is imminent, depending on the orbital paths of existing and future satellites. For example, the US, Russia, and China are reportedly working on "repair" satellites that could closely approach another "friendly" satellite in order to repair its malfunctions and to refuel it for additional missions. However, the technology that permits "repair" satellites to work enables the same orbiters to disrupt or destroy another "unfriendly" satellite, should they choose to do so. To deal with this situation, i.e. a possible form of mutual space vulnerability, states will have to negotiate "keep away" circumferential zones surrounding their satellites and may also need to equip those satellites with self-defense mechanisms.

Ninth, cyberwar might contribute to a mistaken decision for a nuclear first strike or prompt retaliatory launch, on the faulty assumption that the opponent had already taken a decision for attack, or that an attack was actually in progress. Cyberattacks have several properties that are contributory to first-strike fears. First, they are hard to detect. Malware may be inserted into another state's networks months or even years in advance, primed for later activation. Or nearly instantaneous cyberattacks against enemy command-control and communications systems may precede a kinetic attack. Second, cyberattacks are often difficult to attribute.

---

[26]The US Defense Intelligence Agency (DIA) notes that "China and Russia, in particular, are developing a variety of means to exploit perceived U.S. reliance on space-based systems and challenge the U.S. position in space." Defense Intelligence Agency (2019). *Challenges to Security in Space* (Washington, D.C.: Defense Intelligence Agency), p. 7. Available at: https://www.dia.mil/Military-Power-Publications (accessed on October 2020).

[27]Blair, D. C. (2019). "Why the US must accelerate all elements of space-based nuclear deterrence," *Defense News*. Available at: https://www.defensenews.com/opinion/commentary/2019/02/07/why-the-us-must-accelerate-all-elements-of-space-based-nuclear-deterrence/ (accessed on October 2020).

Attackers purposely disguise their identities and some may impersonate third parties, implicating an innocent state actor or others. Third, attacks on critical infrastructure or information systems can create panic among targeted decision-makers who might therefore decide to strike at the plausible sources of the attack before their own systems fail.

To mitigate this danger of deterioration of nuclear deterrence stability by the possibility of mutual cyber destruction, states might attempt to establish certain "rules of the road" with respect to peacetime and crisis-time behavior in cyberspace. One option is increased transparency with respect to the capabilities of states' systems for offensive and defensive computer network operations. Just as nuclear arms control agreements limit the numbers of launchers and warheads available to each side, and provide for monitoring and verification of agreed limits, the broad compass of cyber defense and attack capabilities could be make known without compromising actual code or in-house protocols. This suggestion collides with the traditional expectations of secrecy that mark all states' cyberactivities. On the other hand, in a cyber competitive world, secrets are sometimes perishable: yesterday's secret system is often tomorrow's exposure. Edward Snowden and the Shadow Brokers compromised some of the NSA's most powerful tools for offensive cyber operations, the so-called Tailored Access Operations (TAO) instruction manuals and codes.[28] The Stuxnet worm used successfully against Iran's centrifuges became a *cause celebre* when it unexpectedly mutated into a global problem.[29]

Another option would be the adoption by the US and other major nuclear and cyber powers of an agreement on "no first use" of cyber as well as nuclear weapons during a crisis. Such an agreement would be a declaratory policy that relied upon the good faith of the participants: a cyber "first use" would be difficult to verify, compared to the obviousness of a nuclear first use. The reasoning behind this agreement would be that successful crisis management requires that contending parties fully understand the other side's actual intentions and capabilities, regardless of their disagreements about other matters. An agreement of this sort might be supported by exchanging cyber experts among countries in peacetime and encouraging regular channels of communication between US Cyber Command and their counterparts in other countries.

---

[28] Sanger, D. E. (2018). *The Perfect Weapon: War, Sabotage, and Fear in the Cyber Age* (New York: Crown Publishers), pp. 226–230.

[29] *Ibid.*, pp. 21–25.

9.5. INF, New START and the Control of Escalation

The discussion in Section 9.5 is meant to establish the priority of cyber-related deterrence and risk management in the creation of future viable frameworks for nuclear deterrence and crisis stability. The examples of cyber relationships to nuclear deterrence and crisis stability are only part of the potential for a collision course between nuclear arms races and new technologies. Meanwhile, and apart from new technologies, the nature of the linkage between INF and New START in the minds of US and Russian planners remains an open question. If additional INF deployments are undertaken by either side, these deployments will have a two-sided possibility with respect to the ladder of nuclear escalation. First, they can serve as firebreaks between the initial or early use of tactical nuclear weapons, on one hand, and the employment of strategic nuclear forces, on the other. Second, and in contrast, new INF could serve as conveyors for a slippery slope of escalation that was undertaken in the mistaken expectation that theater nuclear war could be sealed off from strategic nuclear attacks. This two-sided character of the relationship between INF and strategic nuclear forces has an inherent ambiguity that might appeal to some deterrence theorists but, at the same time, alarm policymakers and military strategists looking for "exit ramps" in the event of an outbreak of tactical nuclear warfare.

The political linkage between INF and New START is also subject to diverse interpretations. One school of thought holds that the demise of INF may create a domino effect that has a high probability of toppling New START and creating other negative by-products for nuclear stability. Russian President Vladimir Putin noted in late November 2018 that Russia would not leave unanswered an American withdrawal from the INF Treaty. Russia's military and political leaders will be tasked to develop responses to US abrogation of the treaty, according to Putin. The Russian president cited his previous warnings to the US against its withdrawal from the Anti-Ballistic Missile (ABM) Treaty, which limits missile defenses, and Russia's response, in the form of hypersonic weapons capable of defeating any defense. On the other hand, according to Putin, Russia will not be dragged into a new nuclear arms race: instead, Russia will emphasize "balanced development" of its armed forces.[30]

---

[30] *Russia Today* (2018). "Russia won't be dragged into new arms race, but will respond to US withdrawal from INF — Putin," November 20, in *Johnson's Russia List* 2018 — #203 — November 20.

Other Russian officials, however, have warned that a US departure from the INF Treaty could collapse the entire nuclear non-proliferation system and increase the risk of nuclear war.[31]

However, INF and New START are not peas in a pod. INF is a long-standing agreement that dates from 1987 (going into effect in 1988) and was signed on the eve of the Cold War endgame. It was a historic achievement for its time, creating a security space for nuclear threat reduction in Europe and contributing to the rapprochement between US President Ronald Reagan and Soviet leader Mikhail Gorbachev that helped to end the Cold War peacefully. Although a case can be made for continuing the agreement on arms control grounds, the political winds between the US and Russia have shifted considerably since the halcyon days of the early post-Cold War years and the bromance between US President Bill Clinton and Russian President Boris Yeltsin. Vladimir Putin wants a multipolar world that includes a militarily resurgent Russia, fearful of NATO expansion, of US-supported "color revolutions" in states bordering on Russia or in Russia itself, and of US missile defenses that could pose a threat to Russia's nuclear deterrent.

In this context, extending the New START agreement to 2026 or thereafter neither poses an existential threat to Russia nor requires that Russia invest scarce defense resources that threaten its fiscal solvency. The US nuclear modernization plan for the next several decades anticipates replacement of each of the three "legs" of its strategic nuclear triad of ICBMs, SLBMs, and heavy bombers.[32] However, this plan can be accomplished within the constraints of New START ceilings on warhead and launcher deployments.[33] US planners anticipate that each leg of the triad will undergo qualitative improvement, but not necessarily an increase in the numbers of missile or warhead deployments.

---

[31] Ibid. See also: TASS (2018). "Kremlin concerned over US attempts to reject New START Treaty extension," November 29, 2018, in *Johnson's Russia List* 2018 — #209 — November 29.

[32] Wolfsthal, J. B., J. Lewis and M. Quint (2014). *The Trillion Dollar Nuclear Triad: US Strategic Nuclear Modernization Over the Next Thirty Years* (Monterey, CA: James Martin Center for Nonproliferation Studies).

[33] US Congressional Budget Office (2017). *Approaches for Managing the Costs of U.S. Nuclear Forces, 2017 to 2046* (Washington, D.C.: Congressional Budget Office). Available at: https://www.cbo.gov/publications/53211 (accessed on October 2020).

9.6. Missile Defenses: Meaningful or Malign?

The matter of US and NATO missile defenses remains a point of contention as between Washington and Moscow, with potential side effects for the viability of New START. Russia attempted unsuccessfully to get restrictions on US missile defenses included in the New START agreement of 2010. Russian officials are likely to raise this point again, in connection with any agreement to extend New START. In addition, Russia may also bring into the conversation about New START extension the issues of long-range conventional strike systems and military uses of space. Either the US or Russia might also want to introduce the issue of cyber war and its possible relationship to nuclear strategic stability.[34]

Russia's proclivity for inserting other issues into the New START negotiations, other than the limitations on offensive warheads and launch systems, complicates what might otherwise be a straightforward process. Russia's contention that US missile defenses deployed in Europe could be repurposed as offensive strike systems, part of their quibbling with respect to INF as well as New START, is stronger on military-technical, as opposed to realistic political, grounds. The US Navy has established a program to develop hypersonic boost-glide weapons for multi-service use, including possible deployments on Ohio-class ballistic missile submarines converted to launch cruise missiles or Virginia-class attack submarines with a specialized payload module. Conceivably the hypersonic glide body could also be deployed on cruisers and destroyers, creating a large number of sea-based prompt global strike (PGS) weapons with the range to reach large areas of Russia and China. Although sea-based weapons are not included within the scope of the INF Treaty, weapons that could be launched from the Mk-41 Vertical Launch System (VLS) deployed on ships and submarines could also be launched from the same system deployed on land, including the Aegis Ashore based in Romania (and an additional system planned for Poland).[35] With regard to New

---

[34]On this issue, see Futter, *supra* note 21; Cimbala, S. J. (2018). *Getting Nuclear Weapons Right: Managing Danger and Avoiding Disaster* (Boulder, CL: Lynne Rienner Publishers), pp. 191–205.

[35]Akulov, A. (2018). "More details on reasons behind US decision to leave INF Treaty," *Strategic Culture Foundation*, November 25, in *Johnson's Russia List* 2018 — #206 — November 26. See also: Strategic Systems Programs, Department of the Navy, *FY19 — FY23 Navy Intermediate Range Conventional Prompt Strike (IRCPS) Weapon System*

START, hypersonic glide weapons deployed on Virginia-class submarines would not fall within its jurisdiction, but warheads deployed on Ohio-class ballistic missile submarine launchers for hypersonic boost-glide vehicles could be counted against allowable New START totals. According to RAND Corporation experts, Russian leaders emphasize the US development of advanced conventional capabilities, especially hypersonic glide vehicles and missile defenses, not necessarily because of immediate jeopardy to Russia's strategic deterrent, but because these US systems, "especially if fielded in larger numbers, may become a greater threat to Russia's second-strike capability."[36]

With regard to the preceding military-technical factors, much depends on the specific direction of US research and development efforts as they move toward actual deployment. But it seems clear even now that the US could realize any conventional PGS modernization objectives with sea-based and air-launched platforms, excluding land-based deployments based on repurposed missile defenses. Politics weighs in favor of NATO restraint with respect to ground-based PGS systems of intermediate or larger range. Given the hard work in getting NATO consensus on the European Phased Adaptive Approach (EPAA) to missile defenses, a turncoat operation converting defenses into offensive weapons would be neither politically expedient for NATO nor militarily efficient.[37] A repurposing of Aegis Ashore for offensive missions would alarm Russia without providing a meaningful gain in NATO's already extensive conventional and nuclear strike power. Without EPAA, what deters an Iran or other regional actor from moving faster toward actual nuclear weaponization and deployment? Only deterrence and the threat of punitive retaliation in the case of any hostile nuclear launch: without defenses, there can be no additional threat of deterrence by denial.

The Russians know all this, but they prefer to use American and NATO missile defenses as a bargaining chip because this ploy supports Putin's rhetoric of being surrounded by an advancing West, pulsing with prepackaged color revolutions exportable into Russian security space.

(WS) Development and Integration Presolicitation Notice, Solicitation Number N00030-19-R-0025, November 21, 2018.

[36]Chivvis, C. S., A. Radin, D. Massicot and C. Reach (2017). *Strengthening Strategic Stability with Russia* (Santa Monica, CA: RAND Corporation), PE-234-OSD.

[37]For important background and perspective, see Futter, A. (2013). *Ballistic Missile Defence and US National Security Policy* (New York: Routledge), Chs. 5–7.

Putin's points of argument about US and NATO anti-missile defenses are, at least at the margin, logically inconsistent. On one hand, the Russian President brags of Russia's new hypersonic weapons that will surely defeat any US or allied Western missile defenses. On the other hand, US and NATO missile defenses present a security threat to Russia sufficient to cause Russia's strategic and military-technical hyperventilation.

Russian fears on this point are of two kinds. First, missile defenses themselves, if sufficiently competent and strategically located on a regional and global basis, could nullify Russia's nuclear deterrent by threatening Russia's strategic nuclear second-strike capability. A second Russian concern is that, even if present and immediately foreseeable defense technologies cannot by themselves threaten Russia's nuclear deterrent, defenses might be part of a larger military-strategic schematic for disarming Russia. From this second standpoint, advanced US and NATO missile defenses combined with long-range, conventional strike systems, cyberwar, and space-based or space-enhanced weapons, together with NATO's own version of hybrid warfare, could confer a coercive advantage in crisis management.[38] This more elaborate scenario for putative Russian vulnerability probably has more to do with Russia's history of resistance to foreign invasions and the cultural DNA left by that experience than it does with military-technical or nuclear-strategic realities.[39]

For example, the idea that the US might decide to launch a disarming conventional first strike against Russia's strategic nuclear forces, in the expectation that Russia would somehow accept defeat or retaliate only with its own conventional weapons, strains credulity. From a military-technical standpoint, there is no feasible way for the US or NATO to accomplish Russia's effective nuclear disarmament with conventional strikes only. Russia's launch detection of a massive US attack on its state territory from land- and/or sea-based missiles would be followed almost immediately by an order for "launch on warning" of its available nuclear forces. Russia would not wait to determine whether the fast-flying US missiles were

---

[38] Potential threats, mitigation options, and other aspects of US space operations receive expert consideration in: Astorion-Courtois, A., R. Elder and B. Bragg (2018). *Contested Space Operations, Space Defense, Deterrence, and Warfighting: Summary Findings and Integration Report* (Arlington, VA: Strategic Multilayer Assessment). Available at: https://www.NSIteam.com (accessed on October 2020).

[39] Lourie, R. (2017). *Putin: His Downfall and Russia's Coming Crash* (New York: St. Martin's Press), pp. 130–142 and passim.

equipped with conventional or nuclear-armed warheads — nor, for that matter, would the US. In theory, either side might wait until actual detonations of weapons had occurred on its state territory before responding with nuclear counterattacks. But in practice, that choice is highly unlikely: heads of state will be urged by their military advisors that they face a "use them or lose them" dilemma with respect to silo-based ICBMs.

The competence of US and Russian strategic nuclear forces with respect to deterrence and crisis stability can be estimated and summarized in the following tables. Table 9.1 illustrates plausible New START-compliant force structures for the US and Russia within the constraints of a 1,550 limit on the numbers of operationally deployed warheads on strategic launchers for each side. Table 9.2 summarizes the outcomes of nuclear force exchanges for four different scenarios of operational readiness and launch doctrine:

(1) forces are on generated alert and launched on warning;
(2) forces are on generated alert and riding out the attack;
(3) forces are on day-to-day alert and launched on warning; and
(4) forces are on day-to-day alert and riding out the attack.

Tables 9.3 and 9.4 repeat this process for US and Russian forces limited to a maximum of 1,000 peacetime deployed warheads.

Table 9.1.   US–Russia total strategic weapons, 1,550 deployment limit.

US	2017 Plan	Dyad Without ICBMs	Dyad Without Bombers	Triad 10 SSBN 300 ICBM
ICBM	400	0	400	561
SLBM	1,040	1,407	1,148	880
AIR	109	109	0	109
Russia	**Balanced Triad**	**No Bombers**	**No SLBMs**	**ICBMs Only**
ICBM	758	907	1,412	1,502
SLBM	704	640	0	0
AIR	70	0	88	0

Source: Force structures based on author's estimates and New START counting rules. See also: US Congressional Budget Office (2017). *Approaches for Managing the Costs of U.S. Nuclear Forces, 2017–2046* (Washington, D.C.: Congressional Budget Office), and Podvig, P. "Russian strategic nuclear forces," Blog. Available at: http://russianforces.org/ (accessed on October 2020).

Table 9.2.   US–Russia: Surviving and retaliating warheads, 1,550 deployment limit.

US	2017 Plan	Dyad Without ICBMs	Dyad Without Bombers	Triad 10 SSBN 300 ICBM
GEN, LOW	1282	1219	1290	1297
GEN, ROA	887	1148	966	771
DAY, LOW	948	788	983	1006
DAY, ROA	603	766	659	530
Russia	**Balanced Triad**	**No Bombers**	**No SLBMs**	**ICBMs Only**
GEN, LOW	1303	1335	1335	1352
GEN, ROA	885	816	500	501
DAY, LOW	1080	1164	1290	1352
DAY, ROA	693	645	495	501

Notes: GEN = Generated Alert; LOW = Launch on Warning; DAY = Day to Day Alert; ROA = Riding Out the Attack and Retaliating.
Source: Author, based on Arriving Weapons Sensitivity Model (AWSM@) designed by Dr. James Scouras, who is gratefully acknowledged and is not responsible for any analysis.

Table 9.3.   US–Russia, Total strategic weapons, 1,000 deployment limit.

US	1000 Triad CBO	Dyad Without Bombers	Dyad Without ICBMs	SLBMs Only
ICBM	218	280	0	0
SLBM	672	720	890	960
AIR	109	0	109	0
Russia	**Balanced Triad**	**No Bombers**	**No SLBMs**	**ICBMs Only**
ICBM	318	288	858	1000
SLBM	608	704	0	0
AIR	74	0	76	0

Source: Force structures based on author's estimates and New START counting rules. See also: US Congressional Budget Office (2017). *Approaches for Managing the Costs of U.S. Nuclear Forces, 2017–2046* (Washington, D.C.: Congressional Budget Office), and Podvig, P. "Russian strategic nuclear forces," Blog. Available at: http://russianforces.org/ (accessed on October 2020).

Tables 9.1 to 9.4 show that the US and Russia can modernize their strategic nuclear forces within New START limits on deployed weapons, or at even lower levels, while maintaining deterrence and crisis stability. Neither should be challenged to provide for assured second-strike

Table 9.4. US–Russia: Surviving and retaliating warheads, 1,000 deployment limit.

US	1000 Triad CBO	Dyad Without Bombers	Dyad Without ICBMs	SLBMs Only
GEN, LOW	820	835	800	778
GEN, ROA	572	608	729	778
DAY, LOW	585	643	507	521
DAY, ROA	387	416	485	521
Russia	**Balanced Triad**	**No Bombers**	**No SLBMs**	**ICBMs Only**
GEN, LOW	833	829	828	900
GEN, ROA	614	684	243	226
DAY, LOW	795	829	789	900
DAY, ROA	364	399	239	226

Notes: GEN = Generated Alert; LOW = Launch on Warning; DAY = Day to Day Alert; ROA = Riding Out the Attack and Retaliating.

Source: Force structures based on author's estimates and New START counting rules. See also: US Congressional Budget Office (2017). *Approaches for Managing the Costs of U.S. Nuclear Forces, 2017–2046* (Washington, D.C.: Congressional Budget Office), and Podvig, P. "Russian strategic nuclear forces," Blog. Available at: http://russianforces.org/ (accessed on October 2020).

capability, absent dramatic changes in technology favorable to defenses compared to offenses, and, even then, pessimists can only worry about relative disadvantage in counterforce wars. There is little or no likelihood of removing populations from their hostage conditions to nuclear strikes even by smaller powers, let alone the more sizeable arsenals of the US and Russia. On the other hand, Russia and the US, by dumping New START along with INF, could bring about a new arms race that threatens the basis of nuclear strategic stability and the continued success of the Nuclear Nonproliferation Treaty (NPT).

Russian fears that US missile defenses could nullify their retaliatory strike anticipate missile defense technologies that outperform current capabilities by a considerable margin. However, this does raise another interesting question for the US and Russia, with respect to "how much is enough" when it comes to improving anti-missile and air defenses. Suppose the US and Russia push to develop defenses that *can* offer preclusive protection against nuclear attack based on current missiles and air-delivered weapons. Is the resulting deterrence system more, or less, stable, compared to its predecessor based on secure second-strike capability with survivable offensive weapons? Or, for a more interesting and more practical question: would the US or Russia want to develop and to deploy anti-missile systems that could guarantee, say, 80% effectiveness against any other state's nuclear second-strike forces?

The viability of nuclear deterrence depends on cognitive simplicity and clarity with respect to the expected outcomes of any large-scale nuclear exchange. If states believe that there is no technical escape from mutual vulnerability based on secure second-strike capability, then a choice by any state for a nuclear first strike is self-evidently pointless. On the other hand, if defenses improve to a degree sufficient to create a continuum of possible nuclear exchange outcomes, such that some outcomes are judged acceptable or tolerable compared to others ("winning ugly"), then politicians and their military advisors might mistakenly see a nuclear standoff as a competition for relative advantage, instead of a trapdoor opening the way to mutual suicide.

The preceding statement is a controversial assertion that will be disputed by those who perceive that the threat of nuclear war, as opposed to the actual decision for a nuclear attack, can be used for the manipulation of risk and for nuclear coercion short of war. This counter-argument, that nuclear ambiguity can be more useful that nuclear certainty, is situationally dependent and needs to be carefully qualified.[40] Ambiguity can be used by one state in a coercive bargaining process to its advantage, *provided* the other state can see the difference between *threats short of war* and a *decision to launch an anticipatory attack*.[41] Nuclear ambiguity may characterize a bargaining *process*, but for that process to result in an acceptable *outcome*, nuclear certainty must exist about the effects of a nuclear war.

9.7. Conclusion

The end of the INF is part of a larger problem, which is the need to transition to a new framework for US–Russian nuclear strategic stability.[42]

---

[40]Expert discussion of this issue appears in: Sechser, T. S. and M. Fuhrmann (2017). Nuclear *Weapons and Coercive Diplomacy* (Cambridge: Cambridge University Press).

[41]On the problem of anticipatory attacks, see: Mueller, K. P. *et al.* (2006). *Striking First: Preemptive and Preventive Attack in U.S. National Security Policy* (Santa Monica, CA: RAND).

[42]Sergei Karaganov and Dmitry Suslov argue for a new concept of "multilateral strategic stability" meaning "a state of relations between nuclear powers which enables them to prevent any military clash between them, including intentional and unintentional ones,

The challenge for the Trump Administration and its successors will be to manage the transition in three aspects: first, to maintain the cohesion of NATO and other US alliances with respect to political decision-taking, military preparedness, and arms control initiatives; second, to protect an interim level of strategic stability with Russia while a new Russian–American security framework is being created; third, to incorporate new actors, especially China, into a new framework for nuclear strategic stability; and, fourth, to include recognition of the increased importance of new technologies, including those for the security-related uses of space and cyber.[43]

The costs and benefits of ending the INF Treaty and jeopardizing extension of New START are not only measured in the possibility of renewed nuclear arms race on the European continent — important as that problem is. It is also necessary to consider the impact of a missing INF on the dynamics of crisis management and escalation control. Departure from INF creates a more complicated decision space in several directions: between conventional and nuclear war; between nuclear first use and an expanded theater-wide conflict; and, most important, between theater and strategic nuclear warfare. Sub-strategic nuclear weapons deployed in Europe are two-faced: they are seen as deterrents by their owners, but they also invite preemptive attack on themselves at the earliest stages of a conflict. Or, if you prefer: how many Able Archers can a system withstand?[44] In addition, if a defunct INF is followed by American and Russian refusals

---

because any such clash may develop into a global nuclear war." See: Karaganov, S. and D. Suslov (2019). "The new understandings and ways to strengthen multilateral strategic stability," Higher School of Economics (Moscow), *Russia Matters*, September 16. Available at: https://www.russiamatters.org (accessed on October 2020), in Johnson's Russia List 2019 — # 151 — September 17.

[43]Rose, F. A. (2019). "The end of an era? The INF Treaty, New START, and the future of strategic stability," Brookings, February 12, in *Johnson's Russia List* 2019 — #21 — February 13.

[44]Able Archer 83 was a NATO command post exercise in November 1983, testing procedures for nuclear release and potential use in case of war. The exercise took place during a time of heightened US–Soviet tensions over various issues, including competing NATO and Soviet nuclear missile deployments and an ongoing Soviet KGB intelligence operation (RYAN) to detect signs of a possible NATO nuclear first strike. See Garthoff, R. L. (1994). *The Great Transition: American-Soviet Relations and the End of the Cold War* (Washington, D.C.: Brookings Institution), esp. pp. 138–139, and pertinent references therein. See also: Macintyre, B. (2018). *The Spy and the Traitor: The Greatest Espionage Story of the Cold War* (New York: Crown Publishers), pp. 142–148.

to extend the New START agreement beyond 2021, nuclear arms control will be on a possibly irreversible descent into irrelevance. In this admittedly gloomy scenario, the NPT may feel the tremors from the abdication by the two nuclear superpowers, and events may encourage other non–nuclear-weapons states to reconsider their priorities.[45]

Admittedly, the challenge of keeping INF in place was more complicated for Washington and for Moscow than is the less controversial forwarding of New START, and the demise of INF was foreseeable in the inertial force of US and Russian impatience to be rid of it — albeit for somewhat different reasons Russia's interest in deploying additional land-based medium and longer-range missiles in Europe and in the Far East reflects its perennial fear of encirclement, of additional "bracket creep" in NATO membership, and of China's rising numbers of ballistic missiles of various ranges. Russia also fears an outbreak of next-generation conventional US PGS systems supported by improved anti-missile defenses, space-based weapons, and cyberthreats, although Russia is also modernizing its military capabilities in all of these categories.[46] The US is already planning or developing four land-based missile systems that would have contravened the INF Treaty limits: two of these missiles appear as likely candidates for deployment in Europe.[47] The possible costs of jettisoning INF include reduced stability of the military-strategic balance of power in Europe and, along with this, an unintentional lowering of the nuclear threshold based on confusion between designed flexibility and unintended or inadvertent escalation.[48]

It would be an understatement to say that cyber and information strategies are wrapped around all the arms control issues discussed hitherto. Nuclear strategic stability at, or below, the threshold of general nuclear war requires that certain shared expectations between potential adversaries be cultivated like delicate flowers. For deterrence to hold firm, leaders

---

[45] For pertinent background, see: Sokolski, H. D. (2016). *Underestimated: Our Not So Peaceful Nuclear Future* (Carlisle, PA: Strategic Studies Institute and U.S. Army War College Press).

[46] US Defense Intelligence Agency (2017). *Russia — Military Power: Building a Military to Support Great Power Aspirations* (Washington, D.C.: Defense Intelligence Agency). Available at: https://www.dia.mil (accessed on October 2020).

[47] Pifer, S. (2019). "The death of the INF Treaty has given birth to new missile possibilities," *The National Interest*, September 18, in *Johnson's Russia List* 2019 — #153 — September 19.

[48] For expert commentary on this issue, see the briefing by John K. Warden, Institute for Defense Analysis (IDA), *SMA STRATCOM Speaker Series*, September 12, 2018. https://nsiteam.com/social/wp-content/uploads/2018/09/Limited-Nuclear-War-brief-Warden.pdf (accessed on October 2020).

must have confidence that they have an accurate understanding of their opponents' capabilities and intentions, including their theories of war and assumptions about deterrence. During the Cold War, these shared expectations developed slowly over time as between the Americans and Soviets, and then among their respective alliance partners (for the most part, with unavoidable French pirouettes and Maoist disclaimers offering occasional distractions). Future frameworks for nuclear strategic stability will have to work out similar protocols of reassurance with respect to nuclear deterrence and crisis management: but they will have to do so in the age of cyber. Now the very sources of information and assessment on which strategic reassurance is based are themselves in danger of deliberate or inadvertent compromise. As Sanger warns:

> Cyberweapons are entirely different from nuclear arms, and their effects have so far remained relatively modest. But to assume that will continue to be true is to assume we understand the destructive power of the technology we have unleashed and that we can manage it. History suggests that is a risky bet.[49]

As for New START, its deployment ceilings and other limitations provide sufficient numbers of survivable strategic weapons for the US and for Russia under foreseeable conditions of nuclear weapons modernization. Missile defenses, unless or until they are based on new physical principles or concepts, are unlikely to change this condition. In addition, New START also provides Washington and Moscow with transparency and verification with respect to missile and warhead deployments going forward. As for the relationship between INF and New START on one hand, and nuclear flexibility on the other, much is scenario dependent. The US does not want to be in a position in which it has fewer options for escalation, *and* for escalation *control*, than its opponent does — for the sake of credible deterrence.[50] On the other hand, the US and NATO do not want to permit nuclear flexibility to relax high standards for crossing the nuclear threshold. Nor should Russia wish to do so.

---

[49] Sanger, *supra* note 28, at 296.

[50] Russian non-strategic nuclear weapons play an important role in Russian thinking about how to deter and defeat the West. On the other hand, some Russian military planners and thinkers have sought an additional capability for "prenuclear deterrence" based on long-range conventional strike systems. See Roberts, B. (2018). *The Case for U.S. Nuclear Weapons in the 21st Century* (Stanford, CA: Stanford University Press), esp. pp. 134–136.

Chapter 10

Influence Operations: Combination of Technological Attacks and Manipulation of Content

David Siman-Tov*,‡ *and Ohad Zaidenberg*†

**Institute for National Security Studies, Tel Aviv, Israel*

†*ClearSky, Tel Aviv, Israel*

‡*dudis@inss.org.il*

Abstract

This chapter analyzes a relatively new phenomenon in the world of cyberattacks that combines technological attacks and manipulation of content. While neither the phenomenon of influencing content nor technological attacks on computer systems and computer infrastructure are new in cognitive and cyberwarfare, their combination is a more recent occurrence, especially in light of the attack attributed to Russia during the 2016 US elections.

10.1. Introduction

In this chapter, we will present several models of attacks that combine the manipulation of content and technological attack and cyberattacks and discuss the differences between the varied models in terms of the implications of the attack (knowledge framework and technological capabilities) as these are expressed on the Internet, including social media.

The chapter examines attacks that are attributed to states in which intelligence forces are usually associated with — in other words, activities that include covert aspects. Influence operations that only involve influencing content, e.g. through public diplomacy, are not examined in this chapter.

The importance of analyzing the phenomena that this chapter draws attention to is twofold: it could serve those interested in influencing an adversary and that need to improve their attack capabilities, and it could help those who need to prepare for and thwart such attacks, which are a primary challenge facing democratic processes, especially election campaigns.

Section 10.2 provides a theoretical review that introduces the main concepts in the discourse of cyber influence operations and information warfare. Section 10.3 classifies the attacks found into several groups whose differences are fitting under technological attacks and the framework required for manipulation content. Section 10.4 presents an analysis of the differences between the assorted models.

10.2. Theoretical Background

The development of cyber influence operations, with an emphasis on social media, contains extensive opportunities for leveraging technology as a tool for conveying messages to the masses. While the discussion of cyberattacks whose aim is to disrupt computer systems and infrastructure is familiar in the public and professional discourse, we can distinguish the hybrid and unique nature of attacks for influential purposes that are based on a combination of cyberattacks and the manipulation of content.

10.2.1. *Information warfare in the cybernetic age*

The manipulation of information for political, economic, and military purposes has been a common practice throughout human history. Traditional influence operations used various tools to undermine personal security and public support for state institutions and to damage social solidarity.[1] However, the growing power of non-state actors and the

---

[1]Paikowsky, D. and E. Matania (2019). "Influence operations in cyber — Characteristics and insights," The *Cognitive Campaign — Strategic and Intelligence Perspectives*, INSS Memorandum 197, October, pp. 99–114.

development of the cybernetic realm have led to the development of hybrid information warfare that combines kinetic, political, cultural, and technological aspects within the cognitive campaign.[2] As a result, operations identified with information warfare also include the use of technological developments, elements of subterfuge and deception, and overt digital media tools.[3]

The means that states use to manipulate information and their aims are diverse and based on the accepted political doctrine. For example, the Russian information warfare doctrine is identified in the military-linguistic terminology as an "information struggle." Its goal is to disrupt and paralyze the adversary's systematic efforts by achieving superiority in the realm of information and decision-making processes. The main patterns identified with Russian influence operations include the use of emotional elements, the creation of doubt and uncertainty, use of diverse messages, and exploitation of social weaknesses of the adversary. As a result, the information struggle uses various tools, including psychological warfare, deception, fraud, electronic warfare campaigns, cyberattacks and disinformation campaigns.[4,5]

Unlike the information struggle, Iranian information warfare is a central component of a broader paradigm that is based on non-military political warfare, in light of Iran's conventional inferiority vis-à-vis its enemies. The RAND Corporation defines it as "political warfare," meaning covert warfare that uses the elements of political power to influence decision-making or the shaping of policy in an adversarial state.[6] Iran

---

[2]Danyk, Y., T. Maliarchuk and C. Briggs (2017). "Hybrid war: High-tech, information and cyber conflicts," *Connections*, **16**(2): 5–24.

[3]Brown, R. (2002). "Information operations, public diplomacy & spin: The United States & the politics of perception management," *Journal of Information Warfare*, **1**(3): 40–50.

[4]Adamsky, D. (2015). "Cybernetic operative art: From the perspective of strategic studies and in comparative perspective," *Eshtonot*, No. 11, Israel National Defense College, August [in Hebrew], pp. 39–41.

[5]Michlin-Shafir, V., D. Siman-Tov and N. Shaashua (2019). "Russia as an information superpower," The *Cognitive Campaign — Strategic and Intelligence Perspectives*, INSS. Memorandum 197, October, pp. 115–134.

[6]Robinson, L., T. C. Helmus, R. S. Cohen, A. Nader, A. Radin, M. Magnuson and K. Migacheva (2019). *The Growing Need to Focus on Modern Political Warfare* (Santa Monica, CA: RAND Corporation), pp. 5–24.

uses means including public diplomacy, cyber influence operations, and strategic communications, which help expand its influence in the Middle East, strengthen the impact of its military efforts, and support its ideological and religious principles.[7]

The big data revolution, whose significance is the ability to process enormous amounts of data, makes it much more effective to engage in information warfare and to influence the cognition of the masses extensively. The access of tech giants to big data make them central players in the cognitive campaign. These companies have the ability to target a certain audience relatively effectively and precisely, and to direct the content that users are exposed to, resulting in their status and power as mediators of content and knowledge in the Internet era. Influence operations on large populations aim to change defined opinions of a certain population, and thus information "bombing" and disrupting the information environment on the accepted platforms make it difficult for the individual to understand the reality in which he is living and to formulate a relevant action plan. Thus, the attacking side succeeds in creating a relative advantage in the overall cognitive campaign.[8]

In addition to big data processing, modern information warfare requires understanding the advantages that are made possible by the unique structure of the cybernetic realm. The relevant characteristics include the difficulty in attributing an attack and the anonymity made possible for attackers. In addition, the architecture of the Internet leads to regulatory difficulties in light of the lack of a clear hierarchy and maintaining net neutrality, which creates a veil of anonymization for the user and enables those interested in influencing to exploit the characteristics of the internet world for their benefit.[9]

Furthermore, influence operations in the cybernetic domain are directed toward large populations and tend to use the global scope and messages to shape the public discourse, while emphasizing the creation of personalized content for each Internet user through the act of targeting.

---

[7]Haiminis, I. (2019). "Iran's information warfare," *The Cognitive Campaign — Strategic and Intelligence Perspectives*, INSS. Memorandum 197, October, pp. 135–150.

[8]Assa, H. (2019). "Influencing public opinion," *The Cognitive Campaign — Strategic and Intelligence Perspectives*, INSS Memorandum 197, October, pp. 25–36.

[9]Dunlap, Jr., C. J. (2014). "The hyper-personalization of war: cyber, big data, and the changing face of conflict," *Georgetown Journal of International Affairs*, **15**: 108–118.

This targeting of the individual user creates a reactive modus operandi that establishes a discourse between the attacker and its users, whose results do not depend on the attacker alone. Thus, implementing attack patterns through internet platforms that are accessible to the entire public to a large extent indicate the attacker's ambition to expand the target audience, to enable the victim to "take part," and even to create a force multiplier for the attack. Contrarily speaking, we mention attacks to prevent service or infrastructural weaknesses inside systems that aimed only to shut down computer systems or to cause destruction, as with the Stuxnet malware in Iran in 2010. This is different from attacks that are based on involving the victim in organic discourse on social media or on inserting content within mass platforms, as with Russian intervention in the 2016 US Presidential elections.

In addition to the reactive aspect of the attack, it is important to note the influence of the quantitative aspect in the cybernetic realm in light of the possibility of effectively and precisely targeting large populations on social media. Subsequently, the reverberation and emphasis of content in online influence operations create a kind of viral effect in which the user is exposed to content that is relevant and personalized to him. Consequently, the user chooses how to respond to the content in a voluntary action, which usually is not imposed by the attacker himself. Responses range from writing a response or sharing or tweeting that same content, such that it is preserved to a certain extent among the user's online community. Thus, providing the user with freedom of action in responding to the influence operation establishes the dynamic nature of information warfare in the cybernetic realm, which is dependent on the "reverberation" of the attack and it being maintained by its victims.

The discussion involving the victim in influence operations in the cybernetic realm is reminiscent of traditional attacks based on social engineering, which are known for having cognitive and psychological consequences in the literature on exploiting human vulnerability.[10,11] However, unlike social engineering, which is directed top-down by the attacker to

---

[10]Nurse, J. R. C. (2018). "Cybercrime and you: How criminals attack and the human factors that they seek to exploit," University of Kent, October.

[11]Lively, Jr., C. E. (2003). "Psychological based social engineering," SANS Institute, GSEC Option 1 version 1.4b, December.

aid with traditional online operations, the nature of cyber influence operations depends on the victim's response and the way they relate to the attack pattern, and therefore some identify tend to use the global scope and messages cyber information operation (CIOs) as a combination of top-down and bottom-up processes.

10.2.2. *Cyber influence operations*

A modern prism for looking at the behavior of state and non-state actors in the cybernetic realm is emphasized by the connection points between technological attack types and the cognitive campaign, via content-based influence operations that can serve objectives that are not technological. It is common in the discourse to distinguish between types of cyberattacks based on their objectives — Computer Network Attacks (CNAs), which cause damage and prevent the functioning of computer systems, and Computer Network Exploitation (CNE), for the purpose of stealing information and espionage. A more recent type of attack is cyber influence operations, which may also be referred to as Computer Network Information (CNI).[12] Brangetto and Veenendaal define these as "operations which affect the logical layer of cyberspace with the intention of influencing attitudes, behaviours, or decisions of target audiences."[13] In light of the broad definition of the term, some identify this type of attack in the context of influencing social trends and shaping public opinion, such as concerning elections, by establishing the manipulation of information and distributing false information.[14] Thus, the goal of cyber influence operations is to shape the cognition of the

---

[12]Bren, D. and Y. Levy (2014). "The cyber phenomenon of the Islamic State — What the West must understand," in *Cyber — Challenges and Opportunities in New Spheres, Ben-Haktavim*, Dado Center. December, **3**: 115-137 [in Hebrew].

[13]Brangetto, P. and M. A. Veenendaal (2016). "Influence cyber operations: The use of cyberattacks in support of Influence Operations," *8th International Conference on Cyber Conflict*, May, pp. 113–126.

[14]IAI (2018). "Israel Aerospace industries hosting a think tank as part of the European Union Horizon 2020 Dogana R&D Program," June.

adversary by means that are not kinetic, and to sow feelings of fear and uncertainty among the victims.[15,16,17]

Another study on the issue created a distinction between cyberattacks and espionage on one hand and cyber influence operations on the other hand, where the latter constitutes content-based security threats that involve exploitation of the digital realm in order to influence human cognition. Sander further expands the application of the concept to include any action that is carried out by a state or actors whose behavior is identified with a state according to international law, in which they exploit information in the cybernetic realm in order to influence the political discourse in a foreign state.[18]

Sander adds that strengthening the use and effects of social media has raised the rate of cyber influence operations, as seen in Russian intervention in the American elections in 2016. Consequently, we can distinguish the unique development of cyber influence operations in the social media era, which has strengthened the operational and cognitive capabilities of these activities in terms of quantity and content. Thus, if in the past cyber influence operations were dependent on traditional media and means of communication and on limited access to the target audience that consumed that medium, the evolution of mass media and the possibility of targeting the user in social media have changed the rules of the game in the cognitive campaign. Therefore, we can see social media as an interface that expands the possibilities for conducting influence operations, thus making CNI attacks more common and accessible to significantly larger populations than was the case before the rise of social media.

The internal link between the attacks arises in the traditional characterization of CNE attacks. In the Internet era, the nature of the information gathered about the target is diverse, such as technological

---

[15]Siboni, G. and O. Assaf (2015). "Guidelines for a National Cyber Strategy," Institute for National Security Studies, Memorandum 149, October, pp. 18–19 [in Hebrew].

[16]Pernik, P. (2018). "Hacking for influence — Foreign influence activities and cyber-attacks," International Centre for Defence and Security, February 2018.

[17]Bagge, D. P. (2019). *Unmasking Maskirovka: Russia's Cyber Influence Operations* (New York: Defense Press).

[18]Sander, B. (2019). "The sound of silence: International law and the governance of peacetime cyber operations," in T. Minárik *et al.* (eds.), *11th International Conference on Cyber Conflict*, May, **900**: 1–21.

information for understanding the structure of the computer networks and information for carrying out active operations in the future such as hacking into personal accounts or stealing state secrets or commercial information. Thus, some may see part of the CNE attacks as having the potential to influence and convey messages, similar to CNI attacks. The rationale for the similarity between the attacks is that after exposing the sensitive information, the victim's sense of penetration and vulnerability intensifies, and can be exploited and exposed to all by the attacker and can serve as a tool for exerting influence.[19] Aside from this, there are CNE attacks whose sole objective is to expose, thus the purpose of espionage is not just achieving the information itself, but having the attacker expose the sensitive information and manipulate it.

Consequently, the very distinction between the various cyberattacks and cyber influence operations is becoming further blurred in light of the intensification of the cognitive campaign. Thus, we can say that the traditional division of types of attacks based on their objectives has changed in the Internet era, and they are joined by multi-stage attacks. In these attacks, information gathering and espionage can strengthen cyber influence operations. It is quite possible that a CNA attack leading to considerable damage of a sensitive target that is known to the public could serve as a means of exerting influence, whether intentionally or by chance. This shows the developing relationships between the goals of the attack in the cybernetic realm, with the creation of a hybrid model that combines a mediated attack with an initial attack for achieving the primary and dynamic aims of the attackers.

The fluidity between the goals of the different attacks shows the multiplicity of possible technological patterns that the attacker can use to achieve its primary objectives and even exploit opportunities that are unplanned and depend on the way the attack develops. Figure 10.1 maps out the development of the conceptualization of content-based influence operations, in accordance with the changes that have occurred in the types of attacks in the cybernetic realm, and reflect the above.

---

[19] Sinay, Y. (2016). "Transportation cyber security," *Digital Whisper*, **October**(76): 6–9.

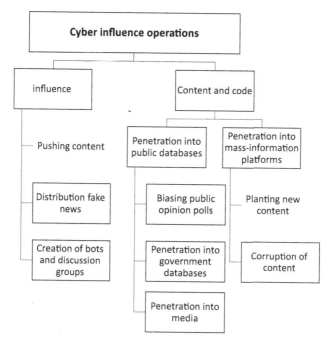

Figure 10.1.   The development of the conceptualization of influence operations based on technology and the manipulation of information.

10.2.3. *Tools, methods, and practices*

Aside from the theoretical conceptualization of cyber influence operations, the review will discuss relevant tools, methods, and practices for attackers. Paikowsky and Matanya[20] relate the nature of online influence operations as the point of departure for psychological operations, the cyber campaign and information warfare, which aim to influence decision-makers by creating a framework of information and narratives. They discuss modern cyberattacks that serve to disrupt social and value-oriented processes, through attacks that combine hostile content with a cyberattack using various technological tools.

---

[20]Paikowsky, D. and E. Matania (2019). "Influence operations in cyber — Characteristics and insights," *The Cognitive Campaign — Strategic and Intelligence Perspectives*, INSS. Memorandum 197, October, pp. 99–114.

A more limited prism for viewing information warfare in the cybernetic realm could refer to the types of attacks that are relevant for use. For instance, there are attacks that enable planting content on varied social media sites or platforms and taking control of the pages displayed to users. In addition, the use of "bots" and "avatars" for furthering influence operations enables uploading content or disrupting it throughout the Internet, thanks to automatization and their great productivity compared to normal human users.[21] Furthermore, attackers can hack into legitimate accounts and websites and disrupt the information on them or distribute alternative information. The issue of intervention in content brings up the phenomenon of disinformation and fake news, which is intensifying in the cybernetic realm, with an emphasis on publication via social media channels or through intentional leaks across online platforms. The objective of misleading information is to strengthen damaging and inciting narratives, thus the use of online platforms helps distribute content on a widespread scale.[22,23]

In conclusion, the review discusses the conceptual development of content-based influence operations by examining basic concepts such as information warfare, information struggle, political warfare, and manipulation of information. In order to understand the development of influence operations in the cybernetic realm, we examined the traditional division of cyberattacks according to the objectives of the attack (CNE, CNA, and CNI), up to the development of the research discourse on cyber influence operations.

10.3. Influence Operations Based on Technological Cyberattacks Combined with the Manipulation of Content

Offensive cyber actions and campaigns can create an influence effect both intentionally and as a deterrent effect after the act of attribution. Such an

---

[21] Ferrara, E., O. Varol, C. Davis, F. Menczer and A. Flammini (2016). "The rise of social bots," *Communications of the ACM*, July, **59**(7): 96–104.

[22] Maasberg, M., E. Ayaburi, C. Z. Liu and Y. A. Au (2018). "Exploring the propagation of fake cyber news: An experimental approach," *Proceedings of the 51st Hawaii International Conference on System Sciences*, pp. 3717–3726.

[23] Gu, L., V. Kropotov and F. Yarochkin (2017). "The fake news machine: How propagandists abuse the internet and manipulate the public," White Paper, *Trend Micro*.

initiative includes the connection between the offensive action and the attacker, whether by indicating a well-known offensive actor within the cyber domain, which is sometimes identified with a state or a stakeholder in such activity, or by pointing the finger at those behind the execution of the attack. Unlike an intentional influence effect, the "delayed deterrent" effect is more trivial, as it includes the deterrence that is generally achieved from such offensive activity.

We can roughly divide the use of digital platforms for malicious objectives, by the state level, into two main axes. The first axis includes "classic" cyberattacks — the use of executed tools for offensive and defensive objectives as in the exploitation of vulnerabilities in existing systems in order to cause some form of damage to the attacked party, such as stealing information, destruction, disrupting processes, and espionage. The second axis includes exploiting the virtual realm for the purpose of influence operations. These operations are based mainly on content and less on technological activity. In recent years, an interface has developed between "classic" cyberattacks and influence operations. We can identify three main ways of combining cyberattacks with malicious content, which we will expand on further in this chapter.

In this section, we will summarize several elements of influence operations that include various cyberattacks. We will begin with a short survey of "classic" cyberattacks, those for which the dimension of influence is not part of the attack's objectives or the tools that are manifested in the attack. We refer to such attacks as "delayed deterrence" attacks — influence operations in which there is no content but the activity creates a delayed deterrent effect among the attacked party and the general public. This is followed by a review of influence operations that include certain cybernetic infrastructure, hacktivist influence operations,[24] and cyberattack events that create influence elements and finally linking offensive cyberactivity and malicious content.

10.3.1. *"Classic" cyberattacks, with an emphasis on CNE and CNA, which have "delayed deterrence"*

These kinds of attacks are the point of departure for cyberattack operations that interface with influence operations via malicious content. These attacks generally do not directly aim to exert any kind of cognitive influence on the attacked party, but rather focus on directly or indirectly

---

[24]Hacktivists are social activist hackers.

damaging it by attaining access for information or in some way damaging its technological asset.

The largest cyberattacks of the past decade (2010–2020) have been characterized mainly by the delayed deterrence effect, especially attacks in which attribution is successful. In this context, we can draw attention to two significant events that manifested status on the attacker who was accused of the attack. The first event of this kind was the attack on the Iranian enrichment site at Natanz through the Stuxnet computer worm, which, according to foreign reports, including that of Edward Snowden, was carried out by the US and Israel.[25] Another event that was characterized by "delayed deterrence" was the NotPetya attack, in which thousands of Ukrainian companies were attacked with malware that were disguised as ransomware. This attack, which took place over the course of two full days and caused extensive damage throughout the Ukraine, was attributed to Russian intelligence (GRU) by the Ukrainian security services (SBU), the ESET Company, and the CIA.[26]

10.3.2. *Cognitive and influence operations — classic disinformation campaigns*

10.3.2.1. *The Global Disinformation Operation*

A significant state in the field of disseminating disinformation via fake news sites is Iran. In 2018, three large-scale disinformation campaigns directed by Iran were exposed, each of which had a different target and used different methods.

(1) The first campaign, Ayatollah BBC, operated for six years, and its goal was to influence the public in Iran, to disseminate false information against Western media outlets broadcasting in the Persian language, and to undermine their legitimacy among the Iranian public. This operation had two branches: a network of websites masquerading as a series of Western media outlets active in Iran and

---

[25] Snowden, E. (2019). "ls Zielobjekt markiert" Der Enthüller Edward Snowden über die geheime Macht der NSA. Available at: https://www.spiegel.de/spiegel/print/d-102241618.html (accessed on 2019).

[26] Nakashima, E. (2018). "Russian military was behind 'NotPetya' cyberattack in Ukraine, CIA concludes," *The Washington Post*. Available at: https://wapo.st/38fjoBC (accessed on January 13, 2018).

broadcastings in Persian, such as the BBC, Voice of America, and Radio Farda, a branch of Radio Free Europe funded by the American Congress. Iran attempted to undermine the legitimacy of these media outlets and frighten readers through deception and implying they have been "marked" by the regime. A large portion of the media outlets that they impersonated were censored by Iranian search engines (such as Yooz and Parsijoo), while the fake sites remained in place.[27]

(2) A network of fake websites posed as unfamiliar independent media outlets that spread disinformation and incitement against the media outlets that they impersonated in the first branch, as well as real incitement against the local journalists who work for those networks.

The second campaign was implemented immediately after the assassination of the Saudi journalist Jamal Khashoggi. As part of this operation, Iran worked to influence Saudi public opinion after the murder of the journalist and to agitate the nation against its regime.

At the end of 2018, a large-scale campaign conducted by Iran was exposed. The campaign aimed to disseminate disinformation that would serve its objectives via a network of fake websites that it operated around the world (i.e. the Global Disinformation Operation, GDO).[28] The global campaign operated unimpeded for six years and succeeded in reaching tens and even hundreds of thousands of people around the world. This campaign included hundreds of fake news and disinformation sites operated by Iran. Each of these sites masqueraded as a fictitious media organization in the target state that Iran's efforts were directed at. The sites were frequently updated, and dozens of fake news articles were uploaded to them that used different methods of disseminating disinformation. In one of these methods, called "false connection," the distributors of the false information connected fake headlines, visual media, and technological media with content that did not match the original content of the website.[29]

---

[27]Clearsky Security (2018). "Ayatollah BBC — An Iranian disinformation operation against Western media outlets," [Blog]. Available at: https://www.clearskysec.com/bbc/ (accessed on 2020).

[28]Clearsky Security (2018). "Global Iranian disinformation operation," [Blog]. Available at: https://www.clearskysec.com/global-iranian-disinformation-operation/ (accessed on 2020).

[29]Jack Stubbs, Christopher Bing (2018). "Special Report: How Iran spreads disinformation around the world." Reuters. Available at: https://www.reuters.com/article/us-cyber-iran-specialreport-idUSKCN1NZ1FT (accessed on 2020).

Each website had its own logo, sometimes even a logo for each language. The fake news media outlet website "Yemen Press" included a completely different logo for its Arabic, Persian, and English version sites. In addition, social media pages identified with the name of the fake media outlet were created for the campaign, along with an extensive network of fake profiles that distributed the operation's articles on different networks and designated applications. Furthermore, many of the fake sites listed a physical address that the media outlet was supposedly located at. A study conducted by *Reuters* on these addresses found places that do not exist or where something exists that is not a newspaper, such as garbage dumps.[30] Unlike the previous campaigns written about in this chapter, this one included many elements whose purpose was to make the sites look innocent.

Hence, we can identify two main aspects of high-quality disinformation campaigns:

(1) Many tools of disguise are needed in order to operate a single disinformation website and present an "innocent" appearance to those exposed to the disinformation and provide the website with a sense of credibility. The more the credibility is needed, the more tools are needed to disguise the website as an innocent one.

(2) In order to carry out a high-level disinformation campaign, considerable resources are needed — both technological resources for operating the website, means for making the website look innocent, and non-technological resources for creating the relevant message and content.

As part of the campaign, the Iranians created a network of fictitious media organizations for the purpose of disseminating the false information and did not impersonate existing media organizations. Despite the large scale and the use of many platforms, including social networks and even designated apps for these websites, it does not appear that, within this campaign, Iran worked to damage the assets of the information's consumers, but only to expose them to information as it understood it or sought to promote.

---

[30]Bing, C. and J. Stubbs (2018). "Special Report: How Iran spreads disinformation around the world," *Reuters*, Available at: https://reut.rs/2YuKHn0 (accessed on November 30, 2018).

Now we will discuss the interfacing between these axes by means of three different kinds of cyberattacks that include a content-based element: CNA and CNE attacks as a basis for CNI attacks based on real content; CNA and CNE attacks as a basis for CNI attacks based on false content; and a combination of CNI attacks with CNE and CNA attacks as a single operation that aims to achieve several goals.

10.3.2.2. *CNA and CNE attacks as a basis for a CNI attack based on real content*

(i) 2016 US elections

The attack on the Democratic National Committee (DNC) that is attributed to the Russian GRU, which apparently took place from January 2015 until the months before June 2016, is an example of a combination of espionage and influence. Unlike the previous attacks, which were characterized mainly by a massive attack that aimed to damage infrastructure and not to exert influence, the attack on the DNC is a significant milestone in combining cyberattacks with influence operations.

As part of this attack, an attack group called Fancy Bear (also called APT28),[31] which is identified with the GRU, took control of digital assets of the Democratic National Committee, such as its email servers. The penetration vector into the DNC's computer systems was via spear-phishing, which included different methods of social engineering and was sent to specific DNC employees. For example, misdepartment[.]com was one of the domains that was created for the purpose of conducting cyberattacks on the DNC employees. One can see that the order of the letters was switched in a way that makes it difficult for those attacked to notice. One of these employees, who fell victim to this spear-phishing attack by the Russian groups, infected the DNC's computer system with malware and enabled the attackers to access confidential information, especially DNC email servers, which included tens of thousands of correspondences. After the relevant information was stolen, it was leaked via an unknown source called Guccifer 2.0 on a website called DCleaks, as well as via a

---

[31] An Advanced Persistent Threat (APT) is a stealthy computer network threat actor, typically a nation state or state-sponsored group, which gains unauthorized access to a computer network and remains undetected for an extended period. In recent times, the term may also refer to non–state-sponsored groups conducting large-scale targeted intrusions for specific goals.

Figure 10.2.   Screenshot from the DCleaks website, which was the main website that the group used to distribute the information about the DNC.

Note: One of the pictures is of the Jewish-Hungarian billionaire George Soros.

Source: Risk Based Security (2016). "DCleaks: Little known site dumps data on George Soros," [Blog]. Available at: https://www.riskbasedsecurity.com/2016/08/13/dc-leaks-little-known-site-dumps-data-on-george-soros/ (accessed on 2020).

designated website that was created by the attackers for the purpose of leaking the information (Figure 10.2).[32]

After about a month of leaks on a limited scale, figures with a fictitious identity contacted the WikiLeaks website and transferred it 19,252 email correspondences and 8,034 attachments. These were publicized on July 22, 2016, for all to see. The information itself included not only dozens of sensitive correspondences that were relevant to the party's activity but also general information that was not relevant to anyone. Even without examining the content of the documents, this attack created several significant influence effects:

---

[32] Threat Connect (2016). "Does a BEAR Leak in the Woods?" [Blog]. Available at: https://threatconnect.com/blog/does-a-bear-leak-in-the-woods/; (accessed on 2019). Trend Micro (2017). "Two years of pawn storm." [Blog]. Available at: https://documents.trendmicro.com/assets/wp/wp-two-years-of-pawn-storm.pdf (accessed on 2020).

(1) The initial leaks damaged the reputation and the standing of the DNC. How could the party manage a country if it was not capable of securing its information? Such questions and others were raised by the candidate of the rival party, who said: "Russia, if you're listening, I hope you're able to find the 30,000 emails that are missing," and were adopted afterward at similar events around the world.

(2) Despite sweeping denials by the Kremlin, which included a declaration by the Kremlin's spokesman, Dimitri Paskov, who claimed: "I completely reject the possibility that the government (of Russia) or a governmental body was involved in this (in hacking into or leaking the email correspondences),"[33] the hack itself situated Russia as a very significant player in the cyber domain and as the leading source of global disinformation. Since the elections, we can identify increasing discussion of Russian attack groups, and specifically APT28, among cyber researchers and journalists around the world. In addition, we can see Russia's position at the frontlines of global disinformation.

Examining other name servers of the group that were exposed at that time indicates efforts on the part of Russia both to prepare infrastructure for a cyberattack but at the same time can also indicate efforts to distribute disinformation through them.[34] For example, the domain vice-news[.]com, which is connected to the attack infrastructure on the DNC, can serve as a website for spreading disinformation, while the domain mail.hm.qov[.]hu masquerades as a website of the Hungarian government, and was apparently a phishing site,[35] perhaps for associates of George Soros, who

---

[33] Roth, A. (2016). "Russia denies DNC hack and says maybe someone 'forgot the password." Available at: https://www.washingtonpost.com/news/worldviews/wp/2016/06/15/russias-unusual-response-to-charges-it-hacked-research-on-trump (accessed on June 15, 2016).

[34] A name server translates domain names into IP addresses. This makes it possible for a user to access a website by typing in the domain name instead of the website's actual IP address. Techterms (2019). "Name Server." Available at: https://techterms.com/definition/nameserver (accessed on 2020).

[35] Phishing is a method of stealing information from the attacked party. Usually users who attack using various social engineering methods in order to fool the attacked party and cause it to provide the sensitive information.

Figure 10.3. Tweet from the DCleaks Twitter account about the Hungarian billionaire George Soros.

Note: The use of a social media platform is another means of not only distribution but also creating credibility among those attacked. In relation to Figure 10.3, please note the location in Manhattan and not in Washington DC or, alternatively, in the attacker's country — Russia.

appeared frequently on this site.[36] That is, the group Fancy Bear operated simultaneously both in terms of classic cyberattacks and in terms of attacks that included malicious content. In addition, it should be noted that this group did not act only via a website. On Twitter, for example, a designated account for DCleaks was created whose objectives could be twofold — on one hand, distributing the website to as many people as possible, and on the other hand, creating another display of credibility for the website.

The main combination of cyberattacks with malicious content was the connection between stealing information through cybernetic kill chain means such as malware and phishing sites, the attacker extracting the information, and the public (and unfiltered) use of this information in order to achieve objectives known only to the attacker. We can see that such a simple cyberattack had global influence, both on the elections, to an extent that perhaps cannot be assessed using quantitative tools, but certainly on the sense of threat of cybernetic intervention in various election campaigns (Figure 10.3).

It should be noted that in these kinds of attacks, there is usually almost no importance in the content stolen, but just in the fact that it was stolen and leaked. These kinds of operations give the victim's opponents the impression that it is vulnerable, does not know how to protect its assets, can

---

[36]ThreatConnect (2016). "What in a name server?" [Blog]. Available at: https://threatconnect.com/blog/whats-in-a-name-server/ (accessed on 2020).

be blackmailed, and even is irresponsible and unfit to lead; while saying that the large volume of the materials does not enable the general public to objectively review all of it, but only to discuss the fact that it was leaked.

10.3.2.3. *CNA and CNE attacks as a basis for CNI attacks based on false content*

(i) Group of Turkish hacktivists
Another event, which is characterized by hacktivist activity against Israel whose goal appears to have been to make waves in the attacker's environment, is the attacks on Israel by a group of Turkish hackers called Ayyıldız Tim that identifies itself as "Turkey's cyber army."[37] As part of these attacks, the group attempted to attain cognitive achievements from the attacks and combined malware, whose purpose was to steal sign-in information for various websites, including Twitter, with the use of the hacked accounts in order to embarrass those attacked or to post various messages of support for the Turkish government in their name.

For example, the Twitter account of the former Director-General of the Foreign Ministry of Israel, Mr. Dore Gold, was hacked by the group using a spear-phishing attack that included malware.[38] The group exploited his account to tweet messages supportive of Turkey and anti-Israel opinions from his account. As part of this wave of attacks, the group also attempted to harm Turkish journalists living abroad, such as a Fox News journalist. The combination of the cyberattack and false messages that were distributed via access to the accounts attacked constitute another way of combining these elements and of an influence operation that combines a cyberattack and malware. Attacks such as these require prior knowledge of the figure who serves as a platform for influencing public opinion. In the case presented above, a hostile message was disseminated on Dore Gold's account, which only included the message itself (the fake and subversive message). This action enables the attackers to easily disseminate their ideas and opinions. In contrast, the effect is relatively minor, as once the account is restored and/or the incident is reported to the relevant social network, the content is deleted from the internet.

---

[37] Witman, A. (2018). "Turkish cyberattack on Israeli sites," *Israel Hayom*, May 21 [in Hebrew]. Available at: https://www.israelhayom.co.il/article/557371 (accessed on 2019).

[38] Spear-phishing is a parallel method to phishing, in which a specific target is attacked using infrastructure that is generally designed for him.

Dr. Dore Gold
@DrDoreGoldTR

Your account is hacked
by the Turkish cyber army
Ayyıldız Tim! Your data and
your DM correspondence
have been captured! The
Turks will never forget,
neither what is done nor what
is evil

Figure 10.4.   The message upon hacking into Dore Gold's Twitter account by the Turkish group Ayyıldız Tim.

Thus, the main success of spreading such content is the very ability to distribute the content and not the content itself. In a different incident in the group's campaign, it distributed a screenshot from the private message page of a single profile from among the profiles discussed. This screenshot proved that one of the people attacked, who was considered an associate of the son of US President Donald Trump, and even publicly supported the President as part of his position as a Fox News broadcaster, muted the President's son on his Twitter account such that he would not see messages received from him. In this incident, the content itself was not fake, but it was carefully chosen to embarrass the person attacked. In such incidents, the attacker does not generally know about the material that the attacked person has, but selects it from among all of the material (Figure 10.4).

10.3.2.4.   *CNI attacks that are combined with CNA/CNE attacks*

In 2019, a campaign called "Endless Mayfly" was exposed, which turned out to be another Iranian disinformation campaign.[39] As part of the report that was distributed on the campaign, two different events were reviewed: the first was GDO, which we discussed earlier, and the second was a disinformation campaign that included websites masquerading as legitimate

---

[39] Citizen Lab (2019). "Burned after reading: Endless Mayfly's ephemeral disinformation campaign," [Blog] Available at: https://citizenlab.ca/2019/09/poison-carp-tibetan-groups-targeted-with-1-click-mobile-exploits/ (accessed on 2020).

media websites around the world, such as *Al Jazeera, Haaretz, The Independent, RT*, and *The Guardian*. These websites are identified as inauthentic websites and inauthentic personas, similar to the wording that Facebook chooses to use when it removes profiles from the social network that aimed to spread disinformation (in addition to being fake).

As part of the campaign, dozens of fraudulent websites were exposed that included the malicious content. These websites generally included only a single article that contained the false information; in certain cases the remainder of the site contained redirects to the original site, while in other cases it presented an error message. The purpose of the fictitious articles that appeared on these sites is not clear, but from the profile of the articles we can learn that they discussed issues at the forefront of the public agenda, and it is evident that the Iranians invested thought in developing the malicious content and in continuously tracking the political mood in the target country. Therefore, the purpose of websites that contained only one article is not clear.

The majority of cases included Iranian impersonation of media organizations and included a fictitious article, sometimes quoting people who never said the things attributed to them. For example, as part of the campaign, a website was created that impersonated Harvard University's Belfer Center. The website was created around the time of then-Israeli Defense Minister Avigdor Lieberman's resignation. The website distributed an article that quoted a speech by former Mossad Director Tamir Pardo according to which Prime Minister Netanyahu wanted to dismiss Lieberman from his position as Defense Minister due to his being a spy for Russian intelligence, things that were never said by the former Mossad Director. However, it should be noted that indeed, a few days earlier, Pardo had given a speech at the Belfer Center, thus we can see the deep knowledge that this campaign's operators had of political events in Israel and the discourse on social media, and we can even learn from this that the operators tried to take advantage of an opportune time to make the post — namely, Tamir Pardo's appearance at the Belfer Center.[40]

The websites were distributed using various social engineering techniques, especially personally contacting specific people identified with different media personalities from specific newspapers (including

---

[40]Bar-Zik, R. (2018). "Fake news campaign against Lieberman: 'Tamir Pardo claimed that he is a Russian Agent,'" *Haaretz*, November 14 [in Hebrew]. Available at: https://www.haaretz.co.il/captain/net/.premium-1.6655180 (accessed on 2020). Note that the domain name of the fake website is belfercenter[.]net, while the domain name of the original site is belfercenter.org

newspapers that they impersonated as part of the campaign). The different distribution platforms included instant messaging platforms such as WhatsApp and distribution through various social media, such as fake Twitter accounts. During the study, the researchers who exposed the campaign found that these attackers had created a fake page for Twitter, the main platform in which the information was disseminated.

The various fake profiles also included a wide variety of techniques for seeming innocent, such as pretending to be a "political analyst and writer" in a profile that misrepresented itself as a woman named Mona A. Rahman and disseminated messages against the Government of Saudi Arabia. This profile tried to get people to go out and demonstrate against the Saudi Government in London, especially after the murder of Jamal Khashoggi. The operators of this profile would tag tweets that were made by a Saudi-American journalist named Ali AlAhmed. Another profile that operated was called Bina Melamed and sent articles to journalists via Direct Messages on Twitter, or, alternatively, also tagged them with the fake articles or with posts calling for action.

The campaign operated in four main stages. The first stage took place between April 2016 and April 2017, during which messages were distributed on Twitter, mainly against Saudi Arabia, by six fake figures who supposedly belonged to the organization "Peace, Security, and Justice Community." The second stage took place between April and October 2017, during which several fraudulent websites were created and disseminated by a number of additional figures, who tried to "hunt" journalists and activists. The third stage began in parallel to the second stage, and in it the campaign's operators started to disseminate fake websites using tags of journalists in responses to these articles, and in addition tried to promote the hashtag #ShameOnSaudiArabia on Twitter. In the fourth and final stage, which took place from December 2017 to November 2018, the fake profiles started to create direct connections with these journalists. It should be noted that after disseminating the malicious content, the fake website was deleted and additional concealment techniques were carried out, such as redirection to the original website, in order to cover the attackers' tracks and try to conceal the attack.[41]

---

[41] These websites shared similar technical details with disinformation websites from the GDO campaign, thus the company connected them. During the technical analysis of this operation, researchers succeeded in finding a technological connection with several applications infected with malware that pretended to be Twitter. This overlap was based on

In conclusion, this campaign included websites that masqueraded as well-known news sites around the world, distributed the information to specific figures via WhatsApp and to broader figures, including journalists and those following journalists on social media, and there is a medium-to-high likelihood that they intended to distribute or did distribute APK files infected with malware. This campaign was more sophisticated than the campaign that was operated in the Russian hacking of the DNC and the GDO campaign that was operated by Iran, in terms of the number of different platforms, and this may have been the first campaign that combined cyberattack efforts using malicious and fake content that was not a clear means of "social engineering."

The purpose of this campaign is not clear. On one hand, it could be claimed that it was not a fake news campaign at all, and that it is in fact a much longer and more sophisticated stage of social engineering. On the other hand, many of the fictitious articles were spread publicly on social media and directed at journalists but also at the general public. Unlike regular phishing sites, in this case the operators also invested in writing a false article that would not only cause the attacked person to want to read it, but also to pass on the message including the disinformation. Thus, we can see this campaign as the one of the strongest example of combining a cyberattack with malicious content.

10.4. Conclusion

The chapter examined several outlines of combinations between technological attacks and the manipulation of content using the virtual realm.

Classic cyberattacks, i.e. CNA-type attacks, demand that the single attacker or group of supporters use several technical attack tools, whether they are based on the independent development of malware by an attack team or whether they are based on "commodity malware" that can be purchased on the internet and used for the attack. The development team generally includes support staff. These can included IT personnel, graphic designers, specific language speakers if the attacker intends to attack targets that are not speakers of his language, economic figures and more. This support staff is not the main component in this kind of attack, as the

---

overlapping infrastructure (e.g. storage of websites on a private, unique server) or, alternatively, complete similarity between the Whois info of these websites.

attacker's main objective is to attain the access he is aiming at vis-à-vis the attacked party. The role of the support staff is to help the attacker achieve his objectives, and therefore, sometimes the attackers themselves constitute the support staff and carry out both of the roles, with their expertise, of course, being the development and/or operation of offensive cyber tools.

In contrast, influence operations in the virtual realm, CNI-type attacks, demand the opposite relation between the support layer and the development team. In many influence operations, e.g. in the disinformation campaign that was carried out from Yemen, the attackers create a fake news campaign that includes a fake website or series of fake websites on which the malicious content is disseminated, but nothing bad happens to the electronic device of the attacked party while using these websites. Therefore, an identical platform is also used on social media — the dissemination of disinformation via fake accounts. Such attacks, thus, require mainly the "support staff" — content writers, graphic designers, disinformation artists, economics experts, and social media experts. There is less of an emphasis on the development staff, if at all (in the case of using social media). This makes CNI attacks common, sometimes carried out by public relations agencies and not by sophisticated cyberattackers.

The analysis carried out in this chapter shows that for cyberattack operations that began a decade ago or earlier and include damaging the functioning of computer systems or espionage operations, only minimal use of content was needed, mainly for the purpose of inserting the malware via social engineering. The second type of attack that was presented in the chapter includes the publication of information attained through cyberattacks. While there is no change in the nature of the attack, a change in its purpose is evident here. It is possible that such publication could also expose attack capabilities or block a breach. In addition, such publication, if it involves large amounts of information, requires creating infrastructure in which it is possible to control the speed and timing of the publication.

The third type of attacks analyzed in this chapter describes an increasing combination of content and technological attack elements at the outset. In this context, we can learn about several characteristics of cyberattacks that involve malicious content:

(1) The familiar platform of malicious websites that distribute malicious content infected with malware is insufficient, and there is a need to

create a framework that complements the cyberattack and includes sample profiles on social media in order to succeed in directly reaching those attacked.

(2) A cyberattack that includes malicious content and aims to exert influence must include several different "layers" that provide credibility to the attacker, unlike the example from classic cyberattacks in which the attacker can use a single e-mail address to distribute a single phishing site. In cognitive-type attacks, the attacker generally incorporates additional elements of credibility — activity on social media or presenting a false image of an existing company, including visual content and even location.

Appendix

Table A.1. The differences between technology-based cyber operations and operations that include the manipulation of content.

Content-only	CNA and CNE attacks as a basis	CNA and CNE attacks as a basis for a CNI	Cyberattack operations
The use of the virtual realm for the purpose of influencing public opinion. The main emphasis in such attacks is on the content that is distributed to the attacked public. In such a campaign, no special technological sophistication is required.	For CNI attacks based on fake, subversive, or carefully selected content — damaging the attacked party using technological tools and cyberattacks, exploiting the damage, and the takeover of assets in order to carry out cognitive and influence operations using the asset. The very distribution of the information about the damage to the attacked party's assets is the main thing, and thus the emphasis is on the use of the virtual realm to exert influence and not on the attack. Such attacks have a low level of sophistication, as the attacker generally identifies itself and stands behind the attack.	Attack based on true content — Damaging the attacked party using technological tools and cyberattacks, stealing sensitive information and exploiting this information for cognitive purposes. The exploitation of the information usually does not involve processing, and it is presented as it is, without manipulation. The theft itself is what is important, thus a high technological level is necessary.	Using technical tools and exploiting the digital platform to damage the target of the attack according to the aims of the attacker. The main emphasis in such attacks is on technological sophistication, bypassing information security mechanisms, and carrying out the necessary technical actions (modules).
	CNI attacks combined with CNA/CNE attacks Same relation between the need for technological sophistication and advanced cyberattacks and the "framework" that provides the capability to distribute false information and influence public opinion, while damaging the targets.		

Chapter 11

The Internet and its Hidden Cyberthreats for Teenagers

Guillermo Arce

*School of Business & Law, Universidad Francisco de Vitoria,
Madrid, Spain*

g.arce.prof@ufv.es

Abstract

Understanding the new environment of cyberspace and how social networks are influencing the future of humankind is critical not only for teenagers but also for their relatives and the society as a whole. This chapter focuses on identifying the explicit, implicit, and more importantly, the hidden threats faced by the present-day society and understanding how these risks can affect our teenagers, who will become the future leaders of governments, companies, and institutions in just a couple of decades from now. Are they aware that everything they are doing now is being been saved permanently and could resurface any time in the future? Privacy is now becoming san utopian concept[1]; we are already living in George Orwell's world and the scary part is that there is not only just one Big Brother watching us, there are many: governments, cyber intelligence agencies, security institutions, and especially mega Cyber

---

[1] Scott McNealy, CEO, Sun Microsystems, once commented: "You have zero privacy. Get over it." Quoted in Solove, D. J., M. Rotenberg and P. M. Swartz (2006). *Information Privacy and Law*, 2nd Edition, p. 635.

International Corporations (CICs), such as Cambridge Analytics, that are controlling and ruling our cyber lives. The terrifying thing is that we, the people and the society, are passively accepting this as part of our daily routine because somehow this hyper–cyber-linked world is satisfying what marketing professionals refer to as a "basic human need[2]": communication, which forms the keystone of our society and human development. At the same time, we are publicly revealing our most hidden needs and our deepest private thoughts (some marketers refer to these as "personal wants") to people and companies that are ruling our cyber lives.

When I was a kid, my parents told me to be aware if anyone was following me, someone could be threatening me. Nowadays, if you don't have at least 500 followers, you are a fool.

Anonymous post on social networks, May 2019

11.1. Introduction

In order to identify and explain the hidden cyberthreats faced by teenagers and the society today, this chapter is divided into the following sections: Section 11.2. identifies the key players ruling the cyberspace; Section 11.3 describes the teenager's behavior, skills, and personality in the cyber world; Section 11.4 provides an understanding of the new rules of cyberspace; Section 11.5 describes the explicit, implicit, and hidden cyberthreats for teenagers; and Section 11.6. provides the discussion and conclusion for the chapter.

11.2. Origins and Key Players in Today's Cyberspace

The present-day cyberspace[3] could be defined as a virtual space based on the Internet and the World Wide Web (WWW) that is present on a

---

[2]Maslow, A., & K. J. Lewis (1987). Maslow's hierarchy of needs. Salenger Incorporated, 14, 987, the hidden wants, and the latest theory about self-transcendence have been discussed in different articles, such as Koltko-Rivera, M. E. (2006).

[3]*The Oxford Language Dictionary* defines cyberspace as: "The notional environment in which communication over computer networks occurs."

computer (or an ICT device such as phone, laptop, tablet, smartphone,[4] etc.) and provides the opportunity to communicate or execute programs (also known as virtual applications or "apps") that allow us to transfer any content (data, images, videos, text, etc.), thereby helping us in our daily personal and professional lives.

Many people, especially teenagers, will say that they cannot exist outside the cyberspace virtual world. Understanding the origins, but especially the reason why society has adopted cyberspace with such enthusiasm, can be only achieved by exploring the origins of our human development as a social group, when they were gathered in small tribes, that used the same codes and communication for creating rules that could help them survive in a wild environment. The amazing capability of communication, i.e. delivering knowledge, sharing ideas, and transmitting information, was the key to humankind's (*Homo sapiens*) outstanding success over other species inhabiting the Earth, even some that are genetically very close to us.

People could share and transfer knowledge to their relatives and descendants, thereby creating strong social tides and what Coleman termed "social capital," that make human beings the stronger species on our planet.[5] The abstract and spiritual world created by our ancestors, as reflected in cave paintings, was born thousands of years ago, and is the precedent of today's cyberspace. Intellectual and communication skills were the key reasons for humankind's successful evolution. Developing tools and using technology were key to our capability of ruling territories, and conquering the best and most useful ones, for survival. Our adaptability to the surrounding environment led to our survival and success, like Charles Darwin[6] described in the 19th century.

The very basic act of communicating knowledge and transmitting complex ideas and information was performed 20,000 years ago, in front of the campfire, by the oldest and the wisest people of the tribe through the medium of storytelling to the youngest, as described by the Spanish

---

[4]Oxford definition of smartphone: A mobile phone that performs many of the functions of a computer, typically having a touchscreen interface, Internet access, and an operating system capable of running downloaded apps.

[5]Coleman, J. S. (1988). Social capital in the creation of human capital. *American journal of sociology*, **94**: S95–S120.

[6]Darwin, C. (1872). *The Origin of Species by Means of Natural Selection, or the Preservation of Favoured Races in the Struggle for Life* (London: John Murray).

Atapuerca's researchers Arsuaga and Martinez[7] in their book *La especie elegida* (trans. The Chosen Ones). This act has the same impact and importance for teenagers and cyberspace users today, as they try to "stand out," and through the very act of telling "stories": that value of power and significance is important for teenagers as a YouTuber[8] or an Instagrammer posting any content in the 21st century. Today's influencers or YouTubers have almost a "god-like power," thanks to the amazing power of the Internet. However, who is controlling them? How can any regulator (companies, parents, governments) enforce or control their right to the "freedom of speech" whenever they cause problems? It all boils down to the matter of balance between this right and the user's right to access accurate information.

The problem is that cyber teens are emotionally connected to these influencers, in an almost spiritual way, mirroring religious faith rather than just a social link, and we do not yet know the effect of this influence in the future. Therefore, this could be classified as a typical hidden threat. As Westenberg[9] says:

> YouTubers are seen as authentic, when reviewing a product or brand. Followers believe that recommendations are honest (…) because they are perceived as equals. The intimate stories about personal lives make them approachable and trustworthy.

The necessity for communication is embedded in our genes and plays a vital part in our culture because it is directly related to the ability of human beings to succeed and thrive. Survival in today's world depends, as did for our ancestors, on the ability to communicate and transmit information. The opinions of other cyberspace users are more important that any advertising.

> Nowadays, personal opinions and experiences have become one of the most valuable sources of information to assist users in their decision-making process.[10]

---

[7]Arsuaga, J. and I. Martínez (1998). *La especie elegida.* (Madrid: Temas de Hoy).

[8]Westenberg, W. M (2016). "The influence of YouTubers on teenagers: A descriptive research about the role YouTubers play in the life of their teenage viewers," Thesis, University of Twente.

[9]*Ibid.*

[10]Chua, A., and S. Banerjee (2015). "Understanding review helpfulness as a function of reviewer reputation, review rating, and review depth," *Journal of the Association for Information Science and Technology*, **66**(2): 354–362.

In order to understand the present-day roles in this global cyberspace, we can focus on three main key players: Users, Regulators, and Companies. The reason for this disruptive proposal is to try and understand that the rules of the game have already changed. The global cyberspace no longer confirms to the traditional boundaries governing social, political, or business arenas, and we are dealing with a completely new environment,[11] where 19th and 20th century laws and regulations do not solve the threats, as described by Dr. Limor Ezioni.[12] The new cyberspace belongs to new "owners" and "players"; we are "playing" in a global virtual field, where one's privacy belongs to others, and where economy and wealth are driven by new rules with new players and different goals, as described by Taspcott in his book *Wikionomics*.[13]

Gómez de Ágreda[14] discussed this situation in his book *Mundo Orwell* (trans. Orwell's World); in his writing, the author updates the statements of the famous British writer about how the world would be like in 1984, contrasting the 1949 novel with the current situation in the first quarter of the 21st century, and dealing with key issues such as information and media manipulation, the concealment of truth, and the obsolescence of the traditional working model. The book opens with an impactful quote that vividly describes the current cyberspace and social situation:

> The real problem of humanity is the following: we have Paleolithic emotions; medieval institutions; and God-power like technology. And it is terrifically dangerous, and it is now approaching a point of crisis overall.[15]

We are facing a completely new approach to this virtual global society and rules; usually your freedom can go as far as meeting others but this is no longer the case in cyberspace, and as Osborne advises, and Dr. Ezioni demands, the society and especially our Institutions is not ready for it yet.

---

[11]Lessig, L. (1999). *Code and Other Laws of Cyberspace* (New York: Basic Books). Lessig declared in his book that: "We will see that cyberspace doesn't guarantee its own freedom, but instead carries an extraordinary potential for control."

[12]Ezioni, L. (2018). "Identity theft and exposure to harmful content. Internet risks for teenagers," *Cyber, Intelligence and Security*, **2**(3), INSS ISRAEL.

[13]Tapscott, D. and A. Williams (2008). *Wikinomics* (London: Penguin Books).

[14]Gómez de Ágreda, Á. (2019). *Mundo Orwell* (Ariel).

[15]Osborn Wilson, E. (2009). Interview. *Harvard Magazine*.

Some other authors, such as Solove,[16] warned about this situation just three years after the social network Facebook was founded (the birth and development of which is perfectly described in Kirkpatrick's book *The Facebook Effect* in 2010)[17] highlighting how the next-generation cyberspace is building a new environment where traditional laws, rules, and codes no longer apply.

Cilluffo, Pattak, and Salmoiraghi[18] already predicted this development two decades ago, after recognizing "the many benefits of information technology and understanding that these benefits far outweigh the risk." They denounced that the "USA Government was prosecuting 21st century crimes with 19th Century laws." They offered very interesting advice and concluded that the government and the corporations (i.e. Washington and Silicon Valley) "as Cillufo, Pattak and Salmoiraghi think side by side and on equal footing." Well, it looks like today this scenery remains the same, and we could even say, that the CICs[19] (Google, Facebook, etc.) are way ahead of any government or country regulation.

Figuring out the key players in this new virtual theater can lead to the understanding that the development of the Internet and the cyberspace has at least the same impact on our global society as all the previous technological and social revolutions that have propelled humans since the beginning of time: the fire, the wheel, the Industrial and Cultural Revolutions, and so on, until we reached Communication Revolution and finally the Internet. This includes artificial intelligence (AI), and the cyber revolution, which is probably the one that will thrust humans into new and unknown frontiers of knowledge.

11.3. The Cyberspace's Main Users: Teenagers

How can we describe the new users of this vast cyberspace, who they are, and what their behavior is, and why do we consider "digital natives" our main target? The global and massive penetration of the Internet and cyber

---

[16] Solove, J. D. (2007). *The Future of Reputation* (New Haven & London: Yale University Press).

[17] Kirkpatrick, D. (2010). *The Facebook Effect* (New York: Simon & Schuster).

[18] Cilluffo, F. J., P. Pattak and G. Salmoiraghi (1999). "Bad guys and good stuff: When and where will the cyber threats converge," *DePaul Business and Law Journal,* **12:** 131.

[19] CIC is a proposed acronym for referring to the cyber conglomerates that are ruling the world in the 21st century. Ref. to Dr. Arce.

networks during the last decade of the 20th century quickly segmented the population and created new terms in order to qualify and describe the cyber users, especially to identify the different generations joining the Internet in the last decades, such as millennials,[20] Z-generation, digital natives, "Google generation,"[21] "blog generation," or "tablet kids."

Either way, we should accept that the new generation, i.e. those born around the 21st century, are intrinsically related to Internet use since they were babies, and we can easily realize that their environment and ways of finding information and communicating are based on the Internet, taking advantage of all the apps, tools, and benefits that the web offers us.

> Online resources can be tools as much as they can be the object of research [...] they can be used to the benefit of single individuals, or organizations, but also communities of practice and learned societies.[22]

We can also conclude that older and mature people ("baby boomers," late "senior boomers," or the X-generation), as described by Alcazar[23] in her book *The New Tribes*, i.e. the so-called "digital immigrants," have embraced this virtual cyberspace with the same enthusiasm but visibly lacking the requisite skills. Today we could say that anyone who has a minimum income in a basic developed country will probably be a user of the Internet and cyberspace. It is surprising, and rather worrisome, that you could find people in rather deplorable conditions, going through hunger and hardship, but possessing a mobile phone. Again, communication and access to the cyberspace seem to be key basic needs for people everywhere, and teenagers are the core inhabitants of this new cyberspace world.

---

[20] The industry has coined the term "millennials" to denote all those born and raised while considered the Internet a fact of life. See: Bátiz-Lazo, B. (2016). "About millennials, new technology and researching business organizations," *Journal of Evolutionary Studies in Business*, **1**(1): 152–156. June.

[21] Solove, J. D. (2007). *The Future of Reputation* (New Haven & London: Yale University Press).

[22] Bátiz-Lazo, B. (2016). "About millennials, new technology and researching business organizations," *Journal of Evolutionary Studies in Business*, **1**(1): 152–156.

[23] Alcázar, P. (2009). *Entre Singles, Dinkis, Bobos y otras tribus* (Barcelona: Planeta Empresa) [in Spanish].

Over the past 15 years, children in a developed country have been exposed to the cyber world and the Internet since they were babies. You could see some of them preferring tablets rather than any other toys, and embracing the cyber world as a vital part of their lives. The 2005 "App Generation" comprises those born almost at the same time as the main social networks like Facebook,[24] Twitter, WhatsApp, or WeChat (in Asia), and they are coetaneous as the disruptive technological advances that have changed the way we communicate and gather information: i.e. the "smartphone."

Teens of this App Generation or "Smarter Generation," due to their smartphone addiction,[25] have embraced technology and the cyberspace as a natural part of their lives. They have grown to be highly skilled in their use, building further steps in the way human beings communicate, not only by transferring or sharing information but also by creating it, using different Internet apps as 21st century tools, and thus becoming "Wikiproducers."[26] For the first time in human history, users are no longer just media consumers but also self-producers and global distributors of information. The way this generation communicates has rocked the rhizomatic perspective of connecting to others, thus influencing every aspect of our lives. Instead of connecting to a dozen or maybe a hundred, any content can be made viral as it travels through the cyberspace worldwide and reaches millions within seconds. We could say that traditional media will probably die, transform dramatically, or even disappear when this App Generation reaches the top echelons of social and entrepreneurial leadership around the world, which would probably occur 20 years from now.

The big question on everyone's mind nowadays is: are these users,[27] i.e. the teenagers of the App Generation, aware of the dangers and threats

---

[24] Facebook, the world's biggest social network, was officially founded in 2004.

[25] The iPhone was officially launched in 2007 by the Apple CEO Steve Jobs. It is considered the first real Smartphone and was based not only on a new understanding of human interaction with the device but also total integration of internet apps built as accessories into the traditional "mobile telephone."

[26] Arce, G. (2015). Thesis "Impacto de las Redes sociales de Internet en la generación net" uses this term in his doctoral thesis to refer to any individual that could create any kind of content, mainly written, graphic, video, or audio short stories (usually using apps as new tools) and communicating or informing others by sharing information through the cyberspace.

[27] Smith, C. (2018). "Cyber security, safety, & ethics education," Doctoral Thesis, Utica College. "Nearly all children, 8 year old and younger have some type of mobile device."

posed by the Internet? The answer is: probably not. Does the Internet use have any benefit on teenagers? The answer is yes, but understanding what this use involves may help develop the tools, educational strategies, and laws that will help them become "safe users" who can take full advantage of the latest technologies. Who are these early 21st century App Generation teens? What are their skills, strengths, and weaknesses? How can the Internet and the cyberspace help them, and how dangerous or harmful can they be for the teenaged users?

The Internet has provided this generation with the most powerful tool possessed by any human being since the advent of humankind: instant access to any kind of information, anytime, and anywhere (as long as there is Internet access); all human knowledge accumulated for centuries can be searched in seconds from different sources and exhibited in various formats.

What are the positive skills acquired by the App Generation? Different sources share the belief that these teenagers are eager to watch and discover new things by themselves; somehow the ancestral human curiosity for learning and knowing everything is one of their main strengths, thanks to their new tools. They own an amazing capacity for social skills, teamwork, and virtual social life, and sharing is now an extension of their personality. Their teamwork skills and ability to achieve a common strategy are amazing (just watch those young teens play online games and cooperate for a virtual goal), as they are used to living in a parallel virtual world that can be perfectly be adapted to their "real" world. It is amazing to see teens sitting together around a table, communicating to each other or to other teens, without saying a word. This rhizomatic network[28] capacity can be the most powerful tool for them; if they focus on demanding or reporting anything, their strength and voice can be felt, heard, and supported by thousands, sometimes millions of people worldwide.[29] They have acquired a great ability of doing "cross-reading" and searching for precise information at lightning speeds and have developed an instant, innate ability to adapt themselves to new

---

[28] Arce, G. (2015). Thesis "Impacto de las Redes sociales de Internet en la generación net." *supra* note 26.

[29] No Communication media has ever had this power. Teens live inside a worldwide rhizomatic link of communication, where you can have support from millions of followers who may never ever meet you personally, but who can trust your statement or idea all the way. Such is the effect of YouTubers and social media influencers.

cyber formats or apps, combined with an amazing capability of self-learning.[30]

We can conclude that we have "super skilled techie" teens who are using the Internet as an amazing cyber tool while probably still in the process of fully developing their cognitive reasoning, before reaching maturity. The standard genetic characteristics of any adolescent — brash, uninhibited, unruly, fearless, experimental, and often not mindful of the consequences of their behavior — usually mean that they might not be aware of how many dangers are lurking in the cyberspace.

11.4. Regulators

When we talk about the cyberspace, we usually refer to WWW[31] and just a small part of it. While the Internet is available globally, most of it is hidden: the dark net (or hidden web, according to Bergman[32]) "is estimated to be 400 or 500 times larger than the common Internet, and while many of its contents are considered criminal," according to Wright,[33] what makes it amazing is that it has no boundaries. Every peer is interconnected freely around the globe, with almost no limitations. This fact makes this amazing and complex computer logarithm the supreme tool for communication, thereby satisfying one of the main human needs.

The Internet was first part of a Cold War military project adopted by the university scientists that helped design it.[34] The strategic military key was based on connecting critical peers, so if any peer was destroyed under a massive attack (in the context of nuclear war), the other ones could

---

[30] Every educational institution (mid, high, graduate, or postgraduate) should consider what their future is going to be like and what added value they can bring to this generation. Top international companies like Microsoft and Google are no longer trusting traditional education and they search and hire people focusing on their personal attitudes and skills rather than grades and official institution titles.

[31] WWW (World Wide Web) is a term and design created by Sir Tim Berners-Lee, a British computer scientist in 1989.

[32] Mike Bergman, a computer scientist and consultant, is credited with coining the term "Deep Web."

[33] Wright, A. (2009). "Exploring a 'deep web' that Google can't grasp," *The New York Times*, December 3.

[34] Internet origin as described in: D. Tapscott and A. Williams (2008). *Wikinomics* (London: Penguin Books).

survive, keeping control and sustaining their counteracting military capability. Once the army dropped the project, it was easily adopted by the faculty members who helped design it as the perfect communication tool for sharing content; this benefit quickly helped expand it in universities and companies worldwide.

Just several decades later, during the 1990s, the cyberspace and the Internet was extended to the whole general population, rocking communication networks around the world and reaching anyone who was able to connect to it. It is probably the latest and fastest universal revolution in human history, but as Osborn[35] stated in his interview, institutions and regulators were not ready to match the speed of this tool and the companies that drove it. Soon new threats, crimes, and ethical or business abuses were taking place, and once again, the cyber world was moving much faster that the regulators. There was no "Global Internet Controller," and every country and justice department had to devise ways to control the power of multinational conglomerates in the field of cyber on their own.

Cybercrime and cybersecurity are definitely some of the most important aspects of the 21st century human security. The universal structure of the Internet *al*low criminals and malicious players to attack and manipulate the cyber network beyond the boundaries of justice, sometimes even supported by government or companies, in an updated version of a new business and strategic Cold War.

Cybersecurity control and responsibility (i.e. protecting your data, information, and most important and personal secrets) no longer lie exclusively with computer specialists. The whole society, i.e. every user and every company, are now unconsciously involved in this "evil play." Some governments and regulators have tried to control the universal personality of the Internet, but the political and justice rules (many from the 19th century) are obsolete and too slow to respond to this threat. If you, as a person or legal entity, or your company, are a victim of a cyberthreat, it is really difficult, if not impossible, to find its origin. Finding the offender and filing a legal attribution is a utopian notion nowadays, as Rid and Buchanan[36] explained in their Q-model proposal. Attribution (and cyber-legal persecution) is usually too large and complex a task for a person,

---

[35]Osborn, J., *et al.* "The suitability of the Risk Matrix 2000 for use with internet offenders." Unpublished manuscript (2009).

[36]Rid, T. and B. Buchanan (2015). "Attributing cyber attacks," *Journal of Strategic Studies*, **38**: 1–2, 4–37.

sometimes even a company, to handle. Cyber attribution is not only a technical problem but also involves a complex analysis, including the strategic, operational, tactical/technical, and communication layers, as described in the Q model. Identifying "hackers" and perpetrators depends on their behavior and personal style, rather than their Indicators of Compromise (IOCs).[37]

The way cyber criminals behave is revealed by their implicit mistakes: when they attack, how they attack, their "cyber style," timing, worlds, the "tech print" used in their programming, their sophistication, or how many people were involved.[38] Every part of the attack draws a trail and leaves a clue that can reveal not only their cyber personality but also intimate details of their attack, such as the origin or supporters, but despite this, even if you do identify the offender, that does not automatically mean they can be persecuted. The universal structure of the Internet allows cyber criminals to attack from remote platforms, where justice or political boundaries prevent them from being reached, or worse, where they are protected by political or business accomplices.

The best way to defend yourself, personally and professionally, assuming that governments, laws, and police are constrained by the slowness and obsolescence of structures unsuitable to follow the speed of the cyberspace, is to understand what the threats are and educate the people around you, especially those who are least knowledgeable and naive with regard to the Internet, to prevent any danger.

Schools, college, and universities are the official institutions that society relies on for the education of their young generations, but most of them are focused on traditional education methods (lectures, homework, essays, exams, etc.) with outdated material (you can still see lots of blackboards, and traditional "face-to-face" classrooms in many schools) led by great teachers and professors, who have extensive traditional knowledge (in history, business, marketing, communication, etc.) but rather low cyber skills compared to their own students.

It is becoming quite difficult to educate the App Generation on how to deal and take advantage of the cyberspace, with its ins and outs. It is a real challenge for 21st century educators, not only the Institutions but the

---

[37]IOCs are technical facts of malicious activity which leave a trail.

[38]Keystroke dynamics and mouse movements can reveal a lot about the individual who is typing. It can identify a betrayal personality trying to impose a fake profile (i.e. sex predator), and stop it (see footnote 36).

parents as well; as digital immigrants, there is a giant gap between them and the App Generation, especially because they do not understand the real threats and dangers faced by teens. As Dr. Ezioni explains:

> There is a big difficulty (all around the world) in finding a mechanism that will prevent invasion of privacy[39] (...) There is an absence of any control, both the party distributing information and the party receiving it, the Internet has become a theater of lawness that victimizes mainly the weak.

We, the society, governments, and educators, have to understand that the Internet is a universally uncontrolled tool, but our regulations and laws are local, and quite often totally obsolete for judging crimes and cyberthreats that only a few decades ago did not exist. How can you litigate someone or something that you cannot reach?

11.4.1. *Parents*

Parents are invariably the last line of defense but ideally should always be the first. School or university education come second only to education imparted at home, but the fact is that most parents either do not understand or have very little concern about what their children are doing on the Internet. Parents are usually late digital immigrants, dealing with highly cyber-skilled teens, who are simultaneously undergoing the natural and genetically naïve and immature process of teenage development, as experienced by others of their age in the previous generations. Roy, Roy and Sinha[40] reveal that, according to a recent survey done by McAfee in India, more than 62% of children shared their personal information and 39% of their parents are unaware of this activity. Also, 71% of the youth keep their online activities a secret from their parents.

---

[39] Privacy is something that a cyber user can control, but few of them do. How many people have accepted the requirements of any new app, without even reading them or leaving the privacy mode unconfigured or accepting any kind of "cookies"? Probably everybody. (Author's note).

[40] Roy, S., Utpal Roy and D. D. Sinha (2017). "ACO-random forest approach to protect the kids from internet threats through keystroke," *International Journal of Engineering Technology*, **93**(S): 2–9.

Relying on schools and teachers for transmitting traditional knowledge through different courses might be suitable, but real in-depth education about moral or religious values, social relationships, respect for others, ethical and especially legal behavior, belongs to parents. Also, giving the right directions and advice for cyber protection is their responsibility. Prevention is the best strategy toward cyberthreats. Prevention could also be the best strategy regarding teaching and influencing the concepts listed — but this could also translate into knowledge and norms related to attackers, malware, and related elements occurring during an attack and awareness on what to do after a cyberattack occurs. Information and norms can be seen as critical support systems throughout all stages. Many institutions[41] have pitched in to help, giving advice and assisting parents on how to supervise their kids with regard to their online activities, but the real problem is that the children are largely ignorant about the dangers and threats they face in cyberspace, and the ensuing problems, until it is too late.

Most parents will first identify their kids' addiction[42] to the Internet in any format (chats, playing games, watching videos, or sharing content) as a natural way of intense communication in the 21st century, and even go so far as to blame themselves for not being part of this cyber world.

As new cyberspace users are increasingly very young,[43] staying away from the cyberspace seems to condemn them to be social cyber "outsiders," and forces them to be apart from their friends circle. Trying to enforce rules requires minimum knowledge and understanding of their cyberspace: one cannot just simply "stop" a game when more than 20 players are involved in pursuit of a virtual goal; it is simply "out of mind" for them (have you ever tried to play soccer without a ball?).

---

[41] A great example is the Spanish guide for parents titled "Teens TIC Protection for Parents" edited by various institutions, concerned about this problem in Valencia, Spain, and published in 2015. ISBN: 978-84-9089-031-8.

[42] Díaz-Aguado, M. J., J. Martín-Babarro and L. Falcón (2018). "Problematic Internet Use, maladaptive future time perspective and school context," *Psicothema*, **30**(2): 195–200. The authors reveal that in order to prevent Problematic Internet Use (PIU), it is important to foster confidence in teens, and their own potential to build the future from the present through positive interaction with teachers.

[43] The age for accessing and using the Internet through various devices has progressively decreased in recent years, and we can easily see children aged as young as five or seven use tablets and smartphones with complete and unsupervised freedom (Author's note).

Their addiction to taking infinite "selfie" pictures goes beyond personal communication and sharing experiences; it is about personal egocentric self-satisfaction, one of the highest hidden "wants": to be recognized and valued as a "winner," just because of what are you doing and who or where you are. Following other people or cyber influencers can create really strong tides that are comparable to being a fan of a traditional popular figure during the last century. However, a "follower"[44] tide is much stronger because one can have instant and sometimes direct, personal feedback and a permanent dialogue with their idols, irrespective of whether they are musicians, athletes, artists, YouTubers, or even the US President! Who could have ever dreamed of that just a few decades ago?

The Internet's attractiveness and the infinite options the cyberspace offers us is too great a temptation to be passed, even for mature, intelligent, and wise people. As cyberspace reaches every corner of the world, we can confirm that older people and highly qualified professionals keep making the same mistakes as immature teens, getting themselves into trouble, sometimes due to a lack of cyber skills, but many times as a result of their naive behavior.[45]

Probably the first instinct for any parent, whose teenaged child is facing cyberthreats, is to confiscate the smartphone as a way of amputating the link to the danger. However, in many cases, it is a lost battle. Mobile phones have become an intrinsic part of youngsters, and their parents are even paying for it. What can parents do to protect their teenagers? Well, it is not so different from basic traditional education; it is about creating norms, being aware of where and who they are connecting to, and delivering norms accompanied by consistent arguments. The so-called, "just don't do it!" has never worked in traditional education, and it is not going to work in cyber education either. The teenagers usually reject orders, just because they are trying to create their own space. A reverse psychology strategy usually works better.

Some great advice[46] for parents is to work as a couple, delivering cyber norms that can help their children understand the threats and

---

[44] A "follower" is someone who follows virtually someone, using any app or cyber connection to be connected to them (Author's note).

[45] Minors engage in immature behavior without worrying about the consequences or how other people will be affected as a result of their actions.

[46] Extracted, adapted and translated from: "Teens TICs protection for parents." See: Pardo, L. S., G. C. Herrador, R. A. Moya, F.-J. Bueno Cañigral, R. A. Benavent, J. C. Valderrama

dangers of the cyberspace. But there is a need for parents to understand that there are dangers in the cyberspace, in order to set the norms for controlling their children. Some parental rules regarding the use of the cyberspace can include establishing norms that can regulate Internet use (where and when to use it), especially not using smartphones when the whole family is together (usually lunch or dinner) and maintaining discreet supervision of your children's activities in cyberspace, same as you will do in real life, by asking which social networks they are using, who their "friends" are, who they are following or linked to, how they have met those people, and what kind of activities or content they are sharing with them. A casual conversation about all these activities, even showing interest in some specific individuals, such as YouTubers, content, or games (show me, teach me), will help a lot. Direct interrogations usually scare them.

You should also not spy on or record your kids, or you might lose their trust (just remember yourself, decades ago, hidden behind the kitchen door, trying to sustain a personal intimate conversation through a fixed telephone line); privacy is important. Talking to them and joining them for "alternative activities" such as sports, music, cultural visits, or traveling (it is sad that these activities should now be called "alternative" by the App Generation) and focusing on developing common sense and judgment toward any danger or threat is critical for their mature use of the cyberspace.

The most important and critical point will be to identify any behavioral dysfunctions: sadness, loneliness, anger, fear, anything that might go beyond your children's standard personality should immediately call for attention, and a direct and honest conversation should take place in order to understand what the problem is and how we can help them. No matter what the problem is, and how big it is, they need to know that you are by their side, supporting them. Remember, parents and home education, not schools, companies, or governments, are the main line of defense against any cyberthreats faced by teenagers.

Zurián. *Los adolescentes y las tecnologías de la información y la comunicación (TIC). Ayuda para padres* (Valencia, Spain: Plan Municipal de Drogodependencias. Unitat de Prevenció Comunitaria de Conductes Adictives (UPCCA-Valencia), Concejalía de Sanidad, Ayuntamiento de Valencia). ISBN: 978-84-9089-031-8.

11.4.2. *The Internet Virtual Society*

The cyber society has also become a new key player in the cyberspace; the traditional society was usually related to your close environment, hometown, relatives, region, culture, and country. Nowadays cyber users belong to a virtual society that extends beyond any physical frontiers. The great advantage of the Internet cyberspace, a virtual place that "has proven to be a place of both, rigid control and unbounded freedom," as Solove, J. D.[47] stated, has given voice to any individual who can not only participate in it but can also be an opinion leader just by sharing his/her thoughts.

At the same time, the society is acting as a global regulator, creating the balance between an individual's right to speech, behavior, and anonymity, which is now in play. Any individual's participation, regardless of whether one is a famous personality or a naive teen, might be judged by thousands, sometimes millions, of other cyberspace users, for good or bad, and there is no way that any individual, even the most powerful one, can control this aspect.

This virtual and global democracy has proven to be really good for controlling any leader's speech or behavior (especially politicians) nowadays. Thanks to certain websites and apps, people can instantly comment, share, discuss, or respond to any statement, activity, or attitude of any personality. Anything that people do can be somehow be recorded and brought back to them at any time. Anonymity in cyberspace is now a utopian concept, and what is scarier is that it cannot be permanently erased.

On the other hand, anyone can pass judgment even lie or make a false statement about you with total impunity. In addition, there are professional profiles and automatic robots ("bots"[48]) trained for these activities; attacking any individual's reputation and creating a disturbing picture of them is really easy nowadays. Just being and participating in the cyberspace means that you cannot expect privacy because you are using the widest public space ever created. Are our teens aware of this? In the 21st century cyberspace, privacy no longer exists, with anything you do, say, or share being somehow recorded. Your reputation and privacy belong to the virtual cyberspace society and the companies ruling it.

---

[47]Solove, J. D. (2007). *The Future of Reputation* (New Haven & London: Yale University Press).
[48]A bot can be defined as an autonomous program on a network (especially the Internet) which can interact with systems or users, especially one designed to behave like a player in some video games.

As Dr. Siboni and Hacohen[49] remark, "the right for privacy, and owing one's personal secrets, has been a critical point in any society. Rabbi Gershom Ben Judah, back in 10th century Jewish society, stated a Takanah (Jewish religious ruling) declaring a Herem (communal shunning) against any person who reads someone else's letters without permission, as it invades the letter writer's privacy." Other ancient cultures, as the Greeks or Romans, have also considered privacy as a pillar of human rights and important in preserving one's reputation. In the US, "the right to privacy" was already discussed in the *Harvard Law Review*[50] in the year 1890. Losing your reputation could be a matter of life and death, and a few years ago, also a perfect reason for dueling in order to defend one's honor, as Samuel Johnson once said, "to prevent someone from being driven out the society."[51] As a social being, this is the harshest sentence that any human being can face.

Today, due to the omnipresence of our virtual cyberspace, cyber users are acting as a regulator, sometimes as a jury, and thousands of virtual participants are "forming" a court, judging and sentencing individuals, condemning or absolving them in a matter of minutes or hours, and reinforcing or ruining people's reputation in a matter of seconds. Traditional law, and international case-law, might be slow and may sometimes seem completely out of fashion, but it surely has the experience, tools, and professionals that can bring real justice to us. Are the people, acting as a virtual court, ready to deliver a verdict? Do they have the knowledge, skills, and what is most important, all the evidence to pass a judgment? The answer is probably not. But every day, hundreds, maybe thousands, are condemned by the "jury" of our amazing worldwide "cyber democracy" on the Internet. Many of those victims are teenagers, whose unique sin is being too naive or unaware of the virtual game rules,[52] and the worst

---

[49]Hacohem, A. and G. Sibon "Ubiquitous presence," *Cyber, Intelligence and Security*, **2**(3). INSS ISRAEL.

[50]Warren, S. D. and L. D. Bradeis (1890). "The Right to Privacy," *Harvard Law Review*, **4**: 193.

[51]Quote extracted from: Solove (2007), *supra* note 16.

[52]Charles, A. T. (2017). "The abuse of teenagers by online predators facilitated through the Internet and social media," Doctoral Thesis, Utica College. Posting a naked or semi-naked picture (e.g. in a bathroom) can be consider a criminal public offense in some US states. How can any teenager control where and how his photo is going to be posted, once it goes viral?

thing is that their sins, and all the data that prove them "guilty" (images, statements, videos, etc.) will remain on the Internet forever and be brought back to them at any time by anyone, facing them with "their own truth." Does this not constitute a life sentence?

11.4.3. *Companies*

Companies are the key players in our 21st "cyber" century, playing the role of Dr. Jekyll & Mr. Hyde[53] perfectly. Thanks to CICs,[54] the world today has an amazing communication network and tools that are helping the society leap forward. The Internet is helping us not only communicate but also deliver wealth, help connect people, deliver knowledge, spread information, thereby making the world easier, wealthier, and more attractive for everyone; in fact, some Internet companies have helped the humankind achieve progress like never before in a matter of decades.

On the other hand, some of these companies have accumulated immense power; some are richer than many countries or regions, and their political and social influence is so widespread that governments have to think about them in formulating their international geopolitical strategy. Some of these multinational companies could easily compete with any highly qualified intelligence agency because of the sheer amount of data they are gathering from their cyber users, who in some case, are in millions.[55]

Facebook has estimated that it is being used by 2.2 billion people worldwide (the biggest network ever), YouTube by 1.9 billion, and WeChat (China's version of WhatsApp) by about 1.3 billion. No company in human history has ever had that diversity and number of "clients/users," for free! The amazing fact of this universal business is that these companies are delivering their services to the users almost for free. Why? How can any company make money offering services for free? That goes against any traditional marketing rule.

The 4Ps that have ruled the foundation of marketing for decades are now obsolete. Products or services are offered now for free (there is no

---

[53] R. L. Stevenson's *Strange Case of Dr. Jekyll and Mr. Hyde* is a 1886 novel that reflects a perfect example of a psychiatric disorder of double personality, which brings back an ancestral debate between good and bad or virtue and evil.

[54] See *supra* note 20.

[55] *Source*: Global Digital Overview (January 2019).

Pricing strategy), Placement is virtual (no brick-and-mortar shops), and no investment in Promotion is needed because there is natural demand. In delving into the benefits of the Internet that companies are creating and offering us, we can easily slip into the dark side. Why are companies so generous? Why are many of them offering their services for free? What is the catch?

The dark side of the cyberspace is not only its hidden space (almost 90% of the internet is not visible or available to standard users); the "evil" part of it comes from some CIC companies leading the cyberspace and the way they are using our data and personal information. The scariest thing is that we are legally allowing them to do it. Companies are using our personal data, compiling everything we do in the cyberspace (shares, likes, location, searches, statements, comments, etc.) to gather information about us, creating a perfect profile picture of each one of us. Our behavior, goals, frustrations, and personal insights are all revealed, thanks to our explicit and implicit activity on the internet. Everyone has personal and intimate secrets, but the internet and the companies ruling us know about them better than your closest relatives.

Companies have found a way to reach the most precious and historic marketing talisman: our life. And we are delivering it to them, almost for free. We are exchanging our life and secrets in order to satisfy the basic need of communication: sharing our most precious information and experiences with others, which is a critical tool for survival that is imprinted in the human gene.

CICs are the updated and more sophisticated version of Orwell's Big Brother. They act as key regulators in the cyberspace. Now they can supervise us, understand our needs, or learn about our hidden deepest secrets, i.e. our "wants." Once they have them all, they can sell that information or use it in order to send us any offers (commercial, political, or social) that can match our needs, desires, or ambitions, satisfying every stage of our personal "Maslow Pyramid."[56] Basic marketing is thus still alive, in a sense, and it is terrifying. Thanks to the simplest action of accepting the registering conditions of any app, we are giving companies permission to access to our whole live, similar to any colonizer abusing over the indians by exchanging precious gold for trifles.

---

[56] Maslow's hierarchy of needs is a theory in psychology proposed by Abraham Maslow in 1943 in a paper titled "A Theory of Human Motivation," based on different stages, starting from basic needs to realizing self-actualization.

11.5. The Rules are Changing

We, as users and professionals, should be aware of the fact that the rules of the cyberspace are different. Marketing is not the only thing that has changed during the Internet era. Adults can understand that we are forfeiting our privacy, or at least part of it, in exchange for a powerful tool of communication. We know that some aspects of our activities might be harmful, but we continue to do them just because something is useful or somehow satisfying to us (eating, drinking, shopping, driving polluting vehicles, smoking, etc.) Somehow, as a mature person, you think you can manage to be involved in such activities without falling afoul. Something similar is happening on the Internet: your life experience helps you take some precautions, supervising and controlling what you do about the three internet main "Ss" (Search, Share, Socialize), but teens, who are the heavy users, are usually too naive and immature; they are highly tech-skilled but not really aware of the price they pay in exchange.

The society is changing; we are now playing a new game, in a giant court, shared by millions, and the referees are no longer the traditional institutions, but companies and the inner internet users. Concepts such as privacy, information, sharing, reputation, intimacy, abuse, free speech, anonymity, and gossip are reaching a new stage of transformation due to the universal influence of the Internet. Not only is "Big Brother" watching you, but everybody is watching, talking, and controlling each other. As Nicholas Emler[57] explains:

> *Gossip doesn't merely disseminate reputational information, but is the very process whereby reputations are decided. Reputation does not exist except in the conversations that people have about one another.*

The Internet provides the opportunity to reach hundreds, or share information with, thousands of people instantly anytime, anywhere, which is the millennial's dream, and something that the App Generation has taken for granted. However, it has also become a huge trap: controlling the game is nearly impossible, and for good or bad, the dimensions and impact of any action cannot be stopped by any individual. If you or your reputation is attacked, there is very little you can do about it, and there is

---

[57]Emler, N. (2001). *Self Esteem: The Costs and Causes of Low Self Worth* (York, UK: York Publishing Services).

no margin for response. This can overwhelm anyone, but especially those who are highly immature in their thought process.

We have to realize that, in the 21st century, we not only play the roles of users, clients, or consumers, as defined by traditional marketing, but also act as creators, juries, controllers, producers, and distributors, all at once. It is a new social perspective, and with it comes great responsibility.

11.6. The Internet and its Cyberthreats for Teenagers

Until the last decade of the 20th century, mass media was considered the fourth power in society. Media could control and balance other traditional powers (legislative, executive, and judicial), especially in Western democracies. Media and journalism could influence the political and social life of any country, so if one could handle or own the media, it meant one could somehow control society. Nowadays, the cyberspace leadership and control can be divided between some CICs and cyberspace users. We could say that the Internet has already become the fifth power, if not the first, worldwide. Are the teens, i.e. the App Generation, ready to understand this epochal change? The digital generation, generally referred to those born since the year 2000, has been exposed to cyberspace ever since their birth. The use of the Internet and cyberspace starts at a very young age, averaging at just 10 years, and is the main way of entertainment, socialization, education, and communication for teens, as Aranda and Sanchez-Navarro reveal[58] in their research. While the cyberspace has become a natural global courtyard for them, the majority of the children and their parents are completely unaware of the cyberthreats faced by them.

From the author's point of view, cyberspace hazards can be divided into three main categories: Explicit, Implicit, and Hidden Threats, depending on the use, impact, time, and consequences, and how harmful they can be for the individual.

---

[58] Sánchez-Navarro, J. and D. Aranda (2011). "Internet como fuente de información para la vida cotidiana de los jóvenes españoles," *El profesional de la información*, **20**(1), enero-febrero [in Spanish]. It is part of a research project on teenage cyberspace use, combined with other government studies in Spain.

11.6.1. *Explicit cyberspace threats*

We could consider explicit internet threats as those that cause direct, immediate, and specific psychological or physical damage due to the frequency and intensity of the Internet use by the teenager. The most common explicit threats for teenagers are those related to physical disruption or damage caused by the extensive (bordering on the abusive) use of the Internet: eye and vision problems, headaches, insomnia, stress, and anxiety. Some teens can develop joint or muscle problems due to wrong postures or excessive time spent in playing games online. The explicit problems can also lead to serious physiological problems like ceasing other healthy activities (especially cultural or sports), isolation, sedentarism and obesity and, in the long term, cyber addiction. One of the scariest explicit cyber problems is related to the development of new bone or anatomical structures (head, neck, fingers, etc.) not related to genetics, and probably associated with a persistent incorrect position or repetitive movements needed for playing games or using tablets or smartphones. The best way to control and prevent explicit cyberthreats and damages is manage the time and frequency of Internet use.

11.6.2. *Implicit cyberthreats*

Implicit cyberthreats are related to the indirect harmful consequences of using the Internet and establishing relationships with other cyber users in a wrong way or with a naive or immature mindset. Most of the implicit cyber hazards are based on a misunderstanding of the "trust" concept. Fukuyama[59] defines trust as "the expectation that arises within a community of regular, honest, and cooperative behavior, based on commonly shared norms, on the part of the members." Implicit threats usually arise from a wrong or naïve management of trust while interacting with other community members. Cyber teens are usually naive, and more prone to opening themselves, and sharing their intimate secrets on the web, exposing their privacy with very little care, and opening a dangerous door to malicious perpetrators. Many hidden threats can be considered as crimes, especially when the cyber user is underaged and the "attacker" is an adult predator. However, other threats arise due to teenagers who are unaware of the extent of damage and pain caused by some online behavior.

---

[59]Fukuyama, F. (1989). "The end of history?" *The National Interest*, **16**: 3–18.

Some of the most common implicit hazards of the internet are related to technical cyberattacks that are hardware- or software-based, as established by Becher.[60] These threats occur due to a very low awareness of technical self-protection, such as weak password protection, that allows intruder access to personal data and private information (images, data bank, personal history, etc.) and result in phishing attacks, which direct the user to false websites, thereby stealing private data. SSL proxy attacks are aimed at revealing the encrypted code of a cyber device, and finally, probably one of the most dangerous, is exploiting a camera or microphone vulnerabilities, which allow not only intruders but also companies to legally spy on the unsuspecting cyber user.

The Internet of Things (IoT) and AI are two of the most disturbing technological advances in recent years. The amazing capacity of communicating and being understood by any cyber device can become a heinous progress if anyone behind it, individuals or corporations, can have access to and unauthorized control over your private life. The most dangerous implicit cyberthreats are related to personal attacks through the Internet, as Garmendia *et al.* explain in their article[61] about Spanish teenagers using the Internet, which can be extrapolated to include other cyber users worldwide.

Teenagers belonging to the App Generation are the main victims, and sometimes unconsciously, the perpetrators. The implicit hazards of cyber are directly inherited from traditionally frowned upon behaviors, such as "bullying," but the amazing power and dimensions of the cyberspace can multiply its devastating effect, producing irreparable damage to the victim. The results can be as serious as suicide.

Some traditional implicit threats have been adapted to the cyberspace, making them really dangerous, because the Internet facilitates anonymity or the ability to misrepresent an identity in order to take advantage of someone, the so-called "grooming," which is relatively easy to achieve and difficult to pin down. "Gossiping" can easily transform into "cyber bullying" and can be devastating for any kid, especially if the attack goes beyond their natural inner circle (usually their class, school,

---

[60]Becher, M. (2009). "Security of smartphones at the dawn of their ubiquitouness," University of Manheim, Curves.

[61]Garmendia, M., C. Garitaonandia, G. Martínez and M. Casado (2011). "Riesgos y seguridad en Internet: los menores españoles en el contexto europeo," EU Kids Online [in Spanish] (Bilbao, Spain: Universidad del País Vasco).

or neighborhood) sometimes expanding on the web, with the victim being harassed by thousands of unknown people. "Sextortion," defined by the FBI as "the act of someone requesting something of value for the item (usually sexual content) not to be released," or "sexting," which refers to receiving or spreading explicit sexual content, without permission, in order to harass or blackmail someone, are some of the dangerous threats. According to the FBI, teenage girls are the main victims of these criminal cyberattacks.

There is a Spanish proverb about harming someone's reputation: "Defame, that something (bad) will prevail." "Cyber defamation"[62] or creating fake news (usually around politicians or celebrities' lives nowadays) is difficult to stop[63] due to the rapid speed at which any viral content, especially morbid ones, can spread on the Internet.

Stealing anyone's personality or impersonating the other person, i.e. "cyber identity theft" is a direct consequence of being naive or lax about cyber protection and can have serious consequences if that profile is used for any criminal act. Being a "follower fan" can easily lead to "cyber stalking," going beyond the boundaries of privacy and respect for personal space. Teenagers are usually going through a complex process, building their personality and developing a self-confidence shield, while they are growing and reaching maturity and developing common sense. Being a victim of any of these practices can completely destroy their self-esteem, or drive them into a "cyber-shame" state, sometimes provoking permanent physiological wounds or rather extreme bizarre behavior.

11.6.3. *Hidden Cyberthreats*

The term "hidden cyberthreats" refers to all those related to personality and behavioral hazards resulting from a reckless use of the cyberspace. The consequences of the hidden cyberthreats are yet unknown because they will emerge in the future, probably along with behavioral changes,

---

[62]Solove (2007), *supra* note 16, on defamation: in order for the Law to act, "a statement must be false and it must harm a person's reputation."

[63]The problem in cyberspace is that is really difficult to find the origin of the defamation, and almost impossible to persecute it, because the origin can be in another country (with different regulations) or a virtual non-existent website. Also, launching an international lawsuit can be really expensive for any individual, so perpetrators stay safe, due to the obsolescence of our regulator and law system (Author's note).

or distort the personal or professional lives of many individuals who are now just teens. Hidden cyberthreats can affect any person, young or old, but the damage might be particularly pronounced for teenagers who are usually unable to anticipate the consequences of their actions. Social reputation, self-esteem, family, and professional problems may arise some years from now, triggered by the naïve cyber behavior.

The first signs of the hidden cyberthreats can be a direct result of cyberspace use. The App Generation has inherited some ideas from the previous generations, the "Millennials" and the "Z-generation," e.g. the idea of being "Wikiproducers":[64] they look for instant satisfaction and gratification, they cannot handle frustration easily, and they are used to searching and finding any content, at any moment, and anywhere in their virtual world. Scanning and sharing information has never been so easy, and they can find, download, and take for granted any content; the entire human history and knowledge are available to them just with a touch of the fingertip. However, there are some hidden dangers to this amazing advantage.

Traditional and highly critical skills such as reading, writing, and comprehension of text are being threatened. When teenagers look for any information, and they are really good at it, they no longer do any in-depth reading and comprehension exercise, they just pick up the first result (out of thousands presented by their favorite cyber search engine),[65] or just the more attractive one (a video tutorial from YouTube), and after a quick scan, not really reading and after a very scarce critical analysis, they take the content for granted, usually assuming that featuring in the first page of any search result automatically means that the content is the "ultimate truth." They are unable to discern whether the information that the search engine is delivering as "best results" is truthful and accurate[66]; it does not

---

[64]Arce, G. (2015). Thesis "Impacto de las Redes sociales de Internet en la generación net." *supra* note 18.

[65]Google is the most popular Internet search engine in the world, followed by others such as Bing and Yahoo. These search engines look for best results on the Internet, based on an advanced algorithm that combines different inputs, out of which one of the most important is how many people have chosen a certain link. However, Google cannot discern the accuracy of the information.

[66]In order to confirm that any information is real, useful, and truthful, the scientific method considers that it must be valid, reliable, precise, verifiable, and representative and usually updated. The Internet and social networks are continuously offering amazing "research results" or solutions, with very little scientific quality or credibility. (Author's Note).

matter if the content comes from a really prestigious scientific research study or a "numb blogger" expressing ideas without any responsibility.

Lack of critical thinking and in-depth reading is something that educators and parents should be aware of, but it is really difficult to re-educate and re-program the habits of the App Generation since they were born and grew up that way.[67] Writing is also a problem, not only because they are no longer trained for handwriting (their handwriting is sometimes as illegible as an Egyptian hieroglyph) but also because, and this is really serious, they are no capable of creating and conforming to a complex text structure.

The "copy and paste" format has become an easy alternative for borrowing someone else's ideas or concepts. It is scary to see that they are really good at searching, quickly scanning, and finding content (some of them really interesting) and just pasting them together, without even thinking about building a coherent discourse. What is even worse, they are copying and adopting another author's thoughts as their own, without any scruples, totally ignoring that they are committing plagiarism. This can be a minor sin, being just homework, but could be a major problem, even a crime, if the App Generation continue this illegal behavior as adults. Indexing, bibliography, and quoting are, unfortunately, not part of their tasks today.

The cyber society can be tougher at meting out punishments than a traditional jury. Solove[68] explains that: "Internet shaming, is often done to punish not just violations of law, but also transgressions of norms (…) the problem with the internet norm enforcement is that, it usually spins out of control."

The lack of traditional basic writing and reading comprehension skills might be a critical point some years from now, with unpredictable consequences, especially for those unlucky individuals that cannot have access to mid or higher education. But who knows, maybe the future society, ruled by today's App Generation will not take all this into account, just as

---

[67] The age of starting Internet use, through computers, smartphones, and tablets, has progressively decreased among kids. Parents are accepting this as part of their children's social life. The Spanish INE (Statistic National Institute) survey in 2013 revealed that most children under 10 years (91.8%) have full access to the Internet. This age is probably even lower in other advanced cyber countries.

[68] Solove (2007), *supra*, footnote 16.

our generation has abandoned the baroque formalism of the 19th century, while writing letters, or the 20th century's strict business dress code.

Writing and reading skills can be trained in different ways. Some advanced countries (such as those in Scandinavian countries, US, and South Korea) have swapped their traditional notebooks and pens for internet tablets and smartphones, assuming that progress is going that way, and training and educating children with future cyber tools is the best response to handling the new cyberspace. But hidden threats in educational skills are not as dangerous as behavioral hidden threats.

It is difficult to evaluate the consequences of all the hazards behind personality and behavioral distortions on the Internet. Usually the App Generation victims are too young to express or reveal how this is affecting their personality development. But we are already detecting some serious problems among them. The influence that some wrong Internet habits are having on young teens is not clear yet. We can easily detect that uncontrolled exposure to some disturbing contents or activities, such as pornography, explicit violence, extreme political speeches, or gambling, can be as dangerous as drugs for them, developing addictions or in some cases extreme criminal behavior (terrorism, sex assault, mass shooting, or homophobic or racial behaviors).

Having uncontrolled access to extreme content is influencing the App Generation, driving them to develop dangerous or criminal behaviors, such as sex abuse and violence, sometimes as a gang, (this is probably a direct cause of immature teens watching porn, where usually the women's role is totally subjected to men) before even attending sex education or engaging in a "classic loving" approach with other person. It is not about sex (which is a natural and healthy instinct) but about having respect for the others. The increasing incidents of rape, gang abuse, or sexting, are some evil individuals' odd practices and are probably inherited from such cyber behavior, but we do not know the massive consequences of a whole generation leading with these problems. Many kids have watched porn,[69] while feeling bad about engaging in such behavior, even before reaching adolescence.

Filming and recording dangerous activities and sharing them constitute another hidden threat. The egocentrism behind the desire to be

---

[69] See footnote 40.

"famous,"[70] admired, or an instant YouTube star attracts immature personalities whose reasoning is eclipsed by the halo of fame and fun.[71]

The result are really dangerous, if not criminal, resulting in activities such as "balconing"[72] and "pool jumping" from higher floors, over speeding, participating in insane challenges to climb high-rise buildings, etc. popping out on the Internet, going viral, and creating a profile that will affect them forever. The worst thing is that they not only apparently record any infraction but also share it publicly, making it easy for authorities to take immediate action and ensure public punishment, resulting in almost a comical end to a potentially life-threatening situation[73]. Some internal force or lack of basic social education prevents them from evaluating the severity of their actions.

The individualistic but intense social engagement on the Internet and some social networks is also creating hidden problems for our teens. The physical isolation (even though they are virtually and socially connected) depending only on virtual communication (chats mainly) has caused some serious social and family problems, like the lack of personal communication (face to face), the incapability to control harmful activities, and some other physiological and physical disorders that might damage or affect the teen's personality.

Some activities can reveal the most serious hidden threat, i.e. addiction, and parents should be aware of them. Common signs include low academic performance, skipping or dropping out of school, lack of physical or intellectual exercise (music, reading, etc.), or inappropriate behavior or contact, revealing a heinous addiction to the Internet[74] that goes

---

[70]"Everybody deserves their fifteen minutes of fame." Quote attributed to Andy Warhol.

[71]Sharing extreme behaviors, sometimes criminal ones, is something that psychologists should focus on. Probably a mix of instant satisfaction, feeling and being different and superior, or being rewarded by social recognition (based on views, comments, and likes) is the clue that links those behaviors to a strong need for reaching Maslow's self-actualization stage (Author's Note).

[72]Stupid behavior includes jumping into a pool from a higher floor, usually with terrible consequences.

[73]"If you are doing something wrong, don't tell anybody...jerk." Anonymous quote (Author's Note).

[74]Roy, Roy and Sinha (2017), *supra* note 42.

beyond the intended natural use of this tool. Amianto and Fassino[75] reveal that "serious cases of Psychopathological problems (inherited from the hidden hazards of using internet) can lead to behavioral externalization disorders as prostitution, misuse of drugs or alcohol, hetero-aggressive behavior, group violence, including sexual one and domestic violence."

Cyber gambling is probably one of the most dangerous activities that teens can have access to, without any parental or governmental control nowadays. Like other hidden threats, online gambling has an extraordinary impact among kids, as a really easy way of raising money, while having fun. Posing as someone's profile or delivering false data (usually to close relatives) while using someone's credit card is not so difficult. The Internet and gambling websites do not really hesitate to stop this, and some commercials are also played through social networks and traditional media such as television by famous celebrities encouraging this activity. As Dr. Ezioni[76] demands, an international law and global prosecution of this kind of content should be enforced.

Regulations in cyberspace are in urgent need of an international review, otherwise laws and regulations will lag behind the real progress of the cyberspace. Siboni and Sivan-Sevilla[77] state that "controlling the resilience of the private sector in the cyberspace, especially for the western world, which reveals a lack of systematic solutions and tools that can alleviate the cyber hazards for the business industry and the political and social life of many countries," while proposing some very interesting regulations in their book. Their statements can be reflected in the explicit violence and extremist social, religious, and political content that can easily be reached by weak cyber teen users, driving them to a dramatic personality transformation that can end in extremist and dangerous behaviors.

The most dangerous thing about any hidden threat, which most teens and some adults are totally unaware of, is that the Internet is recording and storing every single action we do, and it will remain in cyberspace forever, being brought back to us, at any time, or in any critical moment of our future.

---

[75] Amianto, F. and S. Fassino (2017). "Psychiatric problems emerging in teens: The situation for the design of future interventions."

[76] Ezioni (2018), *supra* note 12.

[77] Siboni, G. and I. Sivan-Sevilla (2019). "Regulation in cyberspace," Memorandum No. 190, INSS.

11.7. Conclusion

Years ago, any oral statement, even a written one, could be blown away in the wind or buried for centuries in a library, but today, the virtual cyberspace and corporations not only have the technological capacity to rescue anything, but millions of users are also storing it in their personal cyber storage devices.

Your reputation[78] and past can be exposed and judged, at any time in your future life, no matter how long ago a certain situation happened (even years or decades ago) or what the social rules were.[79] For the cyber Internet users of the future cyber society, or for future hiring companies, that evil deed will be happening at the precise moment that someone is sharing it or searching for it. Your hidden and deepest secrets are going to be exposed, not because you posted them, but because your implicit cyber behavior is showing them.

Is the App Generation aware that the first thing that any company thinks about when hiring them is going to be searching their "cyber bio-resume," written by them during the years and exposed through social networks and posts? There are no secrets or intimacy anymore. The App Generation should be aware that they are writing their life cyber bio-resume at any given time, with their every share, like, and search, and social networks and blogs clearly push them to do that. The lack of judgment and natural immaturity can cost them severely, in the form of reputational damage years from now. The cyber behavior of teens and their cyber profiles, extracted from their Internet activity record, might result in a high payload in their personal or professional future reputation[80] if they do not take care of it now.

Everybody has a double personality. Solove reminds us of a popular myth which goes: "The public self isn't as genuine as the private self,"

---

[78]Nock, S. L. (1993). *The Costs of Privacy: Surveillance and Reputation in America* (New Jersey: Transaction Publishers). Steven Nock, defines reputation as "shared, or collective, perception about a person." The collective perception in the cyberspace belongs to hundreds or thousands of people.

[79]Smoking was a social and well-accepted habit just three decades ago, while being homosexual could end in jail or physical punishment in some countries. Nobody knows about the cyber rules that may emerge in the next two decades, when the App Generation will be leading the society.

[80]Solove (2007), *supra* note 16, considers that "reputation gives people a strong incentive to conform to social norms and to avoid breaching people´s trust."

but "thanks" to the Internet, both are now merging, conforming your new social cyber profile in a permanent "public mode" and building your reputation in front of the audience.[81] The App Generation teens were born that way; their life can be recalled almost completely not only by their own cyber activity (content search, uploads, downloads, shares, etc.) but also by what other people, including their parents, are posting and sharing, since they were born. The CICs are following us and assembling our profile by processing our explicit and implicit cyber activity. The future of people's reputation was already described back in 2007:[82]

> We're heading toward a world where an extensive trail of information fragments about us will be forever preserved on the Internet, displayed instantly in a Google search.

The population can now be behaviorally micro-segmented[83] and classified, thanks to the OCEAN model[84]; the new "Big Bros" can feed the web with content and messages that will satisfy our most intimate needs (our "wants"), those that everyone loves to hear in order to provoke a reaction from them (buying, voting, demonstrating, etc.).

The "perpetrators" focus not only on knowing who we are but also inducing us to act in a certain way. We are a huge virtual social tribe, and like a naive flock of sheep, we just need some individuals to have an initiative to blindly follow them. As Bandura[85] explains, "people identify with models[86] and adopt their behaviors, values, beliefs, and attitudes."

---

[81] Audience matters, but in the cyberspace the audience is composed of millions.

[82] Solove (2007), *supra* note 16.

[83] Ziegler, M., K. T. Horstmann and J. Ziegler (2019). "Personality in situations: Going beyond the OCEAN and introducing the Situation Five," *Psychological Assessment*, **31**(4): 567–580.

[84] The OCEAN model is a behavioral physiology model that can classify people through five personality traits. This model has being applied to people's behavior in social networks in order to identify users willing to change their mind about something (political, social, or commercial situation).

[85] Bandura, A. (1989). "Human agency in social cognitive theory," *American Psychologist*, **44**(9): 1175.

[86] The 21st century "role models" are the YouTubers, influencers, and cyber opinion leaders (Author's note).

There is also a need to understand that companies and corporations are based on people, and all of them are sharing a personal–private and public–professional life at any time. As Rid and Buchanan describe, in the 21st century, the cyber delinquents will be focusing on the weakest point (usually people's personal lives), in order to perpetrate a strategic cyber attack, starting with a tactical approach (which are the technical weakest points) followed by an operative step (what are they looking for) and implementing the strategic plan (who and why are they attacking this way, and what the aim is); finally they will use the information (data, etc.) considering when and how are they going to use it, communicating their attack (making profits or obtaining publicity advantages).

Once an individual or a company detects that its privacy has been violated, or that his/her reputation is tainted, the response should be to identify and denounce the attacker, but that requires identifying the offender first. That is something quite difficult to do in a global cyber world. Identifying a cyber perpetrator implies huge resources, and is usually unreachable for any individual. In order to identify a cyber attacker, you need to have requisite technical skills to reveal the cyberattacker's technological expertise, time to follow and reveal the trail, and finally the cyber intelligence capacity of discerning and identifying a perpetrator for their explicit and what is most important, implicit or hidden behavior, i.e. clues that reveal the cyber attacker's personality, power, and knowledge. Is an immature cyber teen capable of doing this? The answer is a definite no.

The cyberattackers or instigators can be "evil" companies, country enemies, politicians, social rioters, intelligence agencies, or just a cyber user who is a "cool" influencer. The victims will be either older or young and are usually unskilled cyber users, but the short-term and especially long-term damage can be unpredictable.[87]

According to Kadëna, "Everybody wants to protect themselves and their privacy"[88]; in order to do so, they must be aware of the cyber

---

[87]Rid, T. and B. Buchanan (2015). Attributing cyber attacks. *Journal of Strategic Studies*, **38**(1–2): 4–37, explain that final result (prize) of any cyberattack can be indirect and delayed in time (keeping the attack hidden) and using or keeping the information for a long time. They affirm that the more indirect and delayed, the harder (and painful) becomes to quantify it (Author's note).

[88]Kadëna, E. (2017). "Smartphone security threats," *Management, Enterprise and Benchmarking in the 21st Century*, p. 141.

measures required. But the human factor, i.e. our behavior, will remain the main obstacle to fight any cyberthreat. The only way to fight all these cyberthreats, especially the hidden ones, is education and awareness.[89] Combating cyberthreats requires not only cyber training and cyberthreats education, but also critical and ethical thinking, which is the most important human trait and is cultivated by philosophy, moral, religious, and social education.

The cyber tools may constantly evolve, gaining speed and capacity and delivering great advantages to the users, but the pillar of human dignity was written and described by humanistic philosophers and religious leaders[90] of many different cultures a very long time ago and their edicts still remain intact.

---

[89] See footnote 29.
[90] See Siboni and Sivan-Sevilla (2019), *supra* note 77.

Chapter 12

Ethics and Human Rights in the Cyber Domain and Big Data

José María Ortiz Ibarz[*,†] *and Beatriz Vila Ramos*[*,‡]

[*]*Law & Business School, Universidad Francisco de Vitoria (UFV), Madrid, Spain*

[†]*j.ortiz@ufv.es*

[‡]*b.vila.prof@ufv.es*

Abstract

Our society and economy are organized around big data as its storage and handling have become some of the most valuable resources and because it is used in disruptive transversal technologies that, in turn, facilitate increasingly easy and efficient decisions for people. Our daily lives are replete with massive data that facilitate purchase decisions, mobility, etc. Technologies change ways of life and business models, the latter requiring new forms of regulation (tax, labor, civil, commercial, international), which affect fundamental rights because under the law lies an idea of what society and the person is. Big data affects us because its use can change us for better or for worse. Hence the relevance of the question "for what?" — the response to which will help us discover our personal identity. Technology has thus become a great accelerator of ethical and anthropological questions.

12.1. Mastering Big Data is the New "Black Gold"

Data is already perceived as "the black gold of the 21st century," and the fuel that makes companies grow and become more competitive. But the amount of data that companies encounter and the increasingly stringent regulations that ensure the protection of the most sensitive data are forcing these companies and institutions to rethink their structure and work systems.

With similarities to the traditional CEO (Chief Executive Officer), other titles are emerging, such as CISO (Chief Information Security Officer), CSO (Chief Security Officer), CIO (Chief Information Officer), CTO (Chief Technology Officer), and CDO (an acronym used to denote both Chief Data Officer and Chief Digital Officer). New roles are required due to the digital changes[1] in response to the need to acquire, store, and manage massive data in a secure way. With regard to these emerging titles, as important as it is to define their specific roles and responsibilities, it is just as important to design an organizational structure and decision and management systems that facilitate (and if possible, ensure) the necessary autonomy related to decision-making. Good risk management requires what we have come to call the triple defense barrier:[2] correct operational management, an adequate regulatory compliance system, and an effective internal audit are required.

Not long ago, the business world experienced a similar situation when good governance systems began to recommend an organizational structure that facilitated transparency and objectivity in decision-making. Throughout the 1990s, reports by Cadbury, Greenbury, Hampel, Viennot, and Olivencia emerged around the world. Soon after, these companies formed a new regulatory body, focused mainly on legislation related to stock markets. The reason for voluntary recommendations becoming legal requirements

---

[1] In Spain, the contributions of INCIBE (Spanish National Cybersecurity Institute) have been particularly important in this field, especially through the publication of *"Tendencias en el mercado de la Ciberseguridad."* One of these contributions has been the collaboration in the publication of the *"Libro Blanco del CISO."* The publication of the CISO White Paper (2018) was an initiative of the Spanish Association for the Advancement of Information Security (ISMS Forum Spain), which has had the institutional support of INCIBE.

[2] COSO (Committee of Sponsoring Organizations of the Treadway Commission) is a voluntary commission made up of representatives from different organizations in the US and provides criteria for risk management, internal control, and the fight against fraud.

was probably their significance and the importance of their effectiveness. However, not even transparency or independence could prevent the abuses that led to the financial crises we have experienced, as is well known.

Among the rules of good institutional governance, it is usually recommended that those who have effective command over a society be overseen by independent persons and commissions. Thus, among the advisers we find three different types: the executives (who manage the company), the independent advisers (who contribute their personal knowledge and experience, and in some ways constitute a guarantee for small investors and the market), and the proprietary advisers (representing the main shareholders).

"Ownership" comes from "domain" and invokes whomever, by his nature as owner, has the capacity and right to decide. In today's digital world, what exactly does "domain" mean? It is an address that needs a place, a site (and a server), and that can either constitute a territorial reference (.es, .il, .at, .cn, .ru, .eu, .uk, .cat, .us) or be generic in nature (.com, .net, .org, .edu, .gov). That is, it is a "place" that is occupied and that provides to those who possess it an identification and a set of rights. This can become an object of rent, of advertising income, and also of extortion.

Domain, in addition to an address in one place, is a "mode of relationship." But even in the etymology of the term, both aspects are closely linked. First, as we have seen, *dominus* (i.e. lord) refers to the owner. But the Castilian expression "estate" (*señorío*) has always meant both "the dignity of the Lord" and "the hereditary handing down of a set of lands, vassals, and jurisdiction, given free of charge (as a grant) by the monarchs in payment for the services provided."[3] The estate is both a place and its belongings, as a personal quality.

Obviously, this etymology refers to feudal origins in which the relationship was more despotic than democratic, and in that context, determining whether the handing down was the result of merit or whether it is a gratuitous donation does not help us much in determining who gave and who received. The concept of "domain" has been used to explain the root of human freedom as far back as the ancient Greek civilization.

---

[3]Royal Spanish Academy (1992). *Spanish Dictionary*, Edition XXI (Madrid: Royal Spanish Academy).

In the Aristotelian explanation of material things, the relationship between matter and form is "despotic," as each requires the other; the form of a given matter (a concrete, quantifiable substance) will always make up the form of that matter. However, when one form makes up another form (and that is the characteristic of habits), the relationship between the two is "free": there is a surplus of form, and its sole purpose is not to make up the form.[4]

That habitual character of personal being is the foundation of human freedom (which is not determined) and the root of its dignity. Therefore, the question of individuality is not exactly the same as the question of individuation,[5] similar to how "identification" in the digital world is not equal to "identity."

12.2. Technology Drives Innovation and Causes Profound Changes

Returning to the digital world, the emergence of highly disruptive technologies is what fuels innovation. And with data it could not be different: technologies change the ways of life and business models, and these demand new forms of regulation.

An example of the rapid impact that networks and data have on the economy is the emergence of the platform economy. When the network of networks is working, the infrastructure is already underway and improves on its own. Artificial Intelligence learns, and we increasingly need intermediaries. Supply and demand accumulate as never before. That is why our focus has clearly shifted toward new businesses supported by platforms, to the ecosystems they generate, and to the convenience of participating in collaborative models.

Networks connect consumers in order to facilitate exchanges, and companies only have to provide the network, one that is woven with spontaneity, fluidity, and speed that is difficult to match. Consumers are more united than ever, almost without any additional effort needed to achieve the said union. The network works because we are all willing to share, and

---

[4]Polo, L. (1991). *Quién es el hombre. Un espíritu en el tiempo* (Madrid: Rialp).

[5]Haya, F. (2004). "Individualidad e Individuación según Edith Stein," *Revista de Filosofía*, **32**: 159–173.

that is why our focus is increasingly on the collaborative economy.[6] At the same time, it must be said that we are beginning to worry about the power of those who have a greater impact on the evolution and use of the platform business,[7] due to its huge negotiation capacity.

In just a few years, some business models, such as Uber or Airbnb, have achieved that virtually all rights be reviewed: tax and fiscal, labor, civil and commercial, mortgage, and international rights. The new problems and new solutions will always appeal to a transnational vocation because we live in a world separated from the territories and places in which we step foot on.[8] When globalization causes conflicts of laws to multiply, what we probably need to do is rethink how fundamental rights are affected.

It is clear that the use of big data in areas such as law, finance, health, and education has an immediate impact on fundamental human rights: equality before the law, security, honor, freedom of movement, presumption of innocence, privacy, property.[9] On the other hand, with the Internet of Things connecting objects to the Internet,[10] everything can immediately be translated into data. In this way, we can make enormous advances in health, safety, home automation, clothing (everything wearable that is related to comfort), cities, leisure, industry, agriculture; always, of course, depending on whether we are able to guarantee the right to privacy.

The development of Artificial Intelligence (in its different meanings, depending on whether they are systems that think or act similarly to humans)[11] leads us to question what the axis of human rights is. When we say that its root lies in the dignity and inviolability of human life, we presuppose a superiority of human life over any other, a moral

---

[6]Bostman, R. (2017). *Who Can You Trust? How Technology Brought Us Together and Why It Could Drive Us Apart* (New York: Public Affairs).

[7]Reillier, L. C. and B. Reillier (2017). *Platform Strategy: How to Unlock the Power of Communities and Networks to Grow Your Business* (New York: Routledge).

[8]We are faced with the challenge of reformulating taxation, which can no longer be totally linked to a certain territory. *Cf.* Hongler, P. and P. Pistone (2015). "Blueprints for a new PE nexus to tax business income in the era of the digital economy," White Paper, IBFD.

[9]Raso, F. *et al.* (2018). *Artificial Intelligence & Human Rights* (Harvard: Berkman Klein Center).

[10]Weiser, M. (1991). "The computer for the 21st century," *Scientific American*, September.

[11]Russell, S. and P. Norwig (1995). *Artificial Intelligence. A Modern Approach* (New Jersey: Prentice Hall).

superiority.[12] And at this point, the following question emerges: if intelligence is the highest form of life,[13] can there be a higher morality? When machines surpass humans in intelligence,[14] what happens to the superiority of human life?

There are some questions to which those of us who belong to Western culture have serious difficulty in answering, because we remain trapped in that naturalistic fallacy[15] according to which we are neither allowed to distinguish the should-be from the actual being nor extract moral consequences from the data of experience.

12.3. We are Seekers of a Secure Identity

The permanent technology–business–regulation cycle pushes us toward an interdisciplinary understanding, in which interactions produce increasingly less predictable phenomena. For example, one of the consequences of the aforementioned need to implement three differentiated lines of defense for the proper handling of mass data is that we must adjust to working with a type of mainstreaming, which has been unknown until now. We increasingly need more professionals who understand programming languages and algorithms, databases and data sources; who understand the regulatory requirements; and who meet the needs of each business by enhancing all of its resources.

We are also going to have to adjust to a phenomenon of networking business: the important thing is to encourage contact and the use of the network among members. The benefit will become apparent whenever we learn to read what the data teaches us.[16] The unpredictability of what will happen next when we put large amounts of data into context (a phenomenon that we have named "singularity" including, as we have already said,

[12]Risse, M. (2018). *Human Rights and Artificial Intelligence* (Harvard: Kennedy School).

[13]Tegmark, M. (2018). *Vida 3.0. Qué significa ser humano en la era de la inteligencia artificial* (Madrid: Taurus).

[14]Chalmers, D. (2010). "The singularity: A philosophical analysis," *Journal of Consciousness Studies*, **17**: 7–65.

[15]Moore, G. E. (2002). *Principia Ethica* (Barcelona: Crítica); Sidgwick, H. (1874). *The Methods of Ethics* (London: Macmillan).

[16]Becerra, M. (2005). *Red de valor* (*Value Network*) (Madrid: Instituto de Empresa); Stabell, C. and O. Fjeldstad (1998). "Configuring value for competitive advantage: On chains, shops, and networks," *Strategic Management Journal*, **19**: 413–437.

the possibility that at a given moment, Artificial Intelligence might exceed human intelligence) has a similar result in relation to fundamental rights. And that is why data protection has a lot of rights under construction.

In just a few years we have seen how the list of the largest companies in the world — the most admired and most desired to work for — has been changed by stock market capitalization; banking and energy have been replaced by telecommunications. A small number of companies dominate the majority of the world markets (Google, Apple, Facebook, Amazon, Microsoft) and are a growing concentration as they are the largest data collectors which does generate, e.g. any negligible tax, labor, or free competition issues.[17]

Thanks to data and applied Artificial Intelligence, no one knows consumers and market trends better than these companies. Getting data (or keeping it up to date) could become more profitable than charging for a particular product or service.[18] We then consider the need to separate the storage and use of massive data to prevent excessive asymmetric concentration from providing an unprecedented competitive advantage (a position of power). This is a very similar solution to the one we have already experienced when, in defense of free competition, we have forced companies (telecommunications or utilities services) to assign (rent) the use of their networks (e.g. fiber optics, electric networks, water connections, and gas network). But the most complex problems posed by the use of massive data are those that point toward the specifically human, i.e. toward what makes us unique and "unrepeatable." The generalization and effectiveness of search engines has created tension in the relationship between the right to information and the right to privacy, between the good name and the image itself.

Until recently, time and space were the natural ways to forget about certain things; a "short-term memory," allowed people to live without having to permanently carry the burden of their mistakes, their perceptions, or their past. But massive data storage means that the past can

---

[17] Sokol, D. and R. Comerford (2016). "Does antitrust have a role to play in regulating big data?," in *Cambridge Handbook of Antitrust, Intellectual Property and High Tech* (Cambridge: Cambridge University Press).

[18] A summary of the recent literature on these risks and dangers, as well as the effectiveness and limitations of antitrust practices, can be found in Herrero, C. (2018). "Big Data y Derecho de la Competencia," *Sociedad Digital y Derecho* (Madrid: *BOE*): 659–681 [in Spanish].

continue to exist in the present almost without exception, given the infinite memory capacity of the network.[19]

For decision-making, forgetfulness can have harmful effects but it can also be very beneficial. Keep in mind that in every moment everything that has happened to us in relation to other people is not precisely a guarantee of objectivity or success, but probably of excessive anxiety. Although what we call memory on the web may somewhat resemble "collective memory,"[20] the possibility of forgetting that you have human memory is not a limitation, but a true capacity.[21] We need to advance along the path of the right to forget if we want to maintain the principles and values that underpin the right to free development of personality. And we should even combine it with the right to forgive, as this is a (certainly more perfect) way of achieving that. Now, we can also ask ourselves if the right to be ourselves, to have our own identity, includes the possibility of rewriting the past, or if that would alter identity.

Undoubtedly, the answer to these questions escapes the legal sphere and nudges us toward the anthropological one, to the investigation of what remains the most intimate part of a person, through the innumerable changes that we evidently manifest throughout life. Data can alter what we understand by person[22] and by identity.[23] Algorithms can configure a person's identity and design and control it, which undoubtedly calls into question the right to free development; they can even steal an identity.[24] In addition, a digital personality can lead to "death from death," simply considering that the disappearance of bodily properties is nothing but the liberation of the body to access the "immortality" of the world of data. At this point, it is important to remember that identity and identification are not the same[25]; and, even more important, that knowledge (data, information, intelligence) does not represent the highest form of human life.

---

[19] Solove, D. J. (2007). *The Future of Reputation. Gossip, Rumor, and Privacy on the Internet* (New Haven: Yale University Press,).

[20] Halbwachs, M. (2004). *La memoria colectiva* (Zaragoza, Spain: PUZ).

[21] Baddeley, A. (1990). *Human Memory: Theory and Practice* (Boston: Allyn and Bacon).

[22] Solove, D. J. (2004). *The Digital Person* (New York: New York University Press).

[23] Sullivan, C. (2011). *Digital Identity* (Adelaide: University of Adelaide Press).

[24] Ezioni, L. (2018). "Identity theft and exposure to harmful content. internet risk for teenagers," *Cyber, Intelligence and Security*, **2**(2): 3.

[25] Rodotà, S. (2014). *El derecho a tener derechos* (Madrid: Trotta).

The highest form of human life is not intelligence, but love. It should have been previously noted that intelligence cannot be reduced to the ability to solve complex problems, nor does human memory consist only of storage capacity. Human learning is more than a combinatorial function.[26] Together with the capacity for analysis, human intelligence is also developed in the search for meaning, in the capacity for relationship with a purpose; and in the habit of reaching conclusions based on the understanding of the weight of each of the elements and events that must be considered.[27]

Data analysis is very important in decision-making. Massive data also allows us to create user profiles, thanks to which decisions can be made in a way that is certainly much more efficient. But we have the right to receive explanations,[28] to mediate a human intervention when a decision has been based on a pre-established profile. Personal dignity makes us unique and unrepeatable, and it does not always react well to being pigeonholed in a profile or a pattern. If a certain profile, based on millions of other people's data, suggests that there is high probability of us contracting a disease, losing a job, or failing at school, we definitely want to think about insurance, a scholarship, or a loan. In this way, anyone can be judged not by what they have done, but by what others have done. Massive data poses problems not previously contemplated. As we have seen, it seems to generate a new form of discrimination, different from the classical ones related to birth, race, sex, religion, or ideas. This risk leads us to need to regulate the consent for data processing.

Networks work thanks to the value of the data obtained, and privacy is not the only thing at risk. It is also protection against behavior that puts security at risk, as anonymity cannot be a means to preserve immunity. To prevent cyberattacks and cyberwarfare, the limits of privacy must be defined.[29] Anonymity (not knowing the identity of the attacker) is one of

---

[26] See the special volume of *Scientific American* entitled "Learning in the Digital Age" (2013) for the impact that the intensive use of new technologies has on cognitive development.

[27] In classical thinking, the three intellectual habits are intelligence, wisdom, and science. See: Sellés, J. F. (2003). *El conocer personal* (Pamplona: Cuadernos de Anuario Filosófico).

[28] Calo, R. (2014). "Digital market manipulation," *George Washington Law Review*, **82**: 995–1051.

[29] Barrett, E. (2013). "Warfare in a new domain: The ethics of military cyber-operations," *Journal of Military Ethics*, **12**: 4–17.

the great differences between conventional wars and those that occur in cyberspace.[30]

12.4. Cyberspace Has High Capacity for Exercising Power

With very low entry costs, cyberspace has high capacity for exercising power; small actors achieve this in a very short amount of time, and thanks to anonymity, an imbalance capable of causing huge vulnerability gaps.[31] The network is, in short, a human construct that has changed almost everything, and has become the key to understanding power in this new century.

Anonymity, the difficulty in tracking traceability,[32] the ease of obtaining weapons of attack, or international regulatory differences make the main defender of cyberspace the deterrence.[33]

In the defense of cyberspace,[34] it is crystal clear that a chain is almost always broken by the weakest link. And in national security, the weakest link is usually the private sector.[35] Many companies, large and small, are sometimes unaware that their lack of investment, outsourcing of products and services, or lack of control of certain procedures not only puts their safety at stake but also that of their customers and suppliers; in short, that of everyone, and in particular that of the critical sectors.

It is also true that states are usually the protagonists in the emergence of one of the disruptive technological elements that may be more

---

[30]Dipert, R. (2010). "The ethics of cyberwarfare," *Journal of Military Ethics*, **9**: 384–410.

[31]Nye Jr, J. (2010). *Cyber Power* (Harvard Kennedy School: Belfer Center for Science and International Affairs).

[32]Deferred attacks using Trojan horses are much more frequent in cyberattacks than in a conventional war, and their defense demands more complex combined strategies. See: Averbuch, A. and G. Siboni (2013). "The classic cyber defense methods have failed. What comes next," *Military and Strategic Affairs*, **5**(1): 45–58.

[33]Denning, D. (2015). "Rethinking the cyber domain and deterrence," *Joint Force Quarterly*, **77**: 8–15.

[34]Cyberspace: global domain within the information environment consisting of the interdependent networks of information technology infrastructures and resident data, including the Internet, telecommunications networks, computer systems, and embedded processors and controllers (as defined in *DOD Dictionary of Military and Associated Terms*).

[35]Siboni, G. and I. Sivan Sevilla (2019). *Regulation in Cyberspace* (Madrid, Spain: INSS).

destabilizing than stabilizing in the future: lethal autonomous weapons. It seems clear that these weapons are going to be the subject of a growing development by the most technologically advanced countries,[36] and for this reason international regulation will most likely be conveniently expanded.[37]

For all these reasons, it is essential that there is collaboration between the public and the private sectors in the government of the Internet and cyberspace, on the technical level as well as on the social and legal levels. For cybersecurity to be confidential, comprehensive, authentic, traceable, and available,[38] we need initiatives such as the *Charter of Trust for a Secure Digital World*, signed in Munich, Germany, in February 2018, which is a joint commitment between large companies, governments, and institutions.

Cyberspace has elements common to the dominion of earth, sea, air, or outer space. These are all Global Commons.[39] As a result, cybersecurity is a public good.[40] But these public goods also have some obvious differences, such as the fact that after an action or an attack it can be restored, or reset, in order to return to the starting point. In the other dominions, it is not possible to return to the original starting point. But perhaps the biggest difference stems from the fact that while the other dominions (earth, sea, air, space) have been given to man (it is the nature in which he lives), cyberspace is a man-made construct.

The main requirement for dominating nature in a sustainable way is to respect it: to consider that human activity (work, technical, art) should imitate nature in some way, and has as its ultimate purpose to better it. Hence the natural environment and those resources that man generates seek their harmonization and integration.

---

[36]Anderson, K. and M. Waxman (2013). *Law and Ethics for Autonomous Weapon Systems: Why a Ban Won't Work and How the Laws of War Can*, The Hoover Institution Jean Perkins Task Force on National Security and Law Essay Series (Stanford, MA: Stanford University).

[37]Alston, P. (2012). "Lethal robotic technologies: The implications for human rights and international humanitarian law," *Journal of Law, Information and Science*, **21**(2): 35–60.

[38]These characteristics are described by the National Security Framework in the field of Electronic Administration.

[39]de Agreda, A. G. (2010) "Global Commons en la era de la incertidumbre," *Boletín de Información del CESEDEM*, **317**.

[40]Asllani, A. C. White and L. Ettkin (2013). "Viewing cybersecurity as a public good: The role of governments, businesses, and individuals," *Journal of Legal, Ethical and Regulatory Issues*, **16**: 7.

When considering the criteria of the right to war and rights during wars, and when discussing the principles of fair war, particularly in cyber-war, we find this problem of attribution that can justify the necessity of limiting the right to privacy. Not everything is the same in the real world and in the world of data, but is it possible to combine a person's real and virtual identity?[41] The definition of a "super-identity" that combines data from the real and virtual worlds in a robust way would undoubtedly allow for the detection of possible threats.

Beyond whether or not we can differentiate one person from another through biometric data (such as fingerprints, iris scans, facial features, a person's carriage, odor, or tone of voice), or a combination of these virtual behavior patterns, are we in some way defining or describing who this person is? Differentiation, i.e. the capacity of knowing that we are in front of a distinct individual does not seem to be enough to affirm that we have found the most intimate and defining aspect of a human being.

Big data can undoubtedly be transformed into accessible and enor-mously usable information, but its direct use conforms only to human knowledge, the only kind capable of weighing value judgements.[42] Therefore, which criteria will be used in order to decide on correct and incorrect usage? On which principles and values are we going to legislate?

12.5. Can Data Improve Us to the Point that they Substitute Us?

The fundamental rights at stake (personal dignity, moral and physical integrity, freedom to make decisions, equality, the right not to be discrimi-nated against) should be based on principles and values,[43] and ultimately be rooted in a clear idea of human dignity.

---

[41]Black, S. *et al.* (2012). *SuperIdentity: Fusion of Identity across Real and Cyber Domains* (University of Southampton Institutional Repository, 2012).

[42]de la Quadra Salcedo, T. (2018) "Retos, riesgos y oportunidades de la sociedad digital," in T. de la Quadra Salcedo and J. Luis Piñar Mañas (eds.), *Sociedad Digital y Derecho* 2018, (Madrid: Boletín Oficial del Estado), pp. 21–85.

[43]The report published in April 2019 by the High-Level Expert Group on Artificial Intelligence of the European Commission, titled "Ethics Guidelines for Trustworthy AI" indicates the following principles and values: do good, avoid evil, autonomy, fair play, and transparency.

In a report from March 2018 titled "Statement on Artificial Intelligence, Robotics and Autonomous Systems," the European Group on Ethics in Science and New Technologies noted that, for Europeans, as derived from Immanuel Kant's work *What is Enlightenment*, the root of personal dignity is autonomy, i.e. the ability to give us moral laws, and that is the basis of democracy. This idea, however, contrasts with the experience that the human being from birth to death is a radically dependent being: we are relational beings. Autonomy is undoubtedly a very important feature a personal being, but it can't be the root of their dignity.[44]

The Internet of Things and Artificial Intelligence are perhaps the transversal disruptive technologies that will transform our habits, the way we live, work, relate, consume, and are entertained. Every aspect of our lives is affected when data flows around them: the data we create and that we use, that we buy and sell, provides us with new ways of deciding and affects us. Data affects us because its use can make us better or worse as people. Thus, questioning the meaning is significant. The valuable resource, the "black gold," is not the data itself but what it means.[45]

Data needs algorithms to be organized, and this needs a model for the information to be relevant. But the models serve people in their decision-making, and there is always the meaning, the "why," and rationalizing the ultimate goal of the action.[46] Biotechnology, as well as the digital society, seem called upon to improve human capabilities. But these advances, which we have recently begun to call "posthuman" or "transhuman," have consequences that affect the very concept of what it is to be human. For example, it has always been believed that differences in capacities are

---

[44]What we can undoubtedly be sure of, following the principles of Kantian philosophy, is that currently building a better world is a true moral imperative if we do not want to become engaged in a frightening war pitting everyone against each other. See: de Agreda, A. G. (2019). *Mundo Orwell* (Madrid: Ariel).

[45]Oliver, N. (2018). *Inteligencia Arificial: Ficción, Realidad y ... Sueños* (Madrid: Real Academia de Ingeniería).

[46]Everyone who does works does it for an end, which is his good (Tomás de Aquino, *Summa Theologiae*, I-II, q.1, aa 1 and 2). It should also be kept in mind that in making decisions, prudent action is not simply a matter of deliberation (calculation that takes into account all available information); common sense and freedom play a major role when making a decision; and executing what we have decided is strongly conditioned by the freedom of others and the unpredictable nature of the materiality that surrounds us.

distributed by nature, but if some believe they are entitled to a superior improvement, where is the equality? Contemporary thinkers of the stature of Habermas,[47] Fukuyama,[48] and Sendel[49] have considered the problems that can arise for coexistence given the fact that some people exist that have been improved while others have not.

Also, the enormous power provided by technology and data affect the rights of persons in numerous ways; risks are becoming apparent in social media over the analysis and treatment of big data, not only for individuals but also for democracy and the markets to the extent that they produce an unexpected concentration of power that actually alters the equality of opportunities and free competition.[50] The digital world has revolutionized governments and transparency because it offers new ways of participation and control to the citizens. It has also completely changed the panorama of communication media. We are organized in networks, with all its advantages and disadvantages: anyone can create or disseminate a piece of news. The price that we pay for spontaneity is probably suppression of a critical spirit and a lack of rigor. Immediacy does not sit well with criteria and grounds (including, very often, with truth).

In the network, the responsibility can be diluted by anonymity. Also, the assertion that our capacity for dialogue increases with the massive increase in information is more than questionable to the extent that it is the search engine algorithms that dictate what best fits our preference profile. And in this way, we can reach an almost liquid, public life, flat, with few contrasts. If we organize in networks and the algorithms organize us in groups,[51] it seems clear that digital rights have a public dimension, which allows us to talk about true digital citizenship. Data protection is not just an individual right: it is the right of all citizens.[52] Given the constant proliferation of data,[53] citizens have showed considerable confidence

---

[47] Habermas, J. (2009). *El futuro de la naturaleza humana* (Barcelona: Paidos).

[48] Fukuyama, F. (2002). *El fin del hombre: consecuencias de la revolución biotecnológica* (Barcelona: Ediciones.B).

[49] Sendel, M. (2007). *Contra la perfección* (Barcelona: Marbot).

[50] de la Quadra Salcedo, T (2018). *supra* note 42.

[51] Taylor, L. L. Floridi and B. van der Sloot (2017). *Group Privacy: New Challenges of Data Technologies* (Dordrecht: Springer).

[52] Rodotà, S. (1997). *Tecnopolitica* (Roma: Laterza).

[53] The "*data obesitas*," as referred to in: Hildebrandt, M. (2017). "Learning as a machine. Crossovers between humans and machines," *Journal of Learning Analytics*, **4**(1): 6–23.

in the ability of governments to regulate and protect.[54] But we are increasingly being warned of the risks posed by the new ways of participation of public life.

For those most devoted to big data ("dataists"),[55] the policy as we understand it is regulated by Artificial Intelligence. It is a question of efficiently managing the information. But this question only arises in a philosophical *humus* which ignores or bypasses two realities profoundly present in the world in which we live: human freedom and the randomness of all that is material.

The possibility of improving capacities through brain connections to massive data (brain interfaces — computer) introduces problems related with the manipulation and the interference in the life of people, but above all it leads to situations in which subjects can abdicate responsibility or even lose their sense of their own identity.[56] Are we who we are, or are we who Google say we are? Artificial Intelligence can be an enormous help in several professional fields. In fact, we believe that we should prepare to work increasingly with artificial intelligence and robots.[57]

Regulation on the growing development of robotics gives rise to the question of the legal status of robots.[58] Even though a robot is a being that is given a corporeal materiality,[59] this feature does not have to be essential[60] because many systems that use Artificial Intelligence can cause physical harm without having to be robots. It is clear that the increasing functionalities of the most developed robots distance them from the object, from the instrument, and bring them closer to the characteristics of the subjects.

When we ask ourselves how we will work when many everyday tasks are carried out by machines, the question of meaning emerges more

---

[54]Krotoszynski, R. (2016). *Privacy Revisited: A Global Perspective on the Right to Be Left Alone* (Oxford: Oxford University Press).

[55]Harari, Y. N. (2017). *Homo Deus. Breve historia del mañana* (Barcelona: Debate).

[56]Yuste, R. (2017). "Four ethical priorities for neurotechnologies and AI," *Nature*, **551**(7679): 159–163.

[57]In December 2018, the European Commission published the report "Future of Work, Future of Society," prepared by the European Group on Ethics in Science and New Technologies.

[58]And in that context, there is no less concern over whether they will charge the public purse for their work. See: Ford, M. (2016). *El auge de los robots* (Barcelona: Paidos).

[59]Calo, R. (2016). "Robots as legal metaphors," *Harvard Journal of Law and Technology*, **30**.

[60]Balkin, J. (2015). "The pat of robotics law," *California Law Review*, **6**: 45–60.

emphatically, given that a certain daily hyperactivity may only be masking a living emptiness. When we carry out work that machines cannot do, we will probably work fewer hours; will that make us happier?[61] This work will only have meaning if its true vocation is service, if the "what for" is clearly the improvement of the lives of those that surround us.[62] To the extent that the use of massive data becomes an essential element for decision-making, will professionals be forced to limit themselves to ratifying what the algorithms say? The implementation of Online Dispute Resolution (ODR) mechanisms is the first step in that direction, because they allow for the quick, safe, and cheap resolution of specific conflicts related to consumption.[63]

The increase in information should diminish risks and increase confidence,[64] but the tyranny of the use of algorithms to make decisions, decisions that are above all efficient, is another aspect of the tyranny of quantification[65] and the tyranny of the experts that repeatedly emerge in civilizations.[66] The risks are obvious: exclusion, discrimination, violation of privacy, asymmetry of the information owned, manipulation, opacity, and difficulty in distinguishing between truth and farce.

Decisions do not only need data, i.e. "logos." They also need an "ethos" (emotions) and a "pathos" (a context).[67] In addition, at the time of deliberation (prior to the decision itself and the execution), some caution, a good look around, does not need to be the most exhaustive possible: and in any case it is always necessary to rank, order, consider, and prioritize.[68] Common sense tells us that often it is better not to remember, to disregard,

---

[61]Graetz, G. and G. Michaels (2018). "Robots at work," *Review of Economics and Statistics*, **100**: 753–768.

[62]Schwartz, B. (2016). *¿Por qué trabajamos? En busca del sentido* (Madrid: Empresa Activa).

[63]Benyekhlef, K. (2018). *Some Reflections on The Future of Online Dispute Resolution. From e-platform to Algorithms* (Madrid: Reus).

[64]Frankel, T. (2001). "Trusting and non-trusting on the Internet," *Boston University Law Review*, **81**(2): 457–478.

[65]Frey, B. (2017). "Omnimetrics and awards," *CESifo Working Paper Series* 6582.

[66]Khanna, A. and P. Khanna (2012). *Hybrid Reality: Thriving in the Emerging Human-Technology Civilization* (New York: Ted Books).

[67]Waddel, C. (1990). "The role of pathos in the decision-making process: A study in the rhetoric of science policy," *Quarterly Journal of Speech*, **76**: 381–400.

[68]Saaty, T. (2008). "Decision making with the analytic hierarchy process," *International Journal of Services Sciences*, **1**: 83–98.

and to pass over. Data must be considered (or not) in accordance with the criteria. Efficiency must have a goal. But actions are the responsibility of those who carry them out, and they do not seek efficiency at all costs. When we consider the possibility of recognizing artificial persons, with their own responsibilities (in a similar way to that in which we recognize the responsibility of legal persons), this opens up a series of questions related to the capacity for mastery. Can data (organized in an Artificial Intelligence, *machine learning*, or *deep learning*) invent and create? Can they own the effects they produce?

At what point do we consider that they stop being instruments of human beings and become responsible subjects, in strictly speaking efficient causes themselves? *Smart Contracts* already run without human intervention.[69] Will computer programs in the future own their actions? Can they buy and sell? Can they infringe laws?

12.6. Having and Being: From Oblivion to Memory

The meaning that we give data (the "what for") affects both technology and business models and the necessity for regulations. But in order to know this, it is important to have a prior understanding of the mutual influence that these three integrating elements have on each other.

What happens is that "questioning the meaning" can only be done if the "meaning of the question" has already been examined. In other words: to try to develop an ethical or anthropological discourse which explains what our civilization is experiencing can be profoundly false if we do not begin with an understanding from within what we are living. And something similar happens with each of the elements that are involved in the task. It is not possible to delve into the protection and security of data management without understanding how they are affected by technology, business, and meaning.

As we have seen, the new ways of regulation that we need to develop require new forms of organization: not only new roles and functions for those who handle data but also new ways of organizing the work of facilitating the defense and protection that we need.

---

[69]Werbach, K. and N. Cornell (2017). "Contracts ex Machina," *Duke Law Journal*, **67**: 313–382.

On the other hand, when protection and security look to technology new rights appear (or new extensions of basic rights) which should allow us to guarantee ownership and protect privacy. Security also means a limit to freedom: e.g. to the freedom of information and data, not only in order to defend a specific territory but also, and more importantly, in the defense of essential public services (such as energy, telecommunications, or health).

Big data changes the way we live, but the value of the data also depends on its quality, on the models and biases that are provided. Each life is unrepeatable, and human decisions are not mathematically accurate: they are intrinsically affected by the reality of freedom, and by the imperfection of matter. They are based on reason, which means that problems do not have a single solution. In the same way that the question of meaning implicates technology, demanding that the common good is maintained,[70] and questions economic activities by making us aware that we are beings that need to live in relation to each other, before we start regulating, we need to discover where the most personal characteristics of human beings lie. By taking a comprehensive view of all the questions that relate to the control of data, to its possession, protection and use, we allow ourselves to question ourselves with regard to the meaning, and therefore of that being that underlies all actions, and is in some way prior to having everything.

A few years ago, many believed that human history was coming to an end. Not in a strictly temporal way, but rather through an exhaustion of ideas. In the face of Spengler's[71] fatalistic stance, Toynbee[72] suggested that human history needed creative minorities, people who ask themselves the essential questions.[73] Well, the digital society seems to have returned us rapidly once again to the beginning, to the fundamental questions about humanism. Only now, we find ourselves faced not with revolution, but with the final invention: an intelligence that puts an end to the human age.[74]

---

[70]Mayer, C. (2018). *Prosperity. Better Business Makes the Greater Good* (Oxford: Oxford University Press).

[71]Spengler, O. (2011). *La decadencia de Occidente* (Barcelona: Alianza).

[72]Toynbee, A. J. (1998). *Estudio de la Historia* (Madrid: Alianza).

[73]Sacks, J. (2014). "On creative minorities," *First Thinks. A Monthly Journal of Religion and Public Life*, **239** (January): 33–39.

[74]Barrat, J. (2013). *Our Final Invention: Artificial Intelligence and the End of the Human Era* (New York: Dunne Books); Ignacio Latorre, J. (2019). *Ética para Máquinas* (Barcelona: Ariel).

We do not know, as Heidegger[75] seemed to say, whether technology could dominate everything to the extent that it will dominate man himself, causing the complete oblivion of the self. But it seems clear that the key to ensuring that does not happen lies in the memory of the self.

The best way to demonstrate ownership, the best "title deed," is the capacity for giving. To be able to give something, it must be owned beforehand; no one can give what they do not have and what they do not possess. And the ability to give is one of the keys to building trust.[76] The underlying anthropology of the trust and logic of the gift is what can be considered the essential core of a person: the ability to love and the ability to give.

The most intimate part of a human being is neither found in their intelligence nor their will but in their heart. Intelligence seeks truth, will seeks good, but the heart, and love, simply seeks to give. It knows that fulfillment is achieved when it is not sought, or preferably, when the fulfillment is sought for others. Human beings have a mission, which is not blind destiny, because key to this mission are the recipients: those people, those essential relationships without which one's own life has no meaning. We have received a gift, which is only discovered and unpacked once it is given. We are both gift and task, gift and mission, gift and giving; we give what we have, although absolute perfection belongs to the person who has it to give.

From the oblivion that Heidegger mourned, the outcome of a technological progress that has forgotten its vocation of service, we find ourselves through memory, the memory of the gift received. In the original memory of truth and goodness,[77] in the memory that is the recollection and remembrance (*anamnesis*) of our origin, in listening to the given word, that is where the love received that constitutes the most intimate part of our personal selves.

In the personal identity constituted by being loved and loving, the human body plays an essential role, because it also manifested in the

---

[75]Heidegger, M. (2013). *Carta sobre el humanismo* (Madrid: Alianza Editorial).

[76]Many of these ideas are developed in: Luis Martínez, J., J. María Ortiz and M. Schlagg (2019). "How to implement the logic of gift in the managerial decision making process," in *A Catholic Spirituality for Business: The Logic of Gift* (Washington: The Catholic University of America Press), pp. 201–226.

[77]Ratzinger, J. (2010). *El elogio de la conciencia: la verdad interroga al corazón* (Madrid: Palabra).

ability to give. The immaterial is not only a reflection of perfection: the material body symbolizes supreme perfection when it gives, when it surrenders. The corporeal body is part of the human person's identity, it is neither an irritating accompaniment to the spirit nor a source of errors from which we must free ourselves or detach ourselves. The body is neither expendable nor unnecessary.

In 1997, the Deep Blue chess program beat Kasparov, in 2011 IBM's Watson won Jeopardy!, and Google's AlphaGo beat Lee Sedol in a Go competition in 2016, and Artificial Intelligence is developing a superior capacity for evaluation. However, our identity, the experience of our subjectivity, the value of our work, emotional exchange, the meaning of our actions, and even the separation of public and private spheres are anchored in our corporeality.[78]

Without the body, the human dignity is diluted; without empathy, otherness is not possible and there is no brake on selfishness; without the meaning of the body (with its finitude and pain, its pleasure and happiness), technology becomes a *fatum* that annuls freedom. Paradoxically, the more data that we have, the less we can know each other. And when we are capable of forgetting is when we best remember who we are.

---

[78]Lassalle, J. M. (2010). *Civerleviatán* (Barcelona: Arpa).

Index

Printed in the United States
by Baker & Taylor Publisher Services